T0382894

# Mobilities of Labour and Capital in Asia

The mobilities of capital and labour in the global economy are intricately and persistently linked, but they have hitherto mostly been analysed as separate processes. On the one hand, research on capital mobility has largely asked questions that are internal to the logics and motivations of firms, investors, and other movers of capital. On the other hand, studies of labour migration have generally not been concerned with the structures of capital accumulation and mobility that drive most labour processes. This book attempts to bring both types of mobility into the same analytical frame by arguing that the relationship between the two is best conceived as both an interdependency and a tension. In the context of Asia, the chapters examine when and how capital mobility can be generative of labour migration, but also how it can be disruptive of human mobility when the logic of accumulation demands it. Similarly, labour mobility and migration can be a generative precursor to capital flows, but they can also represent a form of disruptive resistance to mobile capital. Asia's growing importance in the global economy as a contributor to major flows of capital, the venue for significant migration corridors, and a context with diverse institutional actors make it a compelling region in which to explore the interconnections between labour and capital mobilities. Drawing on contextualized studies based in China, India, Japan, Nepal, the Philippines, and mainland South East Asia, the chapters in this book collectively make the case that capital and labour mobilities need to be viewed as systemically connected and mutually constitutive processes.

**Preet S. Aulakh** is Professor of Strategy and International Business and Pierre Lassonde Chair in International Business at the Schulich School of Business, York University, Toronto.

**Philip F. Kelly** is Professor of Geography at York University, Toronto, and former Director of the York Centre for Asian Research.

# Mobilities of Labour and Capital in Asia

*Edited by*

Preet S. Aulakh

Philip F. Kelly

# CAMBRIDGE
## UNIVERSITY PRESS

University Printing House, Cambridge CB2 8BS, United Kingdom

One Liberty Plaza, 20th Floor, New York, NY 10006, USA

477 Williamstown Road, Port Melbourne, VIC 3207, Australia

314–321, 3rd Floor, Plot 3, Splendor Forum, Jasola District Centre, New Delhi–110025, India

79 Anson Road, #06–04/06, Singapore 079906

Cambridge University Press is part of the University of Cambridge.

It furthers the University's mission by disseminating knowledge in the pursuit of education, learning and research at the highest international levels of excellence.

www.cambridge.org
Information on this title: www.cambridge.org/9781108482325

© Cambridge University Press 2020

First published 2020

Printed in India by Nutech Print Services, New Delhi 110020

*A catalogue record for this publication is available from the British Library*

*Library of Congress Cataloging-in-Publication Data*
Names: Aulakh, Preet S., 1962- editor. | Kelly, Philip F., 1970- editor.
Title: Mobilities of labour and capital / [edited by] Preet S. Aulakh and
    Philip F. Kelly.
Description: Cambridge; New York, NY: Cambridge University Press, 2020. |
    Includes bibliographical references and index.
Identifiers: LCCN 2019020554 | ISBN 9781108482325 (hardback)
Subjects: LCSH: Labor mobility--Asia. | Capital movements--Asia. |
    Globalization--Economic aspects--Asia. | International economic
    relations.
Classification: LCC HD5717.5.A78 M63 2019 | DDC 331.12/7095--dc23
LC record available at https://lccn.loc.gov/2019020554

ISBN 978-1-108-48232-5 Hardback

# Contents

SECTION II   From Labour to Capital Mobility

# Figures

# Tables

# Appendices

# Acknowledgements

The work of a number of people went into the preparation of this book. Each of the papers was originally presented at a workshop—Asian Connections: Linking Mobilities of Capital and Labour in Theory and Practice—which took place at the York Centre for Asian Research (YCAR), York University, on 12–13 May 2017. A joint initiative of YCAR and the Schulich School of Business, the purpose of the workshop was to bring together scholars working in diverse theoretical frameworks, disciplinary traditions, methodologies, historical periods, and geographical contexts to engage in discussions that would reunite the study of corporate and migrant transnationalism in Asia. Based on the response to a global call for papers, 12 were selected for presentation at the workshop, of which 10 papers appear in this volume, along with the editors' introduction.

Over the course of the two-day workshop, the authors read and commented on all the papers. In addition, a number of other scholars volunteered to participate in the workshop and led the discussions. We are particularly thankful to Derek Hall from Wilfrid Laurier University, who was instrumental in laying out some possible frameworks in the opening panel. His comments and the subsequent engagement with the individual papers were extremely useful in seeing interconnections between scholars from diverse disciplinary backgrounds. We also wish to thank Shubhabrata Basu, Geraldina Polanco, and Nguyen Tran Lam for their participation in the discussions.

The workshop would not have been possible without the excellent skills of Alicia Filipowich at YCAR. We thank her for facilitating the travel arrangements of the participants, the logistics of the workshop, and taking care of the budget. We also would like to acknowledge the diligent note-taking of Cindy Maharaj, which was immensely useful as the participants incorporated comments and discussion from the workshop in their revised papers. All the chapters in the volume subsequently went through multiple revisions, and we wish to thank the authors for their openness in incorporating our suggestions and for their timely revisions. Thanks also to Neil Coe (National University of Singapore) for comments on the introductory chapter.

Finally, we wish to thank our Commissioning Editor, Anwesha Rana, at Cambridge University Press for her enthusiastic response to our initial proposal, her efficient management of the review process, and in helping us manage the deadlines at various stages.

# Introduction

## Conceptualizing Labour and Capital Mobilities In and Out of Asia

PREET S. AULAKH AND PHILIP F. KELLY

Capitalist development has always, and everywhere, been characterized by the restless mobility of both capital and labour. While these two forms of mobility are fundamentally related, it is unusual to combine the study of both or seek connections between them. In an effort to make these connections more than three decades ago, Saskia Sassen commented that the two processes of capital and labour mobility 'have been constructed into unrelated categories' (1988: 12). This assessment still largely holds true. The objective of this book is to explore the links between these forms of mobility with a particular focus on Asia.

While the imperative to be mobile is well established as a systemic feature of capital, it is usually studied through frameworks that try to understand the behaviour of firms, conglomerates, production networks, or investors. An extensive body of literature addresses corporate structures and strategies of capital accumulation. For example, in the field of international business, attention has traditionally focused on the mobility of capital, primarily through foreign direct investment (FDI) (for example, Dunning, 1988). The underlying assumption is the immobility of labour. The multinational corporation, with its proprietary capital and know-how (ownership advantage) and governance within a hierarchical organization (internalization advantage), facilitates the mobility of capital in order to take advantage of location-bound factors of production (including labour). Other approaches have addressed the networks and supply chains in which firms are situated. There have been, for example, significant efforts at understanding the spatial structures of production through the lenses of global commodity chains and global production networks. These bodies of literature point out that significant levels of spatial flexibility and mobility in production capital have been created through non-ownership modes of control such as subcontracting (Gereffi and Korzeniewicz, 1994; Coe and Yeung, 2015). Complementing this work are studies that focus on corporate international expansion trajectories and governance structures to manage globally dispersed investments (for example, Cuervo-Cazurra and Ramamurti, 2014; Ramamurti and Singh, 2009). Labour seldom features centrally in such accounts, except as an in situ characteristic of a particular place, valued for its skills, affordability, or docility. At the human scale, it is usually the investor or manager who is assumed to be mobile, but mostly it is the spatial configuration of capital itself (through FDI, corporate structures, commodity trade, debt, and so on) that receives attention.

Equally, migrant labour is widely studied, but the locus of analysis is usually rendered as the individual migrant worker, the collective (im)migrant community, or the state and other actors that play a role in facilitating or regulating human mobility (for example, Betts, 2011; Rajan, 2011; Faist et al., 2013). Such studies tend to be nationally rooted in certain sending or receiving countries, or concerned with tracing the transnational social, economic, and political linkages built by migrant communities. The focus, however, is usually directed towards specific issues of migrant social life, culture, belonging, and labour processes, or the regulatory and institutional contexts that govern migrant workers' lives. An exception, in terms of making the link between capital and labour mobility, is the literature on global cities where agglomerations of mobile capital come together with the movement of skilled and unskilled labour. Here, Saskia Sassen's work again plays a key role, highlighting the functional linkages between migrant labour and cities' roles as command and control headquarters for the global economy (Sassen, 2001). These themes have been picked up in other studies focusing on the working-class underpinnings of global city formation (for example, Wills et al., 2009; Schiller and Simsek-Caglar, 2010). While this body of work has been successful in drawing together the linkages of mobile capital and mobile labour, it tends to be focused on cities in the Global North.

The relative neglect in explicitly linking capital and labour mobilities is surprising because there are many ways in which the two appear to be empirically interconnected. For instance, migrations, including historical migrations, have been a prelude to capital flows in the form of trade and FDI (Walton-Roberts, 2011). At a micro level, migrants themselves are now major sources of mobile capital for investment in sending areas, spurring residential developments to be purchased and held as assets from afar or creating small-scale enterprises that are capitalized through remittances (Kelly, 2017). Similarly, global capital, in the places where it alights and agglomerates, demands specific types of labour to sustain its competitiveness. Such labour is often less expensive, more dependable, and more exploitable, precisely because it has been disenfranchised through the process of migration across borders (Kelly, 2012). Finally, it has been observed that globalized networks in manufacturing, service, and extractive sectors can differentially transform labour markets, sources of livelihood, and cultural norms, thus facilitating or necessitating both outward and inward migrations from particular places. A key part of Sassen's argument in her earlier work, noted earlier, was the role of FDI in precipitating emigration from the Global South (Sassen, 1988). In all of these various ways, capital and labour mobilities are mutually dependent.

In this volume, we pursue these themes of interdependent capital and labour mobility with a particular focus on Asia. The phenomenal rise of Asia within the global economy during the last few decades—from less than 20 per cent of the world GDP in the 1950s to almost 45 per cent in the second decade of the twenty-first century (Maddison and Eng, 2013)—would be a sufficient reason for this focus. But there are also additional dynamics of capital and labour mobility across Asia that make it distinctive and, therefore, in need of analytical attention on its own terms (Asian Development Bank, 2017; ADBI, ILO, and OECD, 2017).

Perhaps the most epochal change is the regionalization and globalization of Chinese capital, as the country has shifted from being a huge net destination for foreign investment to becoming a significant net exporter of investment. But China is not the only source of transnationalizing capital within Asia, as domestic firms from India, Thailand, Indonesia, the Philippines, and other countries have been developing transnational corporate structures, similar to the ones used by earlier Asian globalizers from Japan, Korea, and Taiwan. Of particular note is the mobility of capital in both South–North and South–South directions, which taken together challenge the traditional understandings of FDI in the literature. New, and rapidly developing, urban spaces have also been a hallmark of Asian development in the early part of the twenty-first century and have included exclusionary enclaves where global capital is guarded, and migrant workers are employed. From the Philippines to Singapore to India, a model of enclave urbanism and manufacturing or service industry development has been implemented, in what Murray (2017) calls the urbanism of exception. This process has created sites of mobility for capital, which are also spaces of discipline and containment for migrant labour.

Asia has also been both the source and destination for some of the world's most significant new migration corridors (Nathan, Tewari, and Sarkar, 2016). Internationally, major migrant labour flows have moved across land borders in mainland South East Asia (primarily into Thailand), and into India from its South Asian neighbours. Other major flows include the deployment of migrant labour to Gulf countries from South and South East Asia. There have also been distinctive patterns of internal migration, with major movements in China and India. It is important to note that the movement of migrant labour involves sending areas as well as destinations. Migrants retain ongoing social and economic ties with their places of origin and so the spatialities of migration include the smallest of villages as well as the more obvious destinations. Furthermore, many migrations are rural-to-rural in nature, and not just transnational or rural–urban.

Asia is also distinctive in the institutional arrangements at multiple levels that enable, produce, and regulate the mobilities of capital and labour. Most obviously, new forms of state power and state–market interactions are being modelled in various Asian contexts, leading to discussions of Asian varieties of capitalism (Carney, Gedajlovic and Yang, 2009; Zhang and Whitley, 2013). These include sovereign wealth funds as major global investors, state-owned enterprises emerging as transnational corporations, new forms of state regulation of migration, and engagement with diasporas as drivers of development. New state forms have also emerged at other scales, including supra-state regional governance structures and cross-border planning frameworks. These include: the Association of Southeast Asian Nations' (ASEAN) role in seeking to integrate the credentialing of skilled labour across South East Asia; the development of an Asian Infrastructure Investment Bank; and, on a grander scale, China's plans to spread its reach through the 'Belt and Road Initiative'.

In this chapter, we elaborate on these emerging dynamics within Asia in three ways. First, we note the varied forms that mobile capital and mobile people can take. On the one hand, this involves noting recent trends in flows of capital in the form of FDI and migrant remittances. Thus, while we refer to capital as a process and structure in the Marxian sense, we will also be referring to empirical flows of money for investment or remittance purposes, as these have the most direct connection with migration processes. On the other hand, we differentiate migrant types according to their degree of legal status and privilege in places of work and settlement. Having established the forms that capital and labour mobilities are taking, the second part of the chapter identifies key institutional actors that shape their movements. In particular, we highlight the role of the state, corporate conglomerates, and the 'migration industry' as three distinctive (although not unique) aspects of the Asian context that need to be considered. The third part of the chapter develops a framework for understanding the interdependent but contradictory relationship between capital and labour mobility. In particular, we will argue that the mobility of each can have both generative (or enabling) effects on the other, but it can also have disruptive (or disabling) effects. The two mobilities therefore exist in tension with each other, but in ways that are played out in distinctive ways in particular contexts.

## Forms of Capital and Labour Mobility

### Capital Mobility

Capital flows can be examined in terms of portfolio investments (such as investments in stock markets, government bonds, pension funds, and so on) as well as through foreign aid and loans from both public institutions (such as the IMF and World

Bank) and private banks. While not discounting these as important vehicles for capital movement, we focus here on those flows that link most directly with labour mobility. In particular, we identify the magnitude and dynamics of FDI by transnational enterprises and remittances sent home by individual migrants.

Foreign direct investment has been an important conduit for capital mobility across national boundaries, and the ability of nation-states to attract FDI is seen as an important indicator of a country's competitiveness. Data on worldwide FDI flows since the early 1990s show some interesting patterns, especially with respect to the relative weight of Asia in both inward and outward FDI flows (see Figures 1.1 and 1.2). First, during the decade 1990–2000, worldwide inward FDI increased fivefold, followed by a dip during the 2001–2004 period, and then a twofold increase from 2004 to 2016. The share of Asia as a recipient of worldwide FDI increased from around 12 per cent in 1990 to peak at about 35 per cent in 2014 (Figure 1.1). More importantly, in terms of the regional variations within Asia, inward FDI in 1990 was primarily in East Asia (including Japan). Over time, and especially since the turn of the twenty-first century, this has spread to South Asia and West Asia as well (UNCTAD, 2017). Much of this reflects the significance of multiple places in Asia as nodes in global manufacturing and service production networks, as well as fast-growing consumer markets.

Data on outward FDI also show an increasing weight of Asia in worldwide FDI flows (see Figure 1.2). Within the overall increase in annual outward FDI flows, Japan's share has declined substantially, from almost 20 per cent in 1990 to less than

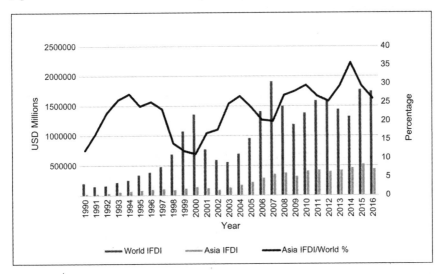

Figure 1.1 | Inward foreign direct investments

*Source*: UNCTAD (2017).

10 per cent a decade and half later. The rest of Asia's share, which was less than 5 per cent in 1990, expanded to 30 per cent of worldwide outward FDI by 2014 before settling in the mid-twenties. Although part of this increase is attributed to the more developed economies such as the Asian Tigers, a large and increasing proportion comes from the developing economies in Asia, with China and India as the leading investors in foreign markets. Furthermore, the outward FDI from Asia has partly followed the paths of the 'third-world multinationals' of the 1960s and 1970s, that is, investing in manufacturing in other developing economies (the primary South–South flows) (Aulakh, 2007; Wells 1983). The recent outward FDI from Asia also encompasses investments to acquire primary resources, including raw materials to satisfy the growing industrial base of Asian economies. However, a particular form of outward FDI from developing economies that challenges some of the traditional assumptions of such capital flows pertains to the geographical spread of investments into other advanced economies and using such investments to acquire established multinationals around the world (Gubbi et al., 2010).

Besides the role of FDI in economic growth, securing strategic assets, and moving up the value chain, other forms of capital flows have been especially significant in Asia. In particular, the role of *remittances* has expanded dramatically. With 247 million global migrants living outside their country of birth in 2013, remittances are increasingly seen as an important basis for economic development at both local and national levels in their countries of origin (*Migration and Remittances Factbook 2016*; Brown 2006; de Haas 2005; Giuliana and Ruiz-Arranz, 2009). Data on

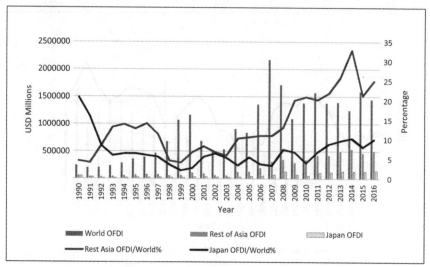

Figure 1.2 | Outward foreign direct investments

*Source*: UNCTAD (2017).

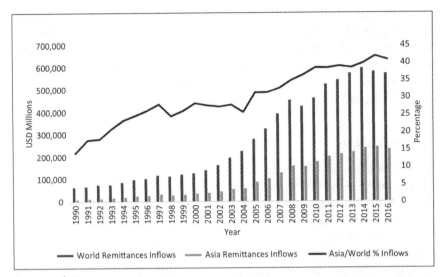

Figure 1.3 | Migrant remittances inflows

*Source*: World Bank (2017).

inward and outward remittances (see Figures 1.3 and 1.4) since the early 1990s show dramatic growth: from less than US$100 billion inflows in 1990 to more than US$600 billion in 2016 (Figure 1.3); from a little over US$50 billion outflows in 1990 to over US$350 billion in 2016 (Figure 1.4). Within this growth in both inward and outward migrant remittances, Asia's share in outward remittances has

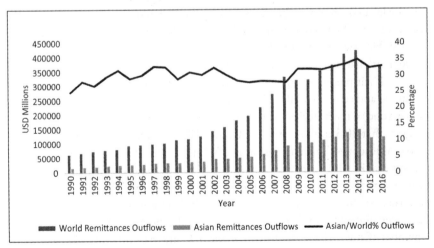

Figure 1.4 | Migrant remittances outflows

*Source*: World Bank (2017).

shown relative stability (staying between 25 and 35 per cent of the world total). However, inward remittances into Asia as a percentage of worldwide remittances have increased substantially, from about 15 per cent to almost 40 per cent. The world's three largest remittance recipients (India, China, and the Philippines), along with the second-largest source of remittances (Saudi Arabia), are all in Asia (World Bank, 2017).

## Labour Mobility

Human mobility can take many forms but our primary focus in this book is on labour mobility—in other words, migration for the purpose of paid employment. Conceptually, the migrant nature of labour is significant for two reasons. First, migration across borders creates a disenfranchisement from the rights that citizens have (at least in theory) within their home countries. By virtue of its deportability, in particular, migrant labour is qualitatively different from local labour. Second, migrant workers usually embody 'otherness' in their destinations, based on intersected identities of gendered, racialized, religious, regional, or linguistic difference. As we will see in this book, such dimensions of difference are often a source of discipline and oppression for migrant workers, but in some instances the construction of co-ethnicity may be a basis for collaboration in facilitating capital flows, as in the case of the overseas co-ethnics or 'returnee entrepreneurs' (Saxenian, 2006).

While migrants are different from locals, they are also different from each other in important ways. In particular, the categories of legal status to which migrants belong can significantly affect where on a spectrum of privilege and marginalization they are located. Here, we identify six forms of human mobility that are particularly relevant in the Asian context and in the case studies presented in this book.

First, historical migrations have created distinct ethnic communities in sites of 'settlement' that may be several generations removed from the original migration process. Their presence can have important implications for contemporary forms of human and capital mobility. The most significant example in the Asian context (and beyond) is the historical migration of Chinese populations. One recent estimate suggests that 40.3 million 'overseas Chinese' live outside mainland China, Hong Kong, Macao, and Taiwan (Poston and Wong, 2016). Poston and Wong (2016) suggest that in 2011 there were almost 30 million 'overseas Chinese' across the rest of Asia, with the largest populations in Indonesia (8 million), Thailand (7.5 million), and Malaysia (6.5 million). Some of these ethnic minority Chinese communities have been embedded over many generations in the 'host' societies. In recent years, a number of studies have identified the role of Chinese communities in facilitating capital flows from Hong Kong, Taiwan, and more recently China itself, as bonds of co-ethnicity facilitated the trust needed to operate at a distance (for example,

Olds, 2001; Mitchell, 2004; Yeung, 2004). In this book, we see the ways in which historical Chinese migrations have facilitated capital mobility in three different settings. Chen, Fu, Zhou, and Xu (Chapter 6) highlight this theme in relation to Chinese communities in the South East Asian region, while Valderrey, Montoya, and Cervantes (Chapter 5) note the history of ethnic Chinese communities in Latin America, and Peru in particular. On a smaller scale, Camba (Chapter 4) shows how ethnic Chinese contacts in the Philippines played a role in facilitating Chinese investment in small-scale mining in provinces far from the metropole.

A second form of labour migration, and perhaps the type most commonly now associated with the term, involves temporary foreign workers who are employed on contracts outside of their home countries. Such workers usually have significantly fewer rights than citizens and permanent residents of the country in which they work and face a range of restrictions in terms of work, residency, mobility, and accompanying dependants. The visas issued to contract workers are generally tied to a specific employer and a particular job category. Furthermore, the legal residency of such migrants is contingent on fulfilling the terms of the contract—if the migrant loses his or her job, he or she also lose the right to reside in the host country. Such workers, therefore, exist in a permanent state of insecurity and precarity. This creates a workforce that is relatively reliable in terms of its docility, stability, and numerical flexibility. When projects are completed, economic growth is slowing, or migrants are too old to do the work any more, they can simply be sent home. The host society bears none of the costs associated with raising and training workers, nor caring for them in their old age.

A workforce of temporary workers of this kind has become increasingly common across the world, but Asian contexts have provided some of the most significant sources and destinations for such migrants. Among the top ten global migration corridors in 2015, the movement of migrant workers from South Asia to the Gulf ranks third and accounts for 6.7 per cent of all global migration (World Bank, 2017). In 2017, over 17 million South Asian workers were employed across Saudi Arabia, the UAE, Iran, Kuwait, and Oman. Cross-border movements within South Asia account for a further 4.2 per cent of global migrants, with migration from Bangladesh to India accounting for the largest single flow. Migrants from low-income countries in East Asia and the Pacific who are moving to high-income countries in the same region or to North America account for a further 7.1 per cent of global migration. The Philippines represents a particular important source of overseas contract workers in diverse sectors and locations around the world. In 2016, over 2 million overseas Filipino workers (OFWs) were formally deployed by the state apparatus tasked with overseeing and marketing them—the Philippine Overseas Employment Administration. Of those, just over 20 per cent were sea-based, providing crews for passenger and cargo ships around the world. Approximately the same number were deployed for land-based work elsewhere in Asia, while 50 per cent worked in the Middle East. Although they have been widely researched, Filipino contract workers in Europe and North America account for less than 2 per cent of global deployments (POEA, 2016).

A third form of migrant labour involves those who do not have (or no longer have) formal legal permission to work in a host country. These workers may have crossed a border legally when first migrating for employment, but their legal status may have changed, for example because of a visa expiration or cancellation. Equally, in movements between neighbouring countries, border crossings without formal documents may be commonplace. Large numbers of workers have, for example, crossed between Laos and Thailand, Bangladesh and India, and the Philippines and Sabah, Malaysia. Whatever the cause of their undocumented status, these workers are highly vulnerable and live under the constant threat of deportation or harassment by security forces. Even basic workplace regulations concerning health and safety and wages and benefits can be flouted by employers. Such workers effectively have fewer rights than any other kind of worker as they cannot risk an encounter with local authorities. And yet they are often integral participants in the labour force. In the case of East Malaysia, for example, where Filipino and Indonesian migrant workers are essential to the operations of oil-palm plantations and other resource industries in the states of Sabah and Sarawak, the Commission on Filipinos Overseas (2014) estimates that almost 800,000 Filipinos are living in Sabah, many of them undocumented.

A fourth, and far more privileged, category of migrants comprises managers and professionals. Mobility among these workers has increased dramatically in recent years as transnational corporations recruit and assign employees from a global pool of talent. Many governments have specific visa categories that ensure the mobility of this type of migrants and they are provided with more freedoms and rights than are available to temporary foreign workers. Singapore provides a very clear example. Among 1.4 million foreign workers who were resident in 2017, around 1 million were temporary foreign workers holding work permits, but a further 400,000 held other categories of migrant visas with calibrated levels of privileges according to their place in an educational and income hierarchy. The assessment of where a migrant is placed in such a hierarchy will determine whether they can bring family members to live with them, whether they can marry a local citizen or give birth in Singapore, and whether they can eventually apply for permanent residency. For very high-earning individuals, there is a 'Personalised Employment Pass', and for entrepreneurs, an 'Entrepass', both of which provide a great deal of flexibility in terms of residency and mobility rights (Yang, Peidong, and Shaohua, 2017).

A fifth category of migrants is what we might call the returnee or the transnational. For these migrants, their movement eventually involves obtaining permanent residency or citizenship rights in their country of settlement. Some countries allow dual citizenship and their emigrants are able to retain a status in their place of origin. With some restrictions, this applies, for example, to Bangladesh, Pakistan, Sri Lanka, and the Philippines. In other cases, such as India, China, and Japan, dual citizenship is not allowed, but diaspora engagement programmes make it relatively easy for former citizens to live, invest, and work there, even if their formal status has been relinquished. In some cases, governments have developed programmes that are specifically designed to lure talent that has migrated abroad. In China, a concerted effort has sought to bring back students who have acquired university degrees and technical experience overseas. For example, the '1000 Talents' programme, launched in 2008, sought to reverse the brain drain to research universities and high-tech companies overseas, especially in North America. The programme sought to bring back elite talent, but a wider programme of attracting overseas students was also underway and in 2009 alone, over 100,000 students returned to China from sojourns abroad (Zweig and Wang, 2013). Aside from the hunt for talent, return migration may be more mundane. In some cases, it represents retirement migration, as immigrants return with pensions that will go further in their homelands. Some may decide to live more transnationally, with property held in both countries and movement between the two. Those seeking property in which to invest for a transient or permanent return are often prime targets for the marketing of new residential developments.

A sixth form of migration, often lost in discussions on a global scale, is internal migration—both rural–urban and rural–rural. In some cases, internal migration within a country can represent almost as profound a challenge to migrants as undertaking international migration. This might be because of administrative restrictions, as in the case of *hukou*, or residence permits, in China that limit access to employment and government services among those moving into a city (Johnson, 2017). Alternatively, the barriers might be related to economic costs involved in getting to and surviving in the city or because of the cultural gulf between cities and rural peripheries. Whatever the case, internal migration presents some analogous forms of marginalization to those who move internationally for work—migrants may find themselves subject to downward mobility in terms of socio-economic class, they may be stigmatized and racialized, and they may lack social capital. For these reasons, they may still be quite dependent on a specific employer, even if they have full access to the entitlements of citizenship.

Figures on internal migration in Asia are unreliable, but there is little doubt that such migrants far outnumber international migrants. In China alone, there were an estimated 253 million inter-county migrants in 2015 (Zhao, Liu, and Zhang, 2018). In India, the figure has been estimated at around 139 million, with 9 million moving every year across state boundaries. Uttar Pradesh and Bihar are the biggest source states, while Delhi, Maharashtra, Tamil Nadu, Gujarat, Andhra Pradesh, and Kerala are major destinations (Sharma, 2017). Kuzhiparambil's case study (Chapter 7) in this volume shows how one form of internal migration is specifically facilitated by government recruitment and training programmes to meet the needs of the export-oriented garment sector.

## Institutions of Capital and Labour Mobility

In expanding our frame of reference beyond the firm and individual migrants, this section addresses various institutional actors that facilitate and govern the mobilities of capital and labour, especially in the context of Asia. Specifically, we will draw attention to the distinctive roles of the state, the business conglomerate, and various actors within the 'migration industry'.

### The State

To a far greater degree than in liberal market economies (Hall and Soskice, 2001), the state has been a key actor in shaping economic processes in Asia. In some cases, Asian contexts have become synonymous with the workings of the developmental state or state capitalisms (Yeung, 2016). In their typology, Musachhio, Lazzarini, and Aguilera (2015) differentiate state capitalisms in terms of government ownership and control of organizations. At one extreme are wholly state-owned enterprises (SOEs), which are directly funded by governments and are usually established to fulfil developmental goals. At the other extreme are private organizations, which operate independently of the state but potentially receive indirect support through preferential capital access, tax breaks, and subsidies. Between these two poles, governments can also participate in economic activities by being majority or minority investors in different organizations. Apart from the level of ownership and control, state capitalism can be distinguished in terms of the importance of SOEs and private enterprises as engines of economic growth (Kohli, 2004). For instance, in the erstwhile communist economies in Eastern Europe, SOEs were the primary vehicles of economic growth. The SOEs received monopolies in different sectors, and their goals were to pursue import-substitution industrialization and to fulfil welfare goals of the state without being subjected to internal and external competition. In contrast, the South Korean economic growth model of the 1960s and 1970s relied on the private sector as the engine of growth. According to Kohli (2004: 13), South Korea's growth model encompassed a 'realization that maximizing production requires assuring the profitability of efficient producers but not inefficient ones'. Such a growth model is 'procapitalist' rather than 'ideologically promarket'. In both types of growth models, domestic firms were promoted through direct and indirect state support, limitations on international exposure (through trade barriers and investment restrictions) and domestic competition (through sector monopolies), and encouragement and support of inter-organizational relationships through the formation of large conglomerates (or business groups). In these pure models, organizations (either private or public enterprises) face coherent state logic and associated institutional expectations. Apart from the pure models, state capitalism can manifest itself through a hybrid organizational model whereby the state maintains economic coordination by encouraging both private organizations and SOEs (Witt and Redding, 2013). In such a case, a state can oscillate between affording primacy to each type of organization in different time periods and/or economic sectors.

The state continues to play an important role in most Asian economies, although the mechanisms through which it influences economic activities, both domestic and international, vary considerably. For instance, in comparing state capitalisms in the two largest Asian economies, Hu, Cui, and Aulakh (2019) suggest that although both China and India share many similarities, such as underdeveloped institutions and historical evolution of development paths, they differ in terms of the interactions between the state and organizational actors as well as the political context within which such interactions take place. China is characterized as a 'state-led business system', whereby a strong state directs most economic activities, but through a controlled devolution of activities to regional levels and private enterprises (see Cui and Jiang, 2012; Nee, 1992; Huang, 2008). Indian state capitalism, on the other hand, is a 'co-governed' one, whereby power is balanced between the state and private business, with state-owned enterprises playing a role in limited number of industries. Similarly, in a large-scale study of 61 economies, Witt et al. (2018) describe Japan as a 'highly coordinated economy', whereby major economic activities continue to stem from state coordination and direction (see also Witt and Redding, 2013).

## Business Conglomerates

Besides the role of the state through direct ownership of major organizations, Asian business systems are also characterized by the prevalence of large conglomerates (or business groups), known as the *keiretsu* in Japan and *chaebol*s in South Korea (Colpan et al., 2010). These groups of firms, 'though legally independent, are bound together by a constellation of formal and informal ties and are accustomed to taking coordinated action' (Khanna and Rivkin, 2001: 47–48). While diverse theoretical perspectives have been applied to study the genesis of business groups, a common insight in the literature is that business groups are formed in response to unique institutional conditions, such as imperfections in factor markets or institutional voids, foreign trade and investment asymmetries, and the important role of the state in economic development. The efficacy of business groups resides in their ability to forge and legitimize certain persistent ties—usually embedded in pre-existing social structures, such as family, kinship, and ethnicity—amongst member firms, which minimizes transaction costs and facilitates information and resource sharing across these firms.

Close and persistent relationships between the state and business groups are evident in most Asian economies. For instance, both the Japanese and South Korean economic growth models relied on the private sector as the engine of growth (Colpan, Hikino, and Lincoln, 2010). In China, the state-led system played an important role in the formation and development of business groups. This organizational form was initiated by the government during its SOE reforms in the mid-1980s, when the key focus was to achieve economies of scale and specialization. Accordingly, the Chinese government emphasized building highly competitive and large business groups in its national economy and promoting their international competitiveness (Lee and Kang, 2010). State-led policy initiatives, such as 'strong-strong combination' and 'national champions', along with strong financial backing from the state, have helped many Chinese conglomerates enter the international stage (Hu, Cui, and Aulakh, 2019). Indian business groups, on the other hand, were primarily initiated by private organizations but with the strong support of the state.

The above discussion shows a strong coordinating role for the state in Asia, in conjunction with organizational actors that include state-owned enterprises directly controlled by the state, and business groups that were encouraged and continue to flourish with direct or indirect support from the state. Given the intertwined goals of these actors in championing national goals, a number of chapters in this volume explicitly incorporate these institutional actors in their analyses. For instance, Chen and colleagues (Chapter 6) and Valderrey and colleagues (Chapter 5) both incorporate the global ambitions of China's state capitalism through the Belt and Road Initiative. Similarly, Camba (Chapter 4) and Cardenas (Chapter 11) discuss the role of transnational linkages of state-supported or sanctioned conglomerates in governing capital and labour flows in the mining and property industries in the Philippines respectively.

## Migration Infrastructure

A final institutional arena is comprised of a network of facilitators that enable human mobility. Xiang and Lindquist (2014: 124) use the term 'migration infrastructure' to capture 'the systematically interlinked technologies, institutions, and actors that facilitate and condition mobility'. They include five dimensions in such infrastructure. First, the 'commercial' dimension (sometimes called the 'migration industry') refers to the various intermediaries who connect workers and employers, often through multiple layers of brokers, recruiters, and agents. This may also include for-profit colleges that train migrants for their roles in the global workforce. In most of Asia, the layers of recruiters operate in nationally specific networks, although transnational temporary employment agencies are increasingly common. Second, the 'regulatory' dimension involves the state apparatus that documents, trains, and licenses migrants for work in specific places and occupations. As noted earlier, the Philippines has perhaps the most developed state infrastructure in the world for this purpose (Rodriguez, 2010). Third, the 'technological' dimensions of the migration infrastructure involve the diverse private (and occasionally state-owned) firms that provide communication and transportation services to migrants. These institutions can range from social media and internet providers to airlines, freight couriers, and remittance agencies. Fourth, non-governmental organizations and international agencies provide services and advocacy for migrant labour in various settings—often stepping in to fulfil protective functions that might properly be performed by the state. Where migrant workers are abused or stranded in their place of work, they are more likely in most cases to approach an NGO rather than an official labour attaché at their country's embassy. Fifth, and finally, migrant social networks are themselves critical forms of infrastructure that shape flows of labour. It is through such networks that direct recruitment, information sharing, and mutual support will usually be manifested.

The role of an institutionalized migration infrastructure in facilitating labour mobility is seen in various chapters in this collection. Walton-Roberts' study (Chapter 10) highlights the role of training institutions and staffing agencies in facilitating global nurse migration, while, in a different segment of the labour market, Conrad and Meyer-Ohle (Chapter 3) illustrate the role of job fairs to attract management recruits to Japan from South East Asia. Similarly, but for the process of internal migration, Kuzhiparambil (Chapter 7) describes the training and recruitment institutions that supply labour to India's regional apparel industry clusters. The institutions created by migrants themselves are also highlighted. For example, both Hari's study (Chapter 8) of Nepalese women migrants and Hastir's work (Chapter 9) on Punjabi migrants show how hometown associations of various kinds are active in directing investments in the homeland.

## Interdependencies and Tensions in Capital and Labour Mobility

It is readily understood that capital and labour are always two sides of the same coin. The process of accumulation of capital inevitably involves labour processes in some way. In line with other classical economists, Marx famously described commodities as 'congealed labour', meaning that they are always the product of past or present value production through human labour. At the same time, while labour processes do not necessarily require capital, or serve the accumulation imperative, they always occur in the context of capitalist accumulation. Labour processes and capitalist accumulation always therefore exist in a state of mutual coexistence and dependence.

Notwithstanding their interdependence, there will be a systemic contestation between the interests of those who own capital and those who sell their labour. Capital seeks to gain the most work, at the highest quality, for the lowest cost from labour. Labour obviously has other priorities, including maximising pay, seeking fulfilment from work, ensuring time for other activities and interests, and securing a safe and at least tolerable work environment. For these reasons, even as there is interdependency between capital and labour, there is always a tension between them as well. It is a dialectical tension in which each, capital and labour, needs the other, but each also has opposing interests. In this book, we see the interaction between capital and labour mobility in the same way—displaying tendencies towards both interdependency and contradiction.

We conceive of that tension as the 'generative' and 'disruptive' implications of each for the other. Perhaps most obviously, capital mobility can be generative of labour mobility by variously incentivising, forcing or enabling it. In some cases, this will be because labour is drawn to the employment opportunities presented by concentrations of capital. In other cases, it is because new capital investment in a place leads to the displacement of existing livelihoods and necessitates outmigration. But mobile capital might also be seen as disruptive to the mobility of labour, so that labour is actually immobilized. Certainly, capital has an interest in fixing its labour in place. Even when labour has been mobile in order to reach an employment opportunity, once there its usefulness to capital is best served by minimizing further mobility until it is no longer needed. Disrupting labour mobility is therefore a tendency as well.

At the same time, labour mobility is an active process within the capital–labour relationship and can be both disruptive and generative for capital accumulation. Labour mobility may be generative for capital accumulation in cases where migrants' remittances become sources of new investment in the homeland. Or, in a rather different scenario, where historical migrations facilitate contemporary capital flows across global space because of bonds of co-ethnicity. Conversely, the disruptive potential of labour mobility for capital accumulation is somewhat limited, but nevertheless present. This might include the impacts of labour mobility for the labour supply available to capital in a given location—after all, perhaps the most reliable form of resistance in the labour–capital relationship is for labour to simply leave in search of more favourable employment.

Table 1.1 summarizes these various dimensions of the generative and disruptive effects of capital and labour mobility on each other. In this section, we take each of

Table 1.1 | Generative and Disruptive Interdependencies between Capital and Labour Mobility

| | Generative | Disruptive |
|---|---|---|
| Labour mobility impact on accumulation by mobile capital | • Supplying disciplined, flexible and low-cost labour for production<br>• Remittances as basis for accumulation in migrant source areas<br>• Historical migrations and co-ethnic communities facilitating investment<br>• Human mobility as a basis for accumulation through the 'migration industry' | • Job-hopping to increase wages and improve working conditions<br>• Migration to escape broader exploitation and oppression based on class, caste and gender |
| Capital mobility impact on labour mobility | • New inward investment prompts migration, either domestic or international<br>• Mobile capital recruiting migrant managers to headquarters<br>• Generation of out-migration as FDI transforms local cultures and economies | • Mobile labour immobilized in workplaces |

*Source*: Developed by the authors.

these possibilities in turn and show how the chapters in this book illustrate these processes through grounded cases studies in Asia.

## Labour Mobility as Generative for Accumulation by Mobile Capital

The mobility of labour as generative for processes of accumulation by mobile capital is perhaps the theme most commonly illustrated in the chapters that follow in this book. First, labour mobility serves to deliver a solution to capital's perennial 'labour problem'—that is, the puzzle of ensuring that capital's labour needs are met in terms of quantities of supply, and qualities of discipline and skill, in order to facilitate the production process. Without labour mobility there can be no assurance that production will be possible. Cumbers, Nativel, and Routledge (2008) frame the problem in the following terms:

> From the perspective of capital, the labour problem sooner or later reasserts itself into the logic of accumulation. That problem—in its simplest terms—is threefold: first, the need to successfully incorporate labour into the production process; second, the need to exercise control over labour time in the production process and third, stemming from this second point, the imperative to exploit labour as part of the process of commodification to realize surplus value. (370)

Migrant labour provides a solution to all three elements of the problem. Uneven development—across national borders, between regions, or between rural and urban areas—ensures that workers will be attracted in sufficient numbers, thereby addressing the first problem, of incorporation. Then, the limits on citizenship rights for migrants, their dependence on employment for the continued residency, and the difficulties they face in asserting their rights, all foster a pliable and disciplined workforce, thus solving the second problem, of control. And finally, migrants' willingness to work for less and their dependence on these earnings to support family members left behind, both render mobile labour readily exploitable in the production process (the third problem).

A clear example of labour migration fostering capital accumulation is found in India's garment and textile industry. As Asha Kuzhiparambil describes in Chapter 7, labour migrants from rural areas provide an essential supply for producers in several key clusters such as Bangalore, Chennai, Tirupur, and Delhi. The training and migration of large numbers of workers from rural hinterlands have made this industrial development possible. Young women from rural villages receive training in skills-development centres created by Indian government initiatives. Investment and capital accumulation in industrial clusters would be impossible without the preparation and movement of labour in this way. Furthermore, the state's involvement goes beyond the establishment of training programs. As Kuzhiparambil notes, village heads have played a key role in persuading rural families to permit their daughters to undertake this kind of migration. Thus, not only is labour mobility a key precursor to capital accumulation in this case, but the state has been intimately supportive in facilitating the process.

A second way in which labour mobility begets capital mobility and accumulation is when labour itself becomes a source of capital, through remittances. As noted earlier in this chapter, remittance flows have become major sources of external investment in many Asian contexts. Cardenas' study (Chapter 11) of urban development in Manila makes this point very clearly. Manila's growth in recent years has taken the form of mixed-use residential, retail, and office development constructed across the metropolitan region. Such developments cater to the desire of overseas Filipinos to buy property in the homeland, as an investment, holiday home, or retirement residence. As a result, the accumulation strategies of major Philippine-owned conglomerates have shifted away from traditional sectors such as banking and food processing, and into real estate. And, alongside real estate development, companies such as Ayala and SM have also invested in the utilities, transportation, and communications sectors that service these new developments. To add a further layer of interconnection, these integrated real estate developments have also served to attract mobile capital in the form of foreign direct investment in the business process outsourcing (BPO) sector (and call centres in particular). The Philippines is now a world leader in the BPO sector.

Remittance flows from overseas migrants are also a feature of Rosy Hastir's work (Chapter 9), which focuses on the links between the Punjabi village of Kharoudi and migrant destinations in Europe, North America, and the Middle East. The landscape of the village has been transformed not just by the private remittances of overseas migrants that have been used to construct new housing, but also through the collective philanthropy of non-resident Indians (NRIs) in the public spaces and infrastructure of the village. Hometown associations of various kinds are active investors in localized development processes. Hastir's study also highlights the fact that transnationalism is a process differentiated by social and economic class. She notes that only upper-caste migrants have generally been able to emigrate to high income countries and settle into professional careers, while lower castes are more likely to be working as contract workers, often with undocumented status. This serves as a reminder that while the possibility of transnationalism exists, the ability of different classes of migrants to engage in the process is differentiated by their uneven power within a network (Sheppard, 2016).

The differential benefits of human mobility are also evident in less tangible ways in Hastir's study. NRIs often return home with 'social remittances' that may be jarring for village residents including new practices, language, household devices and lifestyles. The impact on the village therefore goes beyond the physical landscape and economic capital to generate other kinds of cultural capital that entrench the status of upper castes within the village. Migration may not therefore be a leveller, but can instead lead to deepening economic and cultural inequalities.

A third mode through which labour mobility is generative for capital is in the facilitation of investment through ties of co-ethnicity due to historic migrations. In Camba's study (Chapter 4) of Chinese mining investment in the Philippines, well-established local Chinese communities play a critical role in facilitating investment through joint ventures in small-scale mining. At a time (during the Benigno Aquino administration of 2010–2016) when national government relations between the Philippines and China were strained due to tensions over territorial disputes in the South China Sea, Chinese investors were able to circumvent national politics and get access to Philippine resources by working with local players. Well-connected Filipino-Chinese entrepreneurs were especially important and used their connections and influence with local political elites in peripheral provinces to smooth a path for joint mining ventures. The unrecorded export of ore is also often facilitated by mobilizing such local contacts. In this way, as Camba points out, a long history of Chinese migrations to all parts of the Philippine archipelago becomes—in some circumstances—a useable network of local collaborators to facilitate mining investment. Valderrey and colleagues (Chapter 5) make a similar case—arguing that a well-established ethnic Chinese community in Peru has facilitated Chinese investment in mining and energy sectors. That said, Camba is careful to point out that ties of co-ethnicity are not a determining factor—rather, they facilitate a relationship that is fundamentally based on economic interests.

A final mode through which labour mobility facilitates capital accumulation is through the commodification of migrants themselves. Labour mobility itself becomes a basis for accumulation through the 'migration industry' discussed earlier in this chapter. In Chapter 10, Margaret Walton-Roberts highlights the way in which such an industry exists in the case of nurse migration from India. A multi-layered and transnational network of training institutions, deployment agencies, testing centres, job fairs, and brokers create the space-transcending infrastructure that delivers skilled labour for healthcare facilities in the Middle East, Europe, and North America. A nurse's body becomes, in other words, a value-added commodity and a site for capital accumulation.

## Labour Mobility as Disruptive of Accumulation

The opportunities for labour to disrupt capital accumulation, without undermining its own interests, are limited. Mobile capital, in particular, has certain inherent advantages because the 'threat to exit' always hangs over an employment relationship. Nevertheless, labour has disruptive potential, especially if capital accumulation processes are predicated on tight labour markets and/or integrated supply chains that are spread across space (Theodore, 2016).

On a small scale, mobility between employers—job hopping—can represent a form of resistance in which workers refuse to accept the pay and working conditions that are on offer. The study of Chinese shoe factories relocating to Cambodia by Chen and colleagues (in Chapter 6) notes the wage increases in Guangdong province that have underpinned this imperative for producers to move. As workers in Dongguan and other major industrial centres in China have become more demanding and discerning, and have been able to move between employers, wages have been forced upwards for China's industrial working class. Chen and colleagues note that wages in Dongguan's shoe factories doubled in just two years between 2006 and 2008. In a separate quantitative study, Ariga et al. (2012) found that job hopping in China's industrial workforce, especially by those who were migrants to the coastal industrial clusters, had a significant effect on wages (and in fact brought internal migrants' wages into line with those of local workers). Of course, this form of local disruption to capital accumulation has its own contradictions when employers relocate to cheaper locations such as Cambodia, but it does highlight the potential of labour mobility to interrupt the process of value extraction.

If job-hopping is one form of disruption through human mobility, then a broader sense would include migration away from a place in order to escape exploitation and oppression. Hari's study (in Chapter 8) of Nepalese women's migration to the countries of the Gulf highlights the reality that even out-migration into the harsh working conditions of domestic service may represent a form of resistance. Such resistance may be directed towards the state, which has periodically imposed mobility restrictions on female migrants. Or, it might be towards gender- and class-based forms of exploitation and oppression that exist in the communities from which women are migrating. In some ways, of course, this kind of migration is hardly disruptive of capital accumulation, and labour migrants serve the needs of capital in another location. Nevertheless, as Hari argues, it exemplifies a form of agency and resistance among women with few other options.

## *Capital Mobility as Generative of Labour Mobility*

Capital mobility prompts labour mobility in several ways. Perhaps most obviously, inward investment in a particular place will frequently draw in migrant labour, whether domestic or international, to serve its needs. Since labour and capital are mutually dependent in the production process, it is often difficult to say which is the chicken and which is the egg—that is, whether labour availability begets capital investment, or capital inflows and employment opportunities summon up the necessary labour. In the case of Indian garment and textile production mentioned earlier (and featured in Chapter 7) the active promotion of training and recruitment schemes from rural areas seems to have catalysed and enabled the expansion of production. In Chapter 6, on the other hand, Chen and colleagues show that it has been decisions by Chinese shoe producers to invest in Phnom Penh, Cambodia, that have driven migration from the surrounding countryside into the city. Even more clearly, and again in Chapter 6, we see Chinese investment in infrastructure projects in South East Asia that have brought migrant Chinese labour with them. Gas and oil pipelines from the coast of Myanmar to Yunnan province in China were completed in 2013 and 2017 respectively. A rail and transportation corridor between Laos and China was still under construction in 2019. In both cases, construction labour consisted largely of migrant labour from China. For the Lao rail project, Chen and colleagues suggest that up to 100,000 Chinese workers will be used as construction peaks. These kinds of capital mobility, then, clearly prompt significant mobility of (perhaps temporary) labour in order to serve their needs.

A second, and rather different, case involves the recruitment of migrant managers by transnational corporations from the places where they operate to their home country headquarters. In Chapter 3, Conrad and Meyer-Ohle explain the recent focus by Japanese transnationals on the recruitment of managers and professionals from across Asia. Traditionally, Japanese firms deployed Japanese managers to oversee subsidiaries abroad. A more recent practice, beginning around 2010, has been to recruit talent into the headquarters in Japan from Asian universities, or from among Asian students studying in Japanese universities. The goal is not necessarily for these recruits to return to manage subsidiaries in their home country, but rather to internationalize and diversify thinking at the corporate head office. This new thinking provides important insights because Japanese firms are no longer just internationalizing to create export platforms in the manufacturing sector. Instead, they are increasingly going overseas to service expanding consumer markets in media, retail, and restaurant sectors. For this, a clear understanding of diverse cultural contexts is needed. Migrant managers working in Japan provide these insights. Interestingly, Conrad and Meyer-Ohle suggest that this process has been partly facilitated by the earlier diffusion of Japanese cultural products across Asia. Migrant managers are, they find, often attracted to work in Japan because they have long been exposed to Japanese consumer goods and popular culture, such as comic books, animated characters, music, and film. In some cases, this has also motivated a younger generation to start learning Japanese in order to advance their passion for Japanese cultural products. Migration to the birthplace of iconic pop cultural products is therefore seen as appealing.

A third way in which capital mobility is generative of labour mobility relates to the disturbance of lives and livelihoods by new forms of investment and accumulation in a given place, which in turn prompt migration as old forms of economic life are cast aside. In some respects this returns us to the early work of Saskia Sassen (1988) who drew attention to the role of foreign direct investment in prompting emigration from the Global South. She argued that local forms of livelihood were unsettled by the transformations resulting from integration into global circuits of capital. In Chapter 8 in this collection, Hari makes a similar argument in the context of Nepal. He describes how the transformation of livelihoods, resource access, and cultural practices generates out-migration, especially among women in rural parts of the country. In particular, he shows how the infiltration of global commodities into rural village life creates a demand for monetary income, while also undermining traditional economic practices of informal farming and care work.

## Capital Mobility as Disruptive of Labour Mobility

Capital always has a contradictory interest in labour's mobility and immobility. As noted earlier, the supply of migrant labour to sites of production makes labour mobility a beneficial process for capital accumulation. The docility and vulnerability of people who are working outside the boundaries of their citizenship or cultural home also serves to benefit capital accumulation. But capital also has a strong interest in the immobility of labour. Once engaged in the production process, capital's interest is in locking down labour so that it is immobile until its usefulness is exhausted.

In Chapter 2, Kleibert shows how new forms of bordering, containment, and enclave-formation work to constrain labour. By focusing on special economic zones, offshore service districts, and cruise ships, she shows how each of these transnational offshore spaces have become an important site for mobile capital and accumulation. But, while they give flexibility and freedom to capital, they significantly constrain the mobility of labour. In the case of special economic zones, this is sometimes accomplished through the use of dormitory accommodation which restricts the freedom of movement for industrial workers. In the case of cruise ships, workers are very clearly immobilized even as they ply the world's oceans. In each case, accumulation is predicated on the availability of migrant labour in various forms. But at the same time, these enclaves simultaneously constrain the mobility of the workers who sustain them.

## Conclusions

We started this chapter by noting the separation of labour and capital mobilities in the many studies that exist on each. Research on capital mobility largely asks questions that are internal to the logics and motivations of firms, investors and other movers of capital across the world. Similarly, studies of labour migration are generally not concerned with the structures of capital accumulation and mobility that drive most labour processes.

We have argued here that it is instructive and important to bridge the study of labour and capital mobility and that the relationship between the two is best conceived as both an interdependency and a tension. Capital mobility can be generative of labour migration, but it can also be disruptive of human mobility when the logic of accumulation demands it. Similarly, labour mobility and migration can be a generative precursor to capital flows, but it can also, on occasion, represent a form of disruptive resistance to mobile capital.

In attempting to bring both forms of mobility into the same frame, this book focuses on the Asian context in particular. In part this is because the intensity of economic growth in many parts of Asia have made it the world's most dynamic region in terms of capital flows and labour migrations. For both mobilities, sites in Asia are globally significant. Moreover, these flows take on particular modalities in Asia. As the data presented earlier demonstrate, countries in Asia now represent close to one-third of inward and outward FDI flows globally. Asia also includes the three largest recipients of remittances, and the second largest source country. Every variety of migrant labour is represented through East, West, South, and South East Asia, and they move through some of the world's most significant migration corridors. But Asian contexts also have some qualitative differences that are significant as well. Distinct institutional structures of state regulation, variegated configurations of state–market relations, and particular corporate formations all shape the forms that capital mobility takes. These institutional dimensions of difference also shape labour regimes and policies towards permanent immigration and temporary migrant labour. Asian contexts are important to understand, therefore, not just because of their numerical importance for global capital and labour mobility, but also because of their qualitative differences.

In engaging with the interactions of labour and capital mobility, the chapters in this book necessarily take either labour or capital as the starting point of their analyses. This provides an organizing principle for the ordering of the case studies into two sections. In the first section, capital is the starting point of analysis, in the form of transnational corporate structures and investment flows. In each case, the role of labour is quickly brought into the picture to show that capital mobility is inseparable from human mobility. In the second section, labour is the central actor in each study, as the pathways of migrants are traced and the implications for capital accumulation and mobility are drawn into the analyses. Taken together, the chapters make a compelling case for a contextualized understanding of the interdependency between capital and labour mobility.

# References

Ariga, K., F. Ohtake, M. Sasaki, and Z. Wu. 2012. 'Wage Growth through Job Hopping in China', KIER Working Paper No. 833. Retrieved from Kyoto University, Institute of Economic Research. Available at https://econpapers.repec.org/paper/kyowpaper/833.htm. Accessed on 10 July 2019.

Asian Development Bank Institute (ADBI), International Labour Organization (ILO), and Organization for Economic Co-operation and Development (OECD). 2015. *Building Human Capital through Labor Migration in Asia*. Tokyo.

Asian Development Bank. 2017. *Asian Economic Integration Report 2017: The Era of Financial Interconnectedness*. Manila.

Aulakh, P. S. 2007. 'Emerging Multinationals from Developing Economies: Motivations, Paths and Performance.' *Journal of International Management* 3(13): 235–240.

Betts, A. 2011. *Global Migration Governance*. Oxford: Oxford University Press.

Brown, S. S. 2006. 'Can Remittances Spur Development? A Critical Survey.' *International Studies Review* 8(1): 55–76.

Carney, M., E. Gedajlovic, and X. Yang. 2009. 'Varieties of Asian Capitalism: Toward an Institutional Theory of Asian Enterprise'. *Asia Pacific Journal of Management* 26(3): 361–380.

Coe, N. M. and H. W. C. Yeung. 2015. *Global Production Networks: Theorizing Economic Development in an Interconnected World.* Oxford: Oxford University Press.

Colpan, A. M., T. Hikino, and J. R. Lincoln. 2010. *The Oxford Handbook of Business Groups,* Oxford: Oxford University Press.

Commission on Filipinos Overseas. 2014. *Stock Estimate of Filipinos Overseas.* Manila. Available at http://cfo.gov.ph/program-and-services/yearly-stock-estimation-of-overseas-filipinos.html. Accessed on 18 October 2018.

Cuervo-Cazurra, A. and R. Ramamurti. 2014. *Understanding Multinationals from Emerging Markets.* Cambridge: Cambridge University Press.

Cui, L. and F. Jiang. 2012. 'State Ownership Effect on Firms' FDI Ownership Decisions under Institutional Pressure: A Study of Chinese Outward-investing Firms.' *Journal of International Business Studies* 43(3): 264–284.

Cumbers, A., C. Nativel, and P. Routledge. 2008. 'Labour Agency and Union Positionalities in Global Production Networks.' *Journal of Economic Geography* 8(3): 369–387.

Dunning, J. H. 1988. 'The Eclectic Paradigm of International Production: A Restatement and Some Possible Extensions.' *Journal of International Business Studies* 19(1): 1–31.

Faist, T., M. Fauser, and E. Reisenauer. 2013. *Transnational Migration.* Cambridge: Polity Press.

Gereffi, G. and M. Korzeniewicz. 1994. *Commodity Chains and Global Capitalism.* Westport, CT: Praeger.

Giuliano, P. and M. Ruiz-Arranz. 2009. 'Remittances, Financial Development, and Growth.' *Journal of Development Economics* 90(1): 144–152.

Gubbi, S. R., P. S. Aulakh, S. Ray, M. B. Sarkar, and R. Chittoor. 2010. 'Do International Acquisitions by Emerging-economy Firms Create Shareholder Value? The Case of Indian Firms.' *Journal of International Business Studies* 41(3): 397–418.

Hall, P. A. and D. Soskice. 2001. *Varieties of Capitalism: The Institutional Foundations of Comparative Advantage.* Oxford: Oxford University Press.

de Haas, H. 2005. 'International Migration, Remittances and Development: Myths and Facts.' *Third World Quarterly* 26(8): 1269–1284.

Hu, H. W., L. Cui, and P. S. Aulakh. 2019. 'State Capitalism and Performance Persistence of Business Group-affiliated Firms: A Comparative Study of China and India.' *Journal of International Business Studies.* 50(2): 193–222.

Huang, Y. 2008. *Capitalism with Chinese Characteristics: Entrepreneurship and the State.* New York: Cambridge University Press.

Johnson, L. 2017. 'Bordering Shanghai: China's Hukou System and Processes of Urban Bordering.' *Geoforum* 80: 93–102.

Kelly, P. F. 2012.' Labor, Movement: Migration, Mobility and Geographies of Work.' In *The New Companion to Economic Geography*, edited by T. Barnes, J. Peck, and E. Sheppard, 431–443. Oxford: Blackwell.

———. 2017. 'Migration, Remittances and Development.' *Handbook of Southeast Asian Development*, edited by A. McGregor, L. Law, and F. Miller, 198–210. London: Routledge.

Khanna, T. and J. W. Rivkin 2001. 'Estimating the Performance Effects of Business Groups in Emerging Markets'. *Strategic Management Journal* 22(1): 45–74.

Kohli, A. 2004. *State-directed Development: Political Power and Industrialization in the Global Periphery.* New York: Cambridge University Press.

Lee, K. and Y-S. Kang. 2010. 'Business Groups in China.' In *The Oxford Handbook of Business Groups*, edited by A. M. Colpan, T. Hikino, and J. R. Lincoln, 210–236. New York: Oxford University Press.

Lim, K. F. 2014. '"Socialism with Chinese Characteristics": Uneven Development, Variegated Neoliberalization and the Dialectical Differentiation of State Spatiality.' *Progress in Human Geography* 38(2): 221–247.

Maddison, A. and P. van der Eng. 2013. *Asia's Role in the Global Economy in Historical Perspective* (no. 021), Centre for Economic History, Research School of Economics, Australian National University. Available at https://ideas.repec.org/p/auu/hpaper/021.html. Accessed on 12 March 2019.

*Migration and Remittances Factbook 2016*. Available at http://www.worldbank.org/en/research/brief/migration-and-remittances. Accessed on 13 May 2018.

Mitchell, K. 2004. *Crossing the Neoliberal Line: Pacific Rim Migration and the Metropolis*. Philadelphia, PA: Temple University Press.

Murray, K. 2017. *The Urbanism of Exception: The Dynamics of Global City Building in the Twenty-First Century*. Cambridge: Cambridge University Press.

Nathan, D., M. Tewari, and S. Sarkar, eds. 2016. *Labour in Global Value Chains in Asia*. Cambridge: Cambridge University Press.

Nee, V. 1992. 'Organizational Dynamics of Market Transition: Hybrid Forms, Property Rights, and Mixed Economy in China.' *Administrative Science Quarterly* 37(1): 1–27.

Olds, K. 2001. *Globalization and Urban Change: Capital, Culture, and Pacific Rim Mega-projects*. Oxford: Oxford University Press.

POEA (Philippine Overseas Employment Administration). 2016. *Compendium of OFW Statistics, 2016*. Manila. Available at http://www.poea.gov.ph/ofwstat/ofwstat.html). Accessed on 18 October 2018.

Poston, D. L. and J. H. Wong. 2016. 'The Chinese Diaspora: The Current Distribution of the Overseas Chinese Population.' *Chinese Journal of Sociology* 2(3): 348–373.

Rajan, S. 2011. *Dynamics of Indian Migration: Historical and Current Perspectives*. New Delhi: Routledge.

Ramamurti, R. and J. V. Singh. 2009. *Emerging Multinationals in Emerging Markets*. Cambridge: Cambridge University Press.

Rodriguez, R. A. 2010. *Migrants for Export: How the Philippine State Brokers Labor to the World*. Minneapolis, MN: University of Minnesota Press.

Sassen, S. 1988. *The Mobility of Labor and Capital: A Study in International Investment and Labor Flow*. Cambridge: Cambridge University Press.

———. 2001. *The Global City: New York, London, Tokyo*, 2nd rev. edn. Princeton, NJ: Princeton University Press.

Saxenian, A. 2006. *The New Argonauts: Regional Advantage in a Global Economy*. Cambridge, MA: Harvard University Press.

Schiller, N. G. and A. Simsek-Caglar, eds. 2010. *Locating Migration: Rescaling Cities and Migrants*. Ithaca, NY: Cornell University Press.

Sharma, K. 2017. 'India Has 139 Million Internal Migrants. They Must Not Be Forgotten.' *World Economic Forum Online*. Available athttps://www.weforum.org/agenda/2017/10/india-has-139-million-internal-migrants-we-must-not-forget-them. Accessed on 25 October 2018.

Sheppard, E. 2016. *Limits to Globalization: Disruptive Geographies of Capitalist Development.* Oxford: Oxford University Press.

Theodore, N. 2016. 'Worlds of Work: Changing Landscapes of Production and the New Geographies of Opportunity'. *Geography Compass* 10(4): 179–189.

UNCTAD. 2017. *World Investment Report* 2017. UN. Available at http://worldinvestmentreport. unctad.org/world-investment-report-2017. Accessed on 10 May 2018.

Walton-Roberts, M. 2011. 'Immigration, Trade and "Ethnic Surplus Value": A Critique of Indo-Canadian Transnational Networks'. *Global Networks: A Journal of Transnational Affairs* 11(2): 203–221.

Wells, L. T. 1983. *Third World Multinationals: The Rise of Foreign Investments from Developing Countries.* Boston, MA: The MIT Press.

Wills, J., K. Datta, Y. Evans, J. Herbert, J. May, and C. McIlwaine (2009). *Global Cities at Work: New Migrant Divisions of Labour.* London: Pluto Press.

Witt, M. A. L. R. Kabbach de Castro, K. Amaeshi, S. Mahroum, D. Bohle, and L. Saez. 2018. 'Mapping the Business Systems of 61 Major Economies: A Taxonomy and Implications for Varieties of Capitalism and Business Systems Research.' *Socio-Economic Review* 16(1): 5–38.

Witt, M. A. and G. Redding. 2013. 'Asian Business Systems: Institutional Comparison, Clusters and Implications for Varieties of Capitalism and Business Systems Theory.' *Socio-Economic Review* 11(2): 265–300.

World Bank. 2017. *Migration and Remittances Data.* Available at http://www.worldbank.org/ en/topic/migrationremittancesdiasporaissues/brief/migration-remittances-data. Accessed on 12 October 2018.

———. 2018. *Moving for Prosperity: Global Migration and Labor Markets.* Washington, DC: World Bank. Available at http://www.worldbank.org/en/research/publication/moving-for-prosperity. Accessed on 13 March 2019.

Xiang, B. and Lindquist, J. 2014. 'Migration Infrastructure.' *International Migration Review* 48(s1): S122–S148.

Yang, H., P. Yang, and S. Zhan. 2017. 'Immigration, Population, and Foreign Workforce in Singapore: An Overview of Trends, Policies, and Issues.' *HSSE Online* 6(1).

Yeung, H. W. C. 2004. *Chinese Capitalism in a Global Era: Towards Hybrid Capitalism.* London: Routledge.

———. 2016. *Strategic Coupling: East Asian Industrial Transformation in the New Global Economy.* Ithaca, NY: Cornell University Press.

Zhang, X. and R. Whitley. 2013. 'Changing Macro-Structural Varieties of East Asian Capitalism'. *Socio-Economic Review* 11(2): 301–336.

Zhao, L., S. Liu, and W. Zhang. 2018. 'New Trends in Internal Migration in China: Profiles of the New-generation Migrants.' *China & World Economy* 26(1): 18–41.

Zweig, D. and H. Wang. 2013. 'Can China Bring Back the Best? The Communist Party Organizes China's Search for Talent.' *The China Quarterly* 215: 590–615.

From Capital to Labour Mobility

# 2

# Offshore Spaces

*Multi-scalar Bordering Processes and the Segmented
Mobilities of Capital and Labour in Asia*

JANA M. KLEIBERT

## Introduction: Borderless World or a World of Borders?

The optimistic globalist accounts of the 1990s that painted the rise of a 'borderless' world (for example, Ohmae, 1990; for a critique see Yeung, 1998) are faded myths today. The second decade of the twenty-first century seems to be more adequately characterized by the instigation of new borders and/or the fortification of existing ones. The rise of populist governments around the world, the shift towards protectionist policies in the USA under Trump, the vote of the UK electorate to exit the European Union, and the migration 'crisis' that has emerged in Europe following violent conflicts in close geographic proximity have brought the fortification of borders, fences, and walls back on the agenda of governments and in the broader public view. These borders are generally discussed at the level of the (nation) state. The aim of this chapter is to engage with a less-noticed undercurrent of the multi-scalar process of bordering, often at the subnational level, that is equally structuring a non-borderless world: the enclosure of territories with specific and differential impacts on capital and labour, designed in many ways with the aim to increase the mobilities of one while regulating those of the other. The enclosed territories, or offshore spaces, take the shape of special economic zones (SEZs), tax havens, or cruise ships.

The central argument advanced in this chapter is that the spatial form of globalization is expressed as an archipelago economy that consists of networked offshore spaces, or transnational enclave spaces. These depend on territorial zoning strategies that operate through mechanisms of bordering/enclosure, which are necessary for capital accumulation. The cross-border mobilities of capital and labour do not operate in isolation from each other, but are indeed closely related and intertwined. Intensifying globalization, however, has had a differential impact on these mobilities, generally privileging capital mobility while allowing only regulated and restricted movements of labour.[1] The mobilities of capital and labour should be seen as an intertwined and interdependent process. Offshore spaces for capital accumulation depend on various forms of transnational labour, though labour is integrated in highly uneven and segmented terms.

The chapter explores the spatialities of globalization through a focus on micro-spaces of the offshore. The next section develops the concept of *transnational enclave spaces*, drawing on theoretical backgrounds of the differential mobilities of capital and labour and multi-scalar bordering processes. Then, three examples of different types of offshore spaces from South East Asia are presented as illustrations of the argument, namely SEZs, offshore services districts, and cruise ships as floating offshore enclaves. The chapter concludes by outlining a research agenda for investigating offshore sites and processes of enclave creation in the contemporary global economy.

## Uneven Mobilities of Capital and Labour and Multi-scalar Bordering Processes

The mobilities of capital and labour are often treated as separate empirical processes and have thus rarely been analysed together, despite being in many instances related to each other (Sassen, 1988). They are, moreover, characterized by segmented mobilities, usually regulated and negotiated at the border. On the one hand, international capital mobility has been successively eased over time via policies of financial deregulation and via technological advances in information and communications technology (ICT) that have enabled the ever-faster travel of capital across the globe, for instance through high-frequency trading. Even after the 2008 financial crisis and calls for increased regulation of the financial sector, capital mobility remains high, and recent legislative efforts even point towards increasing deregulation.[2] International labour mobility, on the other hand, remains heavily restricted through national policies and, where internal borders have been dissolved, this has usually occurred at the expense of more intensive border-checks at the outside as the 'Fortress Europe' metaphor suggests. The European integration project, a macroeconomic union aimed at creating a single market and facilitating

---

[1]   The current backlash against globalization in many parts of the world is in favour of stronger regulation of migrant labour (for example, raising a fence against Mexican migrants to the USA), while leaving capital mobility relatively unrestricted.

[2]   Though there are notable exceptions, capital mobility of the Renminbi remains heavily restricted by the Chinese government.

intra-regional free movement of capital, goods, and people, has been crucially negotiated by the financial sector's increased powers through a broadening of the market (Mügge, 2010), whereas increasing the mobility of labour has taken a back seat. Many European governments have negotiated relatively long temporal exemptions from the free inward migration labour from several Eastern European accession countries with lower labour costs, including Romania and Bulgaria. Similarly, the establishment of the Association of Southeast Asian Nations (ASEAN) Economic Community, in 2015, primarily focuses on the abolishment of taxes and duties and capital market integration process, while labour mobility is still subject to extensive licensing regimes in host countries that limit the free flow of workers.

Borders clearly work differently for differently placed actors and bodies. Sassen (2013: 39) has argued that

> we see a simultaneous shift to increasingly open geographic state borders along with transversally closed bordered spaces. The former are far more common and formalized for major corporate economic actors than they are for citizens and migrants; the growing exception is the emergent global class of individuals who are top-level global economic players. [...] Firms and this new global class are now enveloped in multiple new types of institutionalized protections through these new transversal bordering capabilities, while citizens and migrants lose protection and have to struggle to gain such new types of transversal protections.

Labour, like capital and land, is one of Karl Polanyi's 'fictitious commodities', which is made to resemble a 'real' commodity but cannot be reduced to one. Labour differs from other commodities in another regard, as David Harvey famously noted: 'Unlike other commodities, labour power has to go home every night' (1989: 19, cited in Peck, 2000: 141). Labour is embodied, and unable to travel at the speed of light, leading to a physical restriction of its mobility. While certainly not immobile, labour is thus relatively less mobile than capital, given its reproduction in particular places (Peck, 1996). The ICT revolution, however, has expanded the ways in which labour can be integrated into 'global' labour markets through 'virtual migration' as work is conducted on online platforms and integrated into global value chains and delivered in real time to end markets in the geographically distanced markets (for example, Aneesh, 2006). The opportunity for labour arbitrage in services has, however, not led to a flat or borderless world, as even online markets exhibit discriminatory processes and workers are found to receive differential remuneration for similar work based on their geographical location (Beerepoot and Lambregts, 2015).

Much of today's transnationally stretched industrial production arrangements continue to rely on low-cost labour. Paradigmatic 'global industries', above all garments and apparel manufacturing chains, crucially depend on various forms of domestic and international migrant labour. China's domestic migrant labour force of 130 million has moved to the country's booming coastal manufacturing zones, constituting a rural–urban migration on an enormous scale, but other countries equally rely on young, female migrant labour employed in SEZs and disciplined by labour control regimes, including dormitory accommodation (Arnold and Pickles, 2011; Azmeh, 2014; Ngai, 2007). As we will discuss here, the border plays an extremely relevant role in structuring the relations of production and labour at these 'enclave' sites.

National borders have the agency to shape the value of labour, and relatedly, labour power, through migration regimes, through the control over order and space, and through shaping of the terms and conditions of entry and exit (McGrath, 2017). Immigration regimes and semipermeable national borders enable the disembodiment of labour from the migrant worker and spatially separates the sites (and costs) of production and reproduction (Kearney, 1991, cited in Peck, 1996: 10). Dennis Arnold and John Pickles (2011: 1599), studying the emergent labour formations in a border industrial zone in South East Asia, argue that '[t]he convergence of regionalization and globalization is articulated in localized spaces conducive to mobile capital and investment that, on the one hand, straddle and blur national boundaries, and on the other, redefine and reify borders, particularly in terms of flows of migrant labor'.

These borders are, however, occurring not just at the national scale; instead, we see a shifting of borders from the national to subnational scales and the creation of new spatial logics. An intriguing case in point is the instigation of special security zones for logistics as 'new forms of containment', which prioritize flows and where normal civil and labour laws can be suspended (Cowen, 2014). The combined effect of these infrastructural spaces is the 'massive reorganization of where the border works, how, and for whom' (Cowen, 2014: 90). Instead of becoming obsolete, the importance of borders for globalization processes could be argued to be of central importance (though generally hidden) for organizing or 'making' globalization. As Sandro Mezzadra and Brett Neilson convincingly argue in their book *Border as Method*, 'far from serving to block or obstruct global flows [borders] have become central devices for their articulation [… and] regulate and structure the relations between capital, labour, law, subjects and political power' (2013: 6–8). The authors explicitly focus on the subnational level and identify the proliferation of enclave spaces as 'a more general characteristic of the emerging spatiality of globalization' (Mezzadra and Neilson, 2013: 238). Borders are clearly no anomaly in globalization that will dissolve over time but need to be made and unmade precisely for the operation of the contemporary global economy.

An interesting body of research, drawing on actor-network theory, has engaged with the social practices of 'b/ordering' (van Houtum, Kramsch, and Zierhofer,

2005; Berndt and Boeckler, 2009 and 2011). The argument here is that borders do not simply exist but are created and constructed through segmented mobilities that are enforced through the borders' semipermeability in an ambiguous and ambivalent process, thus displaying 'their selective force through their potential to produce a complex amalgam of multiple, often deeply unequal differentiations' (Berndt and Boeckler, 2011: 1062). Again, the mobilization of the border does not necessarily coincide with the red lines marked on atlases and maps. Christian Berndt and Marc Boeckler show, based on the empirical case of tomato commodity chain assemblages along the US–Mexican and the European–Moroccan borders, how these North–South borders as '"inner borders" of global capitalism … move southwards, meandering across rural regions, including some fields and installations and excluding others as market integration's Other' (2011: 1067–1068).

Technologies of zoning and bordering are particularly visible in the creation of SEZs (Easterling, 2014; Ong, 2006; Mezzadra and Neilson, 2013), which constitute exceptions to national legislative territory, permitting enhanced mobilities of capital and deregulated labour laws. Building on Giorgio Agamben's (2005) notion of 'state of exception'[3] Aihwa Ong has argued that 'by deploying zoning strategies, sovereign states can create or accommodate islands of distinct governing regimes within the broader landscape of normalized rule. The political outcome is an archipelago of enclaves, the sum of which is a form of variegated sovereignty' (2006: 103). Offshore spaces, or enclave spaces, are regulatory exceptions that have spatial boundaries and aim to disembed themselves from their local surroundings. James Sidaway has suggested that enclaves constitute a 'new metageography' occurring at multiple sizes and scales, forming a 'heterogenous and disparate array of interlaced and bounded spaces and projects defying easy categorization' (2007: 355). These enclave spaces complicate binary ideas of the Global North/Global South, of 'developed' and 'developing' countries, and are overlapping, interleaved, and intersecting arrangements.

It would be wrong to envision enclaves as hermetically sealed-off spaces. They are semipermeable, and their borders enable the interplay of restrictions and openness, of regulation and deregulation, and of selective embeddedness into transnational flows.[4] While the notion of the enclave works as a metaphor for the enclosed

[3] Agamben's discussion focuses on the 'bare life' of the unprotected individual against the sovereign state who has the power to suspend laws. He draws on Carl Schmitt's discussion of the *Ausnahmezustand*, linking the suspension of laws during a state of emergency into a longer-term arrangement, which finds its spatial expression in prison camps. Ong (2006), however, uncovers more complex state strategies in the face of neoliberalism, leading to variegated sovereignty rather than the simple suspension of laws.

[4] See also Harms (2015) for a discussion of gated communities as 'porous enclaves' in South East Asia.

territories within nations, its territorial understanding falls short of grasping the embeddedness in global networks—the topological dimension. Beyond being the result of mobile technologies of bordering and zones, transplantable and mutating across different places in the world, enclave spaces can be seen as transnationally networked spaces that constitute nodes in transnational networks of capital and labour, the spaces where flows 'touch down'.

I thus suggest the term *transnational enclave spaces* to signify the importance of offshore spaces' embeddedness in global networks, in order to capture the complex relationship of topography and topology that also characterizes Sven Opitz and Ute Tellmann's (2012) discussions of 'global territories' as modulators of connectivity that make global circulation possible, precisely through their particular (re)arrangements of borders, (dis)connectivity, and visibility. Building on Opitz and Tellmann's work on offshore zones as juridico-political constructs, this chapter delves more deeply into the question of how offshore spaces are not only crystallization points of globalization, but also vital technologies for differentiating capital and labour mobilities.

## Offshore Spaces for Capital Accumulation in Asia

Offshore spaces come in a variety of shapes and forms. In order to corroborate the argument that these networked territories constitute important vantage point for understanding global–local encounters and frictions, this section discusses some empirical cases drawn from South East Asia. The analysis does not offer a representative and all-encompassing overview of different types of offshore spaces, but is restricted to a discussion of three illustrative examples of enclosed transnational nodes where transnational migration and capital mobility intersect: (a) offshore production zones, (b) offshore service zones, and (c) (mobile) offshore leisure zones. It will be shown how these offshore, or enclave spaces, do not simply exist but are created through a process of (re)constructing difference at the border through a segmented process of bordering/enclosure to enable capital accumulation. Though embedded in local socio-economic, political, and cultural contexts, these spaces are fundamentally relational and constitute crucial elements in organizing the complex spatial division of labour in the global capitalist economy.

### Offshore Production Zones

SEZs are the paradigmatic example of regulatory exceptions for capital accumulation that are expressed spatially. The genealogy of production zones is long and can be traced from ancient forms of free ports and free trade zones, to the classical tool of export-processing zones (EPZs) that were essential spaces for the 'new international division of labour', to variegated contemporary forms, including extraterritorial zones (Chen, 1995; Neveling, 2015). Though they constitute an incredibly versatile technology, the common feature of most zones is that they constitute a space relatively independent from domestic laws, offering financial incentives (for example, tax benefits, waiver of import/export duties), subsidized infrastructure, and eased regulations for foreign investors to stimulate exports. In many ways, SEZs are thus enclave structures, functioning 'like a country within a country', and often headed by an independent authority and equipped with a special police force (Takeo, 1978). Jonathan Bach (2011: 101), discussing the contemporary transformation of the concept of the zone, argues that the zone is best described as a 'spatial capital accumulation machine'.

SEZs have been rising steadily over the past 50 years. The first official zone opened in Shannon, Ireland, in 1959. From 1975, when there were about 79 zones in 25 countries in operation, SEZs grew rapidly to approximately 3,500 zones in 130 countries in 2006 (Neveling, 2015). More recent figures by *The Economist* (2015) count as many as 4,300 zones globally. Despite the widespread geographies of the phenomenon, absolute numbers show that Chinese labour constitutes approximately 40 million out of a total of 66 million SEZ workers (data for 2006, see Neveling, 2015, for details). The Chinese SEZ strategy, in particular the case of Shenzhen, has come to be known as the 'Chinese model'—an industrialization strategy based on a selective opening to the global economy—which has fundamentally reshaped the coastal regions of the country.

Of China's total SEZ workforce of approximately 40 million, many are migrant workers from the rural provinces (whose lives are vividly portrayed in Lixin Fan's *Last Train Home*). SEZs, in particular, draw on a labour pool of young, single, and mostly female migrant workers, who are housed and disciplined through a dormitory system (Ngai, 2007). The working conditions in the Taiwanese Hon Hai Precision Industry (better known by its trade name Foxconn), a key supplier to Apple Inc. and a producer of electronic gadgets, including the iPhone, received international media attention when a wave of worker suicides prompted the company to install safety nets at worker dormitories as a measure to curb suicides (Merchant, 2017). These tactics show the extent of 'enclosure' of workers in their work places, and the reach of labour control regimes within SEZs that aim to construct migrant workers as temporary 'commoditized placeless labour' (Peck, 1996: 9), exposing the simultaneity of migrant labour both as mobile and fixed in space.

These industrial production sites are crucial nodes within global production networks and thus critical for capital accumulation strategies. In Zhengzhou, China, the world's largest production site for iPhones, a bonded zone has been created, from which products can be 'virtually' imported and exported without actually crossing any borders (Barboza, 2016). It is in these zones that the supplier sells the final product to Apple, which captures the largest share of product value, also through the use of complex tax avoidance schemes (Barboza, 2016). It is estimated that less than 2 per cent of the final retail price of the 'Made in China' iPhone are accrued as direct wages in China (Kraemer, Linden, and Dedrick, 2011).

Other countries not only rely on domestic migrants but also operate production zones staffed with transnational migrants. In Jordanian Qualifying Industrial Zones,[5] for example, the national minimum wage regulations have been lifted. The production and labour regime in these zones critically depends on the disembeddedness and vulnerability of migrant workers from countries such as India, China, Bangladesh, Sri Lanka, and Nepal, whose migration has coincided with the Asian ready-made garment firms, thus forming 'Asian enclaves' in Jordan (Azmeh, 2014). These zones are transnational migration and production enclaves that are only rendered viable as 'exceptional spaces', based on an interplay of regulation and deregulation that differs from the surrounding national legislation.

Border SEZs have been created, for instance, on the Thai–Myanmar border (Mae Sot-Myawaddy SEZ) and the North–South Korean border (Kaesong SEZ), operating with varying levels of success. These are based on a mix of political and economic objectives and enable the incorporation of low-cost labour from neighbouring countries for export production. In his analysis of Mae Sot Special Economic Border Zone, Campbell (2018) shows how 'border capitalism' consists of the production, operation, and struggle over two borders: the geopolitical border dividing Thailand and Myanmar and an internal border drawn around the SEZ that constitute a technology of rule, restrict migrant workers' mobility, and leave them 'trapped' within precarious work arrangements.

Even more explicitly transnational in their reach are extraterritorial SEZs and transnational SEZs, such as the Indonesia–Malaysia–Singapore Growth Triangle (Sparke et al., 2004). Analysing the case of Batam (an Indonesian island that is part of the Triangle), Johan Lindquist (2010: 35) argues that in the Riau islands, the 'transnational mobility of labour and capital have moved in opposite directions'. He explains that instead of breaking down borders as a result of regional integration, these borders persist and continue to perform an important function:

> [T]he position of Indonesian migrant labour in the Growth Triangle should be located at the historically contingent intersections between state regimes of deportation, a gendered transnational labour market, and the emotional economy that keeps migrants on the move. The fact that these national borders are regulated, not closed, makes the position of Indonesian labour more complicated than might first appear. (Lindquist, 2010: 120)

---

[5] Qualifying industrial zones enable preferential access to the US market based on fulfilling Israeli content requirements.

After having shown how SEZs for manufacturing constitute variegated, multi-scalar transnational enclave spaces, the next section turns to the phenomenon of offshore service zones.

## *Offshore Service Zones*

The smooth operation of globalization requires not only the sites of production, as segmented places of capital and labour mobility, but also key sites for circulating the produced goods, for organizing flows of capital and debt, and for controlling and commanding vast commodity chains and production networks. One example is logistics zones, which operate as key nodes of circulation and securitization (Cowen, 2014; see also Stenmanns and Boeckler, 2018).

The term 'offshore' usually conveys images of offshore islands, on which different legal rules apply compared to the 'mainland', and where thus (capital) mobilities are facilitated that would be impossible or unprofitable in the 'mainland'. Sven Opitz and Ute Tellmann (2012) discuss the two disparate but connected cases of offshore finance and migration processing of capital and human mobility, based on two extreme cases of (a) offshore finance in the Cayman Islands and (b) an Australian refugee claims processing centre on Christmas Island. They argue that both use a strategy of zoning that

> shifts accountability and visibility, it re-arranges the relations between inside and outside, it organizes monetary and legal dis/connectivity. [...] The zone is about relations and the access to them: that between subjects and law, between money and 'marked' circulation, between executive power and democratic control, between spaces of control and political contestation. (Sven and Tellmann, 2012: 278)

The two cases also illustrate how zoning technologies renegotiate mobilities of capital and human beings in highly uneven ways.

Beyond the creation of these exceptional territories for global circulation, so-called global cities intermediate between national economies' integration and global flows. Global cities perform a command and control function for globalizing capitalism through a concentration of higher-order service activities in a limited number of 'global cities', including Asian cities like Mumbai (Friedmann, 1986; Sassen, 2001). The global cities literature often seems to suggest an articulation of an entire city into transnational flows, whereas in reality it is only a fraction of these cities, usually the central business districts, that become spatially demarcated 'global city zones' (see also Parnreiter, Oßenbrügge, and Haferburg, 2013). Newly built financial districts, in particular, such as Canary Wharf in London or Marina Bay in Singapore, impose restrictive legislation on the types of activities allowed within these zones. Global cities as crucial sites for capital accumulation also critically depend on migrant labour, both in terms of highly skilled employees to manage the transnationally stretched production networks and as informal and/or low-cost labour that supports these activities (Sassen, 2001).

Offshore finance, in its most obvious form of registered mail-box companies, requires relatively little labour and is primarily organized as a facilitator for capital mobility. The line between offshore finance activities and onshore financial hubs is somewhat blurry, as many traditional international financial centres are successfully based on the regulatory exceptions they provide, including secrecy, low taxation, and specialist advice on tax restructuring and evasion. The list includes European cities such as Luxemburg, Dublin, Zurich, and Amsterdam, as well as the Asian hubs of Singapore and Hong Kong, the latter primarily basing its success on its 'off/onshore' position relative to China.

Finance not only requires the operation of front-office services but also depends on large volumes of back-office services, which are increasingly offshored to countries with educated, English-speaking workforces at relatively lower salary levels. IT and business process outsourcing (BPO) services are delivered from SEZs in urban India as well as the Philippines. Over the past decade, the sector has grown to employ more than 1 million employees in the Philippines (the majority of whom work in call centres) and has become the second-largest foreign exchange earner, after migrant remittances. Eastwood City, the first SEZ for IT-BPO services in the Philippines, is a privately developed and securitized zone within Quezon City (Metro Manila) that follows earlier, large-scale public SEZ industrialization policies of the Philippines. The zone functions as a site of virtual migration. Being connected through telecommunications with primarily North American customers, workers do not leave their home country, but in many instances temporarily abandon their names (using aliases), their language (using 'neutralized' American accents), and their time zones (working the 'graveyard shift' according to the clients' time) when entering the SEZ, which simultaneously has become a site of globalized consumption (see Kleibert and Kippers, 2016). The physical movement of bodies is thus reduced for the operation of digital capitalism, just as the earlier practice of 'body-shopping' of technology experts is replaced by online labour, with only a few expatriate staff and managers living in the zone to oversee operations. Several hundred SEZs for services have arisen in recent years to support the Philippines' efforts at plugging into global flows of capital and, thus, transforming cities and creating urban 'exceptions' to fit an idealized imaginary of a 'global city' (Kleibert, 2017; Murray, 2017; Ortega, 2016; Shatkin, 2008).

A final example moves beyond territorially fixed landscapes and turns to the mobile and the literal offshore.

## Mobile Offshore Leisure Zones

John Urry convincingly discusses cruise ships as 'leisure offshored': beyond functioning as a space for capital accumulation, offshoring enables secrecy, law avoidance, and irresponsibility. As 'floating gated communities that are based on consuming to excess … the offshore consumption zone is based upon the strict separation of local people, except as employees, and mobile visitors' (2014: 181). Who can claim to be 'local' on a mobile cruise ship, however, is questionable. Cruise ships present an almost paradoxical combination of im/mobilities of enclosed spaces, with elite spaces of luxury consumption and labour exploitation within mobile offshore sites.

The global cruise industry is one of the fastest growing tourism sectors. The business association Cruise Lines International Association (CLIA) has recorded global revenues of US$126 billion in 2016 and expected 28 million passengers in 2018—an increase of more than 10 million since 2009 (CLIA, 2017). Cruise ships are 'spaces of containment' specifically built as enclaves that enable monopoly revenue capture of its encapsulated passengers (Weaver, 2005). The industry is extremely concentrated; over 80 per cent of all revenues in the deep-ocean cruise industry are accounted for by the three largest operators: Carnival Corporation, Royal Caribbean Cruises, and Star Cruises (Chin, 2008).

Revenue incomes derive particularly from different on-board extra-fee services, for example exorbitantly priced telecommunications fees, alcohol, and additionally charging 'speciality' restaurants.[6] Moreover, such duty-free shops sell products in competition with land-based, onshore duty-free shops at harbours; however, the bought items (such as liquor) are prohibited to be consumed on board—they are sealed and only handed to the customer at the end of their journey (Weaver, 2005). Duty-free shops are only one way in which cruise operators are extending their reach to onshore locations. Moreover, several of the largest cruise ship operators own or rent 'private' beaches in the Caribbean, fenced-off spaces for revenue containment that are not 'contaminated' by local elements (for example, Princess Cruise's Princess Cays and Disney Cruise Lines' Castaway Cay in the Bahamas, Royal Caribbean International's Labadee in Haiti; see Weaver, 2005). When passengers dock at 'regular' ports, disembarkation is organized in a cargo-like procedure with strict protocol, for which passengers are grouped into coloured and numbered batches, are shuffled into buses and have efficiently-timed photo-stops, before boarding the ship again, thus minimizing opportunities to escape the

---

[6] Some of these insights are derived from the author's own short-term work experience on a cruise ship in 2010.

containment or experiencing interactions with individuals who are not part of the cruise ships' tour operator network. Cruise ships are promoted as 'destinations' rather than as a means of travel.

To reap economies of scale, the size of cruise ships is increasing, with vessels often carrying more than 3,000 affluent passengers and about 2,000 seafaring crew. The cruise industry critically depends on low-wage migrant labour, constructing a segmented workforce at sea that is based on hierarchically ranked intersections of nationality, race/ethnicity, gender, and class (Chin, 2008). Seafaring workers, however, are not 'transnational migrant workers as much as they may be considered "de-nationalized" workers' who sign labour contracts with crewing agencies in country A, work for a cruise line headquartered in country B, on a ship flagged in country C, cruising in international waters and entering the territories of numerous other countries (Chin, 2008: 6). The multitude of overlapping territorial regulations serves to create 'obfuscated labour rights in a complicated chain of fragmented accountability and liability' (Chin, 2008: 10).

Filipino contract workers account for 30 per cent of the world's total seafaring employment. In 2014, there were more than 400,000 Filipino seafarers, of whom close to 80,000 were working on passenger ships according to data from the Philippine Overseas Employment Administration (POEA, 2014). The discursive making of Filipinos as the ideal 'docile service workers', in conjunction with sociopolitical structures and institutions of migration in place in the Philippines, enables the geographical mobility of Filipino workers across the oceans, while simultaneously limiting their social mobility to subordinate positions in the stratified divisions of labour on cruise ships (Terry, 2014).

Thus, apart from being mobile and physically offshore, cruise ships' ability to operate under 'flags of convenience'[7] enables them to select their territorial jurisdictions. As a result, limited taxation and lenient labour regulations apply on most vessels. Working conditions on cruise ships internationally are regulated only by the Consolidated Maritime Labour Convention of the International Labour Organization (ILO), which allows for extended working hours (14 hours daily or 72 hours a week) and substantially lower minimum wages than under most national legislation. Still, not all cruise ship operators adhere to these standards and a court ruling against the Italian cruise ship operator MSC found labour conditions analogous to slave labour (*Zeit Online*, 2016), revealing the sharp edges of the segmented mobilities constituting and coming together in offshore sites.

---

[7] The term is used for ships carrying foreign flags of states with no or low taxation of cruise revenues, like Panama, Bahamas, Bermuda, Liberia, and Malta. See for more information: http://www.itfglobal.org/flags-convenience/index.cfm.

## Conclusions

Offshore spaces constitute crucial sites for capital accumulation under contemporary globalization. This chapter has discussed cases drawn primarily from South East Asia but it should be clear that these are global phenomena. The carving out of 'exceptional' space for the purpose of capital accumulation, the rise of securitized, enclosed, surveilled, gated, or privatized spaces on different scales, and the creation of segmented mobilities of capital and labour can also be observed in other contexts. They are the geographically visible and grounded infrastructures of the expulsing, externalizing, and wealth-transferring forces of global capitalism that a number of sociologists in the past few years have developed metanarratives around (Sassen, 2014; Lessenich, 2016; Urry, 2014). A more micro-level analysis has enabled us to zoom in on the spatial strategies, technologies, and infrastructures that enable the carving out of offshore spaces and assess whose mobilities are enhanced and whose are restricted, or 'who and what is allowed to recombine and gain speed and fluidity' (Opitz and Tellmann, 2012: 278).

The notion of the 'offshore' necessarily takes the view of what lies off-the-shore of sending countries, raising the danger of employing a Eurocentric optic. Every 'offshore' is someone else's onshore. New offshore spaces are rarely uninhabited, *tabula rasa*-like blank spaces, but, instead, are being transformed as efforts are undertaken to cut them out of their local contexts (from fishing villages on tropical islands becoming financial offshore hubs to SEZs on farming lands). We should be careful to not make these, often contested, processes of transformation invisible, by simply locating them offshore, geographically dissociating ourselves from them and placing them out of view, but by developing a grounded understanding of the processes of bordering and enclosure in particular diverse places. Seth Schindler (2015) argues that in many cities in the Global South today, capital and labour exist in relative abundance but remain disconnected. Capital is invested in the creation of elite spaces (such as real estate and infrastructure, rather than in efforts at industrialization), signifying a 'territorial moment' that privileges capital over labour. A future research agenda could thus focus on the processes of re/making offshore spaces and delve deeper into the (subnational) production of borders and enclave spaces, and the actors and technologies involved in the remaking of space. Beyond the cases discussed here, transnational enclave spaces and zones multiply and emerge in a range of fields, including casinos, university campuses, or server centres (Easterling, 2014).

Second, these offshore spaces fulfil a critical function of a 'borderless' financialized capitalism by enabling connections to similar 'global' sites at the expense of forming deeper local ties. Uncovering the global archipelagic structures of these transnationally linked enclave spaces is a vital task. Are these offshore spaces the organizing principles of a 'fragmented globalisation' (Scholz, 2002), an 'emerging mosaic of city-regions' (Scott, 2012), or the 'world city archipelago' (van Meeteren and Bassens, 2016)? It is hoped that future research into the structures of globalizing capitalism, and its variegated mobilities of capital and labour, will benefit from a grounded engagement with the un/making of the offshore and of transnational enclave spaces.

# References

Agamben, Giorgio. 2005. *State of Exception*. Chicago and London: University of Chicago Press.

Aneesh, Aneesh. 2006. *Virtual Migration: The Programming of Globalization*. London and Durham: Duke University Press.

Arnold, Dennis and John Pickles. 2011. 'Global Work, Surplus Labor, and the Precarious Economies of the Border'. *Antipode* 43(5): 1598–1624.

Azmeh, Shamel. 2014. 'Labour in Global Production Networks: Workers in the Qualifying Industrial Zones (QIZs) of Egypt and Jordan'. *Global Networks* 14(4): 495–513.

Bach, Jonathan. 2011. 'Modernity and the Urban Imagination in Economic Zones'. *Theory, Culture & Society* 28(5): 98–122.

Barboza, David. 2016. 'How China Built "iPhone City" with Billions in Perks for Apple's Partner'. *The New York Times*. Available at https://www.nytimes.com/2016/12/29/technology/apple-iphone-china-foxconn.html. Accessed on 10 August 2018.

Beerepoot, Niels and Bart Lambregts. 2015. 'Competition in Online Job Marketplaces: Towards a Global Labour Market for Outsourcing Services?' *Global Networks* 15(2): 236–255.

Berndt, Christian and Marc Boeckler. 2009. 'Geographies of Circulation and Exchange: Constructions of Markets'. *Progress in Human Geography* 33(4): 535–551.

———. 2011. 'Performative Regional (Dis)Integration: Transnational Markets, Mobile Commodities, and Bordered North–South Differences'. *Environment and Planning A* 43(5): 1057–1078.

Campbell, Stephen. 2018. *Border Capitalism, Disrupted: Precarity and Struggle in a Southeast Asian Industrial Zone*. Ithaca, NY: Cornell University Press.

Chen, Xianming. 1995. 'The Evolution of Free Economic Zones and the Recent Development of Cross-National Growth Zones'. *International Journal of Urban and Regional Research* 19(4): 593–621.

Chin, Christine B. N. 2008. 'Labour Flexibilization at Sea'. *International Feminist Journal of Politics* 10(1): 1–18.

Cowen, Deborah. 2014. *The Deadly Life of Logistics: Mapping Violence in Global Trade*. Minneapolis, MN: University of Minnesota Press.

CLIA. 2017. '2018 Cruise Industry Outlook'. Available at https://cruising.org/-/media/research-updates/research/featured/2018-clia-state-of-the-industry.pdf. Accessed on 10 August 2018.

Easterling, Keller 2014. *Extrastatecraft: The Power of Infrastructure Space*. London and New York: Verso Books.

*The Economist*. 2015. 'Special Economic Zones: Not So Special'. 4 April. Available at http://www.economist.com/news/leaders/21647615-world-awash-free-trade-zones-and-their-offshoots-many-are-not-worth-effort-not. Accessed on 10 August 2018.

Friedmann, John. 1986. 'The World City Hypothesis.' *Development and Change* 17(1): 69–83.

Harms, Erik. 2015. 'Porous Enclaves: Blurred Boundaries and Incomplete Exclusion in South East Asian Cities'. *South East Asia Research* 23(2): 151–167.

Harvey, David. 1989. *The Urban Experience*. Oxford: Blackwell.

van Houtum, Henk, Olivier T. Kramsch, and Wolfgang Zierhofer, eds. 2005. *B/ordering Space*. Aldershot: Ashgate.

Kearney, Michael. 1991. 'Borders and Boundaries of State and Self at the End of Empire'. *Journal of Historical Sociology* 4(1): 52–74.

Kleibert, Jana Maria. 2017. 'Exclusive Development(s): Special Economic Zones and Enclave Urbanism in the Philippines'. *Critical Sociology* 44(3). Available at doi:10.1177/0896920517698538.

Kleibert, Jana Maria and Lisa Kippers. 2016. 'Living the Good Life? The Rise of Urban Mixed-Use Enclaves in Metro Manila.' *Urban Geography* 37(3): 373–395.

Kraemer, Kenneth L., Greg Linden, and Jason Dedrick. 2011. 'Capturing Value in Global Networks: Apple's iPad and iPhone'. Working paper. University of California, Irvine; University of California, Berkeley; and Syracuse University, New York.

Lindquist, Johan A. 2010. *The Anxieties of Mobility: Migration and Tourism in the Indonesian Borderlands*. Singapore: NUS Press.

Lessenich, Stephan. 2016. *Neben uns die Sintflut: die Externalisierungsgesellschaft und ihr Preis*. Berlin: Hanser.

McGrath, Siobhan. 2017. 'Dis/articulations and the Interrogation of Development in GPN Research'. *Progress in Human Geography*. Available at https://doi.org/10.1177/0309132517700981.

van Meeteren, Michiel and David Bassens. 2016. 'World Cities and the Uneven Geographies of Financialization: Unveiling Stratification and Hierarchy in the World City Archipelago'. *International Journal of Urban and Regional Research* 40(1): 62–81.

Merchant, Brian. 2017. 'Life and Death in Apple's Forbidden City'. *The Guardian*, 18 June. Available at https://www.theguardian.com/technology/2017/jun/18/foxconn-life-death-forbidden-city-longhua-suicide-apple-iphone-brian-merchant-one-device-extract. Accessed on 20 March 2019.

Mezzadra, Sandro and Brett Neilson. 2013. *Border as Method, or, the Multiplication of Labor*, 6–8, 238. Durham and London: Duke University Press.

Mügge, Daniel. 2010. *Widen the Market, Narrow the Competition: Banker Interests and the Making of a European Capital Market*. Colchester: ECPR Press.

Murray, Martin J. 2017. *The Urbanism of Exception: The Dynamics of Global City Building in the Twenty-First Century*. Cambridge, UK: Cambridge University Press.

Neveling, Patrick. 2015. 'Free Trade Zones, Export Processing Zones, Special Economic Zones and Global Imperial Formations 200 BCE to 2015 CE'. In *The Palgrave Encyclopedia of Imperialism and Anti-imperialism*, edited by I. Ness and Z Cope, 1007–1016. Basingstoke: Palgrave Macmillan.

Ngai, Pun. 2007. 'Gendering the Dormitory Labor System: Production, Reproduction, and Migrant Labor in South China'. *Feminist Economics* 13(3–4): 239–258.

Ohmae, Kenichi. 1990. *The Borderless World: Power and Strategy in the Interlinked Economy*. London: Collins.

Ong, Aihwa. 2006. *Neoliberalism as Exception: Mutations in Citizenship and Sovereignty*. Duke University Press.

Opitz, Sven and Ute Tellmann. 2012. 'Global Territories: Zones of Economic and Legal Dis/connectivity.' *Distinktion: Scandinavian Journal of Social Theory* 13(3): 261–282.

Ortega, Arnisson Andre. 2016. *Neoliberalizing Spaces in the Philippines: Suburbanization, Transnational Migration, and Dispossession*. Lanham, MD: Rowman & Littlefield.

Parnreiter, Christof, Jürgen Oßenbrügge, und Christoph Haferburg. 2013. 'Shifting Corporate Geographies in Global Cities of the South: Mexico City and Johannesburg as Case Studies'. *Die Erde: Journal of the Geographical Society of Berlin* 144(1): 1–16.

Peck, Jamie. 1996. *Work-Place: The Social Regulation of Labor Markets*, 9–10. New York: Guilford Press.

———. 2000. 'Places of Work'. In *A Companion to Economic Geography*, edited by Eric Sheppard and Trevor J. Barnes, 133–148. New York: Wiley.

POEA (Philippine Overseas Employment Administration). 2014. *Annual Report 2014*. Manila. Available at http://www.poea.gov.ph/annualreports/annualreports.html. Accessed on 10 August 2018.

Sassen, Saskia. 1988. *The Mobility of Labor and Capital: A Study in International Investment and Labor Flow*. Cambridge, UK: Cambridge University Press.

———. 2001. *The Global City: New York, London, Tokyo*. Princeton, NJ: Princeton University Press.

———. 2013. 'When Territory Deborders Territoriality'. *Territory, Politics, Governance* 1(1): 21–45.

———. 2014. *Expulsions: Brutality and Complexity in the Global Economy*. Cambridge, MA: Harvard University Press.

Schindler, Seth. 2015. 'Governing the Twenty-First Century Metropolis and Transforming Territory'. *Territory, Politics, Governance* 3(1): 7–26.

Scholz, Fred. 2002. 'Die Theorie der Fragmentierenden Entwicklung'. *Geographische Rundschau* 54(10): 6–11.

Scott, Allan. J. 2012. *A World in Emergence: Cities and Regions in the 21st Century*. Cheltenham, UK and Northampton, MA: Edward Elgar Publishing.

Shatkin, Gavin. 2008. 'The City and the Bottom Line: Urban Megaprojects and the Privatization of Planning in Southeast Asia'. *Environment and Planning A* 40(2): 383–401.

Sidaway, James. 2007. 'Enclave Space: A New Metageography of Development?' *Area* 39(3): 331–339.

Sparke, Matthew, James Sidaway, Tim Bunnell, and Carl Grundy-Warr. 2004. 'Triangulating the Borderless World: Globalisation, Regionalisation and the Geographies of Power in the Indonesia-Malaysia-Singapore Growth Triangle'. *Transactions of the Institute of British Geographers* 29: 485–489.

Stenmanns, Julian and Marc Boeckler. 2018. 'Supply Chain Capitalism and the Technologies of Global Territory'. In *Routledge Handbook on Transregional Studies*, edited by Matthias Middell. London: Routledge.

Takeo, Tsuchiya. 1978. 'Free Trade Zones in Southeast Asia'. *Monthly Review* 29(9): 29–39.

Terry, William C. 2014. 'The Perfect Worker: Discursive Makings of Filipinos in the Workplace Hierarchy of the Globalized Cruise Industry'. *Social & Cultural Geography* 15(1): 73–93.

Urry, John. 2014. *Offshoring*. Cambridge: Polity Press.

Weaver, Adam. 2005. 'Spaces of Containment and Revenue Capture: "Super-sized" Cruise Ships as Mobile Tourism Enclaves'. *Tourism Geographies* 7(2): 165–184.

Yeung, Henry Wai-chung. 1998. 'Capital, State and Space: Contesting the Borderless World'. *Transactions of the Institute of British Geographers* 23(3): 291–309.

*Zeit Online*. 2016. 'Kreuzfahrten: Billig unter fremder Flagge'. Available at http://www.zeit.de/wirtschaft/2016-08/kreuzfahrten-reedereien-steuern-sparen-ausflaggung. Accessed on 17 August 2016.

# 3

# Japanese Multinational Companies and the Control of Overseas Investments

## Expatriates, Foreign Employees, and Japan's Soft Power

HARALD CONRAD AND HENDRIK MEYER-OHLE

## Introduction

On 3 February 2018, over 500 university students assembled for a career fair in Singapore's Expo Centre. Singapore sees numerous career events every year, but what made this 'ASEAN Career Fair with Japan' 2018 stand out was that participating companies were nearly all Japanese and that most of these companies were looking to hire employees into their home operations in Japan. Job seekers came from further afield than just Singapore. The majority of students had travelled from other South East Asian countries, with the fair organizers subsidizing travel for many of the participants. The career event was being held for the sixth time and was competing with several other such events that have come to be regularly organized in Singapore and other countries in Asia to support Japanese companies seeking to recruit foreign personnel into their home operations. What explains this drive by Japanese companies to hire foreign university graduates for employment in Japan, and how can we approach this phenomenon theoretically?

In 1988, Saskia Sassen pointed to a link between investment and human mobility streams, arguing that 'these patterns in the new immigration become particularly acute when we consider that the major immigrant-sending countries are among the leading recipients of the jobs lost in the U.S. and of U.S. direct foreign investment in labour-intensive manufacturing and service activities' (1988: 13). Sassen pointed to Asia as the newly emerging primary source of migrants to the USA and to the existence of a combination of push and pull factors underlying this trend. Moreover, she pointed to the fact that investments, the internationalization of production, and other forms of engagement have created 'linkages that contributed, directly or indirectly, to emigration' (1988: 16). In a similar vein, Massey et al. (1993) have pointed to the importance of economic, cultural, and ideological links in determining the direction and nature of migration flows. The ability of developed core countries to channel migration streams towards themselves might well be linked to former colonial relationships that shape affinities in terms of language, education, and administrative systems. Moreover, the consequences of economic penetration are reinforced by the activities of media and advertising companies as well as the establishment of communication and transportation infrastructures. Based on these insights, they summarize six hypothetical relationships between the expansion of global markets and migration streams that characterize the 'world systems theory' approach to migration (shortened from Massey et al., 1993: 447):

1. International migration naturally results from capitalist market formation in the developing world.
2. The flow of labour reversely mirrors the flow of goods and capital.
3. Colonial powers draw migration from former colonies based on the formation of specific transnational markets and cultural systems.
4. Policymakers face difficulties in limiting migration streams, when such limits go against the interest of transnational corporations.
5. Failure or threats to international investment spheres can lead to migration flows to the core economies.
6. Dynamics of market creation and the structure of the global economy are more important in determining migration than labour market or wage differentials.

Kritz and Zlotnik (1992) and Faist (2000) define the 'systems approach' to migration further by stating that this approach assumes a migration system that is constituted of a group of countries that exchange migrants, often consisting of a central immigration region and one or more emigration countries. They add to the earlier discussion of the concept of weak and strong links, with strong links often being necessary to lead to migration flows. Links between countries can be of an economic, political, security-related, or cultural nature. Links are regarded as necessary and dynamic, but not sufficient to set off and sustain migration streams. Other factors such as brokerage and networks on the meso-level or policymaking on the macro level also need to be considered.

Having for a long time been regarded as a country which views migration unfavourably, Japan has in recent years gradually opened its doors to foreign workers. This has happened incrementally by relaxing rules or opening backdoors, for example, through so-called trainee programmes or generous work regulations for foreign students. Until a reform in December 2018, when Japan came up with a system for bringing in low skilled-workers, there have been no overarching policies for immigration and labour mobility (Aiden, 2011; Vogt, 2013; Kobayashi et al., 2015; Komine, 2018). Foreign workers have found employment as low-skilled labour in Japan's agricultural, manufacturing, and consumer services sectors, with recent initiatives widening this to nursing and household services. At the same time though, as the emergence of recruitment fairs in Singapore and elsewhere shows, Japanese companies have initiated a new mobility stream for higher qualified workers. This initiative involves the systematic recruitment of non-Japanese graduates from Japanese universities as well as other universities in Asia.

In this chapter, we look at the factors that underlie this new migration stream and identify how links between Japan and the emigration countries have shaped labour mobility. We will show that, despite having built up a significant economic presence in other countries of Asia, Japanese companies have not managed to project an image as attractive employers of white-collar managerial workers. Instead, we will argue that the development of a ready pool of applicants for recruitment in Japan is related to the expansion of Japan's cultural capital. We will also argue that a major aim of the newly initiated hiring of foreign young graduates is to internationalize Japanese headquarters from within and to facilitate the investments of Japanese companies abroad in the longer term. Such an internationalization of headquarters, if successful, might eventually lead to the long-demanded localization of human resources in Japanese overseas subsidiaries.

This chapter presents research into the recruitment of foreign fresh graduates that we have conducted over the previous three years. Our findings are based on the review of relevant primary and secondary sources, interviews with the representatives from the human resources (HR) sections of 19 companies (Appendix 3.1), interviews with 33 young foreign employees in Japan (Appendix 3.2), and interviews with representatives of 10 companies that perform functions of labour market intermediation, acting as brokers between applicants and employers. In addition, we have interviewed three representatives of university career offices and visited and observed several recruitment events targeting foreign employees abroad and in Japan.

In the following, we will first describe the link between Japanese overseas investments and human mobility, showing how overseas investments have so far been accompanied by temporary expatriate mobility of Japanese nationals out of Japan. We then look at the new recruitment initiatives by Japanese companies of bringing young foreign graduates to Japan with the longer-term aim of developing Japanese businesses abroad. Following this, we will take a look at the supply side, namely young foreign employees, focusing on their motivations for working and acquiring skills in Japan. This is followed by a discussion of the aforementioned links in the migration system and references to other factors such as government policy, brokerage, and networks. The conclusion summarizes our findings and suggests areas that deserve more in-depth research.

## Controlling Foreign Direct Investments through Expatriates

While Japanese companies have built significant networks of overseas subsidiaries in other Asian countries, they have been found wanting in terms of the localization of their overseas operations. Japanese companies continue to display strong ethnocentric preferences by trying to transfer some of their HR management practices overseas and steering overseas operations through expatriates who work in close cooperation with headquarters in Japan. Tung (1982) assessed this situation early on, and more recent research on Japanese overseas subsidiaries confirms that conditions remain largely unchanged (Legewie, 2002; Harzing et al., 2016). While often criticized, it should not be overlooked that this state is grounded in some rationality, especially in Asia, where Japanese companies initially concentrated on export-oriented production activities, often within networks of other Japanese suppliers, distributors, or providers of finance or other services (Legewie, 2002). In addition, while Japanese companies internationalized sales and manufacturing activities, higher value-added functions, such as research and development (R&D), were not transferred overseas but largely remained in Japan, thus leaving overseas subsidiaries dependent on headquarters. This in turn necessitated subsidiaries to stay in close communications with Japan, with Japanese expatriates acting as the main conduits (Yoshihara, 2000).

Linking foreign direct investment and the movement of people, Japanese foreign direct investments have thus been primarily controlled by expatriates from Japanese headquarters, who are temporarily moved into overseas operations. Most of these expatriates tend to stay only a few years, before they are recalled to headquarters. Only a small number of expatriates stay on, by either setting up their own businesses to service the Japanese expatriate community or by changing to local contracts. Based on their deeper and longer exposure to the host country, such Japanese nationals have come to be seen as playing an important role in bridging differences in attitudes between the host-country staff and Japanese expatriates in terms of workplace behaviour and decision-making (Okamoto and Teo, 2011). Inpatriation, the delegation of overseas subsidiary personnel for a certain period to headquarters in multinational companies' home countries, has become an important tool for many multinational companies to nurture local personnel, driving localization as well as the internationalization of headquarters (Reiche, 2011; Kim 2013). Yet Japanese companies have not so far systematically used inpatriation as an HR development tool. Japanese overseas investments have thus not greatly enhanced labour mobility between subsidiaries and headquarters or among subsidiaries. Companies often cite the incompatibility of employment systems and the low adaptive capacities of home-country operations as major stumbling blocks for such increased labour mobility (Conrad and Meyer-Ohle, 2017). In our interviews, company informants voiced a desire to increase inpatriation, yet also raised doubts whether their overseas subsidiaries were indeed able to attract employees of the right quality and whether subsidiary employees were thus worth bringing to Japan.

> HR manager of a chemical company: I think that it would be normal to bring the strong foreigners from operations overseas to the Japanese headquarter. So, we want to recruit people of the executive class in Japan as well as overseas. That would be good, yet I do not know whether the overseas branches can recruit such excellent people.

In sum, overseas subsidiaries have historically not played a major role in the globalization of the HR of Japanese companies.

However, many Japanese companies are now facing stagnating or shrinking markets at home and increasingly affluent consumer markets in other Asian countries. Moreover, they need to diversify their customer base in B2B markets away from their traditional networks. Responding effectively to the needs of these new markets requires the internationalization of headquarters and the localization of HR in subsidiaries, something that Japanese companies have so far struggled with due to their reliance on expatriate Japanese managers. Furuno (2013), based on interviews with 50 Japanese subsidiaries in Asia, diagnoses the existence of a 'negative spiral' that Japanese companies find difficult to break out of: the reliance on expatriates and a neglect to develop local employees has reduced the attractiveness of Japanese companies as employers (Koop, 1994; Yu and Meyer-Ohle, 2008; Shiraki, 2014), with those working in Japanese companies only seeing limited opportunities for advancement. The resulting high turnover of employees makes it difficult for Japanese managers to justify investing in the training of local employees. This in turn makes it difficult to find local employees who can be promoted to more senior positions in subsidiaries or who can play a role in the internationalization of headquarters. Companies thus need to send even more expatriate managers to their subsidiaries, thereby enforcing the negative retention spiral. Only in recent years have Japanese companies begun to address this situation. Yet a recent survey of 26 subsidiaries in Singapore, all with some responsibility for business functions across Asia, shows that many companies are still in the process of developing coherent HR systems and have not moved to measures that would truly strengthen their attractiveness as employers, reduce turnover, and nurture local executives (Mercer, 2015).

# Fresh Foreign Graduate Mobility into Japanese Company Headquarters

Aiming to address problems of insufficiently internationalized headquarters and localized subsidiaries, Japanese companies have in recent years come up with a new recruitment initiative. As mentioned in the introduction of this chapter, this initiative involves the systematic recruitment of foreign fresh graduates from universities in Japan and increasingly also from overseas.

When trying to trace the employment of foreigners in Japanese companies, we met with some reluctance by company informants to pinpoint when they had begun to employ foreigners. This relates possibly to the fact that members of Japan's long-settled Korean community, while usually indistinguishable in language, appearance, or educational background, also legally count as foreigners. In the past, many large companies discriminated against this group when they recruited fresh university graduates in Japan (Wu, 2003). Yet, based on the answers of our informants as well as other secondary data, the recruitment of foreigners into large Japanese companies since the 1980s can be characterized by the following broad trends. In the 1980s, the focus was primarily on foreigners who had studied at Japanese universities and had applied for jobs via the normal domestic route along with their Japanese peers. Yet these were only singular cases. By the beginning of the 1990s, after Japanese companies had significantly increased their global presence in form of foreign direct investment, companies began to focus on recruiting American employees, either from within Japan or from business schools in the USA. Some companies looked for language or other specialist skills, while others just wanted to demonstrate an international mindset (Miller, 1995: 145). Yet companies found that many of these employees would not stay for long. For some companies this seems to have shaped a preference for employees from Asia, who are assumed to show a higher level of adaptability to Japan and its work practices. Around the turn of the millennium, some companies began to recruit employees from overseas for their technical skills, often for specialist positions and on temporary contracts. At the same time, the number of foreign students enrolled at Japanese universities increased. Companies report that this led to an increase in foreign employees, yet not due to strategic considerations, but rather accidentally, after foreign students began to apply to them alongside their Japanese peers.

The systematic recruitment of young foreign employees into headquarters and operations in Japan began around 2010. Companies began to actively look for foreign employees in Japan itself and later overseas. This led to the organization of specialized recruitment events. An analysis of newspaper reports and websites of recruitment events for non-Japanese people shows the wide popularity of this strategy among large Japanese employers.[1] Among Japan's largest companies in terms of revenues in 2016, 37 had participated in events specifically organized for non-Japanese employees, while 5 more mentioned the recruitment of non-Japanese on their web pages. In our interviews, representatives of HR departments were reluctant to provide concrete numbers, but some hinted at targets for the recruitment of foreigners being between 10 and 20 per cent of the annual intake of fresh graduates, a figure that was confirmed by the interviewed recruitment agents. Considering that large Japanese corporations hire between a few hundred up to over a thousand fresh new university graduates every year (*Nihon Keizai Shinbun*, 2017), those companies have set themselves ambitious targets.

Overall, we propose that these recent activities of Japanese companies constitute a notable and distinct new recruitment and mobility trend for qualified foreign labour due to (a) the focus on newly graduated foreign university students, (b) the broad scope, with companies targeting graduates from the natural and the social sciences as well as the humanities, and (c) the systematic nature of activities in terms of timelines and numerical targets.

Company representatives explain the systematic hiring of non-Japanese employees with reference to needs to globalize their business and to strengthen their competitiveness by increasing diversity in headquarters:

> HR manager of an IT company: Like other big Japanese companies, we cannot expand the market in Japan due to the ageing of the population. Japanese companies need to globalize, especially for our company, sales are basically domestic. Foreign sales are only 20 per cent, it used to be 40 per cent at the peak. However, business has been consolidated. Therefore, we have to be globalized.

> HR manager of a trading company: The way of thinking is different, how things are perceived is different, this is what we want most, this is what is necessary. Our ways can be strict, with only one way of thinking, so it is good to have people who look at things from different perspectives.

---

[1] Companies that have made some efforts to systematically recruit foreigners include retailers (for example, Aeon, Lawson, Muji, Rakuten, or Nitori), electronics companies (for example, Sony, Brother, Toshiba, Fujitsu, Mitsubishi Electric, or Panasonic), chemical companies (for example, Teijin, Kaneka, or Mitsubishi Chemicals), financial institutions (for example, SMBC or Nomura), general trading companies (for example, Marubeni, Mitsui, Mitsubishi, or Sojitz), transport companies (for example, YKK or Yamato Transport), and other prominent companies, such as JT, IHI, NTT Communication, or Deloitte. (Based on articles from the *Nihon Keizai Shinbun* and the participation in recruitment events, such as the Nikkei Asian Recruitment Forum at workjapan.nikkeihr.co.jp/en, ASEAN Career Fair with Japan at asean-career.com/, and Top Career Asia Pacific at www.topcareer.jp/inter/tcap2015/.)

HR manager of an electronics company: In certain areas, Chinese students are better, for certain specialties. We hire based on job vacancies and descriptions. For certain areas we cannot hire in Japan, for certain areas talents in Japan are not so good, not enough.

The objectives to hire for diversity or certain skills lead to the question why companies are emphasizing the recruitment of fresh graduates over recruiting more experienced ones or bringing in more employees from their subsidiaries (inpatriation). Here, companies point to the importance of strong corporate cultures into which new employees should be properly socialized.

HR manager of an electronics company (when asked why the company was not hiring more experienced non-Japanese people): That is one idea, but [long pause] the culture is very important. If we hire fresh graduates we teach them the company's culture from scratch.

HR manager of a trading company: This is related to culture. We hire for life-long employment from the beginning.... Foreign companies do not develop people. For them this is normal. You then have to develop your own skill as an employee. In Japan, since the old days, we bring in young people and develop them over several years. I believe that this has value.

Japanese companies have thus consciously opened their operations to foreign employees in recent years. By recruiting from Japanese universities, companies offer new opportunities to international students. Company objectives meet here with the policy objective of the Japanese government which sees international students as a valuable addition to the Japanese labour market and promotes a two-step migration model for skilled labour (Breaden, 2014). In terms of recruiting young graduates directly from universities abroad into operations in Japan, companies name several motives, one among them being the need for certain skills unavailable in Japan, as well as the aim to recruit from the best universities in Asia, where some universities have caught up or even outperformed their Japanese peers. The beginning of these recruitment activities of Japanese companies in other Asian countries, especially in South East Asia, coincides with a renewed interest in South East Asia as a destination for Japanese foreign direct investment. Some of these investments are still in export-oriented manufacturing, where production becomes more diversified and moves away from China, but many other investments directly reflect a Japanese interest in South East Asian consumer markets and their growing middle classes (JETRO, 2017; Meyer-Ohle, 2014).

## A New Kind of Expatriate Mobility—Improving Localization?

The systematic recruitment of young foreign staff into Japanese headquarters with a view to internationalizing companies from within and to grow international operations is a relatively new trend. The possible outcomes in terms of labour mobility are yet uncertain. What is certain, however, is that companies do not simply hire these foreign graduates into their headquarters as a straightforward means to develop future leaders for operations in their countries of origin.

> HR manager of an IT network/systems company: We actually do not think about someone we hire from India to return [for our company] to India eventually. So, if someone prefers to live in his/her country, we will probably not hire such a person.

Rather than a direct development of future leaders for their home-countries, Japanese companies aim for employees who, while being properly socialized into headquarters operations, come from more diverse backgrounds and are more apt at communicating inter-culturally when working in headquarters or overseas subsidiaries (Conrad and Meyer-Ohle, 2018). Legal and organizational concerns also need to be considered. Once foreign employees are hired into headquarters, it is difficult for companies to switch such employees to local contracts when they are sent to their home countries and to deny their expatriate privileges. This situation will last as long as Japanese companies have no integrated global remuneration and incentive systems.

> HR manager of a chemical company: We have hired Chinese, who became managers and then transferred them to China with local Chinese working under them. The salary difference became enormous, since these people worked as expats at headquarters standards, yet age and skills were not that different. This led to relationship problems that were difficult to manage.

Considering the current situation, one possible future scenario is that more foreign employees among expatriates and more Japanese employees being exposed to non-Japanese employees in headquarters will positively impact the quality of expatriates that Japanese companies use to control their overseas investments. This change in quality might eventually also drive the localization of subsidiaries, as culturally more adaptable expatriates can improve subsidiary–headquarter communications and should be more willing to develop local subsidiary employees. An increased adaptive capacity of headquarters should also increase subsidiary–headquarter mobility through more inpatriation and thus contribute to the career advancement of subsidiary staff. Finally, an additional possible effect of the current recruitment initiative of Japanese companies is an increased pool of skilled employees in host countries through return migration. Japanese companies recruit foreign young graduates with the expectation to employ them long-term, yet we encountered several cases of employees quitting and returning home, because they were dissatisfied with their working conditions or wanted to be closer to their families. Having returned to their home countries, such employees might find that the best places to utilize their Japanese experiences are the overseas subsidiaries of Japanese companies.

## Employee Motivations: Moving to Japan to Study and Seek Employment

In the previous section, we outlined the complex relationship between Japan's overseas investments and human mobility. Japanese overseas investments have so far been accompanied by sustained expatriate movements. Only recently have we witnessed a new form of labour mobility through the recruitment of young foreign employees into Japanese headquarters. As we have argued, this might in the long-term lead to a new quality of expatriate mobility. Yet the activities of companies only tell one side of the story, leaving unanswered the question of which factors attract non-Japanese graduates to work for Japanese companies and to acquire the skills that are necessary to do so.

The foreign students among our informants mentioned a variety of motives underlying their interest in Japan and having sought work with Japanese corporations in Japan. These ranged from a general interest in Japanese culture to attractive financial support. Figures 3.1 and 3.2 show the relative importance of these reasons based on a large-scale official Japanese survey conducted among foreign students and foreign employees in 2014. Figure 3.1 presents the reasons for current foreign employees and current foreign students behind their decision to enrol in a Japanese university. The major reasons are an interest in Japanese culture and the perceived attractiveness of Japanese universities. The nationalities of the respondents of this survey appear to be largely representative of the current foreign student and employee population in Japan. In the student sample, 58.1 per cent of respondents were from China, thereby forming the majority among the overall 81.6 per cent of respondents from Asia; in the employee sample, 66.7 per cent of students were from China and 87.7 per cent from Asia. Figure 3.2 shows the results to the question why foreign students studying at Japanese universities aim to seek employment in Japanese companies in Japan.

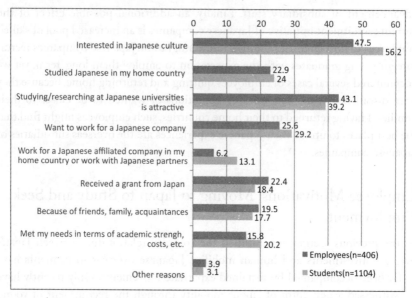

Figure 3.1 | Reasons of foreign students and foreign employees enrolling in a Japanese university (multiple answers in percentage)

*Source*: Keizai Sangyōshō (Ministry of Economy, Trade and Industry of Japan), survey considering the current situation of the employment and integration of foreign students (2015).

*Note*: Translation by the authors.

The graph indicates that the reasons differ among students who study humanities and science subjects. Yet, overall, pure economic factors such as not being able to find work at home or high salary levels do not seem to play a dominant role. Instead, especially young foreign employees with a background in engineering mention the technical strength of Japanese companies, a reason which we also encountered several times in our interviews.

> E28: After graduation in China, I wanted to work in a Japanese IT company. In China, I would have just done programming, not much perspective for growth. In Japan, I am involved in the whole project, every aspect.

This quote illustrates the motivation and adds to our earlier discussion of the characteristics of Japanese companies abroad by highlighting the limited development opportunities in Japanese subsidiaries in China. Moreover, other research has also pointed out that Japanese companies in building up operations in Asia have mainly focused on production and distribution networks, limiting the

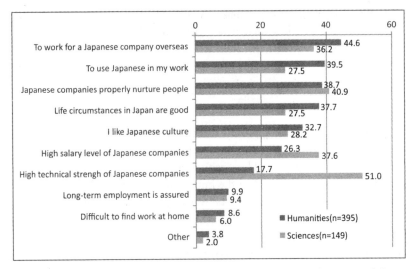

Figure 3.2 | Reasons of foreign students studying in Japan seeking employment with Japanese companies in Japan (multiple answers in percentage)

*Source*: Keizai Sangyōshō (Ministry of Economy, Trade and Industry of Japan), survey considering the current situation of the employment and integration of foreign students (2015).

*Note*: Translation by the authors.

transfer of knowledge by keeping higher functions such as R&D with their home operations (Yoshihara, 2000).

Regardless of their background in the social sciences or humanities, both groups of students appear to value the fact that Japanese companies take time to train young employees. However, our research with young foreign employees has shown that the particular training styles of Japanese companies, favouring vagueness over explicit instructions and egalitarian principles over differentiation by performance, are eventually perceived negatively by many foreign employees. Apart from perceived training opportunities, non-science students are less clear about work-specific advantages of Japanese companies. These students' motivations to work in Japan appear to be more strongly influenced by their general affinity to Japanese culture, life circumstances in Japan, and the opportunity to use Japanese language in their work—factors that have led some of them to study at Japanese universities in the first place (see also Figure 3.1). Figure 3.1 also shows that, when making the decision to study in Japan, the opportunity to work in Japan or for Japanese corporations seems not to have been of major importance. The decision to apply to Japanese companies might therefore involve a good degree of opportunism, especially since job-searching activities have come to be seen as an accepted element of university studies in Japan that should be undertaken while still studying.

E16 ('E' stands for employee number): At Keio University, I was surrounded by Japanese people, a comedy circle, who engaged in job hunting. All of a sudden it felt more real. All people in their suits and you hear stories from people who got *naite* [job offers] in great companies.

## Discussion of Links

The 'world systems theory' approach is regularly mentioned among the possible approaches to explaining migration for its emphasis on linking migration streams to larger global developments. Here, capital flows are commonly emphasized, but some authors have also pointed to the importance of cultural flows (Faist, 2000). In this section, we discuss the links between Japan and emigration countries in qualified labour migration to Japan in more detail and assess how they may have contributed to the movement of people.

Economically, Japan has strong links with Asian emigration countries, as Japanese companies have built up significant operations in the region. Initial engagement was focused on raw material extraction and the development of Asian export markets, followed by the relocation of production activities and the participation in major infrastructure projects in Asia (Edgington and Hayter, 2000). Yet, while there appears to be a close parallel between the countries that Japanese companies have invested in and where they are now recruiting young foreign employees, a closer look shows that the underlying structures and processes are more complex.

First, in terms of the flow of products, the current young generation in Asia has been growing up with Japanese consumer goods. Yet, compared to their parents, for whom Japanese goods often represented the pinnacle of consumption, the younger generation has had more local and other Asian choices, such as Korean goods and cultural products, which have made inroads into areas previously solely occupied by Japan. Large Japanese companies also no longer rank particularly high in Asian employer rankings and have lost grounds in terms of brand rankings.[2] Yet, as we discussed earlier, Japan's businesses seem to have maintained some reputation in terms of their technological prowess.

Second, there are considerable differences in the state of the political relationships between Japan and other Asian countries. While Japan has systematically invested

---

[2] Survey of 87,000 students in South East Asia. Among the top 10 for business in general is no Japanese company, only for engineering, Toyota ranks at sixth and Sony at ninth. See http://universumglobal.com/rankings/asia-pacific/student/2014/business. A ranking of the most popular 100 graduate employers in Singapore has Sony as the only Japanese company at the 66th rank. See http://singapores100.com/Ranking.aspx. A brand survey shows Japanese brands still represented, yet have lost much of their dominance. See http://www.campaignasia.com/Top1000Brands.

in its relationships with countries in South East Asia, where links are commonly strong, relationships with China and Korea are far less favourable. Yet these two countries account for the largest number of migrants to Japan.

Third, the dominance of China and Korea as emigration countries can primarily be explained in terms of language similarities. Chinese and Korean students have less difficulty in acquiring proficiency in the Japanese language due to common characters (Chinese, Korean) and similar grammar (Korean). In terms of the highest official Japanese Language Proficiency Test, the numbers of those taking the test in China, Korea, and Taiwan are thus unsurprisingly far higher than in other Asian countries (Table 3.1). While some companies have been experimenting with employing foreign employees without prior Japanese language skills, most Japanese companies still see Japanese language skills as essential. Moreover, companies expect young foreign employees to undergo the same orientation and socialization programmes as their Japanese peers, which means that they will frequently start work in domestically oriented divisions, such as local sales, where high language skills are a prerequisite to communicate well with customers (Conrad and Meyer-Ohle, 2017).

Table 3.1 | Location and Number of Persons Taking the Japanese Language Proficiency Test (JLPT) (Highest levels, N1 + N2)

| | N1 | N2 | N1 + N2 |
|---|---|---|---|
| China | 38,106 | 32,249 | 70,355 |
| Japan | 29,305 | 33,374 | 62,679 |
| Korea | 10,836 | 7548 | 18,384 |
| Taiwan | 7,552 | 8,272 | 15,824 |
| Vietnam | 1,402 | 4,461 | 5,863 |
| Thailand | 1,021 | 1,755 | 2,776 |
| Hong Kong | 1,157 | 1,179 | 2,336 |
| Indonesia | 500 | 1,542 | 2,042 |
| USA | 756 | 946 | 1,702 |
| Myanmar | 259 | 529 | 788 |
| Singapore | 315 | 426 | 741 |
| Brazil | 298 | 375 | 673 |
| Malaysia | 178 | 440 | 618 |
| India | 127 | 478 | 605 |
| France | 117 | 363 | 480 |

*Source*: Authors' table based on data from Official Worldwide Japanese-Language Proficiency Test website (www.jlpt.jp), Kokusai Kōryū Kikin/Nihon Kokusai Kyōiku Shien Kyōkai (2016).

*Note*: Main test in December 2015 by the test site. The nationalities of participants taking the test in Japan itself are unknown. Some people might take tests in a third country.

Underlying and connected to the language link, there exist strong links around Japanese popular culture. It seems that this shared interest is what unites many young people from other Asian countries and makes them learn the Japanese language and seek education and employment in Japan.

> E22: Well, like everyone, I was first interested in Japanese subculture. Manga, mainly manga, I liked manga.... In Thailand, there are also many Japanese manga, but it takes time before they are translated into Thai, therefore I wanted to read those that I liked earlier. So, I thought if I understand Japanese, I can read them earlier.

Like this employee, most of our other informants had acquired some Japanese language skills in their home countries before coming to Japan, and most reported that they had not done this with future job prospects in mind, but rather motivated by an interest in the popular culture of Japan.

> E30: At my university, there was, apart from English only Japanese, and I wanted to study languages. I also liked Japan, anime, so I studied Japanese for two years. Then, I wanted to go Japan, applied to Japan, and then went to Osaka University, studied for 4 years, and in my fifth year graduated.

> E32: Subculture, mainly subcultures, only at a later stage, after doing JS [Japanese Studies], I realized that Japanese culture was always around. I only had this realization pretty late. And it actually only happened when I was going through the job interviews. The starting point that I came to JS was a particular subculture, and then it expanded. When they [the job interviewers] asked what 'was my first encounter with Japan', I realized that this was when I was quite young, like eight years old.

The apparent importance of Japan's popular culture as a motivator warrants a closer look at how popular culture products have spread across Asia, especially since the underlying processes have differed significantly from the earlier spread of Japanese products, such as consumer electronics, cars, motorcycles, household goods, or food. While some Japanese popular culture content was distributed legally and reached high popularity in Asia (Tang, 2012), this was just a fraction of the overall amount of Japanese popular culture, which was generally not produced with an international audience in mind. Moreover, governments often banned the distribution of Japanese materials, either for their Japanese origin or for their risqué content. Yet Japanese content spread quickly in Asia, often not through official channels but informally or outright illegally (Otmazgin, 2008). Gradually, more content became available through proper commercial channels and in translation, yet Japanese language skills remained necessary to access the content created exclusively for the Japanese market or to be able to follow the latest trends. Thus, somewhat paradoxically, it was and is the non-availability of content through official channels that has contributed to the study of Japanese language among young people in Asia and has thus provided a ready supply of applicants with Japanese language skills to study at Japanese universities and work in Japanese companies in Japan.

This leads to the question of whether, apart from promoting the study of Japanese language, the Japanese popular culture boom has overall raised interest in Japan as a country. Having realized the popularity of its cultural products, Japan has in recent years responded to Joseph Nye's (1990) ideas about soft power complementing, if not replacing, hard power in international relations. Since the 2000s, the Japanese government has engaged in a soft power initiative, even though scholars have largely doubted its ability to strategically shape a positive image of the country through popular culture (for example Lam, 2007). These scholars have pointed out that Japanese products largely became popular because of their artistic quality and novelty, as a general expression of modernity, or precisely because Japanese content and practices do not evoke images of a certain country, thus offering the possibility to be locally accommodated and reinterpreted. Iwabuchi (1998) has pointedly termed this the 'odourlessness' of Japanese popular culture products. Yet, while agreeing that Japan derives limited diplomatic power from the popularity of its popular culture abroad, Otmazgin (2008) argues that Japan's popular culture has added additional dimensions to its image and thereby opened new avenues for people to connect regionally, even though old negative images have not been completely replaced.

> The diffusion of Japanese popular culture products connects individuals and communities in a regional encompassment, and endorses the construction of regional markets for Japanese culture. The accommodating process of consumption incites new interests and appreciations, and encourages young East Asians to develop new images of Japan. (Otmazgin, 2008: 97)

Asian consumers with an affinity for Japan, shrinking consumer markets in Japan, growing middle-class markets in other Asian markets, and the encouragement of the Japanese government have in recent years facilitated a new wave of Japanese investment in Asia. Among the investing companies are retailers, restaurants, and media companies, some of them also being at the forefront of the new recruitment trend of young non-Japanese personnel into operations in Japan (Kawazu, 2013; Meyer-Ohle, 2014).

However, for some people, who developed favourable images of Japan through popular culture, the realities of work in Japanese companies has led to some disillusionment.

> E30: Japanese drama series are also like that. There are dramas that show great feelings and thoughts. Everyone watches this and thinks 'this is Japanese society'.

I now think that it is produced in this way exactly because things are not like this. You see this and it is good for you mentally.

This quote highlights an interesting paradox: For many young people in Asia, their interest in the popular culture of Japan and their study of the Japanese language provide an avenue to engage with counterculture, an opportunity to relatively safely express some otherness within the often quite conservative and restrictive social and cultural environments of their home countries. Survey results (Figures 3.1 and 3.2) show that this interest in Japanese culture might eventually even result in a wish to study and work in Japan. However, the fulfilment of this wish comes at the cost of joining large Japanese companies, which, as our interviewees have described, still constitute very conservative and rigid work environments—the very environments that Japanese popular culture provides the antithesis to.

## Policies, Intermediaries, and Networks

This chapter has introduced the recruitment of fresh foreign university graduates into operations in Japan as a new migration trend. So far, we have focused on identifying the motives of companies and employees and discussed the underlying links between Japan and the emigration countries. Naturally, this approach only provides a limited number of pieces in the complex puzzle explaining the emergence and development of this new migration trend. Proponents of a 'systems approach' to migration have suggested combining the identification of systems of migration with other approaches to the study of migration, such as identifying the situation at the macro-policy level or the role of brokers and networks at the meso-level (Faist, 2000). In this penultimate section, we focus briefly on such issues.

The main policy area relevant to the recruitment of young foreign employees in Japan is the government's strategy to address the relative decline of its universities in terms of local student numbers by increasing the number of foreign students. Japan began early on to bring students from other Asian countries to Japan, with students from South East Asia often receiving financial support from the Japanese government and with the implicit expectation that students would return to their home countries after graduation. Tang (2012: 92) describes this as a form of public diplomacy and notes: 'This form of Japanese public diplomacy had, over the years, served to enhance the human capital stock and raise the level of technical expertise of Southeast Asians at minimal or no cost to their respective governments.' While Japan is still interested in maintaining its influence in South East Asia by playing a role in educating its elites, more recent efforts of the Japanese government need to be considered against the backdrop of the demographic decline of its population. The government has formulated an ambitious plan for 300,000 foreign students to study in Japan by 2020 (Yonezawa and Yonezawa, 2016). Having reached 246,000 students in 2015, this was followed by an announcement in 2016 that the targeted share of foreign students finding employment after graduation in Japan should be raised from 30 per cent to 50 per cent (*The Japan Times*, 2016). Consequently, the government supports Japanese universities in recruiting students abroad and has also introduced relatively generous rules for students to finance their studies through part-time work and to spend time in Japan after graduation for the purpose of finding a job. Moreover, work visas for skilled labour are issued relatively smoothly, and the country has relaxed its requirements for permanent residency (Liu-Farrer, 2009; Komine, 2018).

Employers and employees are supported in their recruitment and job seeking efforts by the emergence of an active and diverse brokerage industry that organizes job fairs and corporate information sessions, especially for non-Japanese applicants inside and outside of Japan, often with some official support from government agencies. Brokers counsel non-Japanese employees in navigating distinct Japanese recruitment and employment practices. Breaden (2014) has termed this the acquisition of 'local literacy'. This literacy becomes of even higher importance when companies decide that they do not want to hire graduates from Japanese universities. Brokers have been essential in building links with overseas universities to secure their help in motivating students to participate in corporate information sessions and specialized recruitment fairs. Over time, with the increasing number of non-Japanese finding work in Japan, networks of foreign employees have also developed around the recruitment of foreigners, so that the trend has become more self-sustaining (Conrad and Meyer-Ohle, 2018).

## Conclusion

This chapter has introduced a new migration trend, namely the initiative of Japanese companies to internationalize their headquarters in Japan from within by recruiting foreign university graduates. The objective of companies is to inject diversity into headquarters and to nurture the human resources necessary for international expansion. We have argued that this has the potential to change the outlook of Japanese companies' headquarters and contribute in the longer term to the localization of overseas subsidiaries, an area where Japanese companies have come under criticism for maintaining a strongly ethnocentric model of international coordination based on the use of Japanese expatriate managers. Employing more non-Japanese in headquarters can improve the communication with overseas subsidiaries, enable the easier temporary inpatriation of overseas staff into headquarters, and, finally, where expatriates still have to be deployed overseas, enable companies to select them from a more diverse and international pool of employees.

Some employees, who have initially found employment in Japan, might also decide to move permanently back to their home countries and there might work for the companies they already worked for in Japan or or for other Japanese employers. Return migration might thus provide Japanese subsidiaries abroad with a valuable pool of employees. This might unintendedly be one of the major outcomes of this initiative. Considering that integration of foreign employees into operations in Japan has not been easy, with foreign employees facing strong assimilative pressures (Moriya, 2012; own interviews with employees), we predict that many will eventually decide to return to their home countries. Looking at return migration of foreign employees or their possible future career paths within Japan should thus provide interesting directions for future research. With a view to understanding the supply side, we also focused on the motivations of young non-Japanese seeking employment in Japan. While Japan's perceived high technological capabilities appear to be a motivation for some job seekers, a more common motivation is a general interest in Japan's culture and the wish to experience this while living in Japan.

Overall, we believe that the attempt to link human and capital flows can contribute substantially to a better understanding of migration flows. For our case, we have shown how human flows into Japan are affected by the aims of Japanese corporations to increase and control overseas investments. The 'systems approach' to migration, while having limitations in fully explaining migration phenomena, has still been useful in shaping our thinking about the sources and directions of Japan-related migration. In terms of the hypothetical relationships between the expansion of global markets and migration streams, which we outlined in the introduction (Massey et al., 1993), we suggest the following connections in the Japanese case. Each of them deserves further research. Japanese companies have contributed to the formation of markets and thus economic and social development in other Asian countries, which in turn have become the main sources of inward-migration to Japan. The migration of skilled labour only became possible after these countries had reached an advanced level of economic and social development, allowing their populations to engage in higher education and to consume Japanese cultural products and study Japanese. Yet, while this might explain the ability to migrate to Japan as a student or skilled labour, it does not explain the motivation to do so. While Massey et al. (1993) point to the flow of goods as well as colonial legacies to explain the attraction of destination countries, we suggest that the wide spread of cultural products, language affinities not explained by colonial legacies as well as income differentials (after all) are more relevant to our case. In terms of government policies, Massey et al. (1993) have argued that policymakers might find it difficult to limit migration streams when such limits go against the interest of transnational companies. In Japan, however, policymakers have first silently and subsequently openly endorsed skilled labour migration. This is a reflection of traditionally cooperative government–big business relationships and also in line with government policies to support universities in their internationalization. The situation around low-skilled labour migration to Japan is far more complex, but as Komine (2018) has shown, even low-skilled labour migration has increased in recent years. While migration research has recently turned towards the micro-level of migration, for example by focusing on the experiences of migrants, networks, and brokers, our approach has demonstrated the merit of a multi-level approach, including the hitherto neglected relevance of HR management policies in destination countries.

# Appendix 3.1: Details of Interviewed Companies

| Sector | Employees (thousands) | Overseas sales as percentage of total sales |
| --- | --- | --- |
| Electronics | 100–150 | Over 60 |
| IT infrastructure/services | 150–200 | Over 40 |
| Trading company | 5–10 | Over 20 |
| Chemicals | 50–100 | Over 40 |
| IT infrastructure/services | 100–150 | Over 20 |
| IT network/systems | 5–10 | n/a |
| Heavy machinery | 25–50 | Over 40 |
| Advertising | > 5 | n/a |
| Logistics | 150–200 | Under 10 |
| Chemicals | 25–50 | Over 20 |
| Engineering | 0.5–1 | n/a |
| Electronics/home appliances | 200–300 | Over 40 |
| IT network/systems | 10–25 | Over 10 |
| IT network/systems | 0.1–0.5 | Under 10 |
| Banking & finance | 50–100 | Over 20 |
| Automobile | 100–150 | Over 60 |
| Trading company | 50–100 | Over 20 |
| Trading company | 25–50 | n/a |
| IT infrastructure/services | 5–10 | Under 10 |

*Sources*: Toyo Keizai (2015) and company websites for employee numbers. Sales data provided by Nomura Research.

*Note*: Employee numbers as well as the overseas sales ratios are only presented in ranges to give an indication of the company size and degree of business internationalization while maintaining anonymity.

## Appendix 3.2: Details of Interviewed Young Foreign Employees

| Nationality | N = 33 |
|---|---|
| Chinese | 16 |
| Korean | 5 |
| Singaporean | 6 |
| British | 3 |
| Other | 3 |
| *Gender* | *N = 33* |
| Male | 14 |
| Female | 19 |
| *Highest degree* | *N = 33* |
| Japanese university | 15 |
| University overseas | 18 |
| *Industry* | *N = 33* |
| IT/communication | 8 |
| Electronics | 6 |
| Finance | 5 |
| Trading | 4 |
| Retail | 2 |
| Chemical | 2 |
| Consumer goods | 2 |
| Other | 4 |
| *Contact method* | *N = 33* |
| Company not involved | 29 |
| Company involved | 4 |

## References

Aiden, Hardeep Singh. 2011. 'Creating the "Multicultural Coexistence" Society: Central and Local Government Policies towards Foreign Residents in Japan'. *Social Science Japan Journal* 14(2): 213–231.

Breaden, Jeremy. 2014. 'Global Attributes or Local Literacy? International Students in Japan's Graduate Employment System'. *Japan Forum* 26(4): 417–440.

Conrad, Harald and Hendrik Meyer-Ohle. 2017. 'Overcoming the Ethnocentric Firm? Foreign Fresh University Graduate Employment in Japan as a New International Human Resource Development Method'. *The International Journal of Human Resource Management Online*. Available at https://doi.org/10.1080/09585192.2017.1330275.

———. 2018. 'Brokers and the Organization of Recruitment of "Global Talent" by Japanese Firms: A Migration Perspective'. *Social Science Japan Journal* 21(1): 67–88.

Edgington, David W and Roger Hayter. 2000. 'Foreign Direct Investment and the Flying Geese Model: Japanese Electronics Firms in Asia-Pacific'. *Environment and Planning A* 32(2): 281–304.

Faist, Thomas. 2000. *The Volume and Dynamics of International Migration and Transnational Social Spaces.* Oxford: Clarendon.

Furuno, Yōichi. 2013. 'Genchi manejimento kyōka ni wa bēsu ni soshiki no shinrai kōchiku ga hitsuyō' (As a base for the strengthening of local management it is necessary to build trust in the organization). *RMSmessage* 30(February): 33–34. Available at www.recruit-ms.co.jp/ research/journal/pdf/j201302/m30_summary.pdf. Accessed on 2 March 2016.

Harzing, Anne-Wil, Markus Pudelko, and B. Sebastian Reiche. 2016. 'The Bridging Role of Expatriates and Inpatriates in Knowledge Transfer in Multinational Corporations'. *Human Resource Management* 55(4): 679–695.

Iwabuchi, Koichi. 1998. 'Marketing "Japan": Japanese Cultural Presence under a Global Gaze'. *Japanese Studies* 18(2): 165–180.

The Japan Times. 2016. 'Record Number of Foreign Students Find Work after Graduating Japanese Universities in 2015'. 16 November. Available at www.japantimes.co.jp/ news/2016/11/16/national/record-number-foreign-students-find-work-graduating-japanese-universities-2015/#.WOrlhGclFzk. Accessed on 30 November 2016.

JETRO. (2017). *ASEAN ni okeru Nihon kigyō no tōshi dōkō* (Trends in the investments of Japanese companies in ASEAN). Available at www.kyushu.meti.go.jp/press/1707/170706_1_s1.pdf. Accessed on 1 March 2018.

Kawazu, Nori. 2013. 'Consumer Trends and Expansion of Retail Markets in Growing ASEAN Economies'. *NRI Papers* 182. Nomura Research Institute. Available at www.nri.com/-/ media/Corporate/en/Files/PDF/knowledge/report/cc/papers/2013/np2013182.pdf?la=en &hash=87A151E28F958FC78745D541531007CA60D35869. Accessed on 1 March 2013.

Keizai Sangyōshō. 2015. *Heisei 26-nendo sangyō keizai kenkyū itaku jigyō hōkoku-sho* (Gaikokujin ryūgakusei no shūshoku oyobi teichaku jōkyō ni kansuru chōsa)' (Report on the 2014 Consignment Survey on economy and industry: survey considering the current situation of the employment and integration of foreign students). Available at www.meti.go.jp/ policy/economy/jinzai/global/pdf/H26_ryugakusei_report.pdf. Accessed on 1 March 2017.

Kim, Heejin. 2013. 'Inpatriation'. *Annals of Business Administrative Science* 12(6): 327–343.

Kobayashi, Tetsuro, Christian Collet, Shanto Iyengar, and Kyu S. Hahn. 2015. 'Who Deserves Citizenship? An Experimental Study of Japanese Attitudes towards Immigrant Workers'. *Social Science Japan Journal* 18(1): 3–22.

Kokusai Kōryū Kikin/Nihon Kokusai Kyōiku Shien Kyōkai. 2016. *2015 nen, dai 2kai, Nihongo nōryokushiken kekka no gaiyō* (Outline of results of the Japanese Language Proficiency Test, 2015, second round). Available at www.jlpt.jp/statistics/pdf/2015_2_9.pdf. Accessed on March 2017.

Komine, Ayako. 2018. 'A Closed Immigration Country: Revisiting Japan as a Negative Case'. *International Migration* 56(5): 106–122. Available at https://onlinelibrary.wiley.com/doi/ full/10.1111/imig.12383.

Kritz, Mary M. and Hania Zlotnik. 1992. 'Global Interactions: Migration Systems Processes and Policies'. In *International Migration Systems—A Global Approach*, edited by Mary M. Kritz, Lin Lean Lim, and Hania Zlotnik, 1–16. Oxford: Clarendon Press.

Lam, Peng Er. 2007. 'Japan's Quest for "Soft Power": Attraction and Limitation'. *East Asia* 24(4): 349–363.

Legewie, Jochen. 2002. 'Control and Co-ordination of Japanese Subsidiaries in China: Problems of an Expatriate-based Management System'. *International Journal of Human Resource Management* 13(6): 901–919.

Liu-Farrer, Gracia. 2009. 'Educationally Channeled International Labor Mobility: Contemporary Student Migration from China to Japan'. *International Migration Review* 43(1): 178–204.

Massey, Douglas S., Joaquin Arango, Graeme Hugo, Ali Kouaouci, Adela Pellegrino, and J. Edward Taylor. 1993. 'Theories of International Migration: A Review and Appraisal'. *Population and Development Review* 19(3): 431–466.

Mercer. 2015. 'Zai Shingapōru Nikkei kigyō kyoten no genjō to kadai—kagi wa saiyō ritenshon kyōka to yakuwari sekinin kengen no meikaku-ka' (Current situation and issues of Japanese-affiliated regional bases in Singapore—the key is a strengthening of recruitment and retention and the clarification of roles and responsibilities). Available at www.mercer. co.jp/our-thinking/2015-talent-management-trend-in-singapore.html. Accessed on 4 January 2019.

Meyer-Ohle, Hendrik. 2014. 'Japanese Retailers in Southeast Asia: Strong Local Partners, Shopping Malls, and Aiming for Comprehensive Internationalization'. *The International Review of Retail, Distribution and Consumer Research* 24(5): 500–515.

Miller, Laura. 1995. 'Two Aspects of Japanese and American Co-Worker Interaction Giving Instructions and Creating Rapport'. *Journal of Applied Behavioral Science* 31(2): 141–161.

Moriya, Takashi. 2012. 'Nihon kigyō no ryūgakusei nado no gaikokujin saiyō e no ichikōsatu' (A study of the employment of foreigners, such as foreign students, by Japanese companies). *Nihon Rōdō Kenkyū Zasshi* 54(6): 29–36.

*Nihon Keizai Shinbun*. 2017. 'Kakusha no saiyō keikaku 2128 honsha chōsa' (The recruitment plans of each company, a survey of 2188 head offices), 21 March, morning edition, 23.

Nye, Joseph S. 1990. 'Soft Power'. *Foreign Policy* 80(Autumn): 153–171.

Okamoto, Kazue and Stephen T. T. Teo. 2011. 'Convergence and Divergence of Role Stress Experience of Locally Hired Japanese and Non-Japanese Host Country Staff: A Qualitative Study'. *The International Journal of Human Resource Management* 22(1): 218–231.

Otmazgin, Nissim Kadosh. 2008. 'Contesting Soft Power: Japanese Popular Culture in East and Southeast Asia'. *International Relations of the Asia-Pacific* 8(1): 73–101.

Reiche, Sebastian B. 2011. 'Knowledge Transfer in Multinationals: The Role of Inpatriates' Boundary Spanning'. *Human Resource Management* 50(3): 365–389.

Sassen, Saskia. 1988. *The Mobility of Labor and Capital: A Study in International Investment and Labor Flow*. Cambridge, UK, and New York: Cambridge University Press.

Shiraki, Mitsuhide (ed.). 2014. *Guroobaru maneja no ikusei to hyōka, Nihonjin hakensha 880 nin, genchi sutaffu 2192 nin no chōsa yori* (Developing and evaluating the global managers, based on a survey of 880 Japanese expatriates and 2192 local staff). Tokyo: Waseda Daigaku Shuppansha.

Tang, Siew Mun. 2012. 'Japan in the Foreign Relations of the ASEAN States'. In *Japan's Relations with Southeast Asia: the Fukuda Doctrine and Beyond*, edited by Lam Peng Er, 84–103. London: Routledge.

Toyo Keizai. 2015. 'Data Services'. Available at http://dbs.toyokeizai.net/en/. Accessed on 15 March 2017.

Tung, Rosalie L. 1982. 'Selection and Training Procedures of US, European, and Japanese Multinationals'. *California Management Review* 25(1): 57–71.

Vogt, Gabriele. 2013. 'When the Leading Goose Gets Lost: Japan's Demographic Change and the Non-Reform of Its Migration Policy'. *Asian Studies* 49(2): 14–44.

Wu, Kenneth C. 2003. 'The Protruding Nail Gets Hammered Down: Discrimination of Foreign Workers in Japan'. *Washington University Global Studies Law Review* 2(2): 469–491.

Yonezawa, Yukako and Akiyoshi Yonezawa. 2016. 'Internationalization of Higher Education as a Response to Globalization: Japan's Policy Challenges since the 1980s'. In *Creating Social Cohesion in an Interdependent World*, edited by Ernest Healy, Dharma Arunachalam, and Tetsuo Mizukami, 191–204. New York: Palgrave Macmillan.

Yoshihara, Hideki. 2000. 'Options for Strategic Change: Screwdriver Factories or Integrated Production Systems?' In *Corporate Strategies for South East Asia after the Crisis*, edited by Jochen Legewie and Hendrik Meyer-Ohle, 57–73. Basingstoke: Palgrave Macmillan.

Yu, Jie and Hendrik Meyer-Ohle. 2008. 'Working for Japanese Corporations in China: A Qualitative Study'. *Asian Business & Management* 7(1): 33–51.

# 4

# Accumulation at the Margins?

## Mineral Brokerage and Chinese Investments in Philippine Mining

ALVIN A. CAMBA

## Introduction

The chapter examines how previous historical migrations, which resulted in diverse Filipino-Chinese communities, facilitated the dynamics and articulations of the People's Republic of China's (PRC) foreign direct investment (FDI) in the Philippine mining sector. In the early 2000s, Gloria Macapagal-Arroyo (2001–2010) set aside the Philippines' territorial claims in the South China Sea in order to strengthen bilateral ties, culminating in more than 20 major investments from Chinese state-oriented enterprises (SOEs) and an increase in smaller private investments across a wide variety of sectors in the Philippines. Private Chinese investors began forming mining companies with Filipino partners in order to take advantage of the Philippines' emerging mineral economy. However, Benigno Aquino III's (2010–2016) stand on the South China Sea led to the deterioration of Philippine–China relations, reversing the previous administrative policy of encouraging Chinese investments. Ironically, his term experienced an upturn in activities from numerous Chinese-funded artisanal and small-scale mining (ASM) firms, which was paradoxical because national political rhetoric and state preference were discursively against Chinese capital. Despite this, Philippine media and civil society organizations reported the rise of illegal ASM funded by Chinese investors. From the perspective of officials in the Aquino administration, the unsanctioned Chinese mineral extraction was part of China's imperial activities in the South China Sea,[1] one with foundations in the unquenched yearning for South East Asia's

---

[1] Interview with a member of the Liberal Party, Mandaluyong City, 5 August 2017.

strategic resources and juridically sanctioned territories. Indeed, Walden Bello, a former congressman during Aquino's term, said that he 'received reports of the rise of illegal Chinese mining activities during Aquino, which was an irony because the increasing international conflict [between the Philippines and China]'.[2]

What accounts for the rise of Chinese ASM during the Aquino administration? I present two interrelated but distinct points on the Philippine mining sector and Chinese FDI from a political economy approach in concert with ethnographic research on three Chinese mining companies in one Philippine province. First, I examine the successive eras of state authoritarianism (1965–1985) and neo-liberalism (1986-onwards) to explain the emergence of ASM in the Philippines. I show how the historical evolution of the Philippine and Chinese economies led to a confluence of factors that resulted in the proliferation of Chinese-funded ASM mining. The crisis of the Philippine mining economy and the neoliberal transition institutionalized the position of regional–local elites to greatly manage the mining sector. For China, the reliance of the Chinese economy on export manufacturing and fixed asset investments led to an economic slowdown and contradictions after the 2008 financial crisis, resulting in the upsurge of Chinese FDI to the developing world. These conditions situate the field research within the Philippines' and China's role in the mineral economy.

Second, I show that Filipino-Chinese, as local intermediaries and shareholders, bridge the economic capital of the PRC's capitalists and the political power of Philippine actors. Here, three factors matter: the type of Chinese company, the owner–broker relationship, and place-based considerations of mines and labour usage. The type of Chinese mining company matters. Those having close ties with Chinese development institutions and the PRC care more about the political impact of FDI on the Philippines. Those with fewer ties care more about making a profit and acquiring the minerals cheaply. In addition, while relationship-building (or *guanxi*) appears to be crucial in linking the Chinese capitalists and Filipino-Chinese businessmen, Chinese capitalists see working with Filipino actors as a practical business opportunity more than an expression of supposedly shared 'ethnic roots'. The identities of both the actors appear fluid, transitional, and contingent on the political and economic conditions of the time. Nevertheless, the existence of regionally diffused Filipino-Chinese brokers and politically embedded Filipino partners determine the diffusion of Chinese mining investments across Philippine provinces. And finally, places and spaces matter. While the movement of labour within and across the provinces occurs because of Chinese capital, the accumulation strategy depends on both the resources and the labour.

---

[2] Interview with Walden Bello, Quezon City, 18 August 2017.

This chapter is structured as follows. First, I explore the crisis of the Philippine mining sector and its transition to a neoliberal mining regime. Second, I situate Chinese mining investments within the broader pattern of Chinese FDI's rise in the world and diffusion during the Arroyo and Aquino administrations. Third, I present the findings of my fieldwork built on my experience with three mining companies in the province of Zambales in 2014 and 2015 in concert with recent field research in 2017. In the concluding section, I discuss the findings of the chapter in relation to capital and labour mobility.

## *The Crisis of the Philippine Mining Economy*

The crisis of the Philippine mining economy and its transition to a neoliberal regime created the conditions for Chinese ASM. First, from the post-war period to the 1980s, many postcolonial states encouraged the build-up of domestic industries, construction of infrastructure, and financing of SOEs, culminating in the state's direct ownership of, or assistance to, companies in various sectors. This programme, popularly known as import-substitution industrialization (ISI), was widespread across the developing world and relied on the state-directed management of enterprises. Like other developing countries, the Philippines borrowed money from commercial banks, paid off the principal, and accrued profit afterwards (Devlin, 2014).[3] Alongside the borrowing and spending spree, these projects needed oil and commodity minerals—copper, nickel, and steel—as basic inputs for import substitution (Eichengreen, 2011). Ferdinand Marcos (1965–1986), a former president who became a dictator and established his family in the Philippine political scene, borrowed money from the international commercial banks to assist the initial construction of the extractive infrastructure of the domestic firms: Marcopper borrowed US$4 million dollars in 1968; Lepanto borrowed US$3 million; and Benguet borrowed a total of US$1.5 million in the 1970s (Lopez, 1992).

A combination of interest rate shocks and global commodity glut gutted the mining sector. When the USA devalued the dollar in 1979, the so-called Volcker shock raised US interest rates three times above the world market average (Panitch and Gindin, 2012). In 1974, petrodollars tied to oil imports parked new capital in the hands of commercial banks. This shock stimulated a movement of capital from development projects in the Third World into the banks of New York and San Francisco. Consequently, development projects in the developing world were delayed

---

[3] It is also worth noting that Korea and Japan relied on these Caribbean banks during the early years of their boom despite following a cheap commodity export strategy. See Bello et al., 2005.

and abandoned afterwards because of an inability to access capital for reinvestment (Bello et al., 2005). Because of the lack of demand, an excessive supply of minerals flooded the world market, pushing down the global prices and forming deficits for mineral exporting states. Oil prices peaked at US$35 per barrel in 1980 but fell below US$10 in 1986.[4] In 1974, the world copper price averaged US$0.93 per lb (Devlin, 2014). With the global commodity glut, copper prices fell to US$0.67 in 1982, and reached an all-time low of US$0.62 in 1986 (World Bank, 1987: 25–26).

The prices of minerals declined drastically, leading to unprofitability and diminished employment, which led to the downfall of the Philippine mining sector. In 1983, Philex Mines, one of the most profitable companies in the Philippines during the post-war period, did not have enough revenue to pay its international loan obligations and workers. In 1983, copper mining companies petitioned a deferment of all tax, duty, and fee payments to the Philippine government. The Marcos regime issued the Presidential Letter of Instruction (LOI) 1416 that allowed payment deferment by five of the financially distressed mining companies (World Bank, 1987: 44). Philippine mining companies of all sizes needed to defer tax and international loan payments to survive. In the aggregate, the share of mineral products in exports fell from 21.33 per cent to 12.3 per cent in 1985 (Camba, 2015). With the political crisis of the Marcos government and the lack of external financial sources, around 14 large- and medium-scale mines had to shut down. Mines started to slow down operations, fire employees, and limit operations (Lopez, 1992). These conditions created a glut of labour in the provinces.

The second significant context is the transition to a neoliberal mining regime, whereby a combination of liberalization policies and domestic politics structured the mining sector. Because Marcos left the Philippines heavily indebted to international lenders after his reign, the Philippine state, national government corporations, and private mining companies needed payment deferment and preferential debt scheduling to survive. The World Bank and the International Monetary Fund (IMF) awarded these concessions in return for the implementation of structural adjustment programmes (SAPs). In 1987, Corazon Aquino (1986–1992) set the initial foundations of the neoliberal restructuring by stressing the role of foreign companies in national recovery. Such emphasis on the neoliberal model became apparent in the National Economic and Development Authority's (NEDA) Medium-Term Philippine Development Plan (1987–1992), which dismantled state monopolies, increased unemployment, and enacted Executive Order (EO) 266, an investment omnibus code that reneges the state's funding commitment to domestic mining companies (Bowie and Unger, 1997). The state thus retreated from its direct management and financing function to make way for private capital.

---

[4] The worth of US$35 in 1980 is US$101 today.

Domestic politics underpinned by Corazon Aquino's need to distinguish her rule from Marcos' shaped this path (Thompson, 1992). Aquino gave additional political power to traditional politicians and competing oligarchs who supported her against Marcos. During the end of Marcos' rule, many of Marcos' loyalists in the national and local governments switched sides in favour of Aquino when the transition seemed inevitable. In return for their support to the post-Marcos government, these politicians were granted significant regional and local autonomy. Aquino gave these national and local governments additional autonomy in their own provinces, which explains the Local Government Code of 1991 (Republic Act 7160).[5] With the SAPs that encouraged the state to delegate powers to local politicians, the traditional corporatist relationship between the national mining companies and the state's development strategy started to crumble. The number of operating mining companies decreased from 39 in the 1980s to 16 in the 1990s (Israel, 2010). In other words, the neoliberal restructuring encouraged the national state to retreat, paving the way for regional and local politicians to attract foreign investments themselves in the extractive sector. As mining companies began to default one by one, workers were terminated from their positions.

Perhaps unintentionally, more progressive political reforms were implemented, for example, the recognition of indigenous peoples' rights through the Indigenous Peoples Rights Act of 1997 (IPRA). However, the centrepiece of Aquino's political compromise with the regional–local politicians was the decentralization of mining-related decisions to local government units (LGUs) to strengthen regional autonomy, especially in mineral-rich Mindanao. Quite contradictory to EO 266, which aimed to restructure the mining sector in favour of foreign capital, the Philippine state eventually passed Republic Act 7076, or the People's Small-Scale Mining Act, giving power to local actors to decide on ASM operations.[6] The bankruptcy and the closure of many mining companies led to the unemployment of hundreds of miners and thousands of other skilled engineers (Verbrugge, 2014). The newly unemployed from state-owned companies and agriculture became the labour force for small-scale mining. Gold was the one and only commodity that remained profitable during the commodity glut years. As demand for gold increased in the world market, small-scale mining in Central Africa, Ghana, Ivory Coast, and many sub-Saharan African states proliferated (for example, Hilson, 2009). In the late 1990s, large-scale intra-regional migration occurred across the Philippines due to the emergence of ASM in pursuit of gold, most notably in Mount Diwalwal (Camba, 2015), which attracted 150,000 ASM miners (Lopez, 1992). In the late

---

[5] Interview with the non-executive director, Quezon City, Philippines, 3 June 2010.

[6] While Marcos also passed the Presidential Decree 1899 in 1984, the RA 7076 was an upgrade in terms of local government autonomy.

1990s, ASM remained a lucrative livelihood strategy in mining regions, and the resultant unsafe and (socially and environmentally) costly extractive activities occurred at the margins of the state (Lopez, 1992).

## Chinese FDI in the Philippines

In the past two decades, China's rapid economic growth was driven mostly by export-oriented manufacturing. As stagflation occurred in the West, China received the largest share of global FDI to jump-start its capital-starved economy (Hung, 2008: 161). The East Asian states, which relied on state-guided capital, similarly reinvested their capital in the PRC's manufacturing sector by the 1980s (Hung, 2015: 187). Specifically, China's currency devaluation and generous tax incentives to foreign investors, particularly after China's accession to the WTO in 2001, led to the movement of capital into the Chinese economy. Manufacturing sectors, originally located in the major markets of the West, transformed China into the 'workshop of the world' by drawing on the huge reserve army of rural migrant labour. Apart from export manufacturing, China also relied on fixed asset investment to bolster its growth. Investment projects by state-owned companies or local governments have been fuelled by cheap credits from state banks. The growing liquidity fostered by China's central banks created the conditions for the explosion of loans, which in turn relied on the rapidly expanding foreign exchange reserve that originated from China's export manufacturing (Hung, 2015: chapter 3). In other words, the expansion of the state-owned investment sector is grounded on China's export growth.

When the bubble of financial expansion and debt-fuelled consumption in the USA collapsed in 2008, driving a deep and long decline of the American economy, the export-driven economy of China also collapsed at the end of the year. However, Beijing successfully engineered a strong economic rebound in 2009–2010 by opening the floodgates of state bank lending to the state sector. The weakening of the export engine and the reckless investment during the rebound of 2009–2010, created a gigantic debt bubble no longer matched by commensurate expansion of the foreign exchange reserve of China. Between 2008 and early 2015, outstanding debt in China skyrocketed from 148 per cent to 282 per cent of GDP, exceeding the level in the USA and most other developing countries. China's foreign exchange reserve ended its long expansion and started to shrink in 2014 (Hung, 2015). In an attempt to restore profitability, China began to export capital. The stock of China's outward FDI jumped from US$28 billion in 2000 to US$298 billion in 2012, though it is still small in comparison with smaller advanced capitalist economies like Singapore (see Hung, 2015: table 5.4). Following China's economic slowdown and leadership transition, Beijing altered the behaviour of Chinese FDI to help rebalance from export-led to consumption-driven growth. As China's reliance on export manufacturing to the developed world and state-led reinvestment experienced a slowdown in returns, the Chinese government and businesses began investing more in other sectors that promised more returns. This included diversifying FDI acquisitions away from solely resource investments to a broad portfolio of strategic assets across a variety of sectors. An analysis of Chinese FDI in the Philippines should be situated within these broader macroeconomic forces.

While Arroyo attempted to increase Chinese foreign capital and FDI in the country, by the end of her term, all but one of these major projects were cancelled or withdrawn. Zhongxing New Telecommunications Equipment (ZTE) Corporation's privatization bid for the Philippine National Broadcasting Corporation (NBN) faced intense political opposition, leading to its cancellation by Arroyo herself (Camba, 2018). The China National Machinery Industry Corporation (Sinomach), which started the construction of a high-speed rail project under partial ownership, received an open-ended moratorium in 2008, while the Industrial Commercial Bank of China (ICBC), which proposed opening more than 24 branches in the Philippines, ultimately decided to withdraw its offer (Camba, 2017a). Similarly, 18 Chinese agribusiness projects were hindered by multiple regional--local elites, leading to their eventual withdrawal. At the start of Benigno Aquino's term as president, Chinese foreign investment was targeted to fund more than 10 major projects. Aquino himself visited Beijing in 2011 and acquired the commitment of the Chinese government to provide more than US$13 billion worth of aid and investment (Camba, 2018). When the South China Sea issue erupted in 2012, these plans were eventually shelved by both the states. At the end of Aquino's term, there were no major Chinese market investments except for the State Grid Corporation of China (SGCC). Most of the Chinese investments were from the smaller, flexible foreign direct investors located in manufacturing, services, tourism, and real estate. Near the end of Aquino's term in 2015, the Philippines had one of the lowest levels of Chinese investment in South East Asia.

China's relatively small share in the Philippine mining sector, despite the economic capacity of Chinese mining companies and the mineral needs of the Chinese economy, can be explained by the politics of foreign ownership and geopolitics in the South China Sea during the Aquino administration (Camba, 2017b). First, greenfield investments and the 100 per cent foreign ownership of assets remain controversial political issues for the Philippine public. Philippine political and economic elites, intent on monopolizing the country's economic sectors, easily unite against national policies that allow full foreign ownership (Camba, 2015). While changes brought about by the Philippine Mining Act (RA 7942) allow full foreign ownership in the mining sector, any Philippine administration risks some degree of political opposition unless there is public support for the foreign investors. This fear is further highlighted in the mining sector given the scale and implication of operations, leading to media emphasis on socio-environmental degradation. In most cases, foreign investors take the limited foreign ownership via joint ventures to evade the potential controversies (Camba, 2017a: 15). Allowing foreign ownership rests on considerable political ties with the ruling administration and economic linkages with Philippine firms.

Second, Aquino's administration stood their ground in the South China Sea dispute. In 2013, Philippine and global media popularized China's bullying, making it increasingly difficult for politicians to endorse Chinese economic transactions in the country, much less support full foreign ownership (Camba, 2017a: 16–17). Philippine politicians ceaselessly highlighted the South China Sea issue to generate political capital, creating negative perceptions on Chinese aid and investment. While Arroyo created joint natural resource development agreements in the disputed area, Aquino rescinded them during his tenure. In concert with these changing perceptions, the constrained space of foreign ownership in the mining sector resulted in support for partnerships with Canadian and Australian companies instead. Mining companies from these countries did not encounter resistance from major political elites at that time. Apart from the Left's resistance to these companies, major Philippine institutions cemented these positive and often misleading perceptions.

Table 4.1 | Chinese Investments in the Philippine Mining Sector, 2010–2016

| Year | Name of the mining company | Type of mineral investment |
|------|----------------------------|---------------------------|
| 2002 | Eramen Minerals | Joint venture |
| 2003 | Hualong International INC. | Joint venture |
| 2004 | China Nonferrous Metal Industry's Foreign Engineer and Construction Co. | Joint venture |
| 2004 | United Philippine and China Mining Corp | Joint venture |
| 2005 | Asia Philippine China Mineral Corporation | Joint venture |
| 2005 | Yinlu Bicol Mining Corporation | Joint venture |
| 2005 | 14th Metallurgical Construction Company INC | Joint venture |
| 2005 | Adnama Mining Resources, INC | Joint venture |
| 2006 | Oriental Synergy Nickel Corporation | Joint venture |
| 2006 | Global Phil-Sino Mining Corporation | Joint venture |
| 2006 | Mega Tsung Mining Corporation | Joint venture |
| 2006 | No. 14th Metallurgical Construction Company of China in Non-Ferrous Metal | Joint venture |
| 2007 | China Acadia Mining Resources Philippines Corporation | Joint venture |
| 2007 | Fil-China Mining Development Corporation | Joint venture |
| 2007 | Hai Cheng Nickel Mining Corporation | Joint venture |

*Contd*

*Table 4.1 contd*

| Year | Name of the mining company | Type of mineral investment |
|------|----------------------------|----------------------------|
| 2007 | China International Nickel Steel Corporation | Joint venture |
| 2007 | Guo Long Mining Corporation | Joint venture |
| 2007 | Konka Fulim Mining and Development Corporation | Joint venture |
| 2007 | Peng Cheng Metallic Resources Corporation | Joint venture |
| 2007 | Singtech Mining & Trading Co. LTD, INC. | Joint venture |
| 2007 | Fujian Sino-Phil Mining Corporation | Joint venture |
| 2008 | Fareast Nickel Mining Corporation | Joint venture |
| 2008 | Eight Circles Mining & Trading Corporation | Joint venture |
| 2008 | Sinosteel Philippines HY Mining Corporation | Joint venture |
| 2008 | Oriental Vision Mining Corporation | Joint venture |
| 2008 | AMD China Starlite Mining Corporation | Joint venture |
| 2008 | Philippine China Friendship Mining INC. | Joint venture |
| 2008 | South China Mining Corporation | Joint venture |
| 2009 | Zhongli Mining Corporation | Joint venture |
| 2010 | China Nonferrous Metal Mining Group | Joint venture |
| 2010 | Oriental Vision Mining Corporation | Joint venture |
| 2010 | China and Philippine Non Ferrous Metal Mining Co. | Joint venture |
| 2010 | China Mining ZBGPH Corporation | Joint venture |
| 2010 | China Philippines Unity Mineral Resources | Greenfield investment |
| 2011 | China International Mining Petroleum Limited | Greenfield investment |
| 2011 | Gold Mountain International Mining Company Limited | Greenfield investment |
| 2011 | China ACLAS Technology | Joint venture |
| 2011 | Yangtze Worldwide Development Corporation | Joint venture |
| 2011 | Philippine China Amity Ventures Corporation | Joint venture |
| 2011 | Sinophil Paracale Mining Inc. | Joint venture |
| 2012 | Libjo Mining Corporation | Joint venture |
| 2012 | Lian Hai Philippines Mining Corporation | Joint venture |
| 2013 | China Nonferrous Mineral Corporation | Joint venture |
| 2013 | Oriental Synergy Mining Corporation | Joint venture |
| 2015 | Techiron Resources INC | Joint venture |

*Source*: Articles of incorporation and shareholder data from Philippine Security Exchange Commission.

The preference for Australian and Canadian mining because of the associated territorial disputes in the South China Sea affected Chinese FDI in the mining sector. On the one hand, the number of Chinese mining companies decreased from the Arroyo to the Aquino administration. Table 4.1, which draws from articles of incorporation and shareholder data in the Philippine Security Exchange Commission (SEC), illustrates this point. The decrease is paradoxical because the overall amount of Chinese FDI worldwide increased after the 2008 financial crisis. In the case of Philippine mining, a Chinese investor said that 'Aquino's actions in the South China Sea scared potential mining investors because he [Aquino] made them feel that the state can take their output or reverse their license.'[7] On the other hand, there were reports on the increase of Chinese illegal ASM operations across the country. In 2013, the Philippines became the top supplier of nickel to China despite the decreasing rates of profitability. Other minerals were also reportedly mined and smuggled out. The next section explores these illicit extractions in the province of Zambales.

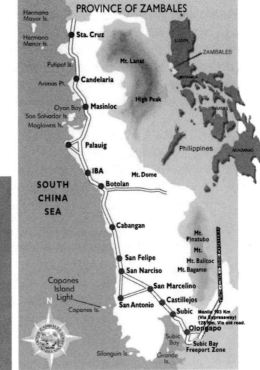

Figure 4.1 | Zambales in the Philippines

*Source*: https://capefoundationinc.wordpress.com/forests/zambales-mountains/. Accessed on 7 May 2019.

---

[7] Interview with Chinese investor, Subic Metropolitan Bay Authority, Subic City, 10 August 2017.

## Case Analysis: Chinese Mining in Zambales

With its capital in Iba, the mountainous province of Zambales is in Central Luzon and borders Pangasinan, Tarlac, and Pampanga (see Figure 4.1). The province has a total population of just over 500,000 living in 1 major city, 13 municipalities, and 230 *barangays*. The three major ethnic groups are Tagalog, Ilocano, and Sambal. The province was incorporated in the Spanish Empire by Juan de Salcedo, leading to the establishment of major towns as early as the sixteenth century. Masinloc, a town in the province, was the capital during the Spanish period but was eventually replaced by other towns. In the post-war period, the Americans established a military base to house the USA's Seventh Fleet. At that time, the base provided a source of jobs for the population, including light manufacturing, retail, and the sex trade. Olongapo, the only major city in Zambales, grew from the American naval station established during US colonial rule. Indeed, for all the problems of the American base, Central Luzon's economic activities were bolstered by the American military bases. When the Philippine Senate rejected the renewal bid for the American military bases in 1991, the Subic Bay Metropolitan Authority, a new institution formed by the post-Marcos Philippine governments, established the Subic Bay Freeport Zone (SBFZ). The first export processing zone, which was established 20 years earlier in the Clark Development Zone (CDZ), became a template and was followed by the SBFZ. Indeed, the SBFZ became a gateway for American and Hong Kong goods in the Philippines.

This explains why the SBFZ was able to attract more FDI than the other export processing zones. Illustrated in Table 4.2, Chinese FDI commitment in the SBMA was vastly higher than all the other Philippine investment promotion agencies

Table 4.2 | Chinese FDI in the Philippine Investment Promotion Agencies, 2003–2015 (US$ million)

| Agency | 2003 | 2004 | 2005 | 2006 | 2007 | 2008 | 2009 | 2010 | 2011 | 2012 | 2013 | 2014 | 2015 |
|---|---|---|---|---|---|---|---|---|---|---|---|---|---|
| AFAB | | | | | | | | | 2 | 4 | | 4 | 3 |
| BOI | 3 | 1 | 1 | 42 | 57 | 51 | 5 | 12 | 18 | 14 | 5 | 25 | 47 |
| BOI ARMM | | | | | | | | | | | 175 | 37 | |
| CDC | 0 | 0 | 3 | 6 | | 0 | 40 | 36 | 3 | 2 | 1 | 4 | 5 |
| CEZA | | | | | | | | | 0 | 1 | 1 | 1 | 1 |
| PEZA | 10 | 33 | 2 | 4 | 16 | 29 | 102 | 6 | 26 | 54 | 31 | 49 | 27 |
| SBMA | 0 | 0 | 0 | 379 | 3 | 0 | 1 | 79 | 452 | 0 | 0 | 209 | 0 |
| Total | 14 | 35 | 7 | 431 | 76 | 81 | 147 | 133 | 501 | 76 | 213 | 329 | 83 |

*Source*: Modified documents from Philippine Statistics Authority and Philippine investment promotion agencies (2010).

that manage the country's export processing zones (EPZs) in the country. Here, Olongapo's infrastructure, educated populace, and historical position as a receiver of migrants from elsewhere in Luzon, contributed to the higher investment rates. As the former host of an American base, the communications, transportation, and disaster infrastructures were far above the standards elsewhere in the country. Ports in, and shipping lines from, the South China Sea also made SBFZ one of the country's main docking stations for imported goods. The city's infrastructure and saliency during the Aquino administration justifies the case selection of in-depth qualitative and ethnographic research. Here, I present the findings of my field research on three Chinese mining companies in Zambales.

## Variations of Chinese Mining Companies

Various kinds of Filipino actors bring up different narratives of exploitation regarding Chinese mining companies. Social movements often interpret Chinese mining companies through the narrative of core–periphery relations, unequal exchange, and global inequality (for example, Singh and Camba, 2016). American mining companies monopolized the sector in the early colonial period, but since the 1980s, Australian and Canadian mining companies have been the most active in working with the wealthiest Philippine mining companies (Kirsch, 2014). Some of the major left-wing organizations see China in the same line of imperialist interest in the country. Leon Dulce, a spokesperson of Kalikasan, one of the major anti-mining organizations in the country, said, 'Americans have historically colonized the Philippines for its resources but recently, other Western countries have taken this role seriously.'[8] A crucial consideration is whether or not the Chinese mining companies conform to this caricature. As researchers have argued, there is no single characteristic 'Chinese investor' (Wang, 2002). Instead, a multiplicity of national and regional SOEs, provincial entrepreneurs, and private investors fall under the general label of 'Chinese investors' (Camba, 2017a; Lee, 2018). Their investment activity varies in terms of asset specificity, sectoral distribution, and investment size (Nyíri and Tan, 2017).

Among the three Chinese mining companies discussed in this chapter, one is the subsidiary of a large Chinese SOE while the other two are smaller private companies. The former can be described as state-backed FDI while the latter can be understood as flexible FDI. State-backed FDI comprises capital with the capacity to transform economies because of its sheer size, the fact that they are often found in strategic sectors, and that they depend on the political relationship of the sending and host states. In the case of China, state-backed FDI usually goes through

---

[8] Interview with an organization's (Kalikasan-PNE) member, Quezon City, 13 June 2014.

crucial infrastructures, mega facilities, and strategic sector agreements via official development assistance (ODA), funded by the Chinese Export and Import Bank (EXIM), or assisted by the Chinese Development Bank (CDB). Chinese SOEs or largely monopolistic Chinese private companies take the lead in projects, which also include material sourcing requirements and Chinese labour usage. Private Chinese companies such as ZTE and Huawei can also spearhead these projects, but the Chinese state usually has the final say on which project to fund (Camba, 2017a).

Flexible FDI, comprised of smaller sums of capital owned by sending country citizens, operates at a scale that makes it unable to direct political or economic change on its own. These investors differ not only by their size and amount of capital but also in terms of their access to crucial political networks in both the sending and host countries. The most common examples of flexible FDI are small and medium enterprises owned by sending country citizens; these are often found in the export processing zones and non-strategic sectors of the host state. Specifically, smaller Chinese companies with little financial reliance on the EXIM bank, the CDB, or the Chinese Communist Party (CCP) are considered flexible foreign direct investors. These investors tend to work *within* the formal rules and structures in the host country, often partnered with local business groups and technocrats. As such business ventures are often smaller, located in non-strategic sectors, and consider profit making above all else, these Chinese investors can continue to increase even in the presence of interstate conflict. Nevertheless, despite having an ostensibly apolitical and profit-motivated behaviour, flexible foreign direct investors still encounter political risk.

I interviewed representatives of the three Chinese mining companies in the province of Zambales in 2014. While their perspectives may be hard to generalize, they do illustrate the ways in which the two types of mining companies follow distinct logics based on their ties with Beijing. From the perspective of the state-backed SOE, 'We wanted to invest in the Philippines and create a win-win situation for both of our countries, but instead, there is a fear of anti-Chinese sentiments in the current Aquino government today.'[9] This investor said that 'It is not about profit, but China wants peace and Asians to help other Asians without ... and we Chinese have the mindset and the acculturation similar to other Filipinos.'[10] Indeed, the political impact of this mining company on Zambales has been helpful to the Chinese cause. An interview with a Filipino middle man posited that 'the Chinese have helped people get jobs and stimulate profit for the local businesses and, without them, the province wouldn't have grown so much'.[11] As C. K. Lee

[9] Interview with a Chinese small-mining firm representative, Zambales, 8 July 2014.
[10] Interview with a Chinese investor, Zambales, 29 July 2014.
[11] Interview with a Filipino middleman, Zambales, 29 July 2014.

(2018) has argued, some Chinese firms in Africa appear to accept losing out on profit in the short-term in exchange for long-term security and political influence.

In an interview with the smaller, second Chinese company, the owner said that 'Chinese investments are good for the Filipino capitalists and the Chinese so that the local economies can be developed.'[12] When the second investor was asked about the practices that circumvent the Philippine national government, the owner said that 'in many parts of the world, these rules are not in place, like in China we have our local government officials deciding where to mine and to what extent'. Both investors also saw the regional–local elites with some degree of optimism due to their practicality. The first firm's investor sees regional local elites as 'partners that cannot be influenced by Western powers and looking after their own [development]'.[13] In an interview with the third mining company, a smaller kind similar to the second one, the representative said that 'it is not about circumventing the rules of the national government, but also giving the local governments power to decide the fates of their people and their lives rather than letting those at Manila decide on what is good'.[14] These sentiments, situated within the broader context of the South China Sea and US intervention, generate the conditions for Chinese investors, Filipino-Chinese brokers, and regional–local elites to create distinct institutional arrangements to devise a quick solution towards the perceived injustice of national regulations. In sum, the aims and motivations of Chinese FDI in the mining sector also depend on the type of Chinese actors.

## Creating Linkages

In a conventional investment process, companies need national government support and local intermediaries to facilitate investments. Between the two, the former is more important than the latter. The CEO of a major mining company noted in an interview that in their investments in the developing world, 'establishing support from the national government is more important than the local politicians or the social groups'.[15] This perspective comes from an interstate framework between the multinational companies and the developing country built on the foundations of contracts, memoranda of agreement, and international dispute bodies. However, when the government is unwilling and unable to support the investment, Chinese mining firms rely on their business networks and personal contacts to expand

---

[12] Interview with a Chinese investor, Zambales, 16 June 2014.

[13] Interview with a Chinese investor, Zambales, 29 July 2014.

[14] Interview with a Chinese representative, Zambales, 30 June 2014.

[15] Author interview with the mining consultant, Geograce Resource Philippines, Quezon City, Philippines, 31 December 2009.

their operations. In these cases, these firms establish their operations by allying with regional–local actors that often circumvent national-level regulation. China's growing economic power has allowed Chinese capitalists to invest in the developing world, but these actors deal with the political-economic structures shaped by postcolonial development paradigms.

In the Philippine context, the South China Sea dispute, Xi Jinping's ascent to power, and China's economic contradictions led to a proliferation of Chinese capitalists in the untapped mineral resources of the Philippines. Arroyo's administration attracted 35 new Philippine and Chinese joint ventures in Mineral Production Sharing Agreement (MPSA) agreements during her tenure. Comparatively, Aquino was only able to attract seven new mining companies despite the far better state of the Philippine economy at that time (Camba, 2017a: 10). Nonetheless, Chinese capitalists respond to their government's tenuous relations with the Philippines by expanding ASM investments. This difference is remarkable because China only really began to export capital at a far higher rate after Arroyo's tenure and it is a testament to the importance of international relations to the strategic sectors.

Chinese investors began to utilize the network of Chinese communities across South East Asian states in order to acquire contacts in the Philippines. Filipinos with full or partial Chinese heritage are not homogenously wealthy and powerful in the country. Indeed, some Filipino-Chinese or Chinese mestizo families, such as the Sys and the Tans, are considered to be the wealthiest economic elites in the Philippines. Following their footsteps, some of the most important families include the Caktiong, the Tan, the Consunji, the Ty, and the Sia (Simbulan, 2005). These families exist in the Philippines' top business association called the 'Makati Business Club', located in the country's wealthiest business district and residence.[16] These families currently dominate the highest echelons of the national economy. Many of these groups tend to oppose or mobilize against Chinese FDI in other sectors of the economy unless they directly mediate or benefit from the deals. These new Chinese elites, known as the *taipans*, control a significant portion of the Philippine economy. Their rise rivalled and to some degree eclipsed the Chinese mestizos and the land-based 'old rich' Filipino elites (McCoy, 2009).

After these elites, thousands of other Filipino-Chinese and Chinese mestizo families occupy a wide range of class backgrounds with differential access to political networks, assets, and wealth. A notch below the Makati Business Club, some Filipino-Chinese or Chinese mestizo families belong to the Philippine Chamber of Commerce and Industry (PCCI), which has regional chapters across

---

[16]    Interview with a political broker, Quezon City, 10 August 2017.

the country.[17] There are also middle to upper-middle class of these families who occupy high-skilled professional jobs, for example in law, medicine, and retail. These families also comprise the lower-middle class where they still work in the service sector, for example in restaurants or small retail establishments.

In this chapter, interviews are drawn from Filipino-Chinese or Chinese mestizo business people in the provinces who have partnered with Chinese investors and the regional–local elites in the country to form distinct institutional structures of mineral extraction, hidden from national regulations. These regional–local elites capitalize on the Chinese investors and the Filipino-Chinese business people to acquire economic capital necessary for their re-elections and political control. These three groups collude and work with one another in order to offset their rivals elsewhere.

Observers in intelligence, business, and political circles believe that many of these families, or local elites with Chinese heritage, remain firmly linked to their East and South East Asian counterparts.[18] Since the Philippine government does not have enough capacity to police the movement of entrepreneurs and their economic capital, Chinese investors can circumvent the national state and work directly with regional actors. Chinese mining firms tap into their networks of middle to upper-middle class Filipino-Chinese or Chinese mestizos. A minimum common denominator among the Filipino-Chinese communities is the use of the local dialect, such as Hokkien or Hakka. Chinese investors cannot capitalize on this because these dialects are only widespread among sub-ethnic Chinese groups. What fosters a common agenda is that many Filipino-Chinese and Chinese investors get connected in a network of Chinese businesses comprising relatives, friends, and acquaintances. Chinese investors then find partners in the South East Asian community or in Fujian to communicate with Filipino-Chinese in their dialect or simply in English.

The first interview is with a Chinese investor who was able to invest in the Philippines in 2007, but their operations were hindered by anti-Chinese mobilization during Arroyo and the South China Sea issue's eruption during Aquino. Indeed, this Chinese investor said that

> during Arroyo, it was already difficult to acquire huge tracts of land because of the anti-Chinese sentiments revolving around ZTE and North Rail ... but after Arroyo, it became harder and harder to negotiate with the officials in Manila because of their worries of strategic resources and territorial conflict with the Chinese government.[19]

---

[17] Ibid.

[18] Interview with a military intelligence analyst, Makati City, 18 August 2017; affirmed by political elite from the Liberal Party, Mandaluyong City, 5 August 2017. The degree that this is true, in which sectors, events, how big, and how expansive remains debatable.

[19] Interview with a Chinese investor, Zambales, 29 July 2014.

As the Aquino government placed a moratorium on the approval of new mining operations in 2012, the strategies of Chinese mining companies also changed. For the second Chinese investor, his firm relied on 'funding ASM mining firms to extract minerals and sell their mines to the existing Chinese mining companies'.[20] This strategy appears to contrast with the large-scale, capital-intensive mining companies of the Australian and Canadians with their Filipino partners. These latter companies resorted to intensifying capital investments in their huge delimited tract of lands to acquire more minerals. The Chinese investor's experience was very different and he narrated his story of arriving in the Philippines in 2012:

> My family comes from Fujian and I had distant relatives in Indonesia. I contacted them about investing in Indonesia, but they did not have any contacts with the Indonesian government or other businessmen. I heard from them that their other family members in the Philippines were looking for people who could invest money in new mining firms. After talking to them, I went to the Philippines using a tourist visa to personally meet them and visit the mines. I visited Zambales, saw the mineral areas, and hired my own engineers and geologist to inspect them. These Filipino-Chinese gave me the assurance that the local officials and the politicians could provide us with protection.[21]

For the Chinese investor of the third mining company, he suggested that 'the Filipino Chinese that I work with are not really family or bloodline members, but simply networks that I had to tap in order to invest in the Philippines ... I'm from Beijing and did not know Hokkien or any of these languages'.[22] The Filipino-Chinese broker in the third firm brought a similar story to the interview: 'We are working with each other not because we have Chinese roots, but because they want minerals and we want money ... we see this as an exchange of sorts rather than some sort of bond or *guanxi*.'[23] The Filipino partner of the third company, a political elite with business ties with the Filipino–Chinese, said that 'expanding mining in the area is necessary but very few people have the means to do so ... getting Chinese investors to fund the ASM firms work because it spread the money around without subjecting these incomes to the corrupt bureaucrats of Manila'.[24]

For these three interviews, it is possible to draw three inferences about this process. First, a common economic goal is necessary for Filipino-Chinese and Chinese investors. The former's political network and embedded relations with

[20] Interview with a Chinese investor, Zambales, 16 June 2014.
[21] Ibid.
[22] Interview with a Chinese investor, Zambales, 30 June 2014.
[23] Ibid.
[24] Interview with a Filipino politician, Zambales, 29 June 2014.

the host country's population combine with the latter's economic capital and their own demand side network. In other words, Filipino-Chinese also need Chinese investors to access the market for mineral exports. Second, their linkages do not appear to be cultural or based on a sense of common identification between the Chinese investors and the South East Asian Chinese. Rather, cultural heritage becomes a tool of using distinct South East Asian Chinese networks to connect with interested investors whose economic opportunities have dwindled given the Philippine–China relations. And finally, there appear to be distinct strategies for the Chinese and Western mining companies. For the former, utilizing existing political connections to fund or purchase mines from ASM firms appeared to be the pattern. This strategy became logical because smaller mining companies often operate on tiny tracts of land and then move elsewhere afterwards. For the latter, many Western mining companies and their Filipino allies acquired huge tracts of land during the Arroyo administration, leading to the intensification of resource extraction with little need to expand to other sites.

Many of these Filipino-Chinese use their connections with regional and local elites whose economic influence and political patronage over communities facilitate and enable Chinese investors to purchase mines or illegally fund ASM. By the twentieth century, the Filipino-Chinese population numbered 1 per cent of the Philippine population or around 1.5 million out of 100 million people in the Philippines.[25] In addition, there were an estimated 25 million people who had partial Chinese heritage. In the late nineteenth and early twentieth centuries, these people were considered Chinese mestizos. In the twenty-first century, many of them are simply known as Filipinos despite having access to the local Chinese dialect. Most of the Filipino-Chinese belong to the professional, business, and retail sectors, but the Chinese mestizos are more widespread across social and class lines (Wickberg, 1965).

In other words, the tendency of Chinese investors to tap into this 'less wealthy' pre-existing network of South East Asian Chinese in the host countries goes back to the historical migration of Chinese people into South East Asia. Chinese migration to the Philippine islands transformed demographic features, population dynamics, and ethnic relations in crucial ways (Tan, 1972). Most South East Asian Chinese come from Hokkien and Hakka roots. While the Philippines has historically been a recipient of huge numbers of these migrants, the Spanish created a system of religious identification based on Roman Catholicism and a racial hierarchy that valorized whiteness (Cullather, 1994). Indeed, these events go back to the numerous 'Chinese massacres' in the sixteenth century and the popular

---

[25]  Philippine Statistics Authority. *Provincial Summary: Number of Provinces, Cities, Municipalities and Barangays, by Region.* (2015).

historical figure of the uncouth Chinese vendor sprawling around the streets of Manila (Wickberg, 1965).

However, these dynamics changed when Spain lost Latin America to independence in 1815. Spain removed the racial barriers, allowing Filipinos, who were owners of land based on the historical socio-economic structures, and Chinese, who had economic capital from China, to intermarry in order to bolster the Philippine economy. This led to the birth of Chinese mestizos who became part of the Philippine social fabric in the nineteenth century, and members of the group even launched the Philippine Revolution against Spain. However, as the intermarriage of Filipinos and Chinese and inflows of new Chinese migrants continued, the nature of the Chinese mestizos started to transform (Tan, 1972).

Chinese investors tap into the network of Chinese communities in the host countries. Filipino-Chinese or the Chinese mestizos are closer to their counterparts in Thailand, where relatively successful assimilation led to the 'Southeast Asianization' of the Chinese descendants (Wang, 1996). In contrast, Chinese populations in Malaysia and Thailand created distinct political-economic communities with their own goals and ideals largely separate from the South East Asian population. Similarly, trans-local Chinese-majority states and political entities, such as Singapore, Hong Kong, and Taiwan, established a distinct Chinese society separate from the PRC and their other South East Asian counterparts (Wang, 1981).

## Place-Based Considerations

There is currently no data set that accurately gauges the overall number of miners and scale of ASM operations in the Philippines, their activities, and variations among them. However, key actors of the Philippine mining sector are aware of their existence and activities.[26] In the formal economy, Filipino mining companies and their Australian and Canadian transnational partners dominate the large-scale mining activities in the country. Their domination goes back to their land ownership or lease and permission to exclusively operate in the largest tracts of land, contribution to taxation, and share of mineral exports (Camba, 2015). Foreign and national firms need to acquire permission from and secure the necessary permits with the national regulatory institutions, such as the Department of Environment and Natural Resources (DENR), the Mines and Geosciences Bureau (MGB), and the National Commission for Indigenous Peoples. In contrast, the state crafted the ASM laws to make communities organize firms, diffuse market competition,

---

[26] My fieldwork in 2010, 2014, and 2015 revealed the perceptions.

and ensure that local governments benefit from mining operations. ASM firms, organized by communities, incorporate their firms in the local government and petition a specific amount of land as their desired mining areas. Even without national supervision, local governments have the power to issue mineral permits and designate lands for mineral extraction due to significant deregulation in the 1990s. The national government does have power to contest these permits under certain circumstances.

Organizing ASM operations needs a considerable sum of money, not within the reach of most rural communities in the provinces. Monetary investments are necessary to purchase the means of extraction, the labour of engineers and miners, and the permission of regional–local politicians. As a result, some ASM firms began to receive considerable foreign capital infusion from other mining companies or investors, exchanging the labour payments and mining equipment for the mineral output.[27] These arrangements between ASM firms and investors exist in a grey area, ranging from commonly accepted practices like selling mineral output domestically to illegal ones such as exporting or smuggling ores to the foreign market.[28] ASM capitalizes on skilled workers left behind by the destruction of state-owned companies, the retrenchment of workers, and the lack of state response to compensate afterwards (Verbrugge, 2014).

ASM is not exclusive to the Chinese, but the access of other multinationals to large-scale mining (LSM)—due to the partnership of Canadian and Australian firms with Filipino companies—makes the ASM an unappealing option for other foreign investors. Instead, Canadian and Australian companies mainly purchase metals from ASM firms. Because they are smaller, Chinese and non-Chinese ASM firms incorporate locals in the employment decision-making structure.[29] Hiring workers in the area generates loyalty in the local population, fostering allies and redistributing patronage to hinder the national government from circumventing these arrangements. Workers are used for various phases of mineral production. In my field research in Zambales, Chinese ASM firms capitalize on the community's local knowledge to know where to explore and hire unemployed residents to survey potential mining areas.[30] During exploratory phases, Chinese ASM firms hire consultants from the Manila or have a non-Filipino Chinese expert with a tourist visa to conduct geological assessments to verify the potential fecundity of the untapped reserves.[31]

---

[27] Interview with a Filipino politician, Zambales, 29 June 2014.

[28] Ibid.

[29] Interview with a Chinese small-mining firm representative, Zambales, 08 July 2014.

[30] Interview with the Bureau of Customs Official, Zambales, 28 June 2014.

[31] Ibid.

On the part of communities, many take it as an opportunity to be employed as labourers due to their embedded position as community members, their 'local' understanding of the geography, and to some, their experience as former miners during the Marcos years. In the second mining company, a local *barangay* (village) captain told me that his family 'had ancestral knowledge of the nickel's source's location, and developed rudimentary yet effective techniques to ascertain these sources'.[32] During the conversation, some degree of uneasiness was apparent due to his involvement in helping the Chinese acquire minerals in the Philippines, yet he feels that 'as community members, they deserve to profit and benefit from the minerals, which the current government has failed to do due to their focus on rent-seeking and acquiring bribes from multinational companies'.[33] In other words, Chinese ASM firms use a variety of labour, ranging from consultants, skilled engineers, and the formerly employed populace with the support of regional–local elites in order to successfully pursue extraction.

Chinese ASM firms also utilize the various modes of household labour.[34] Men provide labour to operate the machines, drill for minerals, or pick the rocks away. Women provide provisions to the men on-site, administering bags of rice alongside plastic bags of cooked vegetables, fruits, and meat during longer working hours. As the wife of a male miner described to me, 'We often help our husbands by cooking and delivering food and provisions to their work because they often travel to sites and not go home for days.' 'Our son helps in the work together with other children.'[35] Children of miners typically assist their fathers by providing auxiliary labour, such as hammering the rocks and carrying waste from one part of the site to another.[36] In gold mines, many of these children pan gold from the tailings. These other forms of labour enable men and women to focus on the more laborious and skill-intensive parts of the extraction.

Gold extraction remains a particularly sophisticated process. In gold extraction, ASM relies on the carbon-in-pulp method and the cyanidation process, which isolates the carbon from the gold through a process called 'elution' and releases cyanide at a high temperature. Before the elution process, gold needs to be extracted or ground (see Figure 4.2). Chinese investors fund the materials and construction of portions of the the the carbon-in-pulp procedure in the mining community, such as the jaw crusher, grinder, and the ball mill.[37] Miners also extract gold outside

[32] Interview with *barangay* captain, Zambales, 21 June 2014.
[33] Ibid.
[34] Interview with a miner, Zambales, 21 June 2014.
[35] Ibid.
[36] Ibid.
[37] Interview with the wife of a miner, Zambales, 21 June 2014.

the working day, but they often do not have the equipment or capital to convert the 'raw' gold into a pure state. Miners can sell the extra gold they extracted for themselves, which means that Chinese ASM can induce extra working hours by creating an output-based incentive to work on mines.[38] In contrast, nickel and copper do not usually use labour in these ways due to the nature of the minerals. Chinese investors fund the equipment necessary for open-pit mining similar to capital-intensive extraction by major transnational mining companies.[39] For the national government, catching unregulated ASM mining is often very difficult. An environmental official in Zambales told me that it is very difficult to monitor the operations and output of small-scale mining.[40] Inspection of the ASM is often conducted by the local government, which may have friends, families, and voters within the firms. The ASM firms are able to move their operations across the mountains and fields, ranging hundreds of hectares at the edges of the land, evading the national regulatory apparatus. The official said, 'We conduct our inspections in the Barangay hall and sometimes visit the site. However, we cannot do that all the time because of the lack of manpower and sometimes the cooperation of the local government.'[41]

Figure 4.2 | Grinder in artisanal small-scale mining site (taken on 7 July 2017)

*Source*: Photograph taken by the author.

---

[38] Interview with a miner, Zambales, 21 July 2014.
[39] Ibid.
[40] Interview with a local government official, Zambales, 26 June 2014.
[41] Ibid.

Furthermore, the national government also cannot stop the transfer of minerals of the ASM to the Chinese firms and have been unable to properly account for the amount of metal exported abroad. An official from the Bureau of Customs said, 'The mining firms get to the ships at the export processing zones but many of the people in those ports are friends or have been bought by the firms.'[42] In other words, the national government's relatively weak capacity to account for the number and type of exported metals enable the illicitness of ASM activities. Additionally, the cutback of state employment at the national level and the increase at the local level created rent-seeking opportunities and the lack of coordination among these government officials. There is often space for smuggling, including but not exclusive to 'finding metals labeled in different boxes and doctored tallying and documents'.[43] Indeed, local government officials with such meagre wages cannot be expected to follow the rules blindly, 'often looking out for themselves through rent-seeking opportunities by following their political patrons'.[44]

In sum, the PRC's demand for natural resources, the inability of their investors to expand due to Aquino's policies, and the capacity of regional–local elites to evade national regulations made them one of the most active investors in ASM. Extracted metals are eventually handled by the middlemen who deliver the goods to relatively unregulated ships and ports in the coastal areas. Due to the Philippine national government's weak capacity, regional–local elites are given the power to oversee these operations and give permits to these ships to leave. These situations allow for mineral smuggling, such that the volume and type of the exported minerals in the ships do not match what is usually written and reported in the formal documents. These arrangements allow the Chinese investors and their Filipino-Chinese or Chinese mestizo and other Filipino partners to satisfy the PRC's demand for minerals and avoid interruption by the Philippine national government.

## Conclusion

Building on historical and ethnographic research, I have attempted to explain the puzzle of Chinese ASM's rise during the Aquino administration (2010–2016). First, I argued that the historical evolution of the Philippine and Chinese economies led to a confluence of factors that resulted in the proliferation of Chinese ASM mining during the neoliberal period. Second, I showed that the Filipino-Chinese, as local intermediaries and shareholders, bridge the economic capital of the PRC capitalists and the political power of Philippine actors. I argued that three factors

---

[42]  Interview with a Bureau of Customs official, Zambales, 28 June 2014.

[43]  Interview with a military intelligence analyst, Makati City, 18 August 2017.

[44]  Ibid.

mattered: the owner–broker relationship, the type of Chinese company, and place-based considerations shaping the subsequent patterns of mineral extraction and labour usage. A process of 'mineral brokerage' occurs, linking the PRC capitalists, Filipino-Chinese brokers, and Filipino informal labour. As a result, Chinese capitalists provide the bulk of the economic capital while Filipino brokers contribute the political network to acquire the support of the local Philippine politicians, the protection of security apparatus, and/or purchase mines from other mining companies. These conditions are enabled by the history of neo-liberalism in the Philippines, the autonomy of regional Filipino politicians, and the regional histories of the provinces.

The argument shows that capital and labour mobility—in this case, Chinese capital and the labour attracted by ASM—formed distinct institutional arrangements drawn from sociocultural specificities and rearrangements of landscapes. The chapter shows historical migrations created co-ethnic networks that facilitate contemporary mining FDI inflows, shaping the way these articulate at the micro level, and the political-economic structures of the Philippines. In the case of Chinese FDI, the chapter agrees with previous findings on the *protean* nature of Chinese FDI: it is able to adapt to different political conditions and historical circumstances. The disaggregation of Chinese and host-state actors also affirms some ethnographic work in Africa and South East Asia conducted to show the difference between Western and Chinese capital (Lee, 2018). My finding is also consistent with the recent ethnographic literature on Chinese outward FDI that stresses the importance of people, places, and ideas (Nyíri and Tan, 2017).

# References

Bello, Walden F., Marissa De Guzman, Mary Lou Malig and Herbert Docena. 2005. *The Anti-development State: The Political Economy of Permanent Crisis in the Philippines*. London: Zed Books.

Bowie, Alasdair and Daniel Unger. 1997. *The Politics of Open Economies: Indonesia, Malaysia, the Philippines, and Thailand*, vol. 4. Cambridge: Cambridge University Press.

Camba, Alvin Almendrala. 2015. 'From Colonialism to Neoliberalism: Critical Reflections on Philippine Mining in the "Long Twentieth Century"'. *The Extractive Industries and Society* 2(2): 287–301.

———. 2016. 'Philippine Mining Capitalism: The Changing Terrains of Struggle in the Neoliberal Mining Regime'. *Austrian Journal of South-East Asian Studies* 9(1): 69–86.

———. 2017a. 'Inter-state Relations and State Capacity: The Rise and Fall of Chinese Foreign Direct Investment in the Philippines'. *Palgrave Communications* 3(1): 1–19.

———. 2017b. 'Why Did Chinese Investment in the Philippines Stagnate?' East Asia Forum. Available at http://www.eastasiaforum.org/2017/12/12/why-did-chinese-investments-in-the-philippines-stagnate. Accessed on 23 May 2018.

————. 2018. 'Duterte and the Philippines' Chinese Investment Boom: More Politics than Geopolitics', New Mandala. Available at http://www.newmandala.org/duterte-philippines-chinese-investment-boom-politics-geopolitics. Accessed on 23 May 2018.

Cullather, Nick. 1994. *Illusions of Influence: The Political Economy of United States-Philippines Relations, 1942–1960*. Stanford, CA: Stanford University Press.

Devlin, Robert. 2014. *Debt and Crisis in Latin America: The Supply Side of the Story*. Princeton, NJ: Princeton University Press.

Eichengreen, Barry. 2011. *Exorbitant Privilege: The Rise and Fall of the Dollar and the Future of the International Monetary System*. Oxford: Oxford University Press.

Hung, Ho-fung. 2008. 'Rise of China and the Global Overaccumulation Crisis'. *Review of International Political Economy* 15(2): 149–179.

————. 2015. *The China Boom: Why China Will Not Rule the World*. New York: Columbia University Press.

Hilson, Gavin. 2009. 'Small-Scale Mining, Poverty and Economic Development in Sub-Saharan Africa: An Overview'. *Resources Policy* 34(1–2): 1–5.

Israel, Danilo C. 2010. *National Industrialization in Philippine Mining: Review and Suggestions* (no. 2010–35). PIDS Discussion Paper Series. Quezon City: PIDS.

Kirsch, Stuart. 2014. *Mining Capitalism: The Relationship between Corporations and Their Critics*. Berkeley, CA: University of California Press.

Lee, Ching Kwan. 2018. *The Specter of Global China: Politics, Labor, and Foreign Investment in Africa*. Chicago, IL: University of Chicago Press.

Lopez, Salvador P. 1992. *Isles of Gold: A History of Philippine Mining*. Oxford: Oxford University Press.

McCoy, Alfred W. (ed.). 2009. *An Anarchy of Families: State and Family in the Philippines*. Madison, WI: University of Wisconsin Press.

Nyíri, Pál and Danielle Tan. 2017. Introduction, 'China's "Rise" in Southeast Asia from a Bottom-Up Perspective'. *Chinese Encounters in Southeast Asia: How People, Money, and Ideas from China are Changing a Region*. Washington, DC: University of Washington Press.

Panitch, Leo and Sam Gindin. 2012. *The Making of Global Capitalism*. London: Verso Books.

Singh, Jewellord T. Nem and Alvin Almendrala Camba. 2016. 'Neoliberalism, Resource Governance and the Everyday Politics of Protests in the Philippines'. *The Everyday Political Economy of Southeast Asia*, 49. Cambridge: Cambridge University Press.

Simbulan, Dante C. 2005. *The Modern Principalia: The Historical Evolution of the Philippine Ruling Oligarchy*. Quezon City: UP Press.

Tan, Antonio S. 1972. *The Chinese in the Philippines, 1898–1935: A Study of Their National Awakening*. Quezon City: R.P. Garcia Pub. Co.

Thompson, Mark R. 1996. 'Off the Endangered List: Philippine Democratization in Comparative Perspective'. *Comparative Politics* (28)2: 179–205.

Verbrugge, Boris. 2014. 'Capital Interests: A Historical Analysis of the Transformation of Small-Scale Gold Mining in Compostela Valley Province, Southern Philippines'. *The Extractive Industries and Society* 1(1): 86–95.

Wickberg, Edgar. 1965. *The Chinese in Philippine Life, 1850–1898*. Quezon City: Ateneo De Manila Press.

World Bank. 1987. *The Philippines Mining Sector Review*, report no. 6898-PH. Country Department II Asia Region. Washington, DC.

Wang, Gungwu. 1996. 'Sojourning: The Chinese Experience in Southeast Asia'. *Sojourners and settlers: Histories of Southeast Asia and the Chinese*, edited by Anthony Reid, 1–14. Sydney: Allen & Unwin.

Wang, Gungwu. 1981. *Community and Nation: Essays on Southeast Asia and the Chinese*, no. 6. Published for the Asian Studies Association of Australia by Heinemann Educational Books (Asia).

Wang, Mark Yaolin. 2002. 'The Motivations behind China's Government-Initiated Industrial Investments Overseas'. *Pacific Affairs* 75(2): 187–206.

# 5

# Soft Power and Transnationalism Affecting Capital and Labour Mobility

## Chinese Diaspora in Mexico and Peru

FRANCISCO J. VALDERREY, MIGUEL A. MONTOYA,
AND MAURICIO CERVANTES*

## Introduction

The rise of China in the international arena is an indisputable fact (Shambaugh, 2013). The dynamics that made its advance and the whole economic reform process possible are well known to scholars, although the role played by 50 million overseas Chinese is the subject of limited discussion. They are probably the most extensive expatriate community in the world, with the potential to become an extended army for the hegemonic plans of the People's Republic of China (PRC),[1] using soft power. Most times, researchers present a narrow view of the Chinese diaspora (or the spread and settlement of the overseas Chinese all over the globe); consequently, the contribution of the diaspora to the achievements of the PRC is still unclear. In our view, a primary goal of China is to gain leadership in global affairs through peaceful means (Mingjiang, 2008). Despite its military power and

---

* Authors would like to thank professors Philip Kelly and Preet Aulakh, as organizers of the seminar 'Asian Connections: Linking Mobilities of Capital and Labour in Theory and Practice' at York University. The comments of professors Derek Hall, Hendrik Meyer-Ohle, Xiangming Chen, Margaret Walton-Roberts, Alvin Camba, Kenneth Cardenas, and Catherine Craven as well as other colleagues from the seminar gave us valuable insights. We also thank Prof. Amy Ferris for her academic advice.

[1] In this chapter we use interchangeably the terms China and the People's Republic of China (PRC), when referring to modern times and after the formation of the PRC. We also use the overseas Chinese and ethnic Chinese as synonyms; a further discussion on the issue goes beyond the scope of this chapter.

economic might, China is resorting to the promotion of its culture, leadership in multilateral organizations, and the use of the network formed by its citizens or descendants scattered around the world.

In this chapter, we explore the bonds between Chinese foreign direct investment (FDI) and migration into Latin America as dual means to exercise and extend soft power. We analyse the linkages between the overseas Chinese and the motherland, within the context of the soft power theory of Joseph Nye. Thus, we bring a new perspective into how capital and labour may be interconnected across the Chinese communities while contributing to the strategic interest of the motherland. We selected this particular region because China 'is getting closer to Latin America due to geopolitical reasons, market expansion, as well as for the need to secure agricultural commodities and raw materials for its industry' (Valderrey and Montoya, 2016: 6). We focus on two Latin American countries that are as remote from one another as appears possible: Mexico and Peru. Thus, we can assess the importance of integration and transnationalism of overseas communities in the two nations as well as to what extent Chinese migratory flows have a relationship with Chinese state-owned enterprises (SOEs) and their investment choices in such contexts. We also evaluate whether or not soft power from the PRC and transnationalism affect capital and labour mobility in Chinese firms seeking business opportunities in the area.

The rest of the chapter is organized into five sections. In the first one, we briefly explain the theoretical concepts of transnationalism and soft power. Following that, we present a historical overview of the diaspora in Latin America, with a glance at the many differences among Chinese communities across Latin American countries. Next, we describe the degree of power that resident overseas Chinese and the PRC hold in Mexico and Peru, with a mutual comparison based on the strength of the local organizations, their economic power, and their closeness to the PRC. Then we scrutinize the economic and business ties between those overseas communities and the motherland, as seen in the cases of Dragon Mart and Chinalco Peru. Finally, we describe how soft power and transnationalism have an impact on capital and labour mobility and present some final remarks.

## Theoretical Aspects

The question of the overseas Chinese is a significant issue in South East Asia, but less so in Latin America. Nevertheless, this region is becoming more attractive to the PRC and, consequently, those communities are playing an increasingly important role in the growing relationship between Latin America and China.

We follow the definition of *soft power* as 'the ability to get what you want' by using forms of 'attraction rather than coercion or payment' (Nye, 2004: 256).

Consequently, the goals pursued by a government willing to use soft power are those that may influence public opinion favourably, both within their country and among other nations. The concept of soft power was first proposed by Nye, although the fundamental idea of resorting to mechanisms of power other than brute force is much older, and may be traced, at the very least, to Gramsci's idea of cultural hegemony and Morganthau's idea of the invisible power (Lin and Xiaonan, 2012). Three factors are at the centre of soft power: culture, political value, and foreign policy. These factors require two main elements, credibility and the ability to persuade, for a nation to carry out the purpose of convincing an opponent without resorting to force. 'These elements also provide legitimacy to the use of power' (Oğuzlu, 2007: 83).

The use of soft power, though, may be part of a strategy that includes the simultaneous use of economic or military power. Soft power and other forms of demonstration of strength are not mutually exclusive. In this sense, there is a divide between a pleasant view of soft power and a more pragmatic one in which there may be the intention to prevail over other people and nations while concealing their long-term goals and intentions.[2] An example of the first approach is the use of soft power by Singapore to show itself as a country that brings together East and West (Mahbubani, 2016). The second method is part of the so-called *smart power* where nations may resort to all means available to pursue their interest (Nye, 2009). Former President Hu Jintao demonstrated the appeal of soft power to the Chinese Communist Party elite in 2007 when he pointed out 'cultural soft power' as 'a requirement for the implementation of scientific development and social harmony' (Guodong, 2017: 1). The message implied that China should look at alternative ways to become an influential and competitive country through a gentler approach to international relations. Our analysis, hence, attempts to see if the overseas Chinese in Latin America have strong ties with PRC and if they act as ambassadors for the motherland.

Our research includes two prominent Chinese communities in Latin America, exploring both their historical background and the economic complexity of local integration and transnationalism. An early definition describes transnationalism as 'the process by which immigrants build social fields that link together their country of origin and their country of settlement' (Schiller et al., 1992: 9). The concept of transnationalism, though, is continually evolving in the literature from the initial focus upon the individual migrant and the reasons behind his or her decision to migrate based on discussions with family members. Eventually, scholars added a view of the organizations that build more solid bonds with the homeland (Portes and Fernández-Kelly, 2015). In our study, transnationalism looks beyond the voluntary

---

[2]   Contrary to popular beliefs, the USA ranks the first in the use of soft power, according to *The Soft Power Report 2016*, while the PRC ranks in 28th place (McClory, 2016).

association of migrants and incorporates the combined influence of individuals and their families, the traditional community in the hosting land, and the intervention of the sending state. Indeed, no matter what the reason for immigration is, the PRC considers itself a stakeholder in any issue involving Chinese people.

Thus, we analyse the full strength of this extended concept of transnationalism in Peru and Mexico and how the organized communities may influence the relationship between the host country and the PRC.

# Chinese Diaspora

The spread of Chinese culture through a large part of the Asian continent testifies to China's long history of emigration, although neither the reasons for the early migratory movements nor the details can be reconstructed with accuracy. The phenomenon eventually extended into other continents and territories controlled by foreign powers. In this section, we present an overview of the diaspora, in general terms, which is necessary to understand the phenomenon in the Latin American region. The diaspora in Latin America is the topic for the second part of the section, while the last part looks at the diversity and the profound differences among Chinese communities in the region.

## *Historical Overview*

Significant emigration from China probably started during the Ming Dynasty (1368–1644) which encouraged the settlement of qualified diplomats in neighbouring countries to improve trade relations (Mote and Twitchett, 1988). After the fall of the dynasty in 1644, the Manchurian invaders initiated the Qing Dynasty and dispossessed the Han Chinese of their land and properties, forcing them to flee. The Ming rebels escaped from the mainland to Taiwan or Nagasaki, and the emperor banned emigration at the cost of the death penalty for all of those who attempted to settle in a foreign country (Atwell, 1986).

The second wave of emigration started between 1776 and 1796, following financial difficulties, rampant corruption, and insurrections. The situation worsened steadily, and by the end of the eighteenth century, China was on the verge of political and economic collapse. The social climate deteriorated even further by 1839, following the outbreak of the First Opium War. China had to open five ports to foreign trade, pay a substantial indemnity to the British, and grant them the right to permanent occupation of Hong Kong. The situation also created an upsurge in the trade of contract workers, which played a noticeable role in Chinese commerce. The first contract workers came from Guangzhou to the British colonies, and other countries began to recruit workers in other open ports (Hoe and Roebuck, 1999:

203–205). In 1847, Chinese workers arrived in California, in 1849 they went to New South Wales and Australia, and after 1850, they migrated to the Caribbean islands.

As competition grew between the external recruiters, the French–British administration of Guangzhou tried to legalize this trade which finally succeeded with the announcement in 1859 that all Chinese contract workers who wanted to go abroad could obtain an exit permit. This sort of labour contract was later called the 'coolie trade' and may be better understood when one considers the economic and social catastrophe at that time. The population had increased from 60 million in 1651 to 450 million people in 1860. Also, the small farmers lost their land to the wealthy landowners, which led to the impoverishment of the former (Deng, 2015).

The economic recession resulted in new political turmoil, especially the Taiping Uprising (1851–1864). The rebels were defeated and had to withdraw to the coast. Many of them were captured and sold to intermediaries of the contract workers' trade. Some were sent to the sugar plantations in Cuba and South America, while many others went voluntarily as contract workers or free emigrants to escape abroad. Although the authorities were able to control the rebellion, they suffered a sudden downturn when the empire came under siege by outsiders during the Second Opium War (1856–1860). Once again, China was defeated and forced to sign the Tianjin Treaty. As a result, all Chinese people could contract with foreigners and take their families abroad (Tan, 2013).

With all obstacles removed, the foreign powers searched for labour across China. Guangdong and Fujian were the primary sources for contract workers. In both provinces, there was rampant unemployment since industrialization and modernization programmes did not reach these territories. Family ties and contacts between migrants and the overseas Chinese contributed to the rise of free migration (Wong-Hee-Kam, 1996). By the turn of the nineteenth century, various internal divisions ended up favouring the Western powers and causing the fall of the Chinese Empire. The end of the Qing dynasty came after the revolution of Sun Yat-sen in 1911 and the proclamation of the republic. Before this event, the overseas Chinese showed their compassion for their fellow citizens in China only through donations and the organization of the reception of new refugees. Afterwards, they became more active, supporting the revolution and playing a significant role in national politics (Fane-Pineo, 1985).

The Sino-Japanese War (1937–1945) produced a stream of refugees and a new migration. After World War II, the civil conflict between communists and nationalists brought new miseries and further outflow of migrants seeking exile. After the end of the civil war and the start of the new republic in 1949, the nationalists fled to Taiwan where they got support from the overseas Chinese. The takeover of the communists put an end to the migration from the PRC, which could only resume after the profound economic changes started by the end of the seventies. The restitution of Hong Kong in 1997 created new waves of migration, with local people fleeing the former colony in fear of the PRC. In the course of globalization, many young Chinese are leaving their home country to study abroad or to pursue a career (Pan, 1998: 160).

## A Diaspora with a Latin American Accent

The ethnic Chinese eventually reached Latin American soil, in particular, between 1868 and 1939. The different migratory waves were a consequence of two opposing sets of events: on the one hand, economic hardship and political unrest compelled many migrants to leave the country, while on the other hand, the American continent offered new opportunities. The abolition of slavery created demand for cheap labour in the plantations or the construction of railroads.

Chinese migrants had to endure stringent working conditions, along with low wages and social isolation. They reacted against hostility and prejudice by organizing themselves in communities, based on the principles of loyalty and mutual trust, which offered newcomers a means of protection and social mobility. Another important aspect were their international and family linkages. Through their networks, they maintained bonds with the families left behind, who provided safety and solidarity nets. At first, immigrants settled in the countryside by the agricultural fields. Progressively, they moved to the cities where they ventured into different sectors. Over time, they were able to build a stable community, well accepted into the various host countries, while keeping essential ties with the motherland (Siu, 2007).

The flow came to a temporary end when the PRC prohibited migration. In the late 1970s, under more favourable policies, new waves of immigrants entered the Latin American region, especially Brazil, Venezuela, and Argentina. Although there are differences from prior flows, more recent immigrants are being favoured by large Chinese enterprises under the official Go Out Policy that encourages Chinese companies to expand operations into foreign markets. They have little resemblance to the old unskilled workers who arrived under contract, and many are employees of large companies. Some are investors, while others seek new opportunities within the network of the communities (Mazza, 2016).

The presence of overseas Chinese is by no means as prominent in Latin America as it may be in South East Asia, and some estimates account for 2.7 million of them in Latin America (CIA, 2017). Those figures are hard to confirm with certainty, as many overseas Chinese do not consider themselves as members of their ethnic group due to weakened cultural ties, the temporary nature of their assignments, or their desire to go back to the motherland. Statistical data may also be unreliable, as many of them enter countries with a temporary permit and later remain illegally for extended periods. In some places, though, the Chinese presence is more evident or the contribution to the local economy is quite significant. Like everywhere else, the overseas Chinese create ethnic and commercial concentration areas, generally known as 'Chinatowns'. Nowadays, Chinese communities in Latin America are made up of business owners and merchants. Among the newcomers, there are investors, white-collar workers, and students.

## Diversity across Communities

A comparison among the Chinese communities in Latin America shows a high degree of diversity. Seven Latin American countries have significant ethnic Chinese minorities: Peru, Venezuela, Brazil, Panama, Argentina, Venezuela, Cuba, and Mexico. By far, the community in Peru is the largest and most influential in Latin America, while it also represents one of the earliest migratory patterns in the region. Ethnic Chinese arrived in four migration waves: the first one was around 1850, a second one at the turn of the twentieth century, a third one in the 1980s, while the last one started in the 1990s and it continues to the present (Tamagno and Velásquez, 2016). Chinese Peruvians have built a well-organized and relevant community, with leverage in different aspects of the local society.

Venezuela hosts the second-largest overseas Chinese community. For many of them, the arrival is recent, although there are four distinct migratory periods. The first wave began in the middle of the nineteenth century, the second one about one hundred years later, the third one during the 1970s, and the fourth migratory wave is still ongoing. The most recent movements follow the strengthening of bilateral relations due to the ideological proximity of their leaders. The group is known for its dedication to retail shops and restaurants, although many newcomers are engineers and skilled workers engaged in the new mining projects (*El Comercio*, 2012).

Chinese immigration in Brazil dates back to the Portuguese colonial period when the local rulers brought them as slaves from Macao and Lisbon. The first mass migration of the Chinese to Brazil came with the outbreak of the communist revolution. The next wave happened after 1974, this time from the PRC, following the re-establishment of bilateral ties. By then, the community had reached both economic and political power, which eventually allowed the offering of considerable support to newcomers into a well-rooted community. They have successfully adapted to the new environment, and the vast majority do not speak Mandarin or Cantonese anymore.

Chinese migrants arrived in Panama from North America in the second half of the nineteenth century. At first, they were brought in to work in the construction of the national railway, but soon they were able to prosper in the commercial sector. Most overseas Chinese in Panama are of Cantonese origin. They have been active in local commerce, although a more recent path of migration has brought wealthy investors from Hong Kong and metropolitan areas of the PRC (Lazarus, 2011). The Chinese-Panamanian community has been able to maintain many of the vernacular traditions.

The overseas Chinese started to arrive in substantial numbers in Argentina in the 1970s, fleeing the communist regime (Sassone and Mera, 2007). Two decades later, the stable economic situation—at that time—attracted many immigrants from Fujian. They ventured into retail activities, and soon they gained a dominant position in the supermarkets of the capital city, Buenos Aires (Grimson et al., 2016).

The overseas Chinese community in Cuba started to emerge during colonial times, when Spaniards brought many of them, either as contract labour or as escapees from poverty. This community is entirely different from others, as their members went through a continuous process of racial intermixing. The reason behind their distinct adaptation is that the Chinese arriving on the island were almost exclusively men. Regardless of their profound adjustment to the local society, the overseas Chinese in Cuba have been able to maintain their cultural identity while being instrumental in the mild transition into a market economy (Hearn, 2012).

The Chinese community is strikingly invisible in Mexico, except in Mexicali, on the Baja California Peninsula. Ethnic Chinese have been emigrating to Mexico since colonial times, although in small numbers. From the beginning, the local population did not welcome Chinese migrants, even if they were permitted to engage in various occupations. They lived through many hardships, suffering severe working conditions before eventually settling down and prospering. Their endurance was proverbial, although in Mexico their conditions were worsened by extreme violence (Dennis, 1979). The hostility encountered probably discouraged new members from migrating into the country and kept the community apart.

As seen from the brief description of the different communities, Chinese presence in the region is far from being homogenous. The differences are many, related to the specific area of origin of the overseas Chinese, the particular point in history where they left their homeland, the degree of adaptation to the hosting nation, and how they interrelate with the local population. The communities vary significantly, and, therefore, the concept of ethnic Chinese in Latin America is, at best, ambiguous. It is important to remember that 'Chineseness cannot be defined by any particular standard' (Tan, 2004: 4).

## Soft Power and Transnationalism in Mexico and Peru

In this section, we examine how the overseas Chinese eventually settled down in two countries, Mexico and Peru, which are at opposing ends regarding integration with the hosting community. We present a brief description of each community, before drawing a mutual comparison based on the strength of the local organization, their economic power, and their closeness to the PRC.

## Overcoming Prejudice in Mexico[3]

Until recently, Mexico had little appeal to the Chinese, and even on a diplomatic and economic level, the two countries maintained a certain distance (Roldán, 2006). As of today, their numbers are not in line with other nations of the region, and there is a lack of an organized community. There are probably 60 different associations serving more than 70,000 ethnic Chinese established in this nation, but not a single entity is capable of coordinating them. There are several reasons behind their dispersion throughout the Mexican territory, although the primary factors probably are the diversity of historical and geographical contexts, their scattering within Mexico, and the language barriers between new and established immigrants. There is a myriad of geographic origins, different cultural heritage, and ideological thinking, depending upon the time of their migration and whether this happened before or after the formation of the PRC. The host country itself is quite complicated, which contributed to further separating the different communities according to local values, economic activities, and cultural influence. Also, Mexico maintained a hostile attitude towards China until recent times; for example, when it opposed its entry into the World Trade Organization (WTO). Today, the bilateral relationship is changing rapidly, as Mexico no longer perceives China as 'a seemingly unmatchable competitor in producing the same kinds of cheap manufactured goods at a fraction of the cost' (Chen and Chen, 2013: 57).

The fragmentation and dispersion of ethnic Chinese did not allow the establishment of a sustainable relationship with China. However, the increasing business opportunities surfacing lately between both nations show the need for a stronger commitment from the associations and their expected contribution to breaking down cultural barriers and animosity. Some of the associations are made up of recent immigrants with higher social status, professional careers, and economic means. Their mediation is focusing now on changing China's perception in Mexico through the promotion of culture and language. The nature of these associations is diverse: in some cases, they have been created directly by the Chinese government, while in other instances they have no support from foreign institutions or even connections with the PRC.

---

[3] The main source for this section is the article by Martinez Rivera and Dussel Peters (2016: 111–143). Therefore, the document will not be further cited in this passage.

## Integration and Transnationalism in Peru[4]

The South American nation hosts over 1.2 million ethnic Chinese, which accounts for approximately 4 per cent of the country's population. Historically, many have pointed out how Chinese communities worldwide favour the interest of the motherland at the expense of loyalty to the host nation. Peru is no exception; associations and family networks of migrant ethnic Chinese have kept fundamental ties with China, providing China with support in business ventures and cultural matters.

In Peru, Chinese organizations operate with the help of the Sociedad de Beneficencia China (SBCH), an influential group with close links to the local elite. The Asociación de Empresas Chinas en el Perú (AECP), which coordinates its activities with the SBCH, deals with economic issues. While the former preserves a humanitarian aura, the latter is involved with business matters. The SBCH started in 1882, and for more than a century, it has assisted relevant institutions such as the prestigious Chinese-Peruvian College. Additionally, it benefits from the unambiguous recognition of the PRC. Founded in 2011, the mission for the AECP appears to be twofold: on the one hand, it provides support to the business community, while on the other, it maintains a permanent bond with the motherland. The synergy from both associations is fundamental for the advance of business interests, promotion of new investments, and keeping formal ties with local authorities. Those organizations maintain a robust relationship with China through the embassy and the Peruvian-Chinese Chamber of Commerce. In the end, people and enterprises enjoy support from the motherland.

China works zealously with the associations, monitoring their activities, with the aim of strengthening patriotic feelings, while also being involved in matters of education, culture, health, and safety. Chinese families assured prosperity at the local level, while the associations have been acting de facto as the international trade representatives of the PRC, with the task of overlooking investments in the most critical sectors in Peru, such as the mining industry.

## Soft Power Makes a Difference

For the overseas Chinese, Peru and Mexico are far away from the motherland. Still, the degree of power for the communities and the PRC varies dramatically, with a possible explanation lying in the use of soft power. Over the course of much of its history, Mexico has developed fundamental ties with the USA, to the point of

---

[4] The main source for this section is the article by Tamagno and Velásquez (2016: 145–166). Therefore, the document will not be further cited in this passage.

being hugely dependent upon its economy. For instance, more than 80 per cent of Mexican exports rely on US customers, with slightly less dependency upon the imports of the most needed products from its northern neighbour. By no means are such strong ties present in the Peruvian relationship with the USA. Instead, during the twenty-first century, Chinese demand for raw materials and mining products have fostered economic growth in Peru. The PRC has a vested interest in securing supplies for its industrial machinery in Peru; most probably, China looks to the Mexican market for its exports and direct investment, but this is a complicated strategy to pursue. A closer Mexican–Chinese relationship will immediately raise concerns, both at a business and at a geopolitical level.

Ever since taking power in China, the Communist Party did target the elimination of its rival in Taiwan at the expense of securing a dominant position in the Latin American region. Consequently, Chinese authorities have avoided confrontations with the USA, the dominant player in all local matters. Presently, though, ill feelings and a possible trade war between the two economic superpowers may overturn the situation. During the last few decades, the PRC has improved its relationship with many Latin American countries through the use of soft power and building upon the leverage of well-established ethnic Chinese communities. Mexico may be the next target.

# Dragon Mart and Chinalco Peru

In this section, we look at the economic relationship of the PRC with Mexico and Peru, as well as to the business weight carried by the Chinese communities in each country. The differences between both groups are remarkable, as reflected in two short cases. The first one is Dragon Mart, a real estate development in the Yucatan Peninsula intended to provide a commercial hub in Mexico for Chinese exports, while the second one, Chinalco Peru, operates successfully in the Peruvian mining industry. The fate of each project varies significantly according to the degree of influence of the PRC in either nation and the influence of the local Chinese communities. Before the case itself, we provide a brief account of the business and trade between either nation and the PRC. We end the section by comparing the degree of economic power of ethnic Chinese in both countries, as well as the influence of the PRC in their markets.

## *Dragon Mart: Failing to Anchor Chinese Exports in Mexico*

During three centuries, from 1565 to 1815, Mexico and China kept a steady trade through a maritime Manila Galleon trade route. Indeed, a Spanish galleon connected the Mexican seaport of Acapulco with the principal seaport of the Philippines, at that time also a Spanish colony. The galleon brought minerals and goods made in the Spanish colonies all the way to Manila, but eventually, most of the products ended up in Chinese soil. Similarly, porcelain, silk clothing, and other products made in Imperial China found their way to the galleon trade route and arrived in Mexico (Schurz, 1918). After the Manila Galleon wound up its operations in the 1820s, bilateral trade between China and Mexico dropped significantly. Only after the PRC´s expansion into international markets during the 1980s did Chinese products find their way into the Mexican market. This fact, along with Mexican perception of China as a direct competitor, kept both nations apart. Eventually, Mexico was the last nation to vote in favour of the admission of China to the WTO, in December 2001, giving its approval only after assuring several protective measures to its home producers.

Recently, both nations have developed stronger commercial ties, favouring exports from both ends of the line and with Mexico luring Chinese investors into a variety of industries. Unfortunately, some of these ventures have been unsuccessful, fostering ill feelings and resentment. In 2011, the project Dragon Mart aimed at creating a huge commercial hub in the Yucatan Peninsula. The plan received recognition as one of the leading projects of the decade in Mexico. Beyond the sizable real estate operation, spanning 1,376.38 acres, including the building of two hotels, a residential area with 722 villas, and commercial premises for 3,040 retail stores, the proposal immediately attracted public attention. Unfortunately, it was perceived by the local merchants as a Trojan horse of Chinese trading companies, eager to compete with local merchants. The funding, about US$180 million, came from different investors. Although only 10 per cent of the money came from Chinese investors, the project was immediately labelled as Chinese, thus raising concerns about the PRC landing a foot on Mexican soil.

No promises or explanations from the developers were sufficient to convey a positive image for Dragon Mart. Indeed, the project was presented as a new tourist attraction where more than one million foreign tourists will be flocking to buy local products. The rationale was indeed to avoid intermediaries and, therefore, facilitate direct contact between manufacturers and consumers (*El Economista*, 2013). As then said, the project could draw from the business connectivity and tourist appeal of Cancun, its enviable geographical position, multicultural environment, aerial connectivity, and prime infrastructure. In summary, Dragon Mart´s project leaders promised the revitalization of the local economy with a commercial hub capable of fostering employment, tourist revenues, and retail sales.

Although the project was envisioned as early as 2007, it was only until 2011 that it was presented to local and federal authorities. The proposal was approved in 2012, albeit subject to certain amendments imposed by the Institute of Impact and Environmental Risk. Many complaints arose, and by 2013, the Mexican Center for

Environmental Law confirmed the nullity of the project. By 2015, the authorities closed down the project permanently, claiming failure to present the environmental impact study or land use change.

What initially appeared as an act of justice in favour of environmental protection came under suspicion for a case that happened about the same time: the cancellation of a high-speed train project between Mexico City and Querétaro City. The Chinese company winning the bid appeared to have a solid case. Unexpectedly, though, the Mexican President Peña Nieto came out on public television announcing the cancellation of the project. The PRC maintained itself at a distance during the cancellation of the Dragon Mart project, not this time though, and Prime Minister Li Keqiang voiced his protest against the Mexican authorities. Soon the National Development and Reform Commission pursued economic compensation and seised on all discriminatory acts against Chinese nationals or enterprises (Dussel Peters and Velásquez, 2015). From that date, the bilateral trade and business exchanges have not much improved.

To some experts, Dragon Mart encountered unexpected legal barriers and the fierce opposition of the local enterprises, probably acting upon 'negative perceptions of the economic and environmental impacts of China investments elsewhere' (Downie, 2017: 1). The Chinese community in Mexico was no match against such opposition and did not issue formal complaints.

*Chinalco Peru: A New Blueprint for Chinese Companies?*

Members of the ethnic Chinese community established in China are known as Tusan, and they are a pillar of the Peruvian society and the local economy. They migrated to Peru since the Spanish colonial times, although in limited numbers. It was only during the second part of the nineteenth century (1849–1872) when they arrived in significant numbers. They performed heavy tasks that were shunned by the locals or any other migrants. Tens of thousands worked in the new railway construction, in mines, farming jobs, or other physically excruciating tasks. As in other countries, ethnic Chinese proved themselves in the most demanding occupations. Afterwards, Peru established diplomatic ties with the Chinese empire, although immigration slowed down considerably (Aquino Rodríguez, 2016). After the Second World War, different waves of migrants arrived, especially during the second part of the last century. The fabulous wealth amassed by mining activities eventually allowed Peru to import Chinese products since early times while exporting precious metals across the Pacific. Trade between Peru and Imperial China was subordinated, though, to the Manila Galleon route, therefore, privileging commerce with Mexico.

In recent times, the situation has reversed, with China becoming the largest trade partner of Peru. The country hosts 170 enterprises from the PRC with an aggregate investment of over US$14 billion (*El Debate*, 2016). Mining has been the cornerstone of the Sino-Peruvian trade relation, with China growing its presence through FDI and its complete control of the Peruvian mining operations and shipment of mineral products to serve its own demand for raw materials. An example is Toromocho, located in the Judín area in Peru, where Chinalco, the Peruvian branch of the giant Aluminum Corporation of China, operates. Toromocho has large deposits of silver and other minerals, and it accounts for the largest and most productive copper mine in the world with close to 2,000 million tonnes of ore/copper reserves. Despite the voices arguing for state ownership of the mine, in 2006, the Peruvian government was more than willing to accept a US$3 billion offer in cash from the foreign company (Simpson, 2008). The deal was finalized by 2007, but an unexpected problem arose: the need to relocate an entire community of 5,000 people in the town of Morococha. During the negotiations, none of the relevant actors had paid much attention to the issue (Poulden, 2013).

The mutually agreed upon solution required Chinalco to move the inhabitants of Morococha into the nearby area of Carhuacoto. The company granted a lump sum payment of US$2,000 and accommodation to entice the native population. Chinalco is already compromising with a new investment of US$1,355 million to expand the current production of Toromocho. Voices favourable to Chinalco presented the handling of the Toromocho relocation as 'a new template for Chinese companies' (Poulden, 2013). Many would disagree with such a statement, but there were many improvements in the way of embracing the community. As a starting point, almost all managers and workers were Peruvian. The Company went to a great length to foster positive relations with the local district, including a vast social programme and joint decision-making over major issues.

## Mexico and Peru Tell a Different Story

The relationship between the two Latin American countries with the PRC has distinctive characteristics. In modern times, Peru's economy has been largely dependent upon the export of mineral products to China. Mexico, instead, is recently building a commercial relationship with China through a more diversified array of import and export products. Table 5.1 shows bilateral Chinese trade with both economies and the significant import-export product categories.

The failure of Dragon Mart and the success of Chinalco tell an entirely different story. Whereas, the Chinese community had no intervention on the Mexican case, it was helpful in Peru, at least throughout the initial stages of the project.

Table 5.1 | China Bilateral Trade with Mexico and Peru, 2016: Most Traded Products

| | Chinese import | | | Chinese export | | |
|---|---|---|---|---|---|---|
| | *Products* | *Percentage* | *Import (USD)* | *Products* | *Percentage* | *Import (USD)* |
| **Mexico** | Machines | 35 | 2.6 billion | Machines | 66 | 42.2 billion |
| | Mineral products | 26 | 1.89 billion | Instruments | 5.2 | 3.28 billion |
| | Transportation | 16 | 1.22 billion | Metals | 4.9 | 3.13 billion |
| | Instruments | 6.7 | 499 million | Textiles | 4.2 | 2.67 billion |
| | Metals | 6.6 | 493 million | Miscellaneous | 4.1 | 2.61 billion |
| **Peru** | Mineral products | 79 | 6.73 billion | Machines | 41 | 3.37 billion |
| | Metals | 9.5 | 810 million | Metals | 11 | 940 million |
| | Foodstuffs | 8.8 | 755 million | Textiles | 11 | 900 million |
| | Vegetable products | 1.1 | 96.8 million | Transportation | 6.6 | 536 million |
| | Wood products | 0.7 | 60.6 million | Chemical products | 6.5 | 533 million |

*Source*: The Observatory of Economic Complexity.

*Notes*: Data are in US$ and percentage as per the total of bilateral trade.

The fundamental difference, though, came from the intervention of the Chinese government. The PRC had no involvement in the first case. Dragon Mart had little participation from Chinese investors but even in the much larger project of the high-speed train connecting Mexico and Querétaro, the PRC did not have enough muscle to reverse the decision of the Mexican government. Instead, Chinalco was always considered part of a geostrategic project for the PRC, as demonstrated during the 2016 visit of President Xi Jinping to Peru, where he endorsed a new bilateral relationship based on mutual respect, including improved governance of Chinese mining companies in the South American nation (*El Debate*, 2016). Table 5.2 shows some of those commitments by Chinalco.

Although Chinese find Mexico attractive for business, the 'almost nonexistent Chinese community in Mexico is a crucial factor for the lack of investment' (Dorantes, 2017: 1). Chinese migration has a considerable impact on Peru's culture and social structure (Flannery, 2013). Consequently, it appears that ethnic Chinese have an impact on the bilateral relationship but not strong enough as to change the flow of investments or trade with the motherland. Most probably, the community can slightly bend some decisions, but the critical ones belong to the realm of the PRC´s geostrategic interest.

Table 5.2 | A New Governance for Chinese Mining Enterprises in Peru

| Policy | Description |
| --- | --- |
| Revenue transparency and distribution | Chinalco will not be paying income taxes for several years |
| Voluntary social investment | Chinalco created a 'company town', Nueva Morocha |
| Voluntary social investment | Project *Obras por impuestos*. Chinalco is the only Chinese firm participating |
| Corporate guilds and multi-stakeholder fora | 'Chinalco: Dialogue Roundtables for a Peaceful Settlement in Morococha' |
| Labour | Chinalco is apparently paying wages above the market average |

*Source*: Adapted from Sanborn and Ching (2017: 183).

## Capital and Labour Mobility

The final focus of our analysis involves the role of the PRC's use of soft power through the diaspora and its impact on capital and labour mobility. Mexico and Peru offer unique scenarios due to the power asymmetry of both nations versus the massive resources of the Chinese government to influence established migrants in foreign markets. Traditionally, soft power has guided the impact of the PRC in the region, which along with the weight of transnationalism, affecting to some extent capital and labour mobility.

Before analysing the PRC's involvement in those matters, it is necessary to comment on the type of Chinese enterprises going overseas. Those are—for the vast majority—SOEs with a lesser degree of independence from the government than any private companies. The latter ones face profound difficulties when operating in foreign markets; after all, many of those organizations reached success in a protected domestic environment. Though in both cases, the management lacks the expertise or the negotiation skills necessary to deal with local authorities or the marketing expertise to reach consumers. Hence, the presence of the overseas Chinese in Latin America has an impact on entry strategies into those markets. Whether acting as translators, mediators, advisors, and partners or lobbying for the PRC and its enterprises, those people have been fundamental in protecting the interest of their motherland. Indeed, the diaspora provides a contributing factor to the international strategies of SOEs having an impact on financial flows and labour allocation. Their support comes mainly from strengthening the international political and economic role of the PRC, preparing fertile ground for investments in new markets, and attracting migration flows to and from China, which involves returnee talents and highly qualified people (Pieke and Speelman, 2013). In the case of Peru, for instance, they were vital for the take-off of bilateral relations with China and for setting up investments in the energy and mining sectors.

The overseas Chinese of Peru, through the various cultural associations and networks, also serve as a reference point for newcomers. Therefore, immigration favours new capital flows, which in turn generate subsequent migratory flows. The PRC has an interest in collaborating with overseas communities while developing their human resource programmes for international assignments. For instance, incentivizing young Chinese to study abroad or hiring newly graduated foreigners is becoming an essential cause of migration flows. Whereas students in international exchange programmes are much welcome in the host countries, a different kind of immigration raises eyebrows. As the PRC pours more resources into infrastructure and construction projects, it also finds it convenient to include their own workers. Consequently, there is a growing perception that Chinese workers replace the local ones, due to lower wages, fewer demands, and imposition from the PRC. In some cases, legal visa permits come together with generous donations from the PRC of sports stadiums or public buildings (Mazza, 2016).

From the start of the Go Out Policy, the PRC has carefully chosen FDI projects after considering economic or geopolitical factors. Decisions on market selection and countries for direct investment follow a review of the local Chinese communities. In the end, Latin America provides a clear example of the distortion of capital and labour allocation based on national interest. In this case, the use of soft power modifies migrant flows occurring during the PRC`s expansion into the Latin American region.

There are several reasons for such policies, such as the necessity to find new markets or the urgency to secure industrial inputs. A most obvious result was the different role of Chinese companies in Africa and Latin America: the first region offered a wide array of commodities, while the second one also provided an appealing market for finished goods. Such presence came immediately under scrutiny, often due to a lack of international experience from Chinese managers and the unrestrained focus on benefits. Numerous problems eventually weakened the global acceptance of the PRC, such as ill-turned relationships with neighbouring nations or commercial disputes. Hence, the need for a foreign policy which would generate more positive feelings towards China became evident.

The most straightforward solution to the controversy arising from exploitation and mismanagement at those enterprises came from the use of soft power. The soft power allowed the PRC to create permanent links with their partner countries, mainly counting on millions of people ready to favour the interest of the motherland. Their impact on the new prosperity is hard to measure, but we can intuitively say that much of the overseas Chinese are already acting on behalf of the PRC. Perhaps, the importance of the relationship between China and Latin

America has been exaggerated (Cornejo and García, 2010), and experts point out how the region has no impact on the New Silk Road project,[5] but the area is gaining attention from the PRC. Furthermore, the region offers a formidable laboratory to test the interaction between local interests and foreign investors while providing distinct market scenarios (Valderrey, 2016). Unexpected events, such as the hostility found with the Trump administration, may further reshape the geopolitical strategy.

## Conclusion

The comparison between Dragon Mart and Chinalco increases our understanding of the linkages between Chinese FDI and Chinese migration into Latin America as dual means to exercise and extend soft power. Yet the results are not conclusive, mainly due to the lack of reliable data on recent immigration from China into Mexico and Peru. Trade flows are also meagre and it is difficult to point out an indisputable connection between flows of capital and labour. Additionally, Latin America is not a preferred destination for Chinese migrants. In any event, the Chinese communities in Latin America are providing support and mediation for the motherland. Thus, the PRC benefits from an advantageous position regarding representativeness, inclusion in the political process, and experience in trade with Latin America.

Through the study, we could learn about the main issues at stake in the diaspora. We found out how the overseas Chinese in Peru forged a secure network of associations with loyalty links with the homeland. We also learned how those communities played a parallel diplomatic role supporting consular activities, preparing fertile ground for Chinese investments. Their use of the *guanxi-* guarantee created links with local business and government. Additionally, they were fundamental to the building of a national 'brand' which includes cultural elements easily recognizable around the globe. All those contributions previously mentioned, though, do not happen in case of all overseas communities, as the case of Mexico demonstrates.

No matter what their specific degree of local power, Chinese communities in Latin America are both propagators and receptors of cultural values that are used by the PRC for its geopolitical plans. Indeed, China is prepared to provide full assistance to any community that embraces its old culture and a shared destiny. Since the beginning of Den Xiao Ping's reforms, different mechanisms ensure the

---

5  The New Silk Road is the largest international project in which the PRC is currently involved. It attempts to recreate the traditional Silk Road, providing international routes to facilitate trade among more than 60 countries in Eurasia and Africa.

propagation of a message to the overseas communities stating that all overseas Chinese belong to a transnationalized group of people (Barabantseva, 2005). The diaspora is as relevant as ever for the Chinese government. Having such a sizable community away from home may bring all the benefits previously described, but the diaspora itself may become a double-edged sword. As seen in different historical events, the overseas Chinese may also turn against those in power in the motherland. As an example, those communities established in the USA created substantial obstacles on the eve of the 2008 Beijing Olympics (Li, 2012). The diaspora in Latin America provides adequate support for the geopolitical interest of the PRC in this region at present, using soft power strategies. The caveat, though, is to make sure that immigrant ethnic groups perform as expected.

The PRC certainly needs a major facelift for its operations in the Latin American region. There is no shortage of negative publicity for Chinese investments and their low and adverse impact on the labour market environment. The country itself is falling behind expectations as a driver of social and environmental changes, with labour and investment following separate paths (Ray et al., 2017). As China leverages on growing economic influence in the region amid dissent of Latin American countries and the USA, other options become more enticing than the soft power. At present, there is little chance for the PRC to become a definite threat to North and South America, but the time may come for China to explore different strategies. The use of smart power, which encompasses a variety of tools to impose decisions on less powerful nations, may slowly become China's preferred path in the region, instead of the current soft power approach, enhanced with generous economic incentives. No matter what the future may bring, it will be challenging to see capital flows and labour mobility unaffected by the PRC or the diaspora in the Latin American region.

# References

Aquino Rodríguez, Carlos. 2016. 'El soft power de China en el Perú' *Pensamiento Crítico* 21(2): 2.

Atwell, William S. 1986. 'Some Observations on the "Seventeenth-Century Crisis" in China and Japan'. *The Journal of Asian Studies* 45(2): 223–244.

Barabantseva, Elena. 2005. 'Trans-nationalising Chineseness: Overseas Chinese Policies of the PRC's Central Government'. *Asien* 96(S.): 7–28.

CIA (Central Intelligence Agency). 2017. 'The World Factbook: Overseas Chinese in Latin America'. Available at https://www.cia.gov/library/publications/the-world-factbook/geos/cu.html. Accessed on 20 March 2017.

Chen, Kayla and Xiangming Chen. 2013. 'China and Latin America: Connected and Competing–Analysis'. *The European Financial Review* February–March.

Cornejo, Romer and A. N. García. 2010. 'China y América Latina: recursos, mercados y poder global'. *Nueva Sociedad* 228: 79–100.

Deng, Kent. 2015. 'China's Population Expansion and Its Causes during the Qing Period, 1644–1911', Economic History Working Paper Series, 219/2015. London: The London School of Economics and Political Science.

Dennis, Philip A. 1979. 'The Anti-Chinese Campaigns in Sonora, Mexico'. *Ethnohistory* 26(1): 65–80.

Dorantes, R. (2017). Por qué los mexicanos no estamos preparados para comerciar con China. Available at https://www.altonivel.com.mx/empresas/los-mexicanos-estamos-preparados-comerciar-china/. Accessed on 26 August 2018.

Downie, E. (2017). 'The Dragon Mart Fiasco Still Haunts China–Mexico Relations'. *The Diplomat*. Available at https://thediplomat.com/2017/01/the-dragon-mart-fiasco-still-haunts-china-mexico-relations/. Accessed on 26 August 2018.

Dussel Peters, Enrique and Samuel Ortiz Velásquez. 2015. 'Monitor de la Manufactura Mexicana 10(11)'. *Facultad de Economía de la UNAM y CECHIMEX-UNAM, México* year 10-number 11–February. Available at http://economiamexicanaennumeros.blogspot.com/2015/02/monitor-de-la-manufactura-mexicana-ano.html. Accessed on 26 August 2018.

*El Comercio*. 2012. 'Ola migratoria china en Venezuela'. 19 April. Available at http://www.elcomercio.com/actualidad/mundo/ola-migratoria-china-venezuela.html. Accessed on 20 March 2017.

*El Debate*. 2016. 'Visita del presidente Chino'. 21 November. Available at https://www.debate.com.mx/mundo/Presidente-de-China-visita-Peru-y-firma-convenios-20161121-0154.html. Accessed on 17 August 2018.

*El Economista*. 2013. Dragon Mart, proyecto de capital mexicano: inversionistas. 9 January. Available at https://www.eleconomista.com.mx/empresas/Dragon-Mart-proyecto-de-capital-mexicano-inversionistas-20130109-0058.html . Accessed on 17 August 2018.

Fane-Pineo, Huguette Ly Tio. 1985. *Chinese Diaspora in Western Indian Ocean*. Ed. de l'océan indien.

Flannery, N. 2013. How China's Relations with Peru Explain Its Approach to Diplomacy. *The Atlantic*. 12 September. Available at https://www.theatlantic.com/china/archive/2013/09/how-chinas-relations-with-peru-explain-its-approach-to-diplomacy/279618/. Accessed on 14 September 2018.

Grimson, Alejandro, Gustavo Ng, and Luciana Denardi. 2016. 'Las organizaciones de inmigrantes chinos en Argentina'. *Migración y desarrollo* 14(26), 25–73. Available at http://www.scielo.org.mx/scielo.php?script=sci_arttext&pid=S1870-75992016000100025&lng=es&tlng=es. Accessed on 10 February 2018.

Guodong, Du. 2007. 'Full Text of Hu Jintao's Report at 17th Party Congress'. Available at http://news.xinhuanet.com/english/2007-10/24/content_6938749.html. Accessed on 22 March 2017.

Hearn, Adrian H. 2012. 'Harnessing the Dragon: Overseas Chinese Entrepreneurs in Mexico and Cuba'. *The China Quarterly* 209: 111–133.

Hoe, Susanna and Derek Roebuck. 1999. *The Taking of Hong Kong: Charles and Clara Elliot in China Waters*. London: Routledge.

Lazarus, Leland. 2011. 'China-Taiwan and the Battle for Panama'. Global Conversation. Available at http://www.globalconversation.org/2011/12/01/china-taiwan-and-battle-panama. Accessed on 20 March 2017.

Li, H. 2012. 'The Chinese Diaspora and China's Public Diplomacy: Contentious Politics for the Beijing Olympic Float'. *International Journal of Communication* 6: 35.

Lin, L. I. and H. O. N. G. Xiaonan. 2012. The Application and Revelation of Joseph Nye's Soft Power Theory. *Studies in Sociology of Science* 3(2): 48–52.

Mahbubani, Kishore. 2016. 'Seven Pillars of Singapore's Soft Power'. *The Straits Times*. Available at http://www.straitstimes.com/singapore/seven-pillars-of-singapores-soft-power. Accessed on 14 May 2017.

Martinez Rivera, Sergio and Enrique Dussel Peters. 2016. 'La diáspora china en México. Asociaciones chinas en el Distrito Federal, Mexicali y Tapachula'. *Migración y Desarrollo* 14(26): 111–143.

Mazza, Jacqueline. 2016. 'Chinese Migration in Latin America and the Caribbean'. *The Dialogue: Leadership for the Americas*, October.

McClory, Jonathan. 2016. *The Soft Power 30: A Global Ranking of Soft Power*. London: Portland Communications.

Mingjiang, Li. 2008. 'China Debates Soft Power'. *The Chinese Journal of International Politics* 2(2): 287–308.

Mote, Frederick W. and Denis Twitchett. 1988. *The Cambridge History of China, Volume 7: The Ming Dynasty, 1368–1644*. Cambridge: Cambridge University Press.

Nye, Joseph S. 2004. *Soft Power: The Means to Success in World Politics*. New York: Public Affairs.

———. 2009. 'Get Smart: Combining Hard and Soft Power'. *Foreign Affairs*, 160–163.

Oğuzlu, Tarik. 2007. 'Soft Power in Turkish Foreign Policy'. *Australian Journal of International Affairs* 61(1): 81–97.

Pan, Lynn (Hrsg.). 1998. *The Encyclopedia of the Chinese Overseas*. The Chinese Heritage Centre, Singapore. Singapore: Archipelago Press/Landmark Books.

Pieke, Frank N. and Tabitha Speelman. 2013. *Chinese Investment Strategies and Migration: Does Diaspora Matter?* MPC Research Reports 2013/06. Robert Schuman Centre for Advanced Studies, Fiesole, Italia. European University Institute.

Portes, Alejandro and Patricia Fernández-Kelly, eds. 2015. *The State and the Grassroots: Immigrant Transnational Organizations in Four Continents*. New York: Berghahn Books.

Poulden, Gervase. 2013. Morococha: The Peruvian Town the Chinese Relocated. *ChinaFile*. 16 April. Available at http://www.chinafile.com/reporting-opinion/environment/morococha-peruvian-town-chinese-relocated. Accessed on 26 August 2018.

Ray, R., K. Gallagher, A. López, and C. Sanborn 2017. 'China in Latin America: Lessons for South-South Cooperation and Sustainable Development'. In *China and Sustainable Development in Latin America: The Social and Environmental Dimension*, edited by R. Ray, K. Gallagher, A. Lopez, C. Sanborn and A. López, 3–30. London: Anthem Press.

Roldán, Eduardo. 2006. Las relaciones económicas de China, OMC, Mèxico, Estados Unidos, Taiwan y la Unión Europea (2006): 47–81.

Sanborn, Cynthia and V. Ching. 2017. *Chinese Investment in Peru's Mining Industry: Blessing or Curse?* London: Anthem Press.

Sassone, Susana and Carolina Mera. 2007. 'Barrios de migrantes en Buenos Aires: Identidad, cultura y cohesión socioterritorial'. In *Fifth European Congress CEISAL of Latin American Experts , Brussels*, vol. 11.

Schiller, Nina Glick, Linda Basch, and Cristina Blanc-Szanton. 1992. 'Transnationalism: A New Analytic Framework for Understanding Migration'. *Annals of the New York Academy of Sciences* 645(1): 1–24.

Schurz, William Lytle. 1918. 'Mexico, Peru, and the Manila Galleon'. *Hispanic American Historical Review* 1(4): 389–402.Shambaugh, David. 2013. *China Goes Global: The Partial Power.* Oxford-Nueva York: Oxford University Press.

Simpson, John. 2008. Cobre peruano en manos chinas. BBC News. Available at http://news.bbc.co.uk/hi/spnish/latin_america/newsid_7461000/7461072.stm. Accessed on 16 September 2018.

Siu, Lok. 2007. *Memories of a Future Home: Diasporic Citizenship of Chinese in Panama.* Standford, CA: Stanford University Press.

Tan, C. B. 2004. *Chinese Overseas: Comparative Cultural Issues*, vol. 1. Hong Kong: Hong Kong University Press.

Tan, Chee-Beng. 2013. *Routledge Handbook of the Chinese Diaspora*. London: Routledge.

Tamagno, Carla and Norma Velásquez. 2016. 'Dinámicas de las asociaciones chinas en Perú: hacia una caracterización y tipología'. *Migración y Desarrollo* 14(26): 145–166.

Valderrey, Francisco J. (2016). 'International Business Diplomacy: Lessons from Latin America'. In *Multinational Enterprise Management Strategies in Developing Countries*, edited by Mohammad Ayub Khan, 295–315. Hershey, PA: IGI Global. doi:10.4018/978-1-5225-0276-0.ch015.

Valderrey, Francisco and Miguel A. Montoya. 2016. 'China to Finance Infrastructure in Latin America'. *Network Industries Quarterly* 18(2): 6–9.

Wong-Hee-Kam, Édith. 1996. *La diaspora chinoise aux Mascareignes: le cas de la Réunion*. Paris: Université de la Réunion/L'Harmattan.

6

# The Spatial Decoupling and Recombination of Capital and Labour*

## Understanding the New Flows across the China–South East Asia Borderlands

XIANGMING CHEN, NA FU, SAM ZHOU, AND GAVIN XU

## Introduction

The association between capital and labour varies spatially and shifts temporally. Post-1980 China represents arguably the most striking and largest-scale reconfiguration of international capital and domestic labour. China not only has become the largest recipient in the developing world of foreign direct investment (FDI), most of which has flowed into manufacturing, but has also experienced the largest domestic movement of rural labourers, over 500 million, into city-based factories in history. As this massive combination of capital and labour transformed China into a global economic superpower with abundant foreign reserves and surplus capital, it has turned China into a major new source of capital outflow, mostly into the Global South. Conventional capital mobility is driven primarily by private multinational corporations towards both safe and profitable markets in the Global North and emerging economies with lower production costs and greater

* This chapter originated from a presentation by Xiangming Chen at the workshop 'Asian Connections: Linking Mobilities of Capital and Labour in Theory and Practice', York University, Canada, 12–13 May 2017, with a complete draft presented at the workshop 'China's Belt & Road Initiative', Fudan University, Shanghai, 7 July 2018. We thank Preet S. Aulakh and Philip Kelly at York University for co-organizing the workshop and its participants for the stimulating discussion that helped framing this work. We also thank the Henry Luce Foundation for an institutional grant to Trinity College that brought Na Fu from China to Trinity as a visiting scholar in Spring 2017 and facilitated the collaboration and completion of this chapter. The Luce grant also provided supplementary funding for Trinity's Summer

market potentials. But China has introduced a new mode of outward capital mobility directed by a strong party-state that also acts as a global capitalist-state. China challenges the prevailing market-capitalist principle and patterns of global capital and labour mobility by unleashing a large wave of capital flow from China to the Global South and thus triggering potentially new but uncertain labour movements within and across national boundaries.

With its powerful role in reshaping a new era of global capital and labour mobility, China offers a timely case for exploring and understanding the spatial reconfiguration of capital–labour relations across a much more expansive swath of the Global South compared to the previous dominance of capital investment from the Global North. By pushing heavy investment into the Global South through such government channels as state development banks and state-owned companies, China presents new questions concerning how a powerful state deals with its weakening domestic economy by sending and steering capital flows to neighbouring national and subnational recipients with weak governance capacities.

This chapter has three purposes. First, we focus on China's heavy capital investment in the Global South, primarily in the least developed part of South East Asia, to understand the formation and consequences of a new zone of cross-border infrastructure-driven regional development. Second, we conduct a two-fold analysis of how Chinese investment in South East Asia differs between a powerful state channel and a more flexible conduit and how this simultaneous but bifurcated capital mobility leads to varied labour movement. Finally, we explore how the institutions and cultures of China and its South East Asian neighbours interact to produce uneven development across their borderlands and beyond.

# China in South East Asia: A New Regional Nexus of Capital and Labour Flows

China and South East Asia have shared multiple and complex connections for a long time, while separated by various physical barriers of land or water.

programming in China and Cambodia in June 2017 that allowed field visits to Company A's factories in both Dongguan and Phnom Penh. We also acknowledge the Paul E. Raether Distinguished Professorship Fund and the Center for Urban and Global Studies of Trinity College for supporting Sam Zhou's and Gavin Xu's on-campus and field research that has contributed to this chapter. We are also grateful to the general managers of Company A's two factories and other knowledgeable shoe-industry professionals in Dongguan and Phnom Penh for talking with us and helping us understand the global and local aspects of the shoe business from the ground up. Last, we have benefited from the comments and suggestions by the two editors and two outside reviewers in completing this chapter. The subsection titled 'The China-Laos Transportation Corridor' draws from X. Chen (2018b).

China–South East Asia links by sea reached a high point between 1405 and 1433, when Admiral Zheng He led several Ming government-sponsored maritime expeditions of large fleets to various parts of South East Asia, such as Java and Brunei, and all the way to the Horn of Africa through the Indian Ocean. Also, in the fifteenth century, China's connection to maritime South East Asia was highlighted by the marriage of a Chinese princess named Hang Li Po to Sultan Mansur Shah, the ruler of Malacca. This predated and seeded the later migration of Chinese to maritime South East Asia, especially to the Malay Peninsula in the eighteenth and nineteenth centuries, which extended into the subsequent wave of Chinese migration including refugees to Sarawak, North Borneo, Malaya, and Singapore due to civil wars and other domestic turmoil during 1927–1949. More recent and contested China–South East Asia connections have revolved around the territorial disputes over a number of islands in the South China Sea. These long and varied maritime connections tend to characterize much of the external imagination and perception of China and South East Asia.

Less known but increasingly important today is a set of China's connections with mainland South East Asia that also go back a long way. In ancient times, the main route of the 'South Silk Road' originated from today's Chengdu through Xichang in Sichuan province, extended south-west to Qingling (today's Dayao in Yunnan), Dabonong (today's Xiangyun in Yunnan), Yeyu (Dali in Yunnan), wound through Baoshan and Tengchong in Yunnan, and connected to Myitkyina in today's Myanmar before reaching into northern India (Wang and Li, 1998). Across the longest land border with Burma or present-day Myanmar, Chinese migrated to Myanmar as early as in the time of Song and Ming dynasties from the eleventh to the fourteenth century. Some Chinese moved to Myanmar from China during the earlier Qing Dynasty around the mid-sixteenth century to leave the Manchu rule. In the eighteenth century, Qing dynasty princes settled in Kokang in northern Myanmar. There is a dual regionality to both the origin and destination of Chinese migration to Myanmar. The Chinese who settled around Yangon and Lower Myanmar were from Fujian and Guangdong as part of the migration to parts of maritime South East Asia. However, the Chinese who traditionally populated areas around Mandalay and Upper Myanmar originated from Yunnan over the land border (Chen, 2006). These past ties provide the background to the current infrastructure and manufacturing connections that are spatially distinctive and intensive across the China–mainland South East Asia borderland.

While historical ties may not translate into contemporary ones directly, in conjunction with geographic proximity they continue to undergird a variety of cross-border connections from China's coastal and inland border regions to many places of South East Asia. The earlier connections described above formed through an extensive movement of Chinese labourers such as traders in northern Myanmar and workers on rubber plantations and tin mines in Malaysia. The sequential waves of Chinese migration to South East Asia added up to very large numbers of settlers and their descendants over time. While they were primarily petty merchants and poor labourers to begin with, some of them gradually accumulated greater capital as successful entrepreneurs and business people who would eventually dominate many sectors of the South East Asian economies despite their small shares of the host-countries' national populations (Chua, 2004; Haley et al., 2009). The various earlier and spatially expansive China–South East Asia connections featured a heavy flow of Chinese migrants to South East Asia, especially from southern China. This form and scale of labour mobility facilitated capital accumulation in South East Asia that began to flow back to China after its reform and opening around 1980. In fact, while this initial and largest flow of capital into China came from Hong Kong and Taiwanese companies, a good number of large and small Chinese-owned firms in Singapore, Malaysia, and Thailand were also part of this capital flow (Chen, 1994).

The earlier pattern of labour and capital mobility between China and South East Asia took an important new turn in the 2000s. This shift began with a reversal of capital flow from China to South East Asia, driven by a mixture of expected and unexpected domestic and external factors. In the original and already dated 'Flying Geese' model of development, the four 'Asian Tigers' (Korea, Taiwan, Singapore, and Hong Kong) followed Japan the 'Lead Goose'[1] by receiving Japan's surplus capital and using their cheaper labour to catch up as the second formation of the pack of flying geese. China and some South East Asian countries, especially Thailand, Malaysia, Vietnam, and Indonesia, would and did follow the development step of the four Asian Tiger economies by absorbing the latter's no-longer competitive manufacturing capital and utilizing cheaper domestic labour (Deyo, 1987; Wade, 1994). This perspective received some confirmation from Taiwan's strategy of 'going west' to invest in China and 'going south' to invest in South East Asia in the 1990s (Chen, 1996).

If China was comparable to the more developed economies of South East Asia in developmental stage and labour cost, it was not expected to send capital and labour to the latter. In fact, China's gross domestic product (GDP) per capita

---

[1] The 'flying geese' was a model for international division of labour in East Asia based on dynamic comparative advantages attributed to the Japanese economist Kaname Akamatsu who published a series of articles about it from the 1930s to the 1970s (see Korhonen, 1994). The model postulated that Asian nations will catch up with the West as a part of a regional hierarchy where the production of commoditized goods would continuously move from the more advanced countries to the less advanced ones. The lead goose in this pattern was Japan itself, the second-tier of nations consisted of the newly industrializing economies (South Korea, Taiwan, Singapore, and Hong Kong).

trailed Malaysia and Thailand and tracked most of the other South East Asian economies except Singapore through the early 2000s. Its growth accelerated around 2005 until China's GDP per capita surpassed that of Thailand in 2011 (US$5,634 versus US$5,491). By 2016, China's GDP per capita not only closed in on Malaysia (US$8,123 versus US$9,508) but also left Thailand behind, while GDP per capita for all other South East Asian countries, such as Cambodia, Laos, and Myanmar, remained low as a group, at below US$3,500.[2] As these relative development positions of China and South East Asia shifted to favour the former, China's earlier unexpected role to be a capital investor has become more expected in light of what has happened inside China.

Domestic regional rebalancing and restructuring since around 2000 has also shaped China's growing and considerably stronger connections to South East Asia with a new spatial focus and impact. China's open policies favoured the south-east coast in the early 1980s and the entire eastern seaboard into the 1990s. Its interior regions including Yunnan province in the south-west, bordering mainland South East Asia, fell much behind. The central government actually imposed strict control on this border region on the premise of it being militarily insecure, especially after the China–Vietnam border war of 1979. For example, the central government limited the purchase of goods by Chinese farmers across the border to 30 Chinese yuan (about $US4) per transaction and the exchange boundary was restricted to a 10 kilometre stretch from the borderline (Kuah, 2000). The early 1990s, however, saw a shift of Chinese development focus to the less developed border regions, extending financial incentives that had previously been granted exclusively to the coastal areas. This policy adjustment was intended to narrow the growing regional disparities and appease the leaders of the inland and border areas who felt that they had been neglected. This regional rebalancing produced quick results. By 1997, Yunnan's foreign trade had grown 20 per cent annually and amounted to US$15 billion. Foreign trade as a share of provincial GDP rose from 1.8 per cent in 1978 to 10.3 per cent in 1997. Yunnan's border trade grew from a cumulative total of US$24 million during 1978–1984 to US$431 million in 1994, averaging an annual rate of over 30 per cent (Chen, 2006).

The launch of the 'Go West' campaign in 2000, parallel to and reinforced by China's 'Go Out' strategy, was instrumental in creating a striking regional focus for China's engagement with South East Asia. This large-scale policy shift from the centre unleashed a new wave of opportunities for Yunnan to expand its cross-border interaction with South East Asia. On 6 May 2011, China's State Council issued

---

[2] These GDP per capital figures are from the World Bank's online data, see https://data. worldbank.org/indicator/NY.GDP.PCAP.CD?end=2016&locations=TH-CN-KH-ID-LA-MY-MM-VN&start=1960, acessed on 30 April 2019.

'Supporting the Accelerated Construction of Yunnan as the Important Outpost for the Southwest Region', which tasked the capital city of Kunming to become the international hub and 'bridgehead' for China's south-western region. Symbolically, Yunnan's tallest building rose in Kunming's Panlong district, which would serve as the financial and commercial zone for the local presence and regional expansion of multinational companies. Yunnan government approved the establishment of six border economic cooperation zones in May 2012, giving them the autonomy to offer financial incentives and approve investment projects. This provincial initiative augmented the central government's approval of opening three border economic cooperation zones in 1992 when the Greater Mekong Subregion (GMS)[3] initiative was launched through the Asian Development Bank.

The GMS has facilitated trade across the China–South East Asia borderland and bilateral trade between China and the South East Asian economies. China's trade with each of the GMS countries has grown since 1990, most rapidly since 2000 (Figure 6.1). The total volume of China–Myanmar trade rose by almost US$10 billion from 2001 to 2015, while China–Laos trade increased by US$2 billion. Much of China's growing trade with Myanmar and Laos occurred across land borders. In value terms, the transit across the Yunnan border accounts for over half of China–Myanmar trade. Over 80 per cent of Myanmar's exports to China and 40 per cent of its imports from China came across Yunnan's border (Singh, 2016). From 1992 to 2004, China's average share in Myanmar's total cross-border trade was about 63.2 per cent, whereas Yunnan's shares of Myanmar's total exports and imports were 59 per cent and 70 per cent, respectively (Than, 2005). As the most important subnational Chinese unit of the GMS, Yunnan is China's primary space and player shaping cross-border economic ties between China and mainland South East Asia (X. Chen, 2018b).

Yunnan's dominant position and role in China's connections with South East Asia reflect both a horizontal and vertical shift in domestic economic restructuring, driven by a powerful and purposeful state. The shift of favourable policy and development focus from the coast to the interior and the border represents a spatial horizontal rolling or scrolling from leading regions to lagging regions (X. Chen, 2018a). Allowing border provinces like Yunnan to create special border zones with financial incentives constitutes a decentralization or decentring of vertical administrative power to the subregional level. This regional convergence of policy mobility in China's coastal region and downward shift of economic decision-making in Yunnan has accelerated economic growth through border trade and cross-border

---

[3] The Greater Mekong Subregion (GMS) comprises China's Yunnan province (with the addition of Guangxi Zhuang Autonomous Region in 2005), Cambodia, Laos, Myanmar, Thailand, and Vietnam.

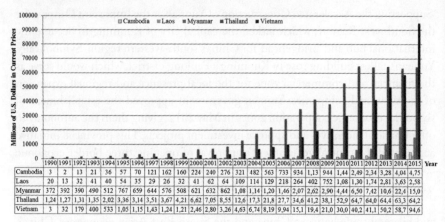

| Year | 1990 | 1991 | 1992 | 1993 | 1994 | 1995 | 1996 | 1997 | 1998 | 1999 | 2000 | 2001 | 2002 | 2003 | 2004 | 2005 | 2006 | 2007 | 2008 | 2009 | 2010 | 2011 | 2012 | 2013 | 2014 | 2015 |
|---|---|---|---|---|---|---|---|---|---|---|---|---|---|---|---|---|---|---|---|---|---|---|---|---|---|---|
| Cambodia | 3 | 2 | 13 | 21 | 36 | 57 | 70 | 121 | 162 | 160 | 224 | 240 | 276 | 321 | 482 | 563 | 733 | 934 | 1,13 | 944 | 1,44 | 2,49 | 2,34 | 3,28 | 4,04 | 4,75 |
| Laos | 20 | 13 | 32 | 41 | 40 | 54 | 35 | 29 | 26 | 32 | 41 | 62 | 64 | 109 | 114 | 129 | 218 | 264 | 402 | 752 | 1,08 | 1,30 | 1,74 | 2,81 | 3,63 | 2,58 |
| Myanmar | 372 | 392 | 390 | 490 | 512 | 767 | 659 | 644 | 576 | 508 | 621 | 632 | 862 | 1,08 | 1,14 | 1,20 | 1,46 | 2,07 | 2,62 | 2,90 | 4,44 | 6,50 | 7,42 | 10,6 | 22,4 | 15,0 |
| Thailand | 1,24 | 1,27 | 1,31 | 1,35 | 2,02 | 3,36 | 3,14 | 3,51 | 3,67 | 4,21 | 6,62 | 7,05 | 8,55 | 12,6 | 17,3 | 21,8 | 27,7 | 34,6 | 41,2 | 38,1 | 52,9 | 64,7 | 64,0 | 64,4 | 63,3 | 64,2 |
| Vietnam | 3 | 32 | 179 | 400 | 533 | 1,05 | 1,15 | 1,43 | 1,24 | 1,21 | 2,46 | 2,80 | 3,26 | 4,63 | 6,74 | 8,19 | 9,94 | 15,1 | 19,4 | 21,0 | 30,0 | 40,2 | 41,1 | 50,2 | 58,7 | 94,6 |

Figure 6.1 | China's trade with five Greater Mekong Subregion countries in South East Asia, 1990–2015

*Source*: Trade statistics from the International Monetary Fund and World Bank (various years).

investment with broader and longer-distance benefits (Chen and Stone, 2017). This process has created a new spatial nexus of capital and labour flows, involving both state and non-state actors operating in their respective cross-border spaces. The combination of both actors and their realms has produced a bifurcated and recombined nexus of capital and labour mobilities (Figure 6.2).

Figure 6.2 has two purposes. One is to propose a new and integrated framework for understanding the changing relationship between capital and labour mobilities as being shaped by China's approach to engaging with the Global South. The other is to use this framework to guide a two-tiered empirical study of China's role in creating both misalignment and recombination of capital and labour flows into mainland South East Asia. From a two-dimensional perspective on factor mobility over geographic space, China plays a new dual role in shaping cross-border capital and labour flows through both the state/public and market/private channels. As Figure 6.2 shows, the Chinese state not only invests heavily in South East Asia's infrastructure sector through its state-owned enterprises but also brings a lot of Chinese workers to the projects. While this approach brings much domestic capital and labour to South East Asia, it creates a kind of capital–labour divergence in the latter in terms of little or insufficient local employment. On the other hand, growing investment by Chinese private companies in South East Asia's manufacturing sector translates into an almost exclusive employment of local workers. This recombination of Chinese capital with South East Asian labour through the market mechanism is similar to the established mode of spatial factor mobility featuring international

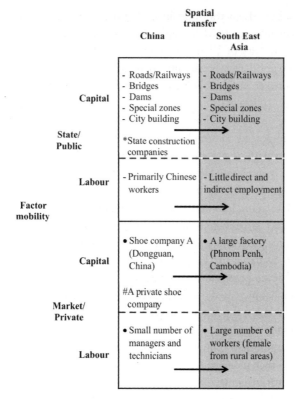

Figure 6.2 | The movement of capital and labour from China to South East Asia

*Source*: Conceived and drawn by the authors.

capital and local labour. Unlike Western developed countries, including Japan and Korea, that have invested in China and South East Asia, China has introduced an unusual strategy in steering and pushing both state and private capital into South East Asia but with different labour flows and usages between the origin and destination. It challenges and will enrich our understanding of new pathways of capital and labour mobilities and their institutional and spatial recombinations.

## State-Led Mobilities: Energy and Transport Infrastructure Connections

In analysing how the Chinese state has shaped new capital and labour mobilities over its border with mainland South East Asia, we focus on the China–Myanmar energy and China–Laos transport links that originate from Kunming, the capital city of Yunnan province, to Myanmar's port town of Kyaukpyu on the Bay of Bengal and Laos' capital city of Vientiane, respectively. The flows of capital and labour through this pair of cross-border infrastructure connections reflect the cumulative interaction between rapid urbanization and regional restructuring inside China and its growing global integration culminating in the Belt and Road Initiative (BRI).

In speeding up urbanization and building large cities, China has created a huge demand for imported commodities and energy, mostly from the Global South. From a country with no private cars to the largest auto market in the world, China has dramatically accelerated its petrol consumption. With millions of high-rise and lower buildings shooting up in its hundreds of large cities that have to be cooled and heated, China has led energy consumption by the world's cities. The scale and speed of China's urbanization drive its huge demand for imported commodities and energy. This has led to a push to 'go out' (inside-out), in search of energy from wherever it is available and keeping it cost-effective in transmission (outside-in). The shift of development and manufacturing from the coast to the interior and border regions has increased the demand for energy in major cities in western China. This regional rebalancing in turn has created more geographic points and untapped opportunities for international trade with China's overland neighbours. In addition, the overall saturation of China's domestic construction market, albeit less so in its western region than its coastal region, has generated a new pressure and opportunity for building infrastructure projects in overseas markets. The BRI's launch since 2013 has added and sustained a much bigger push to this outgoing construction of diverse infrastructure projects, especially those that would physically connect China's western region and border cities to neighbouring countries and beyond.

## The China–Myanmar Energy Nexus

Given its heavy dependence on Middle Eastern oil by sea, China has worked hard with Myanmar in building and operating both a gas and an oil pipeline from the Bay of Bengal to Kunming (Figure 6.3). Agreed upon in 2008 and signed in 2009, the construction of the gas and oil pipelines began in 2009 and was completed in 2013 and 2014, respectively. While both projects involved other international companies such as Daewoo of South Korea, their primary builder, financier, and operator has been South-East Asia Pipeline Company, a Hong Kong-based subsidiary, owned by China National Petroleum Cooperation (CNPC). Despite an initial, combined price tag of US$2.5 billion, the pipelines actually cost almost US$4 billion (Gaung, 2012). The gas pipeline became operational in 2013 and carried 2.86 million tonnes of gas in 2016, accounting for about 5 per cent of China's total

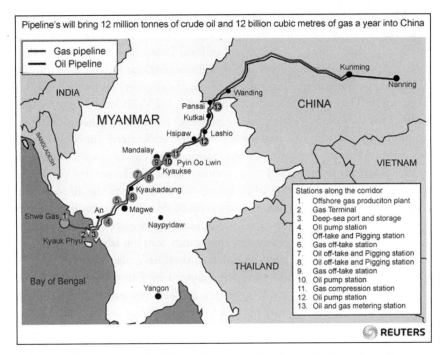

Figure 6.3 | The cross-border China–Myanmar oil and gas pipelines, from Kyaukpyu to Kunming and beyond

*Source*: www.shwe.org.

*Note*: Map not to scale and does not represent authentic international boundaries.

imports. The pipeline will extend further from Kunming to Guizhou and Guangxi provinces in China, running a total of 2,806 kilometres. The oil pipeline opened in 2017 after a long delay, and the Myanmar government had agreed to lower the transit fees. The 770-kilometre pipeline is designed to carry 22 million tonnes of crude oil per year (about 442,000 barrels per day) for the Kunming-based refinery that can process 13 million tonnes annually.[4] This new pipeline allows China to move crude oil from the Middle East overland faster, instead of through the slower and potentially risky narrow and crowded Straits of Malacca.

Given the strategic importance and benefit of the oil and gas pipelines of China, it is not surprising that the Chinese government, through the CNPC, has partnered

---

[4] *Bloomberg News*, 'China Opens Delayed Myanmar Oil Pipeline to Get Mideast Crude Faster', 18 April 2017, available at https://www.bloomberg.com/news/articles/2017-04-11/ china-opens-delayed-myanmar-oil-link-to-get-mideast-crude-faster, accessed on 28 March 2018.

with Myanmar's Ministry of Energy through the Myanmar Oil and Gas Enterprise (MOGE) for this project since the beginning. While the oil and gas pipelines are heavily capitalized projects, their record of local labour benefits has been mixed at best. A small number of local fishing villages obtained jobs to help upgrade the Kyaukpyu–Yangon road as indirect employment generated by the pipelines' construction. They worked for about US$1.5 per day. While this paid more than double what they made weaving fishing nets, they laboured long hours under the hot sun but got very little or nothing for overtime work after 5 pm when the sun goes down. Although some workers were fortunate enough to work more directly for the oil and gas pipelines and were promised to earn US$6 per day, they ended up getting paid only half of it while losing the other half to the employment-contract agent.[5] In addition, the oil and gas pipelines called for acquiring a lot of agricultural land with compensations, which, however were not sufficient to offset the permanent loss of land and eroded opportunity for farm labour.

As the pipelines have been completed, they have also become parts of the Kyaukpyu Special Economic Zone financed by China's state-run China International Trust Investment Corporation (CITIC) for nearly US$10 billion. The zone will cover more than 17 square kilometres and include the US$7.3 billion deep-sea port and a US$2.3 billion industrial park, with plans to attract industries such as textiles and oil refining to create 100,000 jobs in the north-western state of Rakhine, one of Myanmar's poorest regions. Given this planned, huge capital investment, it is expected to have a larger job creation effect, much beyond those directly tied to the oil and gas pipelines. Villagers in Kyaukpyu, however, fear the project will not contribute that much to the area's development, because the operating companies employ mostly Chinese workers. While over 3,000 people live on the Maday Island, the entry point for the oil pipeline, only 47 have so far landed a job with Petrochina, whose Chinese employees are more than double that number (Lee and Lone, 2017).

The above offers some evidence for a weak relationship between capital and labour as shaped by Chinese state-investment in Myanmar. To diversify its overseas sources of oil and gas for national economic security, China has committed heavy capital investment to building a major energy supply route from Kyaukpyu on the Bay of Bengal and a large special economic zone there for affiliated and extended local development. The massive scale of capitalization of these linked projects, however, has not yet generated the expected amount of local employment. This represents heavy cross-border capital mobility from China to Myanmar accompanied by some Chinese labour but with a relatively little use of local labour as suggested by Figure 6.2.

---

[5]  See note 3.

## The China–Laos Transportation Corridor

To further explore the Chinese state's role in shaping and channelling a powerful capital flow into mainland South East Asia with weaker labour connections, we turn to the second case that carries additional insight into the top-half of Figure 6.2. It pertains to the emerging China–Laos transportation corridor anchored to the China–Laos Railway. The line will start in Kunming and travel southward to Jinghong and Mohan until entering Laos through the Lao border city of Boten. It will then travel past Luang Prabang and Vang Vieng before arriving in Vientiane. China envisions this railway to extend from Vientiane to Thailand's border and capital cities of Nong Khai and Bangkok, respectively (Figure 6.4) and then all the way to Singapore via Malaysia and feed into the Trans-Asian Railway linking to Europe. Like the China–Myanmar energy nexus, the China–Laos Railway has a distinctive cross-border regional footprint as an extension from China's rail network from Kunming in Yunnan. Sharing a crucial similar feature with the China–Myanmar energy nexus, the China–Laos Railway bears out China's strategic engagement with mainland South East Asia as a key spatial segment of the BRI that reaches towards its maritime route. The BRI, in conjunction with and reinforced by the railway's route through the Yunnan–Laos borderland, elevates the project's prominence, regarding its level and scale of financing and construction.

Figure 6.4 | The planned route of the cross-border China–Laos Railway

*Source*: Reprinted from X. Chen (2018a: 48).

*Note*: Map not to scale and does not represent authentic international boundaries.

Primarily financed, built, and operated by China, the China–Laos Railway carries an estimated price tag of around US$6.3 billion which is more than one-third of Laos' GDP that stood around US$16 billion in 2016. China will be responsible for 70 per cent of the investment, while Laos will be responsible for the remaining 30 per cent through a China–Laos joint venture company, of which the Lao government will contribute roughly 30 per cent, or around US$700 million. Of the remaining amount, China agreed to give a low-interest twenty-year loan of US$480 million from its Export-Import Bank to Laos to help the latter covering its portion of the cost, with no principal due during the first five years of the loan period. The remaining US$220 million will be drawn from Laos' state budget (Hutt, 2018). As China's biggest investment project in Laos so far, the bulk of this railway's financing is shouldered by China but in somewhat opaque terms, and there is speculation that China will wrest concessions from Laos by collecting future revenues as returns on its massive upfront investment.

Given the scale of investment in the project relative to Laos' GDP, a heavy debt trap looms on the horizon for Laos as a small and weak recipient of capital inflow. From one optimistic perspective, a Lao government official believes that the country will be able to pay the loan back within five years by selling to China minerals from five potash mines that are yet to be excavated. In equally optimistic projections, the Lao government expects roughly 4 million Lao passengers a year to use the railway's 420-kilometre route at first after its completion in 2021, with the figure growing to 6.1 million passengers in the midterm and 8.1 million passengers in the long run. According to the deputy prime minister of Laos, a total of nearly 10 million passengers from China and five other Association of Southeast Asian Nations (ASEAN) countries are expected to use the railway annually, with that figure rising to 11.9 million passengers per year in the midterm and 16.5 million in the long term.[6] Another Lao official of the Laos–China Cooperation Commission predicted that the railway will transport hundreds of thousands of Chinese visitors to neighbouring countries and create a reliable way for Lao products to access vast Chinese, regional, and global markets (Tian and Rong, 2016).

The current fiscal reality for Laos is less optimistic. The government's gross debt was estimated at 67.8 per cent of GDP in 2016. Nearly 65 per cent of Laos' external debt is owed to bilateral creditors, primarily China, up from from 35 per cent in 2012. This reflects the cumulative funding by China for Laos' other infrastructure and power projects, especially the hydropower dams on the Mekong River. Laos' high debt ratio forced some Chinese developers to postpone the construction

---

[6]    *Radio Free Asia*, 'Laos and China Come to Terms on Loan Interest Rate for Railway Project', 4 January 2016, available at http://www.rfa.org/english/news/laos/laos-china-come-to-terms-on-loan-interest-rate-for-railway-project-01042016163552.html, accessed on 28 March 2018.

of hydropower dams on tributaries of the Mekong that were planned to export electricity back to China. As the most expensive and leveraged infrastructure project, the railway is expected to escalate the financial risks for Laos.

While it is too early to know the long-term financial prospect for Laos, or China, the railway project has already created a mixed picture of labour flow and usage. The railway will pass through 72 tunnels with a total length of 183.9 kilometres, representing 43 per cent of the project's total length. The line will also have 170 bridges measuring 69.2 kilometres, accounting for 15.8 per cent of the total line. Therefore, tunnels and bridges combine for around 60 per cent of the total length. Over 200 million litres of fuel is expected to be consumed in the construction.[7] On the one hand, given the sheer amounts of materials needed, the project should create a lot of demand for Lao labour through subcontracting relations and supply chains involving local companies manufacturing materials such as cement and gravel. However, the initial local employment effect was limited. On a less crucial construction site between Luang Prabang and Vang Vieng in northern Laos, local workers outnumbered their Chinese counterparts. Of more than 300 people in nearby hilly villages, only around 20 were hired to work on a subsidiary project and learning the advanced technology and management from their Chinese colleagues.[8] On the other hand, given the technical difficulties in drilling through many tunnels and erecting over a dozen viaducts and numerous bridges, the railway's builder, China Railway Group, brings its workers, technology, equipment, and even some construction materials. At the peak of construction, there will be an estimated 100,000 Chinese workers (X. Chen, 2018a). While a small number of them will be middle-level managers and engineers, most are likely to be line construction workers who tend to come from rural areas and small cities of interior China. If the latter type of workers were Lao, it would lead to an expected combination of foreign (Chinese) capital and national (Lao) labour, similar to how private capital from China has generated employment in Laos (see next section).

While the project's labour benefit has fallen short, so far, it is similar to the China–Myanmar oil and gas pipelines in that the railway is linked to a joint government plan to build the Saysettha Development Zone near the planned railway freight station in Vientiane. Signed into agreement in 2010, soon after the railway project was conceived, this zone aims to attract around 150 enterprises to

---

[7] *Xinhua* (Asia & Pacific Edition), 'China-Laos Railway Construction to Consume 200 Million Liters Fuel: Official', 28 March 2018, available at http://www.xinhuanet.com/english/2017-03/28/c_136164243.htm, accessed on 28 March 2018.

[8] *China Daily*, 'Laos-China Railway Brings Changes to Laos', 7 August 2017, available at http://www.chinadaily.com.cn/business/2017-08/07/content_30359991.htm, accessed on 28 March 2018.

operate from the hub with a total output value to reach US$6 billion and to create about 30,000 new jobs for locals by 2030 after its full development. After 2013, 32 companies were reported to have entered the Saysettha Development Zone and had already brought new operating and management ideas to the local plants.[9] The ultimate scale of indirect job creation will depend on the realized potential of the railway. For landlocked Laos to become land-linked, the railway makes sense for connecting to outside markets, especially if the planned industrial zone near Vientiane's terminal can stimulate manufactured exports and if millions of high-spending Chinese tourists will cross the border on the train. While this cross-border shift of Chinese spending power can create more local commercial and service jobs along the railway in Laos, it can pave the way for even faster Chinese migration southward into South East Asia, complicating the long-term implications for cross-border versus domestic labour mobilities.

## Market-Driven Cross-Border Capital Mobility and Localized Labour

The above pair of case studies distinguishes a new connection between capital and labour mobilities, reflective of how the powerful and capital-rich Chinese state approaches cross-border investment in large-scale infrastructure projects in neighbouring South East Asia. Regardless of the opposite directions of the intended infrastructure connections in terms of oil and gas flowing from Myanmar into China versus a railway extending from China to Laos, they reflect the interaction between China's domestic economic and regional restructuring and external development strategy. The same underlying logic has also induced capital flows from China to South East Asia through the market mechanism instead of the state's channels, with quite different implications for and links with labour dynamics between the capital sending and receiving countries, cities, and companies (Figure 6.2).

To understand this market-driven capital mobility and its impact on labour, we undertake an extended analysis of a Chinese shoe company with its investment in Cambodia. We focus on the combination of the shoe industry between China and Cambodia for two reasons. First, Cambodia, together with Laos and Myanmar, is one of the three poorest South East Asian economies in terms of GDP per capita in 2016 (US$1,270 for Cambodia, US$2,339 for Laos [which only surpassed Vietnam's slightly in 2014], and US$1,196 for Myanmar).[10] They share a large gap from China in developmental stages and comparative advantages such as lower labour costs. Unlike Laos and Myanmar's geographic contiguity with China, Cambodia

---

[9]  See note 6.

[10]  See note 1.

does not border China by land, although it has the Port of Sihanoukville with a strong Chinese connection besides the strong Chinese presence in its capital city of Phnom Penh (see later). Second, by examining the Chinese shoe industry's capital and labour connections to Cambodia, we can offer comparable and complementary evidence on how fierce market competition among labour-intensive companies such as those making shoes produces new cross-border capital mobility with consequences for labour that differs from the state-led cases of large and capital-intensive infrastructure projects in energy and transportation sectors.

## Shifting Urban and Regional Competitive Advantages

Similar to the China–Myanmar and China–Laos cross-border infrastructure projects, primarily with state-investments, there is an urban–regional dimension to the market-driven capital and labour mobilities between China and Cambodia. While Kunming in Yunnan province is the destination and origin of the China–Myanmar energy supply lines and the China–Laos Railway, the city of Dongguan in Guangdong province is the home for a growing China–Cambodia shoe-manufacturing nexus. From the South East Asian aspect, just as Kyaukpyu and Vientiane anchor the Myanmar and Laos' ends of the cross-border infrastructure connections, Phnom Penh serves as Cambodia's main destination for Chinese shoe companies' investment. Unlike the other Chinese and South East Asian cities as nodes of the energy and transportation corridors, the Dongguan–Phnom Penh manufacturing nexus reveals more completely the analytical importance of subnational spatial units and their shifting competitive advantages for understanding cross-national capital and labour mobilities from China to South East Asia. This focus not only highlights the convergence between the spatial and organizational aspects of the capital–labour association (Figure 6.2) but also calls for assessing the facilitating effects of national and local state policies on firms' decisions on how to redeploy capital versus labour between discrete and diverse places.

Almost completely unknown outside China 40 years earlier, Dongguan was a very unlikely place to be closely linked to today's Phnom Penh through shoe manufacturing. Given its relatively short or compressed history of labour-intensive manufacturing, Dongguan carries an inherent logic for eventually being connected to an emerging centre of low-end industries like in Phnom Penh. Overshadowed very early on by Shenzhen, which became China's first and largest special economic zone bordering Hong Kong in 1979, Dongguan still grew quickly as a collection of villages and towns and from the heavy influx of labour-intensive manufacturing from Hong Kong and Taiwan into the Pearl River Delta region. Located east of the Pearl River, Dongguan, bordering Guangzhou to the north-west and Shenzhen to the south, is positioned at the centre of the Guangzhou–Hong Kong economic corridor. With its abundant supply of cheap land (over 2,500 square kilometres) and migrant labour from the vast interior, Dongguan rose to a large manufacturing centre of labour-intensive goods for export in the early 1990s when it made more than 60,000 types of products across 30 different industries (Lu, 2013a).

While Dongguan reached its first peak of manufacturing with the moniker as the 'world's factory', it relied on an economic model of operation called 'three imports and compensation trade' or '三来一补' in Chinese.[11] This policy represented a state-led strategy to attract overseas investment to a most conveniently located city-region with tax incentives and combine it with China's tremendous comparative advantage in low-cost land and labour to make competitive exports for the world market. Characterizing Hong Kong as the 'shop window' and Dongguan as the 'factory floor', this model produced rapid growth and urbanization of Dongguan in terms of rising population, government revenue, and household income. Yet since raw materials, parts, and half-finished and finished components, for example, of electronics products, came from and went through Hong Kong, Dongguan was stuck in the low value-added middle section of what Gereffi (1994) called buyer-driven commodity chains with few inter-firm supplier–manufacturer links that could benefit the local economy more broadly and deeply (Chen, 1994).

The mid 1990s ushered in a more advanced stage for Dongguan's manufacturing sector, which began to take advantage of more Taiwanese IT companies moving more complete production networks to the Pearl River Delta due to greater price pressure for original equipment manufacturing (OEM)[12] orders from multinational corporations, and growing competition from South East Asian IT firms. This process involved a core Taiwanese IT company with either original brand manufacturing (OBM) or original design manufacturing (ODM)[13] relocating to Dongguan first and then bringing a group of its small and mid-sized suppliers of parts and components over to form a complete production and assembly network (Chen, 2007). This was also reflected in the gradual decline of the 'three imports and compensation trade' enterprises in Dongguan and a steady increase in jointly

---

[11] This is a shorthand for enterprises that (a) process imported raw materials, (b) manufacture products according to imported samples, (c) assemble imported parts, and (d) repay loans for imported equipment and technologies with products.

[12] OEM refers to suppliers making certain products according to the designs and specifications and with equipment from generally multinational corporations as buyers. It makes companies engaged in OEM who are largely dependent on multinational corporations that contract the OEM production to them.

[13] ODM refers to companies engaged in OEM also providing designs, whereas OBM refers to companies owning their own brands and using them to deal with buyers of their branded products. ODM is an important upgrade over OEM, and OBM is another major advancement beyond ODM.

or fully foreign-invested companies in other industries that also began to build up regionalized supplier networks. Accompanying this process was the steady spatial concentration of varied industries in a number of Dongguan's towns that made a disproportionately large share of particular products such as furniture or garments. One of the largest shoe-making bases in China and the world, the town of Houjie had more than 400 factories involved in shoemaking and over 800 engaged in the supply of raw materials, machinery, and leather for the industry. In 2010, 600 million pairs of shoes were made in the town, with sales revenues of approximately RMB 20.9 billion or US$3.3 billion (based on current exchange rate) (Lu, 2013a).

While Dongguan remained a vibrant manufacturing centre, the early 2000s marked the onset of a new and increasingly uncertain and more competitive period that has continued into the present. Having recognized the rising local labour and land costs, the Dongguan government in 2004 initiated a drive to upgrade its manufacturing industries. It launched the Songshan Lake High-Tech Park as a new designated space for high-tech manufacturing and research and development (R&D). The park has recently lured large tech firms like Huawei to relocate some of their R&D facilities from neighbouring Shenzhen. In 2008, even before the full impact of the global financial crisis, the Guangdong provincial government introduced a more ambitious policy of industrial upgrading called 'emptying the cage for new birds' or '腾笼换鸟' in Chinese. It was designed to move out declining labour-intensive factories and replace them with more capital- and knowledge-intensive ones, making competitive high-tech projects. In the meantime, the looming global financial crisis worsened the problem of rapidly rising costs in such labour-intensive industries as shoes where factory wages rose from about US$100 per month in 2006 to US$200 per month in 2008. This combination forced 15 per cent of shoe manufacturers in Dongguan to shut down or relocate in 2007, with a large shoe factory owner predicting that 40 per cent of Dongguan's shoe factories would move inland, albeit slowly (Mitchell, 2008). In Houjie alone, the number of shoe-making factories decreased from more than 600 in 2007 to only around 400 in 2011, and the number of employees in the industry dropped from 150,000 to 100,000 (Lu, 2013b). The crisis of the shoe industry continued as more owners closed their money-losing factories without paying some employees who ended up protesting against both the companies and the local government. Some of the protesting workers only got back compensation worth less than half of the pay they were owed (Fang, 2014).

As its shoe industry was losing much of its competitiveness, the Dongguan government pushed forward an ambitious plan to turn the city into a new and more advanced manufacturing centre. Although its labour-intensive and low-end manufacturing base was too wide and deep to be turned around quickly, Dongguan was able to make some progress in upgrading and reorienting its industrial structure.

Its export share of high-tech products in the processing industry rose from 38.1 per cent in 2008 to 49.4 per cent in 2011. Foreign-invested enterprises in Dongguan more than doubled the domestic sales levels from 2008 to 2011. Domestic sales of foreign-invested enterprises increased from RMB 133.9 billion (US$21.3 billion) in 2008 to RMB 247.9 billion (US$39.4 billion) in 2011, taking up 34 per cent of the total sales in 2011 from 26 per cent in 2008 (Lu, 2013b). In the '12th Five-Year (2012–2017) Plan for Dongguan's Economic and Social Development', the municipal government planned to transform the city into an important production base for national, strategic, emerging industries such as advanced information, electric vehicles, solar energy, and semiconductors. Dongguan's ambitious and accelerated industrial upgrading has added heavy pressure on its traditional industries like shoes to find alternative ways and outlets to stay competitive.

A main outlet or destination for Dongguan's shoe companies has turned out to be Cambodia. Together with Vietnam's, Cambodia's footwear sector has recently grown a lot primarily due to its duty-free access to the European Union (EU) and its lower cost factors of production, especially labour, relative to China's. In 2014, the Cambodian government approved 78 new garment- and footwear-investment projects capitalized at US$452 million, which accounted for 28 per cent of its total new investment in fixed assets. In 2015, Cambodia's footwear exports rose by 21.8 per cent to a total of US$538 million, mainly destined for the EU market (Karim, 2017). Most of the new footwear projects involved investment from China and Hong Kong. A recent survey of 640 labour-intensive companies in the Pearl River Delta showed that 27 per cent of the shoe companies either have already invested overseas, mostly in South East Asia and even in Africa, or are planning to do so in three years.[14] A growing number of international companies in China, both labour-intensive industries like shoes, and more advanced electronics like digital cameras and LCDs, have relocated operations partially or entirely to Cambodia and Vietnam. In 2018, Ditto Denko and Nikon shut down their factories in Suzhou, near Shanghai. As Samsung has increased investment in Vietnam, in 2018, it laid off almost all the Chinese employees at its large factory in Shenzhen, which in turn affected its extensive supply chain into Dongguan and beyond (S. Chen, 2018). In comparative terms, while total FDI in China continued to dwarf that in Cambodia, the latter received more foreign investment per person than China in 2012 for the first time since comparable record-keeping began in the 1970s. Labour cost differential was a main driver of this relative shift from China to Cambodia.

---

[14] *Afrindex* (a survey by the China-Africa trade research center), 'China's Light-Industry Companies Move Production to Southeast Asia and Africa', a survey by the China-Africa Trade Research Center, 6 December 2017, available at http://news.afrindex.com/zixun/article10001.html, accessed on 30 April 2019.

Despite being 15–30 per cent less productive, Cambodian workers on average earned less than one-third of Chinese workers (Bradsher, 2013), although this gap has shrunk more recently.

As capital and labour dynamics move from China to South East Asia, especially Cambodia, they have reshuffled the fortunes of major Chinese and Cambodian industrial cities such as Dongguan and Phnom Penh, respectively. While Shenzhen, Dongguan, and Suzhou are first-tier or top second-tier cities in China, they have risen to become major global manufacturing centres. Although these cities rank below New York or Shanghai in the global urban hierarchy, they qualify as important secondary 'global cities' as important global–national economic hubs (Kanna and Chen, 2012).

Despite not being near the same demographic size and economic scale as Dongguan, Phnom Penh has become the most popular place for Chinese manufacturing investment, especially by Dongguan's shoe companies. According to the 2011 Cambodia Economic Census, with only 11.2 per cent of the national population, Phnom Penh Municipality accounted for 19 per cent of the total number of registered businesses, 33.3 per cent of the total employment, 55.4 per cent of the total annual commercial sales, and 57.4 per cent of the annual government expenses of Cambodia.[15] Phnom Penh's business employment was 3.6 times larger than the second-ranked region, in surrounding Kandal province, while its business sales were 10 times as large as Kandal's.[16] By these indicators, Phnom Penh is Cambodia's primate city— occupies disproportionately large shares of the national population, employment, and economic resources. Within Phnom Penh, Dangkor district (Langge in Chinese spelling) is the largest manufacturing base with approximately 150,000 workers which accounts for almost half of the city's total workforce. Phnom Penh plays host to the bulk of Chinese manufacturing investment, especially in shoes, although Cambodia's seaside or port city of Sihanoukville has attracted heavy Chinese investment in commerce, casinos, real estate, and tourism. Upon tracing the spatial shift of the domestic regional and international comparative advantages of China versus South East Asia, we have revealed Dongguan and Phnom Penh as the two place-anchors of the China–Cambodia shoe-manufacturing connection.

## Surviving through Organizational Split and Capital–Labour Reconfiguration

The eroding competitive advantages in making shoes in Dongguan deteriorated considerably during the global financial crisis starting in 2008. The heavy

---

[15] National Institute of Statistics, Ministry of Planning, *Economic Census of Cambodia 2011: Provincial Report*, Phnom Penh, February 2013.

[16] Ibid.

concentration of shoe factories in Dongguan, which created and has sustained a crowded and fiercely competitive environment, struggled to survive. Irrespective of the additional pressure and squeeze from government policies of industrial upgrading, some shoe companies in Dongguan have taken the risk of moving some production to Cambodia rather than the less risky movement to China's interior cities. To understand the microscopic characteristics and consequences of capital and labour flows from China to Cambodia, we conducted a field study of a shoe company in Dongguan labelled Company A (Figure 6.2). We interviewed the general manager of the company twice in Dongguan and its new factory's general manager in Phnom Penh. These interviews were supplemented and enriched by a complete tour of the company's home factory in Dongguan and new factory in Phnom Penh.

Company A is jointly managed by three partners, two Chinese who moved from the neighbouring province of Hunan to Dongguan more than 20 years ago as workers at Taiwanese shoe companies and the other, a Taiwanese shoe-making veteran. Started in 2004 with this Taiwanese, Company A has run into increasing cost pressures to compete and survive in the more unfavourable local environment discussed earlier, especially after the global financial crisis. In the late 2000s, Company A expanded to two factories in Hunan and Guangxi provinces respectively to cut the cost of making the more labour-intensive upper part of shoes. The company also outsourced other accessories to four more factories outside Dongguan. While these measures were cost-saving, Company A found it difficult to find enough workers for its Dongguan factory to finish the shoes as there were fewer workers interested in shoemaking while labour cost continues to rise.. Other challenges included (a) the growing imperative of quality coordination and control over the longer supply chain into other provinces and (b) the rising cost in shipping accessories and other parts to Dongguan for the final assembly of shoes.[17]

Still unable to stabilize its production with any cushion of profitability, Company A took a big gamble in 2016 when it opened up a large factory in Dangkor district of Phnom Penh. While this move was partly motivated by the much lower labour cost in Cambodia, it was a necessary response to the Canadian shoe company, ALDO's, support for a new factory in Cambodia for two reasons. First, Cambodia benefits from Canada's Market Access Initiative for Least Developed Countries, which allows qualifying states quota-free and duty-free access to the Canadian market. Second, Cambodia enjoys tariff- and tax-free trade with the EU, which in 2016 imported almost US$4 billion worth of goods, mostly footwear, from Cambodia as the latter's largest export destination (Hutt, 2017). In connecting the two regional trading dyads, ALDO agreed to provide relatively stable orders

---

[17] Authors' interview with the general manager of Company A, Dongguan, June 2017.

for leather shoes for women from Company A's new factory in Cambodia to be exported directly and duty-free to the EU markets. Through this organizational split, Company A rebalanced and diversified its product lines by moving the low(er)-end, mostly synthetic-leather shoes to Phnom Penh and upgrading its production in Dongguan to make more expensive real leather shoes for women that included brands, such as Nine West, DKNY, Karl Lagerfeld, Donna Karan, and better ALDO shoes (Figure 6.5). To improve the design of these branded shoes and potentially develop its own brands, Company A has also set up an R&D office on its premises in Dongguan. Relative to lowering some labour costs versus incurring other new costs, Company A's new factory in Phnom Penh was geared to be more competitive through diversifying products, capturing higher values, and spreading risks beyond its home base.

To achieve these goals, Company A took a big risk in pulling and then sinking different sources of capital into the new factory in Phnom Penh that has amounted to around RMB 10 million (US$1.6 million), a huge sum for a small private company of around 500 employees. Since the semi-rural land was cheap in the part

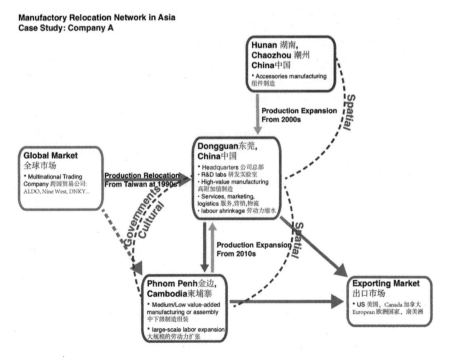

Figure 6.5 | A China–Cambodia-based global shoe production and distribution system

*Source*: Drawn by Na Fu, based on interviews and field work.

of Dangkor district designated by the Cambodian government for concentrated footwear (and garment) manufacturing, Company A was able to lease a sizeable piece of land and erect a sprawling one-level factory building on it. It quickly hired around 1,000 workers within six months through 2016 to work flexibly on two to three assembly lines. Company A sent over 20 managers and technicians from Dongguan to Phnom Penh, who report to one of its two Chinese partners as the factory's general manager. By the end of 2017, the factory expanded to more than 1,300 workers and five assembly lines (Figure 6.6). Most of the workers have migrated from villages in northern rural provinces like Battambang. They are generally young and almost exclusively female, which is similar to the prevailing work force in Dongguan in its earlier years (Chang, 2009) but quite different from the profile of workers at Dongguan's shoe factories today, including Company A's home base (Figure 6.6 (b)). In fact, the labour-creating effect of capital flow from China to South East Asia is larger and broader once we factor in the transnational corporations (TNCs) operating in China and moving production facilities to South East Asia (discussed earlier). As additional examples, H&M, a European retailer, recently shifted sweater production from China to Yangon, Myanmar. In 2013, Japanese investment doubled in South East Asia and shrank by 40 per cent in China. While China's labour force of more than 800 million was more than double ASEAN's combined workforce of just over 300 million (Yang, 2016). The combination of ASEAN's lower wages and sufficient skill will lead to more people working in response to capital moving from China.

As expected, Company A's decision to hire over 1,000 workers was based on Cambodia's manufacturing wage being about one-third of China's. However, Cambodia's minimum wage has risen rapidly since 2012, from about US$60 per month to roughly US$180 per month in 2018. In fact, the actual monthly wage of Cambodian factory workers ranged US$238–260, according to a 2018 survey.[18] While this labour cost has already reached about 50 per cent of the prevailing Chinese factory wage, it remains competitive considering that the average Cambodian worker at Company A's Phnom Penh factory is about 70–75 per cent as efficient as her counterpart at the Dongguan factory.[19] However, the Cambodian workers at the Phnom Penh factory are expected to become more efficient or

---

[18]  A survey of over 30 factories was conducted by the National Trade Union Commission of Cambodia in February 2018. The survey shows that if bonuses were included, some workers could earn as much as US$480 a month, available at http://news.ctei.cn/bwzq/201802/t20180224_3681293.htm, accessed on 15 April 2019.

[19]  Authors' interviews with the general manager of Company A, Dongguan, June 2017 and December 2017. The same source as in note 20 reported similarly that Cambodian workers sew 15–30 per cent fewer sleeves per day than their counterparts in Shanghai.

(a)

(b)

Figure 6.6 | The scale and type of a Chinese shoe company's two factories in Cambodia and China: (a) away factory in Phnom Penh and (b) home factory in Dongguan

*Source*: Photos taken by Xiangming Chen.

productive with training by the managers and technicians from Dongguan. If this will happen, Company A will gain more from the continuing but shrinking labour cost differential between Cambodia and China.

A focused look at the comparative labour costs of Company A's two factories is telling but not sufficient. As recent as the 1990s, the three partners of Company A, and the other shoemaking professionals in Dongguan were making money and betting on a long and prosperous future for their industry where it was. Now they are concerned about the accelerated rise of Cambodian wages over the short period of their new and adventurous operation in Phnom Penh. Despite having a quarter of China's GDP per capita today (discussed earlier), Cambodia's manufacturing wage is approaching half of China's. Factoring in the costs of moving 20 experienced Chinese supervisors and technicians from Dongguan, including some of their family members, and shipping almost all of the materials and intermediate goods by sea to Phnom Penh through the port of Sihanoukville, the total cost of Company A's new factory in Phnom Penh approximates three-quarters of the production cost in Dongguan. Balancing against all these costs, the Phnom Penh factory, through a full exploration of the new location advantages, can secure an average of 5–8 per cent in profit, which already exceeds the shrinking profit margin back in Dongguan. The general managers of both factories told us that they are planning to sustain, if not further expand, the Phnom Penh factory for the next few years or longer, and they are already considering Myanmar as a possible future location for extended or supplementary operation.[20]

Company A is cautiously optimistic about staying in Phnom Penh, but its confidence and comfort in surviving to thrive through increasing competition is anchored back to its home base in Dongguan. Company A continues to receive overseas orders through its trading arm at home, run by the seasoned Taiwanese shoe executive among the three partners. The three work closely together to control all facets of the costs in both Dongguan and Phnom Penh, especially the backward supply chains within Dongguan, extending into the villages in Hunan province (Figure 6.5).

## Conclusion: Towards a China-Centric Capital–Labour Recombination

Through a series of coupled analyses of infrastructure and manufacturing connections between pairs of dyadic macro and micro units: China–South East

---

[20] Authors' interviews with both general managers of Company A, Dongguan, and Phnom Penh, June 2017.

Asia (Myanmar, Laos, and Cambodia), Yunnan (Kunming)–Kyaukpyu, Yunnan (Kunming)–Vientiane, Dongguan–Phnom Penh, and a Chinese shoe company's pair of factories in the latter two cities, we intend to portray a composite trend of China shaping the global and regional landscapes of capital and labour flows and recombinations. This layered shift consists of a correlated crossover of two trend lines. First, China surpassed the USA as the world's largest manufacturing nation around 2009, from lagging behind by US$1,000 billion in gross value added in 2005 to reach ahead by US$1,000 billion in 2016. Second, China's labour cost rose sharply in 2009 from a level comparable to that of Thailand and a little higher than in Indonesia and Vietnam in 2005, to more than triple these countries in 2016 (Morrison, 2017). This is further macro evidence to go along with our subnational- and firm-level analyses earlier. In another significant shift, China's outward investment accelerated in 2005 and exceeded its inward investment in 2015. This makes China today both the largest recipient and source of foreign investment among all developing nations (Morrison, 2017: Figure 12). The BRI's launch in 2013 obviously boosted the latter shift and reinforced the other trend lines. These have led to a historically unprecedented era in which China, as the world's second-largest but still developing, middle-income economy, has begun to drive a new nexus of capital and labour movements to, and in, the Global South.

The most striking feature of an increasingly global China-centric capital–labour regime is the combined power and reach of both the strong and internationally oriented Chinese state and private firms. There is a clear institutional dimension to this outside-inside combination that goes back to the developmental state perspective but extends beyond it with new insights. From the domestic vantage point, institutional reform and market opening and their coevolution, which were instrumental in China's escape from the poverty trap (Ang, 2016), have helped to rebalance regional uneven development, first through the 'Go West' campaign and then through the BRI. These policies in turn have stimulated and incentivized large state-owned companies to turn away from the crowded domestic construction market to build infrastructure projects overseas, such as the China–Myanmar energy pipelines and the China–Laos Railway in order to relieve overcapacities at home. In focusing on pursuing these large-scale infrastructure projects, the Chinese state may capture more hidden capital value from the large tracts of land in Myanmar and Laos that may not lead to much employment benefit.

While the original developmental state in Japan, South Korea, and Taiwan evolved to facilitate rather than drive national firms to operate in the global economy (Yeung, 2016), the Chinese state at the central and local levels has indirectly pushed its private firms like labour-intensive shoe companies in Dongguan to invest abroad through aggressive industrial upgrading policies that targeted the Pearl River Delta. However, it was the shifting competitive conditions of the global shoe manufacturing and market that motivated private companies like Company A to invest in Phnom Penh while upgrading its Dongguan factory. While both the state and the market have channelled Chinese capital flows into South East Asia, they have produced divergent labour outcomes across and within places.

The second distinctive feature of Chinese capital flows into South East Asia is a new spatiality that reflects the increasing involvement of smaller and secondary cities in stitching border-intensive and place-specific infrastructure and economic connections. As China's domestic regional economic restructuring has unfolded, it has unleashed the growth potential of its interior regional hubs and small border cities into new centres for cross-border regional connections between China and South East Asia (Chen, 2005). The city of Kunming, capital of Yunnan province, receives the China–Myanmar oil and gas pipelines that are routed through the small border city of Ruili. In a somewhat similar role, Kunming is the originating point for the China–Laos Railway that needs to be serviced and monitored by the small border town of Mohan (Chen and Stone, 2017). Dongguan's relative decline as a global shoe-making centre has helped Phnom Penh to become the hub of Cambodia's increasingly important shoe manufacturing through the relocation or expansion of Chinese shoe companies. In this sense, the traditional dominant city status of Phnom Penh is both a location advantage and functional beneficiary of the Chinese shoe companies based in Dongguan. By hiring large numbers of young female workers from rural areas, Chinese-invested factories in Phnom Penh like Company A have reproduced the same impact on local labour as Dongguan in the 1980s and 1990s. For these workers from the Cambodian countryside, wages that have risen faster than the Chinese migrant workers would imply an improved living standard 20 or so years ago, but growing food and housing costs prevent many workers from fully benefiting from rising wages (S. Chen, 2018).

Finally, there is a cultural undercurrent to China's growing role in shaping a new capital–labour connection in South East Asia. Part of this cultural underpinning is deeply embedded in the historical trade, ethnic, and migration ties across the current China–South East Asia borderland mentioned at the outset. Once severed or suppressed by the political redrawing and rigid control of borders, these resilient ties have resurfaced to foster border trade, investment, and tourism (Chen and Stone, 2017). While the ethnic Chinese ties are less important for the large-scale infrastructure projects such as the China–Laos Railway, they underpin the growing wave of Chinese migration associated with commercial and manufacturing investment in South East Asia, especially in Cambodia. The congested highway from the city centre of Phnom Penh to where Company A's factory is located in an industrial zone on the outskirts is lined with numerous Chinese restaurants, shops, and other small businesses. This resembles the spatial make-up of the earlier factory cities and towns in China such as Dongguan. Not having enough Mandarin speaking staff, Chinese companies in Phnom Penh provide Mandarin language training. Cambodian workers in Chinese-owned factories who can speak Mandarin can get paid US$400 or even US$500 per month as opposed to US$200–300 per month (Reddick and Co, 2017).

Through a bifocal lens (Figure 6.2) on Chinese capital mobility to three least developed South East Asian nations, we have shown the disruption or disconnect between Chinese state capital and local labour in the large-scale infrastructure projects. The market mechanism, however, has channelled private Chinese capital to recombine with local labour. Between these two different capital–labour relations across borders with South East Asia, China exerts a growing influence on national and regional development in Myanmar, Laos, and Cambodia. We end by calling for further research on the institutional, spatial, and cultural variations of a China-centric capital–labour regime in order to better understand China's broader role in shaping the course of development across the Global South.

# References

Ang, Yuen Yuen. 2016. *How China Escaped the Poverty Trap*. Ithaca, NY: Cornell University Press.

Bradsher, Keith. 2013. 'Wary of China, Companies Head to Cambodia'. *The New York Times*. 8 April. Available at https://www.nytimes.com/2013/04/09/business/global/wary-of-events-in-china-foreign-investors-head-to-cambodia.html. Accessed on 30 April 2019.

Chang, Leslie T. 2009. *Factory Girls: From Village to City in a Changing China*. New York: Spiegel & Grau.

Chen, Sijin. 2018. 'Large Japanese and Korean Companies Leave China Consecutively'. Available at http://blog.sina.com.cn/s/blog_5ef1fe090102xqxp.html?tj=fina. Accessed on 7 May 2018.

Chen, Xiangming. 2005. *As Borders Bend: Transnational Spaces on the Pacific Rim*. Lanham, MD: Rowman & Littlefield Publishers.

———. 1994. 'The New Spatial Division of Labor and Commodity Chains in the Greater South China Economic Region'. In *Commodity Chains and Global Capitalism*, edited by Gary Gereffi and Miguel Korzeniewicz, 165–186. Westport, CT: Greenwood Press.

———. 1996. 'Taiwan Investments in China and Southeast Asia: "Go West But Also Go South"'. *Asian Survey* 36(5): 447–467.

———. 2006. 'Beyond the Reach of Globalization: China's Border Regions and Cities in Transition'. In *Globalization and the Chinese City*, edited by Fulong Wu, 21–46. London: Routledge.

———. 2007. 'A Tale of Two Regions in China: Rapid Economic Development and Slow Industrial Upgrading in the Pearl River and the Yangtze River Deltas'. *International Journal of Comparative Sociology* 48(2–3): 167–201.

———. 2018a. 'Globalization Redux: Can China's Inside-Out Strategy Catalyze Economic Development Across Its Asian Borderlands and Beyond'. *Cambridge Journal of Regions, Economy and Society* 11(1): 35–58.

———. 2018b. 'Rethinking Cross-Border Regional Cooperation: A Comparison of the China-Myanmar and China-Laos Borderlands'. In *Region-Making and Cross-Border Cooperation:*

*New Evidence from Four Continents*, edited by Elisabetta Nadalutti and Otto Kallscheuer, 81–105. London: Routledge.

Chen, Xiangming and Curtis Stone. 2017. 'Rethinking Border Cities: In-Between Spaces, Unequal Actors and Stretched Mobilities across the China-Southeast Asia Borderland.' In *The SAGE Handbook of the 21st Century City*, edited by Suzanne Hall and Ricky Burdett, 479–501. Thousand Oaks, CA: Sage Publications.

Chua, Amy. 2004. *World on Fire: How Exporting Free Market Democracy Breeds Ethnic Hatred and Global Instability*. New York: Anchor.

Deyo, Frederic C. (ed.). 1987. *The Political Economy of the New Asian Industrialism*. Ithaca, NY: Cornell University Press.

Fang, Wang. 2014. 'Chinese Shoe Manufacturers Fall on Hard Time'. *Epoch Times*. 12 November. Available at https://www.theepochtimes.com/mkt_ca/chinese-shoe-manufacturers-fall-on-hard-times_1068847.html. Accessed on 30 April 2019.

Gaung Juliet Shwe. 2012. 'Employment, Complaints Flow from Pipeline'. *Myanmar Times*. 30 July. Available at https://www.mmtimes.com/business/318-employment-complaints-flow-from-pipeline.html. Accessed on 31 April 2019.

Gereffi, Gary. 1994. 'The Organization of Buyer-Driven Global Commodity Chains: How U.S. Retailers Shape Overseas Production Networks'. In *Commodity Chains and Global Capitalism*, edited by Gary Gereffi and Miguel Korzeniewicz, 95–122. Westport, CT: Greenwood Press.

Haley, George T., User C. V. Haley, and Chin Tiong Tan. 2009. *New Asian Emperors: The Business Strategies of the Overseas Chinese*. New York: Wiley.

Hutt, David. 2018. 'Laos on a Fast Track to a China Debt Trap'. *Asia Times*. Available at http://www.atimes.com/article/laos-track-china-debt-trap/. Accessed on 31 April 2019.

———. 2017. 'Why the EU is Dallying Over Possible Cambodia Sanctions'. *Forbes*. 3 November. Available at https://www.forbes.com/sites/davidhutt/2017/11/03/why-the-eu-is-dallying-over-possible-cambodia-sanctions/#17d3fec361a0. Accessed on 31 April 2019.

Kanna, Ahmed and Xiangming Chen. 2012. 'Introduction: Bringing the Less Familiar Cities in and Together'. In *Rethinking Global Urbanism: Comparative Insights from Secondary Cities*, edited by Xiangming Chen and Ahmed Kanna, 1–14. New York: Routledge.

Karim, Mehrin. 2017. 'What Drives Footwear Exports of Vietnam and Cambodia'. *The Financial Express*. 30 April. Available at http://print.thefinancialexpress-bd.com/2017/04/30/171259.

Korhonen, Pekka. 1994. 'The Theory of the Flying Geese Pattern of Development and Its Interpretations'. *Journal of Peace Research* 31(1): 93–108.

Kuah, Khun E. 2000. 'Negotiating Central, Provincial, and County Policies: Border Trading in Southern China'. In *Where China Meets Southeast Asia: Social & Cultural Change in the Border Regions*, edited by Grant Evans, Chris Hutton and Khun Eng Kuah, 72–97. Bangkok: Institute of Southeast Asian Studies.

Lee, Yimou and Wa Lone. 2017. 'China's $10 Billion Strategic Project in Myanmar Sparks Local Ire'. *Reuters Business News*. 9 June. Available at https://www.reuters.com/article/us-china-silkroad-myanmar-sez/chinas-10-billion-strategic-project-in-myanmar-sparks-local-ire-idUSKBN18Z327. Accessed on 30 April 2019.

Lu, Yang. 2013a. 'Dongguan, the World's Factory in Transition, Part I'. *China Briefing*, 27 February, Business Intelligence by Dezan Shira & Associates. Available at http://www.china-briefing.com/news/2013/02/27/dongguan-the-worlds-factory-in-transition-part-i.html. Accessed on 28 March 2018.

————. 2013b. 'Dongguan, the World's Factory in Transition, Part II'. *China Briefing*, 28 February, Business Intelligence by Dezan Shira & Associates. Available at http://www. china-briefing.com/news/2013/02/28/dongguan-the-worlds-factory-in-transition-part-ii. html. Accessed on 28 March 2018.

Mitchell, Tom. 2008. 'China's Shoe Industry Under Pressure'. *Financial Times*, 25 February. Available at https://www.ft.com/content/4ed810c0-e3c8-11dc-8799-0000779fd2ac. Accessed on 28 March 2018.

Morrison, Wayne M. 2017. *China's Economic Rise: History, Trends, Challenges, and Implications for the United States*. Washington DC: Congressional Research Service.

Reddick, James and Cindy Co. 2017. 'In Cambodia's Chinese-Language Schools, a Hard Push for Soft Power'. *The Phnom Penh Post*. 18 December. Available at https://www.phnompenhpost. com/national-post-depth/cambodias-chinese-language-schools-hard-push-soft-power. Accessed on 30 April 2019.

Singh, Swaran. 2016. 'Rebuilding Lifelines of Its Soft Underbelly: China Engages Its Southwest Frontiers'. In *The New Great Game: China and South and Central Asia in the Era of Reform*, edited by Thomas Fingar, 147–170. Stanford, CA: Stanford University Press.

Tian, Liu and Zhongxia Rong. 2016. 'China's Belt and Road Initiative to Unlock Laos Economic Potential'. *Global Times*. 4 September. Available at http://www.globaltimes.cn/ content/1004596.shtml. Accessed on 30 April 2019.

Than, Mya. 2005. 'Myanmar's Cross-Border Economic Relations and Cooperation with the People's Republic of China and Thailand in the Greater Mekong Subregion.' *Journal of Greater Mekong Subregion Development Studies*, 2(October): 2005, 37–54.

Wade, Robert H. 1994. *Governing the Market: Economic Theory and the Role of Government in East Asian Industrialization*. Princeton, NJ: Princeton University Press.

Wang, Rong and Ping Li. 1998. 'Lancangjiang xiayou diqu kouan jianshe guihua yanjiu baogao' (A research report on the construction and planning for the crossings at the lower reach of the Lancang river). *Jingji Luntan* (*Economic Forum*) 107: 24–50.

Yang, Chun. 2016. 'Relocating Labor-Intensive Manufacturing Firms from China to Southeast Asia: A Preliminary Investigation'. *Journal of the Global South* 3(3): 1-13. Available at doi:10.1186/s40728-016-0031-4.

Yeung, Henry Wai-chung. 2016. *Strategic Coupling: East Asian Industrial Transformation in the New Global Economy*. Ithaca, NY: Cornell University Press.

# From Labour to Capital Mobility

# 7

# Skills Development Initiatives and Labour Migration in a Secondary Circuit of Globalized Production

## Evidence from the Garment Industry in India

ASHA KUZHIPARAMBIL

## Introduction

Global circuits strategically organize production processes across new sites through the conjoint actions of a set of actors such as firms, cities, states, and other sectors (Beaverstock et al., 2002). These actors perform important functions in production circuits and shape the geographies of capital and labour at global, national, and subnational scales. A city centre becomes a critical node in the circuits of production by facilitating an environment for the consolidation of hyper-mobile capital and for the provisioning of skilled labour, depending on its strategic positioning and its partnership with other actors. The highly specialized cross-border circuits corresponding to specific industries, more precisely those components of industries that are operating across national borders, connect a series of cities embedded within a nation to the global city network (Sassen, 2001). Therefore, the opening up of economies to the global market and the increasingly interconnected space of flows of labour, capital, knowledge, and goods have secondary consequences within a nation. At the same time, the relentless search for new sites of production and service activities across borders by the new transnational lead firms reproduces more globally integrated and sophisticated production networks by consolidating capital and labour for value creation under different systems of production and by promoting regional development through strategic partnerships between actors (Coe et al., 2010; Coe and Hess, 2013).

Therefore, the global production networks framework calls for a dynamic approach to understand the complex and evolutionary nature of the relationship between state and firm as well as the relationship between fluidity and fixity of both labour and capital (Rainnie, Herod, and McGrath-Champ, 2011; Yeung, 2013). This framework also recognizes the inevitable linkages of households, enterprises, and states to one another in the circuits of production (Gereffi, Korzeniewicz, and Korzeniewicz, 1994; Coe and Yeung, 2015) and provides helpful insights into investigating the capital–labour dynamics and the spatialities of new sites of production within a nation. In this context, this chapter attempts to integrate the study of the concentration of capital in urban spaces and the mobility of labour from rural to urban areas in India. The chapter illustrates how the garment production circuit connects a series of urban spaces with their rural counterparts by examining the consolidation of capital and mobilities of labour, with a particular focus on the institutional governance and the socio-economic and cultural forces influencing labour mobility within India.

First, the chapter examines the consolidation of capital in the garment industry since the Multifibre Arrangement (MFA) regime. For this purpose, the study identifies the district-wise garment clusters by mapping the Apparel Export Promotion Council's (AEPC) new database of 8,953 registered manufacturers and merchant exporters across India. The major export-oriented garment production clusters are located in urban centres, such as Bangalore, Chennai, Tirupur, and Delhi (Figure 7.1). These clusters attract circular migrants from nearby villages to a large extent.

Second, the chapter examines the importance of state policies in facilitating regional labour mobility to these garment clusters. The chapter analyses the strategic sourcing of workers from rural areas to garment clusters in urban centres through state policies, using a new database of 133,216 garment trainees across India. The primary data on the trainees and employed garment workers under the Skill Development Initiative Scheme (SDIS) were collected from the Ministry of Rural Development. The data comprise details about the trainees, training centres, and job placement across India. The training and placement of unemployed rural youth are organized through a public–private partnership between the Government of India and the garment manufacturers. The chapter shows that state-sponsored SDIS in collaboration with private institutions and garment manufacturers are critical nodes that facilitate provisioning of skilled labour for garment clusters in urban agglomerations and counter-magnet areas.

Third, the chapter examines the socio-economic and cultural context in which the garment workers from the villages are trained and employed in the urban industrial clusters by providing specific insight into the recruitment, training, and job placement of the trainees.

The rest of the chapter is organized as follows. In the next section, I provide an overview of garment clusters in India and the geographic concentration of garment producers in urban and peri-urban regions and explain the dependence of these clusters on circular migrants from rural areas. The following section examines the relevance of skills development policies for the rural population in order to illustrate the ways in which the supply of skilled labour to garment clusters across India is sustained. This is followed by an examination of the nuances involved in the recruitment of rural unemployed youth to the skills development centres in order to facilitate regional labour mobility from rural to urban areas. The final section provides concluding remarks on linking mobilities of capital and labour in the Indian garment industry.

# Indian Garment Clusters: Consolidation of Capital in the Urban Centres

The Indian garment industry is heterogeneous in nature with a network of diverse actors linking the formal to the informal sectors, multiple production centres strategically diversified across different regions, and significantly contributing both to the export and domestic market. The garment industry has undergone structural changes with the dismantling of quantitative restrictions imposed under the MFA regime (1974–2004). The MFA governed the export of textile and garment from Asian countries to Europe and the USA by imposing quota restrictions. The Agreement on Textiles and Clothing (ATC) at the General Agreement on Tariffs and Trade (GATT) in the Uruguay Round completely terminated the quota system on 1 January 2005. A consolidation of capital has taken place in the post-MFA regime favouring the large Tier-1 garment manufacturers globally (Merk, 2014). India is one of the leading exporters of readymade garments after China, Bangladesh, Italy, Germany, and Vietnam (Ministry of Textiles, 2016). The Indian garment industry consists of domestic manufacturers, manufacturer–exporters, fabricators, and merchant exporters and traders (Unni and Bali, 2002). Although there is consolidation at the upper tiers of the industry post MFA, state policies of reserving of readymade garment making for Small and Medium sized Enterprises (SME), and the local management of the MFA quota, led to industrial fragmentation and informalization (Mezzadri, 2010 and 2014a). However, informality is an intrinsic feature of the Indian economy with 93 per cent of the labour force working in the unorganized sector and contributing around 60 per cent of Gross Domestic Product (Harriss-White and Gooptu, 2009). Therefore, public policies are deliberated on the basis of the historical prevalence of India's decentralized production that integrates formal factory regimes with the varied informal systems of production, involving even home-based workers in villages—a system organized and integrated into its cultural context.

Figure 7.1 illustrates the regional concentration of the AEPC-registered manufacturer and merchant exporters in India. The number of registered exporters in the AEPC during the quota regime was very high as the manufacturers tended to register multiple units to accrue benefits through the quota system. For example, the registered members in AEPC were 17,504 in 1990 and that rose substantially to 27,312 by 2000. By 2013, out of the 8,953 registered garment exporters (Figure 7.1), 60.24 per cent are manufacturer exporters. The AEPC has classified the garment exporters across India into four regions: north, south, east, and west. Mostly the exporters registered in the southern region are in the states of Tamil Nadu (32.35 per cent) and Karnataka (3.49 per cent). In Tamil Nadu, the manufacturers are concentrated in Tiruppur (2,152), Chennai (384), Coimbatore (107), Erode (66), Karur (51), Salem (38), and Madurai (23). Tiruppur is the fifth-largest urban agglomeration in Tamil Nadu and is also known as the cotton-knitwear capital

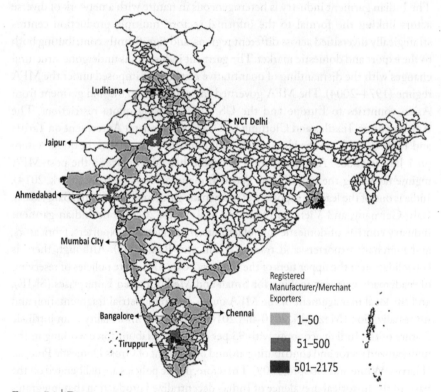

Figure 7.1 | District-wise registered garment manufacturer/merchant exporters

*Source*: Author's calculation using AEPC Exporter Directory, October 2013.

*Note*: Map not to scale and does not represent authentic international boundaries.

of India. The Tiruppur textile and garment industry, a cluster classified under the SME scheme, consists of 7,010 units specialized in garment making, fabric knitting, dyeing, bleaching, printing, embroidery, and other ancillary activities. This cluster provides employment to more than 200,000 workers. The other urban agglomerations such as Chennai, Coimbatore, Erode, and Madurai are also major sourcing destinations for textile products and woven garments. In Karnataka, the manufacturers are registered in the Bangalore Urban district (300) with the maximum concentration of factories in the suburban industrial areas of Peenya, Yeswanthpur, Bommasandra, Bommanahalli, and Rajajinagar. According to the Annual Survey of Industries 2016 (ASI) in Karnataka, there were 6,765 factories and 35,798 people were employed in the manufacturing of wearing apparel and dressing and dyeing of fur (Department of Planning, Programme Monitoring and Statistics, 2016). In the same year, 2,769 units were engaged in the manufacturing of textiles, employing 16,855 people (Department of Planning, Programme Monitoring and Statistics, 2016). The number of workers and units are, however, grossly underestimated due to the large-scale subcontracting and informal work involved in the garment industry across these clusters.

In the northern region, garment manufacturer exporters are concentrated in the National Capital Territory of Delhi (NCT) (24.33 per cent), Uttar Pradesh (5.56 per cent), Haryana (5.31 per cent), Rajasthan (4.09 per cent), and Punjab (7.40 per cent). The maximum concentration of manufacturers is in the National Capital Region (NCR) that consists of NCT Delhi and many surrounding districts from the states of Haryana, Uttar Pradesh, and Rajasthan. NCT Delhi has 2,175 manufacturers. Gautam Buddha Nagar and Ghaziabad in Uttar Pradesh have 384 and 30 manufacturers respectively, and Gurgaon and Faridabad in Haryana have 351 and 103 manufacturers respectively. The NCR Planning Board has selected nine counter-magnet areas that have the potential for growth, and those are the zones for possible migration. One of the identified counter-magnet areas for NCR is Jaipur in Rajasthan. Jaipur has 345 manufacturers and is an important centre for power loom textiles, hand block printing, and readymade garments. Ludhiana in Punjab has 603 registered manufacturers and contributes significantly to domestic and export markets from the northern region. The Ministry of Micro, Small and Medium Enterprises (MSME) recorded 14,000 manufacturing units employing 400,000 workers in the textile and garment industry in Ludhiana.

The manufacturers in the western region are concentrated in states like Maharashtra (11.9 per cent) and Gujarat (0.93 per cent). Mumbai city, Mumbai Suburban, Thane, Pune, and Kolhapur are the major centres of production in Maharashtra. The state has 2,068 textile units and 1,045 wearing apparel units (Directorate of Economics and Statistics, 2016). Ahmedabad and Surat in Gujarat have 52 and 17 garment manufacturers respectively. In the eastern region, the manufacturers are mainly located in West Bengal (3.17 per cent) with the highest number of manufacturers in Kolkata (248 manufacturers) producing primarily for the domestic market.

Each of these regional zones comprises several clusters with product specializations. For example, Tiruppur in south India and Ludhiana in north India specialize in the production of knitwear. Jaipur in Rajasthan in north India specializes in the manufacture of handicrafts and traditional prints. Bangalore in Karnataka and Chennai in Tamil Nadu within the southern region specialize in the production of trousers and structured garments. Apart from the specific historical origins of these clusters in these regions, recent location choices by manufacturers are also affected by state-led industrial and land-use policies. However, the geographical concentration of garment exporters around urban centres and low-cost peri-metropolitan areas clearly indicates the existence of agglomeration economies including the advantages of buyer–supplier linkages resulting from co-location of industries and the availability of labour through migration from the peripheries and rural hinterlands.

The garment industry employed 12.3 million workers, and it constituted 43 per cent of total textile exports from India in 2015 (Ministry of Textiles, 2016). Garment manufacturing, the middle segment of the fashion chain, is the most fragmented, least technologically sophisticated, most geographically dispersed, and most labour-intensive part of the industry (Figueroa, 1996). This leads to the possibility of subcontracting production processes from large-scale factories to small units as well as to home-based workers. Thus, garment workers consist of subcontracted workers in home-based production units and workshops and formal and casual workers in the small, medium, and large-scale manufacturing units.

Garment clusters in specific geographical settings entail a specific set of local labour relations (Mezzadri, 2014b). Within south India, labour–capital relations vary from Bangalore in Karnataka to Tiruppur in Tamil Nadu. In the city of Bangalore, most of the large garment factories are located in the city peripheries, and these units employ local workers and migrants from nearby rural hinterlands. The workers come from within a radius of 250 kilometres from the city, which also includes some districts in the neighbouring states of Andhra Pradesh and Tamil Nadu (Pani and Nikky, 2014). A large number of migrant workers come from Bangalore Rural district. The factory-based production in this garment cluster enables recruitment of female workers in large numbers. The workers belong to socially and economically deprived sections of society and a majority of them live in rented houses with shared sanitation facilities and public standposts for drinking water (Rajasekhar, Suchitra, and Manjula, 2007).

The Tiruppur cluster in Tamil Nadu, known for the export of cotton knitwear, comprises an interconnected dynamic network of small firms primarily owned by a single caste group, the *gounders*, a former peasant and industrial working class who migrated from nearby villages (Chari, 2000). Increased job opportunities during the export boom in the late 1970s led to the inflow to this cluster of young male migrants from agrarian districts in the south such as Tirunelveli and Tanjavur (de Neve, 2003). During the 1980s and mid-1990s, female migrants within Tamil Nadu, who followed their families, and young female migrants from Kerala, were employed in stitching units (de Neve, 2003). The cluster has attracted many migrants from the rural hinterlands as well as impacted the transformation of the local rural economy (Heyer, 2013). Thus, apart from local workers, the Tiruppur cluster attracts migrant workers from different regions, castes, and classes. These workers are uniquely embedded in the garment industry through caste, kinship, and friendship ties.

Though labour–capital relations in different clusters vary within a regional zone, the garment industry depends on a large number of migrant workers across these clusters in India. It is also evident that there is a scarcity of skilled operators in the export-oriented garment clusters in the post-MFA regime. The migrant workers from rural hinterlands who come to the cities in search of job opportunities get recruited by the large-scale garment factories without any stitching skills or work experience. These garment factories are an attractive option for the young female migrants who are searching for their first job. The migrant workers hardly have access to any formal skill training in their villages. To bridge this skill gap, to upgrade labour conditions, and to increase the labour mobility from rural to urban, many skill development policies are undertaken by the Government of India. The next section will examine the SDIS for the garment industry in the context of demographic changes in the country.

# Skill Development to Meet the Demands of Global and Domestic Capital in India

After independence in 1947, the Indian economy was primarily dependent upon agriculture and its allied activities with the majority of the population residing in villages. The 1951 Census reported that 82.7 per cent of the population were rural and 69.7 per cent of the total workforce were agricultural workers consisting of cultivators and agricultural labourers. India continues to transition from an agriculture-dependent workforce to an industry-led workforce. To expand the role of private sector enterprises and accelerate foreign direct investment, the Government of India initiated an economic liberalization programme in the 1990s that consisted of a range of policies to deregulate industries, to amend the Industrial and Foreign Exchange Act, and to reform the financial sector. These policies were a major shift from the inward-oriented and protectionist *license raj* regime to outward and market-oriented policies and had far-reaching implications for accelerating the rural–urban transition. However, the 2011 Census reported a rural population that still represented 68.9 per cent of the national total, with agricultural workers representing 54.6 per cent of the labour force.

At the same time, the total population of India increased from 0.36 billion in 1951 to 1.21 billion in 2011, offering a demographic dividend with the ratio of working population rising from 55 per cent in 1991 to 60 per cent in the 2011 Census (Bhagat, 2014). The young population below the age of 29 years is projected to be 49.9 per cent by 2021, and the demographic dividend will continue until 2040 (Chenoy, 2013). There are several challenges to actively harnessing the growing working-age population, which include providing skill training to the workforce and increasing female workforce participation (James, 2011; Thomas, 2014). The 61st National Sample Survey, July 2004–June 2005, (NSS) results reported that in India only 2 per cent of the workforce in the 15–29 age group had received formal vocational training and 8 per cent had received non-formal vocational training, compared with 96 per cent in Korea, 75 per cent in Germany, 80 per cent in Japan, and 68 per cent in the UK (Planning Commission, 2008). This presents many implementation challenges for 'India's massive skills development ambitions' (King, 2012: 665).

To benefit from the demographic transition, state-led development policies have to focus on training the youth, both male and female, to ensure that the excess labour supply in the country is effectively channelized for economic growth and sustainable development (Chandrasekhar, Ghosh, and Roychowdhury, 2006; Bhagat, 2014; Talreja, 2014). The 11th Five-Year Plan (2007–2012) proposed to launch the National Skill Development Mission (NSDM) to create a pool of skilled personnel to cater to domestic demand from growing sectors of the economy as well as to benefit from the growing global demand for skilled labour. Consequently, the first National Policy on Skill Development (NPSD) was formulated in 2009 and superseded by the National Policy on Skill Development and Entrepreneurship (NPSDE) in 2015. The National Skill Development Corporation (NSDC) was established in 2009 to promote collaboration with the private sector to implement short-term skill training programmes. The skill gap study conducted by the NSDC between 2011 and 2014 indicated a requirement of 109.73 million skilled workers by 2022 in 24 key sectors (NPSDE, 2015). The study also reported the need to reduce the human resource requirement in agriculture from 240.4 million in 2013 to 215.6 million by 2022.

Some of the sectors that require additional skilled workers are automobile and automobile components, food processing, telecommunication, IT and information technology enabled services (ITES), electronics and IT hardware, and pharma and life sciences. One of the key sectors is textile and garment with a projected human resource requirement of 21.54 million by 2022 (NPSDE, 2015). The textile and garment industry, both organized and unorganized, provides employment to many workers with poor socio-economic backgrounds. Special skill development schemes were initiated by the Ministry of Rural Development and Ministry of Textiles for training the unemployed, rural youth to equip them with employable skills in the industry. The training and job placement of the unemployed youth were organized through public–private partnerships between the Government of India, training institutions, and garment manufacturers.

The Ministry of Textiles, through the Apparel Training & Design Centre (ATDC), initiated a special project called Skills for Manufacturing of Apparel through Research and Training (SMART) in October 2010. The ATDC founded 196 training centres across India. The objective of the SMART project was to train a total of 235,000 trainees by 2017. These were short-term courses of 45 days sponsored by the Ministry of Textiles under the Integrated Skill Development Scheme (ISDS). The aim of this programme was to remove entry-level barriers for unskilled workers by providing them training in industrial sewing machine operation, and thus creating an industry-ready skilled workforce. From October 2010 to May 2014, ATDC-SMART trained 116,296 trainees, of which 16.30 per cent were in Rajasthan, 15.85 per cent in Tamil Nadu, 12.89 per cent in Odisha, 8.90 per cent in Madhya Pradesh, 6.90 per cent in Karnataka, 5.63 per cent in Bihar, and 4.53 per cent in Uttar Pradesh. Out of all the trainees, 85 per cent were women, and about 79 per cent were from rural and semi-urban areas. The trainees were from different social backgrounds with 35 per cent belonging to the General category, 31 per cent to Other Backward Castes (OBC), 20 per cent to Scheduled Castes (SC), 7 per cent to Scheduled Tribes (ST), and 6 per cent to minority communities (Ministry of Textiles, 2014). The focus of the project was to provide skill training to underprivileged sections of the society with very low levels of education. Therefore, the educational requirement for the SMART short-term courses was elementary schooling for sewing machine operator and secondary schooling for apparel finisher and checker.

Similar to the SMART project, the Ministry of Rural Development partnered with private enterprises to implement special projects for skilling the below poverty line (BPL) youth under the Swarnajayanti Gram Swarozgar Yojana (SGSY) to alleviate rural poverty. One such special project was the Skills for Employment in Apparel Manufacturing (SEAM) by Infrastructure Leasing & Financial Services Private Limited (IL&FS) implemented under the IL&FS Cluster Development Initiative Limited. The SEAM project envisaged a thirty-day course to train shop floor workers from the villages for the garment industry. The SEAM project was conducted in 11 phases and the first phase, SEAM 1, was initiated in August 2007. The target group for the free training was unemployed rural youth from BPL families and socially deprived sections of society who were in the 18-30 age group.

A centrally planned and locally organized skill development programme in collaboration with the private sector has implications in shaping the geographies of labour–capital dynamics within India. The next section will examine the SEAM in detail to provide insights into the specific socio-economic and cultural context in which the recruitment, training, and job placement of the trainees into the garment clusters took place.

## Skilled Labour for Garment Clusters from Rural Milieu

The SEAM training centres were set up in 129 districts in 20 states. The total number of trainees recruited between 2007 and 2014 included 70 per cent female trainees. The SEAM recruited the trainees with the help of mobilizers that included NGO workers and school teachers. The canvassing and mobilization of trainees from villages required managerial skills to communicate and convince the block- and village-level officials. The role of village *sarpanch* (elected head) was crucial in convincing the families to send their young daughters to the training programme. Nambiar (2013) provides a detailed description of the processes of mobilization, advertisement and job fairs, with field studies from Tamil Nadu, New Delhi, and Rajasthan. These trainees belonged to poor households. Among the total SEAM trainees, 33.27 per cent were from General category, 26.28 per cent belonged to OBC, 25.05 per cent were SC, 12.57 per cent were ST, and 2.83 per cent were minorities. After successful completion of the course the candidate would be placed in garment factories across India, and, therefore, they should be willing to migrate for work outside their state. Figure 7.2 provides education details of the SEAM trainees. These trainees belonged to socially and economically deprived sections of society, and, as a result, most of them could not afford education. Out of the total trainees up until 2014, 61.55 per cent had only primary education and 28.15 per cent had secondary education. This meant that 89.70 per cent of the trainees did not have schooling higher than eighth standard.

Figure 7.3 illustrates the district-wise presence of the SEAM training centres across India. In south India, the SEAM centres are in Karnataka, Tamil Nadu, Kerala, Andhra Pradesh, and Telangana. Out of the 133,216 trainees, 30.19 per cent were trained in Tamil Nadu, 19.54 per cent in Karnataka, 8.82 per cent in Andhra Pradesh, 1.67 per cent in Telangana, and 0.93 per cent in Kerala. Tamil Nadu has training centres in its 22 districts with a large number of trainees from the districts of Kancheepuram, Tiruppur, Coimbatore, Virudunagar, Madurai, and Thiruvallur. In Karnataka, the training centres are in 12 districts with the trainees mainly coming from Bangalore Urban, Bangalore Rural, Kolar, Bagalkot, Mandya, Chamrajnagar, and Mysore. In Andhra Pradesh, training centres are in eight

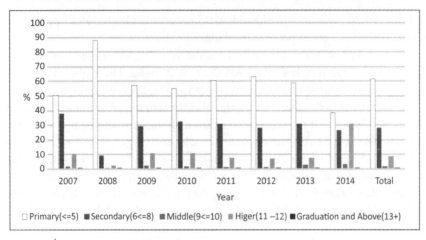

Figure 7.2 | Education of SEAM trainees

*Source*: Author's calculation using SEAM data.

districts with trainees registered from Visakhapatnam, Chittoor, West Godavari, Anantapur, Guntur, and Nellore. SEAM trainees in Telangana came from Ranga Reddy, Hyderabad, and Nalgonda. Kerala has training centres in Wayanad, Thrissur, Kannur, Thiruvananthapuram, Ernakulam, Kozhikode, and Kasaragod. The SEAM trainees from north Indian states of Haryana, Uttar Pradesh, Punjab, Rajasthan, and Uttarakhand were only 5.96 per cent of the total. In western India, the SEAM centres are in Gujarat (1.49 per cent) and Maharashtra (2.96 per cent). In eastern India, SEAM centres have been set up in Bihar (8.24 per cent), Odisha (8.93 per cent), Jharkhand (2.99 per cent), and West Bengal (1.79 per cent). In central India, trainees were trained from the SEAM centres in Chhattisgarh (2.12 per cent) and Madhya Pradesh (2.61 per cent).

Figure 7.3 shows two significant patterns. First, 61.15 per cent of the total trainees were trained in centres set up in the south Indian states of Tamil Nadu, Karnataka, Andhra Pradesh, Telangana, and Kerala. There exists in those south Indian states a large concentration of registered exporters (Figure 7.1). This clearly means that training centres are strategically located to cater to the requirements of these garment clusters. Second, the SEAM centres are present in the east Indian states, such as Bihar, Jharkhand, and Odisha, and central Indian states, such as Chhattisgarh and Madhya Pradesh that have the largest BPL populations. The purpose of skill training sponsored by the Ministry of Rural Development under the SEAM project was to alleviate rural poverty by enabling employment opportunities. Most of the trainees in these states belonged to socially and economically deprived sections of the society. In particular, the percentage of trainees belonging to OBC, SC, ST, and minority communities in these states was very high: 84.68 per cent in Bihar; 99.20 per cent in Jharkhand; 91.15 per cent in Odisha; 96.81 per cent in Chhattisgarh; and 86.06 per cent in Madhya Pradesh.

Figure 7.4 presents the district-wise enrolment of SEAM trainees across India. The trainees were recruited from 406 districts in India. The higher number of training centres in south and east India enabled more trainees from these states (and adjacent districts from other states) to enrol in the training programme. Figure 7.4 clearly points out that the trainees come from all the surrounding regions to the districts where the SEAM training centres are located (Figure 7.3). A field study of Hinjilicut's SEAM training centre at Ganjam district in Odisha (Kuzhiparambil, 2015) revealed that the trainees came from villages, and, therefore, the village *sarpanch* played a crucial role in convincing the families to send their children for the training. Although the SEAM training centres were only in 8 districts in Odisha,

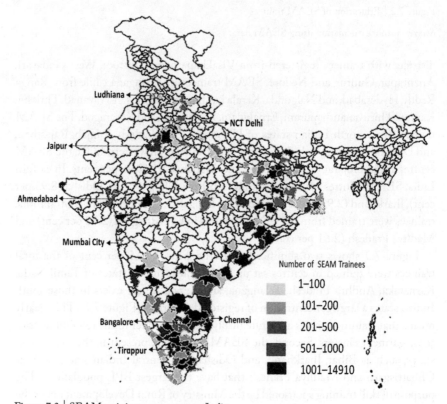

Figure 7.3 | SEAM training centres across India

*Source*: Author's calculation using SEAM data, Ministry of Rural Development.

*Note*: Map not to scale and does not represent authentic international boundaries.

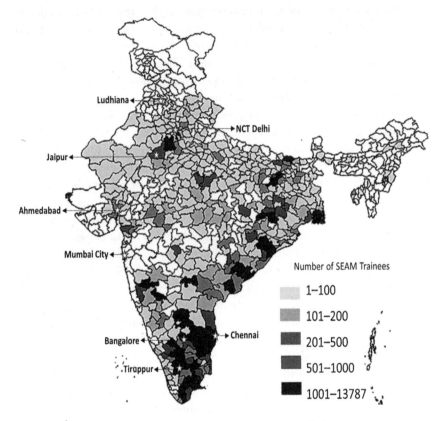

Figure 7.4 | District-wise enrolment of the SEAM trainees across India

*Source*: Author's calculation using SEAM data, Ministry of Rural Development.

*Note*: Map not to scale and does not represent authentic international boundaries.

namely, Ganjam, Sundargarh, Kandhamal, Khordha, Gajapati, Balangir, Malkangiri, and Subarnapur, the trainees were recruited from all the 30 districts of the state.

The garment industry is known for its feminized workforce. There is an increasing feminization in the garment factories in the organized sector in the major south Indian garment hubs, such as Bangalore, Chennai, and Tiruppur, producing for the export market. In south India, the female enrolees for the SEAM training were 87.27 per cent of the total trainees. Similarly, states such as Odisha, Chhattisgarh, and West Bengal in east India; states such as Gujarat and Maharashtra in west India; and states such as Manipur and Tripura in north-east India also had high proportions of female trainees. In the primary study of a SEAM centre in Odisha, Kuzhiparambil (2015) noted that parents were not willing to send their daughters for the skill training and employment in the garment factories due to cultural norms. Through successful mobilization and canvassing by the SEAM workers and assurances from *sarpanch*es in the villages, more and more parents started sending their daughters over the years. These mobilizers also advertised the case of successful trainees, their job placement, and how they could financially help their families through this programme.

The gender profile of trainees was quite different in north and central India, with states such as Bihar, Jharkhand, Rajasthan, Haryana, Uttar Pradesh, Uttarakhánd, Punjab, and Madhya Pradesh, recording mainly male trainees. Out of the total SEAM trainees, 20.29 per cent of the trainees were from these states. The female trainees from these states constituted just 20.63 per cent of the total. The workers from these states mainly find work in the Delhi NCR and its counter-magnet areas. A primary study in Delhi by Neetha and Mazumdar (2010) reported that female workers in the garment factories ranged between 8 and 27 per cent. They also reported that many female factory workers were married, with children, and were 26 to 35 years of age. Another survey in the region by Srivastava (Mezzadri and Srivastava, 2015) reported that a majority of the workers were male and first-generation migrants from rural areas. In the organized factory sector, the garment industry provides the largest source of employment for women in Delhi. However, when considering both organized and unorganized segments, most of the workers in the garment industry are men. The selection criterion for the SEAM trainees is the age group of 18 to 30 years. Therefore, apart from the social and cultural norms dictating female labour force participation in the north, the lower proportion of female trainees also needs to be seen in the context of the higher average age of female factory workers in these regions.

When the SEAM training was initiated in 2007, the average age of female trainees was 24 years and that of male trainees was 23 years. By the year 2014, the average age of female trainees reduced to 21.5 years and that of male trainees was reduced to 22 years. The selection of trainees based on the age criterion was designed to ensure youth training. In the garment industry, such selection criteria have positive effects. The younger the skilled workforce joining the garment industry, the higher their productivity and longer the duration of their service to the industry. A study of female workers conducted in the KINFRA Apparel Park at Thiruvananthapuram in Kerala identified many young and unmarried female migrants from Odisha (Kuzhiparambil, 2015). These workers were trained by the SEAM training centres in Odisha and later migrated to Kerala through the industry-led placement programme to work in the garment factories. The average age of the Odia worker in KINFRA Apparel Park was 21 years when compared with the age of Keralite workers (30 years) who were not trained and placed through the training programme (Kuzhiparambil, 2015).

Figure 7.5 presents the job placement of the trained workers in different garment clusters. Out of the 111,559 employed workers, 79.65 per cent of the them were placed in the south Indian clusters, consisting of states such as Tamil Nadu (43.10 per cent), Karnataka (25.95 per cent), Andhra Pradesh (5.73 per cent), Kerala (2.89 per cent), and Telangana (1.98 per cent). In Tamil Nadu, the workers were employed in Kancheepuram, Coimbatore, Tiruppur, Virudunagar, Madurai, Erode, Karur, Chennai, Thiruvallur, and Tiruchirappalli. In Karnataka, they were mainly placed in Bangalore Urban, Bangalore Rural, Mandya, Mysore, Belgaum, Kolar, and Ramanagara. In Andhra Pradesh, they were placed in Visakhapatnam, Guntur, Chittoor, West Godavari, Prakasam, and Nellore. In Telangana, they were placed in Ranga Reddy, Nalgonda, Medak, and Hyderabad. In Kerala, they were placed in the industrial parks in Ernakulam and Thiruvananthapuram.

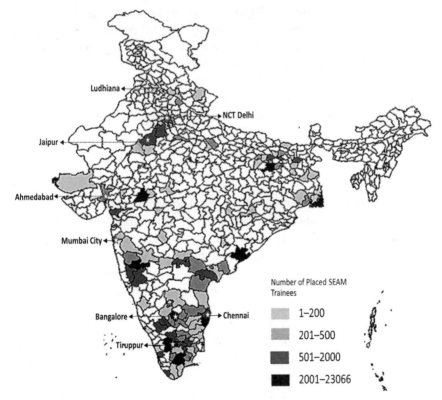

Figure 7.5 | District-wise job placement of SEAM trainees

*Source*: Author's calculation using SEAM data, Ministry of Rural Development.

*Note*: Map not to scale and does not represent authentic international boundaries.

In north India, the total placed workers were 5.24 per cent with placement in Alwar and Jaipur in Rajasthan; Gautam Buddha Nagar, Agra, and Unnao in Uttar Pradesh; and Faridabad and Gurgaon in Haryana. These districts come under the Delhi NCR and its counter- magnet areas. In western India, 4.97 per cent of the trainees were placed in Surat, Ahmedabad, and Gandhinagar in Gujarat and Sangli and Kolhapur in Maharashtra. In east India, 6.67 per cent of the trainees were mainly placed in Bihar in the districts of Gaya, Patna, Bhagalpur, Aurangabad, Buxar, Samastipur, Nawada, and Jehanabad. The trainees from Odisha, Chhattisgarh, and Jharkhand were employed majorly in the garment clusters in other states. Only 3.14 per cent were placed in central India, mainly in Madhya Pradesh.

Out of the total placed trainees, 21.81 per cent of the workers were placed outside their home state. In Tamil Nadu, 18.32 per cent of the workers were migrants. In Kerala, 85.14 per cent were migrant workers from Odisha, Chhattisgarh, and Jharkhand. In Karnataka, 26.67 per cent were migrants. From Figure 7.5, it is clear that a large number of the SEAM trainees are employed in the garment clusters in south India. The sourcing of labour through the skill development centres are strategically located to cater to the needs of the garment clusters. Training the workers at their native place through the SDIS ensures a steady supply of skilled and productive workforce to the garment industry. Therefore, the current pattern from Figures 7.1, 7.3, 7.4, and 7.5 shows that labour migrates to the centres of production in the urban agglomerations and counter-magnet regions where capital consolidates.

## Conclusion

This chapter adds to the literature on the role of extra-firm actors in facilitating the mobilities of labour and capital through SDIS and favourable industrial policies for value creation in global production networks. Using the case of the garment industry in India, this chapter has explored the role of state development policies in shaping the regional geographies of labour and capital. For this purpose, the study identifies and maps the district-wise garment clusters and the sources and destinations of garment workers. The state becomes an active agent in governing regional labour mobility and in complementing global production networks by enabling the processes of identifying, canvassing, training, and placing workers in the garment clusters. The chapter also contributes to the literature on labour–capital dynamics and the spatialities of new sites of production by examining locally embedded labour–capital relations and rural–urban linkages in garment clusters across India. The study identifies the geographic concentration of garment manufacturers around urban centres and the state-induced mobility of skilled workers from rural areas to the industrial clusters. To conclude, the study points out that the strategic partnership between actors in the production network can shape the fixity and fluidity of labour–capital relations resulting in different regional development outcomes.

The SDIS by the Government of India aim to channel the country's demographic dividend into the growing sectors of the economy by providing industry-specific skill training to youth and thereby prepare the nation to become a key site for global production circuits. The state-sponsored planned intervention to smoothen the transition from an agriculture-dependent economy to an industry-driven economy requires a focus on imparting skills to rural youth and facilitating their mobility into the urban areas. This development strategy depends on transferring surplus labour from agriculture and its allied activities to the industrial sector to ensure an adequate supply of labour for production centres. The trainees in the SEAM centres are unemployed rural youth from poor households who are willing to migrate to other states. The job creation through the SDIS can be viewed as opportunities for unemployed youth from the rural hinterlands to integrate into globalized production circuits. At the same time, the transformation of the rural economy depends partly on the connections it is making to the urban centres via skilled labour supply. To conclude, the state-sponsored SDIS in collaboration with private institutions and garment manufacturers is a critical node which facilitates the provisioning of skilled labour to urban garment clusters.

# References

Beaverstock, Jonathan V., Marcus A. Doel, Phil J. Hubbard, and Peter J. Taylor. 2002. 'Attending to the World: Competition, Cooperation and Connectivity in the World City Network'. *Global Networks* 2(2): 111–132.

Bhagat, Ram B. 2014. 'The Opportunities and Challenges of Demographic Dividend in India'. *Jharkhand Journal of Development and Management Studies* 12(4): 6099–6113.

Chandrasekhar, C. P., Jayati Ghosh, and Anamitra Roychowdhury. 2006. 'The Demographic Dividend and Young India's Economic Future'. *Economic and Political Weekly* 41(49): 5055–5064.

Chari, Sharad. 2000. 'The Agrarian Origins of the Knitwear Industrial Cluster in Tiruppur, India'. *World Development* 28(3): 579–599.

Chenoy, Dilip. 2013. 'Public–Private Partnership to Meet the Skills Challenges in India'. In *Skills Development for Inclusive and Sustainable Growth in Developing Asia-Pacific*, edited by Rupert Maclean, Shanti Jagannathan and Jouko Sarvi, 181–194. New York: Asian Development Bank and Springer.

Coe, Neil M., Peter Dicken, Martin Hess, and Henry Wai-Cheung Yeung. 2010. 'Making Connections: Global Production Networks and World City Networks'. *Global Networks* 10(1): 138–149.

Coe, Neil M. and Martin Hess. 2013. 'Global Production Networks, Labour and Development'. *Geoforum* 44(1): 4–9.

Coe, Neil. M. and Henry Wai-Chung Yeung. 2015. *Global Production Networks: Theorizing Economic Development in an Interconnected World*. Oxford, UK: Oxford University Press.

Department of Planning, Programme Monitoring and Statistics. 2016. *Economic Survey of Karanaka*. Government of Karnataka.

Directorate of Economics and Statistics. 2016. *Economic Survey of Maharashtra*. Mumbai: Government of Maharashtra.

Figueroa, Hector. 1996. 'In the Name of Fashion Exploitation in the Garment Industry'. *NACLA Report on the Americas* 29(4): 34–41.

Gereffi, Gary, Miguel Korzeniewicz, and Roberto P. Korzeniewicz. 1994. 'Introduction: Global Commodity Chains'. In *Commodity Chains and Global Capitalism*, edited by Gary Gereffi and Miguel Korzeniewicz, 1–14. Westport, CT: Praeger.

Harriss-White, B. and Nandini Gooptu. 2009. 'Mapping India's World of Unorganized Labour'. *Socialist Register* 37(37): 89–118.

Heyer, Judith. 2013. 'Integration into a Global Production Network: Impacts on Labour in Tiruppur's Rural Hinterlands'. *Oxford Development Studies* 41(3): 307–321.

James, K. S. 2011. 'India's Demographic Change: Opportunities and Challenges'. *Science* 333(6042): 576–580.

King, Kenneth. 2012. 'The Geopolitics and Meanings of India's Massive Skills Development Ambitions'. *International Journal of Educational Development* 32(5): 665–673.

Kuzhiparambil, Asha. 2015. 'Dynamics of Labour Relations across Different Circuits of Globalisation: Evidence from Garment Making and Cashew Nut Processing Circuits in Kerala'. Unpublished PhD dissertation. School of Social Science, NIAS/Manipal University.

Merk, Jeroen. 2014. 'The Rise of Tier 1 Firms in the Global Garment Industry: Challenges for Labour Rights Advocates'. *Oxford Development Studies* 42(2): 259–277.

Mezzadri, Alessandra. 2010. 'Globalisation, Informalisation and the State in the Indian Garment Industry'. *International Review of Sociology* 20(3): 491–511.

———. 2014a. 'Backshoring, Local Sweatshop Regimes and CSR in India'. *Competition & Change* 18(4): 327–344.

———. 2014b. 'Indian Garment Clusters and CSR Norms: Incompatible Agendas at the Bottom of the Garment Commodity Chain'. *Oxford Development Studies* 42(2): 238–258.

Mezzadri, Alessandra and Ravi Srivastava. 2015. *Labour Regimes in the Indian Garment Sector: Capital-Labour Relations, Social Reproduction and Labour Standards in the National Capital Region*. Report of the ESRC-DFID research project 'Labor Standards and the Working Poor in China and India'. Centre for Development Policy and Research. Available at https://www.soas.ac.uk/cdpr/publications/reports/file106927.pdf. Accessed on 23 March 2017.

Ministry of Textiles. 2014. *ATDC-Blue Print: Up-Skilling Apparel Sector: Imparting Skills, Improving lives*, Available at http://www.atdcindia.co.in/docs/Shortterm/ATDC_SMART_ Training_Project.pdf. Accessed on 11 January 2017.

———. 2016. *Annual Report 2015–2016*. Government of India. Available at http://texmin.nic. in/documents/annual-report. Accessed on 28 April 2019.

Nambiar, Divya. 2013. 'Creating Enterprising Subjects through Skill Development, the Network State, Network Enterprise, and Youth Aspirations in India'. In *Enterprise Culture in Neoliberal India: Studies in Youth, Class, Work and Media*, edited by Nandini Gooptu, 57–72. New York: Routledge.

Neetha, N. and Indrani Mazumdar. 2010. *Study on Conditions and Needs of Women Workers in Delhi.* New Delhi: Centre for Women's Development Studies. Available at http://www.cwds. ac.in/wp-content/uploads/2016/11/StudyonConditionsandNeedsofWomenWorkersinDelhi. pdf. Accessed on 11 February 2017.

de Neve, Geert. 2003. 'Expectations and Rewards of Modernity: Commitment and Mobility among Rural Migrants in Tirupur, Tamil Nadu'. *Contributions to Indian Sociology* 37(1–2): 251–280.

NPSDE (National Policy on Skill Development and Entrepreneurship). 2015. *National Policy for Skill Development and Entrepreneurship 2015.* Ministry of Skill Development and Entrepreneurship, Government of India. Available at http://www.skilldevelopment.gov.in/ assets/images/Skill%20India/policy%20booklet-%20Final.pdf. Accessed on 25 February 2017.

Pani, Narendar and Nikky Singh. 2014. *Women at the Threshold of Globalisation.* New Delhi: Routledge.

Planning Commission. 2008. *Inclusive Growth,* vol. 1 of *Eleventh Five-Year Plan, 2007–2012.* New Delhi: Oxford University Press.

Rainnie, Al, Andrew Herod, and Susan McGrath-Champ. 2011. 'Review and Positions: Global Production Networks and Labour'. *Competition & Change* 15(2): 155–169.

Rajasekhar, D., J. Y. Suchitra, and R. Manjula. 2007. 'Women Workers in Urban Informal Employment: The Status of Agarbathi and Garment Workers in Karnataka'. *Indian Journal of Labour Economics* 50(4): 835–846.

Sassen, Saskia. 2001. *The Global City: New York, London, Tokyo,* 2nd edn. Princeton, NJ: Princeton University Press.

Talreja, Chaitanya. 2014. 'India's Demographic Dividend: Realities and Opportunities'. *Indian Journal of Labour Economics* 57(1): 139–155.

Thomas, Jayan Jose. 2014. 'The Demographic Challenge and Employment Growth in India'. *Economic and Political Weekly* 49(6): 15–17.

Unni, Jeemol and Namrata Bali. 2002. 'Subcontracted Women Workers in the Garment Industry in India'. In *The Hidden Assembly Line: Gender Dynamics of Subcontracted Work in a Global Economy,* edited by Radhika Balakrishnan, 115–44. CT: Kumarian Press.

Yeung, Henry Wai-chung. 2013. 'Governing the Market in a Globalizing Era: Developmental States, Global Production Networks and Inter-firm Dynamics in East Asia'. *Review of International Political Economy* 21(1): 70–101.

# 8

# The Counter Geographies of Globalization

*Women's Labour Migration along the Nepal–Persian Gulf Migratory Corridor*

HARI KC

## Introduction

Although migration to India has remained an important source of people's livelihoods in Nepal for years, migration trends beyond India have massively increased in recent years with over 500,000 Nepalese migrating abroad for employment annually (ILO, 2018). A large segment of this migrant population comprises women who originate mainly from Nepal's small rural villages, where most people have adopted traditional mixed livelihood strategies that combine subsistence farming, livestock, and the extraction of local natural resources. The entrenched patriarchy and its various forms of gender-based discriminations and violence, and the penetration of the unregulated global markets even in the smallest of the villages are exerting a tremendous pressure on women's traditional livelihoods, lifestyles, and aspirations that now demand a monetary mode of production while most Nepalese women have been traditionally engaged in informal agricultural sectors and unpaid care and domestic work. The traditional, informal work that women perform does not get recognized even as 'work' in society, let alone monetarily paid. There is thus a disjuncture between the mode of production that Nepalese women have been traditionally involved in and the capitalist monetary mode of production required to address the transformed realities wrought by globalization. This disconnect operates as a powerful catalyst for pushing women out of the villages. Succinctly, Nepalese women's outmigration is a phenomenon resulting from an interplay between various intersecting and interlocking pre-existing systems of oppressions and the newly emerging pressures from global markets and climate change. In such a situation, migration has become a key survival strategy for many Nepalese women, despite the legal and institutional barriers created by the state to contain their mobility and the sociocultural stigmas associated with women's migration for work. It should, however, be noted that for women's migration to happen, there is a simultaneous ongoing twin process, the process of women becoming politically aware of the systems of domination on the one hand and their agentic responses and resistance to those systems on the other.

Against the backdrop of the rapidly shifting socio-economic structures spurred on by globalization, this chapter focuses on the phenomenon of women's labour migration along the Nepal–Persian Gulf migratory corridor. Three dimensions of women's labour migration constitute the key contents of the chapter. First, I examine how the fast-paced outmigration of Nepalese women from the country's previously isolated rural spaces has created new spatialities of migration and distinct forms of governmentality. Second, I discuss the dual and dynamic process in which global capital has necessitated women's outmigration by disrupting their traditional livelihood systems while also acting as conduits for capital inflows into the country's rural spaces and women's lives in the form of monetary and non-monetary remittances. The inflows of remittances reaching the nooks and corners of the country—although no exact amounts of capital generated by women migrant workers are available—have created significant tangible microeconomic outcomes at the grassroots. And third, I chart out how the inflows of capital in the form of monetary and non-monetary remittances have simultaneously produced what Sassen (2002) calls the 'counter geographies of globalization' that heighten the risks, precarities, and vulnerabilities faced by women. These counter geographies get further deepened when they intersect with the state's governance strategy of containing women's migration through the enactment of differential forms of governmentality.

To write this chapter, I employ an auto-ethnomethodological approach and a discourse analysis of the available literature and policy documents, combined partly with qualitative data collected from interviews with women migrant returnees and government officials in Nepal. The genesis of this chapter, however, was the first-hand experience of hearing the complex and heartbreaking stories of women migrants returning from the Middle East while working for a radio drama[1] produced by the BBC Media Action in Kathmandu in 2010. This chapter, divided into four sections, proceeds as follows. The first section briefly zeros in on some of the myths and realities of economic globalization, pertaining particularly to the mobilities of women's labour and capital along the Nepal–Persian Gulf migratory corridor. The second section examines the inflows of capital in the form of remittances sent home by women migrants and their contributions to the empowerment of themselves and to the country's micro– and macro-economic well-being. The third section discusses the counter-geographies—albeit largely invisible and underdiscussed—that intersect

---

[1] The radio drama titled 'Katha Mitho Sarangiko' in the Nepali language was produced by BBC Media Action in Kathmandu, Nepal. It was a weekly improvised drama recorded entirely on location in Nepal and aired from the BBC Radio in London. The drama mainly dealt with the issues of women and gender-based violence in the Nepalese society.

and interlock with the state's governmentalities to produce the lived experience of the Nepalese women migrants and also, the acts of agency and resistance exercised by women migrants against the new vulnerabilities. The fourth section concludes with a succinct summary of the chapter.

## Myths and Realities of Globalization: Women's Labour Migration along the Nepal–Persian Gulf Migratory Corridor

Globalization has engendered often-conflicting outcomes in developing countries, and these contradictions are manifested even in the smallest of rural locations, impacting people's lives in subtle, significant ways. Sassen (2007) contends that subnational spaces should constitute the analytics of globalization, since those small villages are the sites where globalizing processes happen. Similarly, Sachs (2013) emphasizes that the impacts of globalization are not just confined to the 'global cities'; they are prominently evident in the rural localities of poor countries. Antithetical though the 'global' and the 'local' seem, and even conceived as such, globalization has intricately woven them together. This weaving indeed dismantles the notion of the global–local dichotomy. Further, the mobility of capital and labour constitutes an integral part of globalization. However, the intensity, quantity, and spatiality of capital and labour mobilities have been extremely uneven across the globe. Economic globalization has accorded more freedom to the mobility of capital and commodities than that of people and labour (Sassen, 2008; Devries and Sylvain, 2012; Oso and Ribas Mateos, 2013). Anderson, Sharma, and Wright (2009) argue that the process of simultaneously granting more freedom to capital and less to migrants is an important feature of global capitalism and the global system of nation-states. The state, through various im/migration policies and surveillance systems, constrains the mobility of people and labour. Even the supranational governing institutions such as the World Trade Organization (WTO), through deregulations of financial sectors, intellectual property rights, and trade dispute resolutions, have served the interests of the mobility of capital (Oso and Ribas Mateos, 2013). Globalization of labour is thus disproportionately weaker than the globalization of capital (Massey et al., 1993). The greater freedom accorded to the mobility of capital has augmented the power of transnational corporations (TNC), through investments of their capital in lower wage and less unionized countries (Massey et al., 1993). The mobility of capital and labour as well as the shrinking of spatio-temporality are not self-generative but need to be produced with 'capital fixity, vast concentration of highly mobile material and less mobile facilities and infrastructures' (Oso and Ribas Mateos, 2013). Globalization is thus a political project that requires the efforts of the WTO, International Monetary Fund (IMF), and the World Bank and other multinational corporations to push it forward (Massey, 2002). Globalization is not an 'undifferentiated unity'; it is rather a 'geographically articulated patterning' of global capitalist activities and relations (Cox, 1997).

Moreover, the mobilities of the rich and the poor hugely differ in terms of nature, degree, and purpose. The rich people, especially in the Global North and the newly industrialized countries in the Global South, travel out of volition while the poor, particularly temporary labour migrants, move for survival. Bauman (1998) observes that 'tourists travel because they want to, the vagabonds because they have no other bearable choice'. The mobility of even those who are forced to migrate for livelihoods is often rendered immobile due to the securitization of migration and restrictive laws (O'Neill, 2007). Migrant workers are 'flawed consumers', enticed into migration by the promise of material affluence that they can never achieve (O'Neill, 2007). The migrant workers from South Asia, particularly women migrants who migrate to the Persian Gulf to work there as domestic workers, constitute a massive portion of this category.

Labour is not only less mobile; it is segmented and graded. There exists, Castells (2009) argues, a deep divide between 'self-programmable' labour and 'generic labour'; the former refers to the labour that demands advanced training and education and the ability to be attuned to the changing complexity of technology, while the latter refers to the traditional labour-intensive work which is increasingly being displaced by machines. One of the outcomes of the segmented and graded global labour system is the 'feminization of work', although the 'feminization' of work has historically existed. The 'feminization' of work has devalued labour and demeaned women migrants. Most of these women migrants work in the 'care industry' and are poorly paid (Peterson, 2012). Women are more exposed to informal employment in most low- and lower-middle-income countries and are more often found in the most vulnerable situations (ILO, 2018). Neoliberal markets and global capitalism have added further to the precariousness, informality, and flexibility of the work (Peterson, 2012; Oksala, 2013). Vulnerabilities and precarities multiply when the 'feminized' work in the developed and newly industrialized countries is performed by temporary women migrants from poor countries (Peterson, 2012). Lan (2008) contends that domestic labour migration is akin to 'colonial encounters' and has formed 'interior frontiers' that are 'built within the national frontier and in the intimate spheres of marriage and domesticity'.

In recent years, the labour migration of women is not only a South–North but also a South–South phenomenon. Peterson (2012) observes that women from areas with deteriorating economic conditions in the Global South migrate for employment to the Global North where a 'care deficit' exists. However, the South–North divide that existed earlier no longer remains the same. Globalization and global capitalism have indeed created a 'global middle class' in both the South and the North (Hosseini Hamed, Gills, and Goodman, 2016; Sachs, 2013). The Global South has 'formed a thin layer of society that is fully integrated into the economic North' while the North is 'generating its own internal South' (Cox and Sinclair, 1996). The South is thus divided into the rich South and the poor South. Along with the dismantling of the North–South divide and the 'feminization' of work, the dynamics of the gendered division of reproductive labour has massively changed. In particular, the reproductive labour of women in the middle-class households of the newly industrialized countries has been transferred to women migrants from the 'peripheral' countries of the South (Parreñas, 2001; Kilkey, 2013).

As Figure 8.1 shows, most women migrants from Nepal go to the Persian Gulf countries.

The South–North and South–South care chains as well as the inter-regional and intra-regional care chains in the Global South have markedly different characteristics in which most women migrate primarily through informal channels, leading to their undocumented status and employment in unregulated sectors (Hennebry, 2016). The women migrant domestic workers engaged in the South–South care chain are more vulnerable to exploitation and abuses than their South–North counterparts (Kofman and Raghuram, 2010). Nepal can be taken as an example since the number of the 'undocumented' Nepalese women migrants, particularly in the Middle East, is more than that of the documented (Kharel, 2016; ILO, 2015a; Kofman and Raghuram, 2010). What is, however, important is to avoid reducing the perspective on Nepalese women migrants to the homogenizing, monolithic subject without considering the intersectional differences based on caste, class, marital status, and

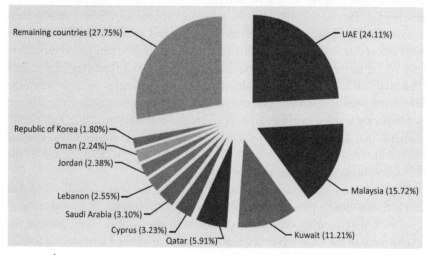

Figure 8.1 | Top destination countries for women migrant workers, 2008/09–2016/17

*Source*: Ministry of Labour and Employment (2018).

geographic regions. According to a study, 43 per cent of women migrating for work were from indigenous communities while the lower-caste women and the higher-caste brahmin and chhetri women occupied 24.1 per cent and 19.2 per cent respectively (Simkhada et al., 2018). Most women migrant returnees interviewed during my fieldwork in Nepal were either from lower-caste Dalit communities, or divorcees, or those whose husbands had died, and this suggests that sociocultural factors play a prominent role in women's outmigration for work.

However, there exists a difference between women migrants from upper-caste rich communities and those from the lower-caste poor in terms of the destination countries; the former category of women can afford to migrate to Europe, North America, Japan, or Australia and migration to these countries carries a social-symbolic value, while the latter choose the relatively more accessible countries in the Middle East. Women's labour is thus highly hierarchized in Nepalese society in terms of social class and even marital status, caste, geographic location, and education level. Since the intersectional differences among women persist, one fundamental challenge, Mohanty (2003) argues, is to reconcile the 'woman' as 'a cultural and ideological composite other constructed through diverse representational discourses' and the 'women' with 'real, material subjects of their collective histories'. The discourse that considers all Nepalese women as a single unified political subject, therefore, entails the risk of eschewing the *lived experiences of difference* among Nepalese women migrants.

No precise figures exist on the magnitude of transnational women's labour migration from Nepal to the Persian Gulf countries. Women migrant workers, according to Nepal's Central Bureau of Statistics (2012), occupy only 12.4 per cent of the total migrant population in the Gulf countries. Similarly, UN Women estimates that 15 per cent of the migrant workers in Nepal are women, and if those working in India are included, their numbers will considerably increase; however, those migrating to India are neither incorporated into the migrant population nor does the state have any data on their numbers. Further, a recent ILO report presents the proportions of women migrants to be much lower vis-à-vis male migrants (see Figure 8.2).

However, since most Nepalese women migrate through unofficial channels and routes due to the state's restrictive policy, the data that the state maintains lack reliability. Simkhada et al. (2018) claim that over 90 per cent of women migrants from Nepal are undocumented, and these women often use informal channels and routes, using India as a transit (kharel, 2016; Amnesty International, 2011; Gurung and Khatiwada, 2013). Since the ILO report is based only on the data of the women migrants who used formal/official channels and routes, the report under-represents women migrants' presence in the Persian Gulf. Gurung and Khatiwada (2013) estimate that 30 per cent of the total Nepalese migrant workers abroad are women migrants, and their total numbers are estimated to have exceeded 2.5 million (Simkhada et al., 2018).

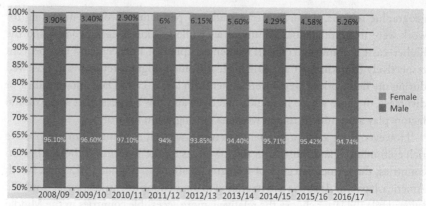

Figure 8.2 | Share of total labour migrants by sex, 2008/09–2016/17

*Source*: Ministry of Labour and Employment (2018).

Over 66 per cent of Nepalese women migrants in the Persian Gulf work as domestic workers (Gurung and Khatiwada, 2013), and they experience 'terrifying and shocking ordeals yet have been unable to hold accountable their abusers' (ILO, 2015a). The *kafala* system in the Gulf, which Johnson and Wilcke (2010) describe as a 'state-produced and -sanctioned relation' between migrants and employers, grants its citizens unregulated power over domestic workers with impunity. The Gulf states have created 'a distinct sort of labouring body that is low-cost, productive, hyper-mobile, disposable, and held in—liminal status—everywhere and nowhere, constantly available to work yet never permitted to live' (Baey, 2010; Aldama, 2002). Many domestic migrant workers are deprived of basic needs and met with physical and sexual assaults from their employers, and many are trapped inside the employer's house with their mobility completely curbed (Weissbrodt and Rhodes, 2013). Domestic women migrants work as forced labourers with their passports confiscated and salaries withheld (ILO, 2015a). Thus, the mobility of women from the origin country has ironically created their immobilities in the destination countries of the Gulf.

Despite the highly oppressive systems in the Gulf countries, the question as to why such large numbers of women from Nepal still continue to migrate needs further elaboration. Most Nepalese women migrating to the Persian Gulf countries for employment come from extremely impoverished situations. These women have the choice between 'un-freedom of poverty' or the 'un-freedom of servitude', and for them, the latter is a much better deal (Sunam, 2014). Sassen (2008) emphasizes the convergence of three factors behind women's labour migration: unemployment of men, shrinking opportunities for traditional forms of profit-making, and the fall in government revenues. In the context of Nepal, the unemployment of men not only adds to the pressures on women to find ways to ensure household survival; more importantly, the unemployed men whose mentalities are deeply rooted in patriarchal values perpetrate physical and psychological violence against women. For many Nepalese women, thus labour migration becomes a means to escape gender violence (Kharel, 2016; ILO, 2015b; Massey et al., 2010).

Similarly, the infiltration of unregulated global markets has destroyed women's traditional livelihoods. As a result of the state adopting the policy of economic liberalization following political change in the 1990s, global commodities have penetrated what Castells calls the 'spaces of places' (2009), and these global goods have jeopardized women's traditional livelihood systems while changing their lifestyles, aspirations, and needs. The mode of production that most Nepalese women have been engaged in is the age-old informal farming and domestic care work while the global commodities demand a monetary mode of production. Likewise, the impacts of climate change—such as recurrent droughts, floods, landslides, and altered precipitation and hydrological disruptions—have severely affected agricultural productivity and food security (Tiwari and Joshi, 2015; Bohle and Adhikari, 1998). Deforestation and climate change-induced phenomena, such as declining agricultural productivity, have produced gender-differentiated vulnerabilities.

Economic globalization has led states to what Sassen (2008) calls a 'two-way traffic': they open national economies to foreign firms while also participating in global markets. However, Nepal's participation in the global economy has rather become a one-way traffic. Nepal has opened doors to global markets and commodities, while its contributions to the global economy are predominantly lower-skilled labour exportations. Nepal's high dependence on the global economy is evident through the country's trade deficit that increased by above 27 per cent in the fiscal year 2018 vis-à-vis the fiscal year 2017 while exports further shrunk by more than 11 per cent (Department of Customs, 2018). Wichterich (2000) states that the integration of poor countries into the global economy has become a means of expanding the reach of the neoliberal market economy to the most far-flung parts. For instance, Nepalese women involved in traditional farming produce potatoes that they sell in the local markets; however, when they return home in the evening, they bring home the products such as potato chips and noodles manufactured by large multinational companies. At the same time, due to the excessive use of pesticides, even the land that would produce plenty for the family can no longer yield enough to make ends meet. Even the use of firewood has been replaced with LPG and local millet-bread with flashy noodles. The infiltration of the multinational companies into the villages has thus destroyed Nepalese women's traditional ways of life and economic bases, necessitating the alternative survival strategies such as 'foreign' employment. Scholz (2010) calls it 'neocolonialism' referring to the multinational corporations' colonizing effects through the power they create by providing commodities to people of the poor countries, leaving in turn impoverishing cultural effects of the Western values and goods. Globalization has thus created conflictual interactions between women's traditional economic activities and livelihood systems and the global markets and multinational companies. It can be argued that women's outmigration is a phenomenon resulting from an interplay between various intersecting endogenous oppressive systems and the newly emerging exogeneous pressures from global markets and climate change.

It should, however, be noted that Nepalese women are not just passively subject to the new forms and patterns of vulnerabilities and fragilities. There are two simultaneous processes happening to create a tipping point for women's outmigration: (a) women are increasingly becoming politically aware of the oppressive systems that they want to escape from, and (b) they are, through the power of their agency, resisting against the new challenges, seeking ways out of them. The act of recognizing migration as an alternative livelihood strategy is in fact a response to the intersecting systems of domination (Bohra-Mishra, 2011; Dixit et al., 2009; Shrestha and Bhandari, 2007). Similarly, women's courage to migrate for survival is an expression of the very angst of existence against all kinds of pre-existing and newly unfurling systems of oppression. Through labour migration, some Nepalese women have gained economic independence and empowerment, which in turn empowers women socially and culturally. Further, migration has provided Nepalese women an escape and some degree of counter-power against patriarchal systems of domination in society and within the family (Kharel, 2016; ILO, 2015a; Massey et al., 2010). Some women migrants, through their agency, transformed their vulnerabilities into sources of power, and it is crucial not to completely discount women's agentic power even in the face of global–local systemic constraints, nor to simply romanticize their migration as a source of sheer 'pleasure, desire, and new subjectivities' (Constable, 2014).

## Capital Mobility, Nepal's Remittance-Economy, and Women Migrants' Remittances

In the context of developing countries, remittances constitute significant forms of capital and are more stable than private capital flows. Remittances have become an important source of financial flux, after foreign direct investment, surpassing the volume of official assistance (Comes et al., 2018). Remittances are 'nearly three times the size of official development assistance and larger than private debt and portfolio equity flows to developing countries' (World Bank, 2013). The macroeconomic effects of remittances studied in different developing countries demonstrate mixed results. An IMF study demonstrates that remittances have positive macroeconomic effects on developing countries through macroeconomic stability, poverty reduction, and the mitigation of the impact of adverse shocks (Adams and Page, 2005). Remittances reduce households' credit constraints and boost the depth of the financial sector (Aggarwal, Demirgü-Kunt, and Pería, 2011). However, remittances spent in consumption create an increase in the monetary mass in the country of origin, thereby generating the appearance of inflationary processes (Ratha, 2005). Remittances can have negative effects on the recipient economy through their adverse influences on income distributions (Orrenius and Zavodny, 2010), household's labour supply, savings rates (Chami, Fullenkamp, and Jahjah, 2005). Sustained levels of remittances can be associated with the Dutch disease effects,[2] (Amuedo-Dorantes, Bansak, and Pozo, 2005; Rahman, Foshee, and Mustafa, 2013), and an increase in conspicuous consumption instead of productive investments (Chami, Fullenkamp, and Jahjah, 2005).

In the context of Nepal, remittances sent home by migrant workers have become an important fixture of Nepal's frail economy. Adhikari and Hobley (2015) describe remittances in Nepal as 'driving social changes in the hills, in ways that revolution and development have really failed to deliver'. As Figure 8.3 shows, Nepal in 2015 received 31.4 per cent of its national GDP in the form of remittances, while the share of the GDP in 2016 was 31.2 per cent (World Bank, 2019).

Apart from helping address issues of unemployment, foreign labour migration has also contributed to poverty alleviation as evidenced by the significant contribution of remittances to individual households and the national economy (ILO, 2015a; Sijapati, 2012). Foreign employment, therefore, works as a safety valve for the huge unemployment problems. Due to inflows of remittances, even net primary school enrolment in Nepal increased from 64 per cent in 1990 to 96.6 per cent in 2015–2016 (National Planning Commission, 2016). Similarly, remittances have become a source of capital in Nepal through various small- and large-scale investments as well as community development projects. Remittances lead to hometown or village construction booms with houses, temples, and meeting halls and to the openings of small village businesses (Nonini, 2002). For example, the Non-Resident Nepali Association (NRNA), which is an umbrella association of all Nepalese living outside the country, registered the 'NRN Infrastructure and Development Limited' in Kathmandu in 2012 with an objective of promoting collective investment through smooth inflows of capital investment in Nepal. The

---

[2] Dutch disease refers to an adverse economic effect caused by high inflows of capital into the country in the forms of remittances or foreign aid. Dutch disease results in appreciation of the real exchange rate, a decline in tradable sectors and surge in non-tradable sectors. Such a situation in the country's economy would create growth in retail trade and construction, but production sectors would be negatively impacted. Such an economy is vulnerable and may suffer if the inflows of capital stop.

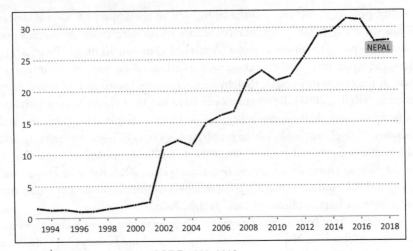

Figure 8.3 | Remittance as share of GDP, 1993–2018

*Source*: World Bank (2019).

company has made substantial investment in four medium hydropower projects in Nepal which is currently confronting a huge power crisis.

A review of the available literature on the inflows of remittances to Nepal reveals three dominant dimensions. First, most research adopts either a micro or a macro approach; second, the contributions of women migrants through inflows of remittances are largely absent from the existing literature; and third, the social remittances women migrants bring home have been underemphasized. Most research focuses on the impact of remittances on poverty reduction (Panday and Williams, 2011; Wagle, 2012Michael and Glinskaya, 2010), agricultural production (Bohra-Mishra, 2013), and economic growth through increases in demand for goods and services (Basnet and Upadhyaya, 2014). In contrast, others stress upon the negative impacts of remittances such as trade deficits (Bhatta, 2013), exchange rate appreciation, a decline in production of tradable goods, and a shift to production of non-tradable goods (Sapkota, 2013).

The mainstream analysis adopts a dualistic approach to look at remittances as having either microeconomic or macroeconomic outcomes which are mutually exclusive, but such a dichotomized lens to look at the various monetary and non-monetary forms of remittances cannot rightly gauge the contributions of women migrants (Dow, 2017). In the context of Nepalese women migrants, the approach that bifurcates the micro and the macro is problematic on two grounds. First, the micro and the macro, although studied as mutually exclusive spheres in most research, are closely intertwined. The micro configurations and outcomes, though they do not appear significant in the larger context of national economy, eventually add up and explain the macroeconomic aggregate figures and variables. Second, adopting such a binary view of the impacts of remittances is at the exclusion of women migrants and their contributions to the country's economy. For example, a substantial portion of remittances may go to consumption, but the investments in better nutrition, schooling, and health will ultimately contribute to human capital formation (Gupta and Wagh, 2009). The investment of remittances in consumption can have significant multiplier effects, encouraging more capital accumulation and growth through spillover effects (Ratha, 2003; Gupta and Wagh, 2009). Likewise, even multinational companies appraise the long-term sustainability of their investments through human capital measures such as education of the working-age population, health indicators, and so on (Basnet and Upadhyaya, 2014). Ali and Alpaslan (2017), therefore, emphasize that remittances form a long-run bidirectional link with domestic investment.

On women's labour migration, in particular, some studies focus on the negative impacts women's labour migration and remittances have on people's traditional agrarian and rural livelihoods. Sunam and McCarthy (2015) argue that labour outmigration from Nepal has increased rural poverty instead of alleviating it, stating that outmigration has changed rural people's relationship to the land and agriculture through the 'commodification' of land and through processes of 'deactivation' and 'repeasantization'. The lack of human capital has reduced livestock which, in turn, has led to scarcity of manure. Replacing manure with chemical fertilizers can adversely affect the quality of land and food. The women who stay behind have excessive workloads, resulting in the 'feminization of mountain agriculture' (Tiwari and Joshi, 2015).

However, at the household level, women's remittances have provided much needed financial resources to supply food, clothes, medicines, and children's education while the women migrants themselves feel empowered and have a sense of self-esteem that comes with the financial freedom. At the national level, the remittances women migrants sent home comprised 11 per cent of the total contributions from remittances while the remittances covered almost 32 per cent of the country's GDP in 2016 (Simkhada et al., 2018). However, as discussed earlier, there exist significant paucities of gender-disaggregated data and discrepancies even in the existing data. For instance, given the fact that large numbers of women migrants migrating to the Gulf countries use informal channels and routes, and stay and work there as 'undocumented' migrant workers, the amounts of remittances these women migrants send home are largely invisible and undocumented. Further, the microeconomic and macroeconomic conclusions drawn by discounting these invisible women migrants fail to take their economic contributions into account. As Nelson (1995) argues, the main problem for women is not about economics being 'too objective'; the important issue is about economics not being 'objective enough'. Seddon et al. (2002) contend that the scale of women migrants' remittances could be at least ten times greater than official estimates indicate. Moreover, the gender of the remitter has an effect on the volume, frequency, and the sustainability of resources (Prakash Nair and Pfutze, 2009). The effects of the investment of women migrants' remittances on education, consumer goods, health, durable goods, and food are macroeconomically and microeconomically significant, contributing positively to both economic and human development (Prakash Nair and Pfutze, 2009).

Besides monetary remittances, women migrants have significantly contributed to the accumulations of various forms of social capital.[3,4] Gartaula argues that, besides the flows of capital and labour, there are other forms of remittances such as social remittances in the form of diffusion of social practices, ideas, and values; knowledge and technology remittances; and the accumulations of all of these social capitals brought back home by returning women migrants contribute to changing identities and political awareness (Gartaula, 2009). Migration has thus created what scholars call 'brain circulation' that refers to the exchange of ideas with people from other countries, and such an opportunity can potentially influence gender, caste, and class relations (Poertner, Junginger, and Müller-Böker, 2011). To highlight the social remittances of migration, Appadurai uses the term 'ideoscape' to refer to the transference of values and ideas across cultures and Schille employs 'long-distance nationalism' to indicate the social capital gained from migration (Nonini, 2002). Sunam (2014) contends that the Nepalese migrants from the lower-caste Dalit community have contested caste institutions through the mobilization of financial, human, and symbolic capitals accumulated through migration. Such remittances that build symbolic and human capitals are significant for migrants from marginalized communities (Sunam, 2014), since the accumulation of those capitals enables them to enact 'a counter- hegemonic praxis' that is 'a symbolic and material vocabulary for challenging ruling ideologies' (Gidwani and Sivaramakrishnan, 2003). The higher consumptions created by inflows of remittances may be 'social transgressions' in the eyes of the dominant, but all of these behaviours help enhance their symbolic capitals (Sunam, 2014).

---

[3] Bourdieu's (1986: 241) conceptualization of social capital is based on the recognition that capital is not only economic and that social exchanges are not purely self-interested and need to encompass 'capital and profit in all their forms'. Bourdieu saw social capital as a property of the individual, rather than the collective, that enables him/her to exert power on the group or individual who mobilizes the resources.

[4] For example, economic, social, cultural, institutional, and symbolic capital based on Pierre Bourdieu's definition of human capital, 'the stock of knowledge, habits, and social and personality attributes ... [including] creativity embodied in the ability to perform labour so as to produce economic value' (1985: 19).

# The Counter-Geographies, Governmentalities, and Resistance

As discussed earlier, large numbers of women, especially from Nepal's small rural villages, migrate to the Persian Gulf countries every year. Studies show that the level of women's outmigration is consistently increasing (ILO, 2018)The women migrants, along their journeys from Nepal to the Persian Gulf, use a variety of transnational networks and circuits which in Sassen's (2002) words serve as sources of 'livelihood, profit-making and the accrual of foreign currency'. Some of the phenomena that compose globalization such as the global markets, transnational and trans-local networks, and the advanced technologies of communication build, sustain, and strengthen such migratory circuits (Sassen, 2002). In the sustenance of these transnational economic circuits, women migrant workers, as discussed earlier, confront different forms and patterns of vulnerabilities resulting from an intersection of various endogenous and exogeneous factors. Sassen (2002) argues that the women migrants are thus the 'truly disadvantaged' group of people who sustain revenues and profits for the advantaged. These lower-skilled women migrants from the Global South act as disposable bodies (Ong, 2006) through their unprotected flexible labour to ensure profits and sustenance of the circuits (Sassen, 2002). While considering the new spatialities of migration produced by the phenomenon of Nepalese women's labour migration, it is also crucial to discuss these invisible geographies that machinate sometimes in overt and covert interactions and association with various global, regional, transnational, and local structures and systems of domination.

For example, Nepal has a policy in place that restricts women's labour migration to the Middle East. The Department of Foreign Employment (2014), which is one of the main state bodies to manage labour migration and execute labour migration policies in Nepal, states that the intent of the bans is to 'protect women from many risks, including long working hours, sexual violence, physical abuse and economic exploitation.' It is though evident that when the media reports abuse and exploitation of Nepalese women migrant workers abroad, and an uproar and resistance among the public is triggered, the government tightens the policies through bans, but the purpose is to allay public resentment and anger. However, when the public resistance subsides, the government lifts bans and releases restrictions. Policy restrictions have indeed acted as a façade for the state to escape public criticism and show that it is committed to protect its women migrants going global. Grossman-Thompson (2016), however, describes this as a 'perverse self-perpetuating dynamic' that enables the state to 'set the stage for unsafe migration conditions and then rush the stage as the rescuing hero'.

Table 8.1 shows the unstable policy of the state towards women migrant workers through various legal bans and restrictions.

Table 8.1 | Restrictive Policies Enforced by the Government of Nepal on Women Migrant Workers

| Time frame | Nature of restriction |
| --- | --- |
| 1985–1998 | Women require consent of a 'guardian' (parent, husband, or other relative) to go for foreign employment |
| 1998–2003 | Complete ban on migration of female workers to Gulf countries |
| 2003–2010 | Partial ban on migration of female workers to Gulf countries |
| January 2009–May 2009 | Complete ban on female domestic workers going to Lebanon |
| 2012–May 2014 | Prohibition on women under 30 years of age to work as domestic workers in the Gulf |
| May 2014–April 2015 | Complete ban on female migrants to be recruited for domestic work in the Gulf countries |
| April 2015 onwards (pending implementation) | Prohibition on women under 25 years of age to work as domestic workers in the Gulf countries |

*Source*: ILO (2014).

The constant policy oscillations of the state towards women migrants shows the ambivalence attitude of the state. The contradictions between the liberalization and the restrictions on women's labour migration should be examined in the context of both history and contemporaneity. The restrictions aimed at containing the mobility of women have intersected with a distinct and differential form of governmentality. To a large extent, the embodied lived experiences of Nepalese women migrants in the destination countries are linked and produced as a result of the intersections between the global–local systems of domination. This protectionist labour migration policy that purports to protect women migrants has given rise to what Sassen (2000) calls the 'counter-geographies of globalization' that consist of brokers, human traffickers, and private 'manpower' agencies, run by people in power (Kharel, 2016; Lohani-Chase et al., 2008).

Historically, Nepalese women were confined to household chores and reproductive work, and the mobility of unaccompanied women would be associated with sexual promiscuity or loss of innocence (ILO, 2015b; Rai, 2008; O'Neill, 2001; Mahapatro, 2013; ). Women in Nepal would require consent from their guardians along with permission from a state authority to obtain a passport during the party-less panchayat system, and those travelling even within the state territory had to be accompanied by a male guardian (ILO, 2015a; Rai, 2008). Women are considered as an asset but as a threat to the nation-state if they cross social and cultural boundaries (Allison, 2017). The containment of women's mobility demonstrates the state's anxiety for protecting the 'purity' of the female body. The possibility of women migrating and working and living independently 'frequently elicit fears about uncontrolled sexuality, promiscuity and prostitution' (O'Neill, 2001). The creation of the discourse of women migrants' 'vulnerability' has given rise to a rescue industry, and many civil society and non-government organizations (NGOs) have contributed to the consolidation of the female migrant 'vulnerability' discourse. The state's restrictive labour migration policies against its female population is largely based on this public perception as well as the representation of women migrants in the Nepali media. O'Neill (2001) argues that the Nepali NGOs and the media, by conflating women's labour migration with forced prostitution, have deployed a compelling discourse that undermines the agency of women migrants (O'Neill, 2001).

After the political change of 1990, Nepal adopted a policy of economic liberalization and the marketization of the economy (ILO, 2018). These circuits are systemically linked with the conditions spurred by economic globalization in the developing countries (Sassen, 2002). Nepal opened its economy to multinational companies and the global markets to accommodate the conditions of the Structural Adjustment Programs of the IMF. This liberalization paved the way for global market commodities to infiltrate into the country's smallest of villages, thereby destroying women's traditional livelihood systems (ILO, 2014). The growing immiseration of governments and whole economies in the Global South has promoted and enabled the proliferation of survival and profit-making activities that involve the migration and trafficking of women (Sassen, 2002).

Although the state claims that the legal restrictions are meant for protecting women from being exploited abroad, doing so has produced a boomerang effect that many women resort to informal/irregular circuits and channels of migration, which are operated by intermediaries at different levels ranging from the village to the country of destination. Differential forms of governmentality have liberalized women's labour migration, but also on occasion contained their mobility. 'Gray areas' were created in the governance of labour migration where private recruitment agencies could tap in for their profits. Large numbers of women use informal and 'illegal' circuits and channels of migration; having to use these circuits of migration with the help of the local *dalal*s[5] has multiplied the vulnerabilities, precarities, and risks of the women migrants (Kharel, 2016). The trans-local and transnational networked circuits, operated by new actors consisting of brokers, traffickers, and contractors who have transnational networks, are thriving on the backs of the Nepalese women migrants, resulting from the state's overt or covert collusion with for-profit private recruitment agencies. Many such actors who run the circuits have collaborations with corrupt politicians. Nepalese women migrants are thus exposed to multiple vulnerabilities resulting from the multilayered invisibilities of the migration circuits.

---

[5] The Nepali word *dalal* literally means an agent who works as a broker between prospective migrants and employment agencies; in common parlance, the word has gained derogatoriness.

Even in the face of such institutional barriers and systems of oppression, the will of the Nepalese women migrants to make their migration journey to the Middle East by circumventing barriers should be taken as clear acts of their agency and resistance against the state. Women's determination to cross the borders, despite all the barriers, should be taken as a form of resistance, the resistance against the state and against the patriarchy. As hooks (1990) argues, the margins are both sites of oppression and resistance, the state's restrictive policy and discriminatory institutional practices and the resistance exercised by the Nepalese women migrants demonstrate this twin process. The Nepalese women migrants, as active subjects, simultaneously resist and reproduce systems of power. The 'illegal' migration of Nepalese women, therefore, demonstrates an intricate interplay between the structure and the agency.

## Conclusion

In this chapter, I have examined the phenomenon of women's labour migration from Nepal to the Persian Gulf, focusing mainly on how the increasing trend of migration has resulted from the interactions and intersections between various long-standing oppressive systems of gender domination and the incursion of global capital and global commodities into the lives of rural women and even into the smallest of the rural spaces of Nepal. These interlocking interactions have, in turn, created new livelihood challenges for women as well as new forms and patterns of vulnerabilities. The new vulnerabilities have resulted largely from the pressures of global markets and multinational companies creating a disconnect between the traditional mode of production, participated in by Nepalese women traditionally, and the capitalist mode of production, required to fulfil the changing needs and necessities wrought by globalization. These rapidly transforming socioeconomic realities faced by Nepalese women have necessitated labour migration as a viable alternative survival strategy.

The increasing feminization of labour migration in Nepal has also produced counter-geographies, consisting of transnational and trans-local illegal circuits, channels, and networks operated by a host of intermediaries who make profits on the backs of women migrants. The counter-geographies operating at the intersections of the state and the private recruiters are largely invisible; however, the lived experiences of the Nepalese women migrants are to a large extent the by-products of such nexuses. The women migrants, despite the existing systems of domination, have nevertheless used their agency to resist those systems; two processes are simultaneously ongoing: women are becoming politically aware of the systems of domination and they have the agency to act and resist against them. Nepalese women's labour mobility abroad thus entails the inflows of capital into the smallest of the villages in forms of various monetary and social remittances, and these capital inflows have empowered women in many ways and significantly contributed to the country's microeconomic and macroeconomic health.

# References

Adams, H. R. and J. Page. 2005. 'Do International Migration and Remittances Reduce Poverty in Developing Countries'. *World Development* 33(10): 1645–1669.

Aggarwal, Reena, Asli Demirgü-Kunt and Maria Soledad Martinez Pería. 2011. 'Do Remittances Promote Financial Development?' *Journal of Development Economics* 96(2): 255–264.

Aldama, Arturo. 2002. *Biopower, Reproduction, and the Migrant Woman's Body. Decolonial Voices: Chicana and Chicano Cultural Studies in the 21st Century.* Bloomington, IN: Indiana University Press.

Ali, A. and B. Alpaslan. 2017. 'Is There an Investment Motive behind Remittances? Evidence from Panel Cointegration'. *The Journal of Developing Areas* 51(1): 63–82.

Allison, Gill. 2017. 'Preserving Patriarchy: Birthright, Citizenship and Gender in Nepal'. In *Global Currents in Gender and Feminisms: Canadian and International Perspectives*, 1st edn, edited by G. Bonifacio. Bingley: Emerald Publishing Limited.

Amnesty International. 2011.'Nepal: False Promises: Exploitation and Forced Labour of Nepalese Migrant Workers', index number: ASA 31/007/2011. Available at https://www.amnesty.org/en/documents/ASA31/007/2011/en/. Accessed on 13 December 2011.

Amuedo-Dorantes, C. and S. Pozo. 2004. 'Workers' Remittances and the Real Exchange Rate: A Paradox of Gifts'. *World Development* 32(8): 1407–1417.

Amuedo-Dorantes, Catalina, Cynthia Bansak, and Susan Pozo. 2005. 'On the Remitting Patterns of Immigrants: Evidence from Mexican Survey Data'. *Economic Review* 90(1): 37–58.

Anderson, Bridget, Nandita Sharma, and Cynthia Wright. 2009. 'Editorial: Why No Borders?' *Refuge* 26(2): 5–18.

Adhikari, Jagannath and Mary Hobley. 2015. '"Everyone is Leaving. Who Will Sow Our Fields?" The Livelihood Effects on Women of Male Migration from Khotang and Udaypur Districts, Nepal, to the Gulf Countries and Malaysia'. *HIMALAYA, the Journal of the Association for Nepal and Himalayan Studies* 35(1), Article 7.

Baey, Grace H. Y. 2010. 'Borders and the Exclusion of Migrant Bodies in Singapore's Global City-state. MA thesis. Ontario: Queen's University, . Available at https://libproxy.wlu.ca/login?url=https://search-proquest. Accessed on 3 February 2018.

Bansak, C. and B. Chezum. 2009. 'How Do Remittances Affect Human Capital Formation of School-Age Boys and Girls?' *The American Economic Review* 99(2): 145–148.

Basnet, H. and K. Upadhyaya. 2014. 'Do Remittances Attract Foreign Direct Investment? An Empirical Investigation'. *Global Economy Journal* 14(1): 1–9.

Bauman, Z. 1998. *Globalization: The Human Consequences.*European Perspectives. New York: Columbia University Press.

Bhatta, G. R. 2013. 'Remittance and Trade Deficit Nexus in Nepal: A VECM Approach. *NRB Economic Review* 25: 37–50.

Bohle, Hans-Georg and J. Adhikari. 1998. 'Rural Livelihoods at Risk: How Nepalese Farmers Cope With Food Insecurity'. *Mountain Research and Development* 18: 321–332.

Bohra-Mishra, P. (2013). 'Labour Migration and Investments by Remaining Households in Rural Nepal'. *Journal of Population Research* 30(2): 171–192.

———. 2011. 'Migration and Remittances during the Period of Civil Conflict in Nepal'. PhD dissertation. Princeton, NJ: Princeton University, Wilson Woodrow School of Public Policy and International Affairs.

Bourdieu, P. 1986. 'The Forms of Capital'. In Handbook of Theory and Research for the Sociology of Education, edited by J. Richardson, 241–258.Greenwood, NY.

Buch, C. and A. Kuckulenz. 2002. 'Worker Remittances and Capital Flows'. IDEAS working paper series from RePEc.

Comes, Calin-Adrian, Elena Bunduchi, Valentina Vasile, and Daniel Stefan. 2018. 'The Impact of Foreign Direct Investments and Remittances on Economic Growth: A Case Study in Central and Eastern Europe'. *Sustainability* 10(1): 1–16.

Castells, Manuel. 2009. *Communication Power*. Oxford, NY: Oxford University Press.

Central Bureau of Statistics. 2012. . Kathmandu.

Chami, R., C. Fullenkamp, and S. Jahjah. 2005. 'Are Immigrant Remittance Flows a Source of Capital for Development?' *IMF Staff Papers* 52(1): 55–81.

Constable, N. 2014. *Born Out Of Place: Migrant Mothers and the Politics of International Labor*. Berkeley, CA: University of California Press.

Cox, R. and T. Sinclair. 1996. *Approaches to World Order*. Cambridge Studies in International Relations, 40. Cambridge: Cambridge University Press.

Cox, R. (1997). *The New Realism: Perspectives on Multilateralism and World Order*. International Political Economy Series. Multilateralism and the UN System. Tokyo and New York: United Nations University Press and St. Martin's Press.

Department of Customs. 2018. 'Nepal Foreign Trade Statistics Fiscal Year 2017/18'. Ministry of Finance. Available at https://www.customs.gov.np/upload/documents/Foregin%20Trade%20 Statistics%202074-75_2018-11-30-13-57-48.pdf. Accessed on 3 July 2019.

Department of Foreign Employment. 2014. *Monthly Progress Report*. Available at http://dofe. gov.np/new/pages/details/34. Accessed on 22 April 2018.

Devries, Samantha May and Renee Sylvain. 2012. Master's dissertation. *Mobility Matters: Tamang Women's Gendered Experiences of Work, Labour Migration and Anti-Trafficking Discourses in Nepal*. Guleph: University of Guelph.

Dixit, A., M. Upadhya, K. Dixit, A. Pokhrel, and D. R. Rai. 2009. *Living with Water Stress in the Hills of the Koshi Basin, Nepal*. Kathmandu: ICIMOD.

Dow, Sheila. 2017. 'Gender and the Future of Macroeconomics'. Institute for New Economic Thinking. Available at https://www.ineteconomics.org/research/research-papers/gender-and-the-future-of-macroeconomics. Accessed on 6 February 2018.

Gartaula, Hom Nath. 2009. 'International Migration and Local Development in Nepal'. *Contributions to Nepalese Studies* 36(1): 37–66.

Gidwani, V. and K. Sivaramakrishnan. 2003. 'Circular Migration and the Spaces of Cultural Assertion'. *Annals of the Association of American Geographers* 93: 186–213.

Grossman-Thompson, B. 2016. 'Protection and Paternalism: Narratives of Nepali Women Migrants and the Gender Politics of Discriminatory Labour Migration Policy'. *Refuge* 32(3): 40.

Gupta, Pattillo and Smita Wagh. 2009. 'Effect of Remittances on Poverty and Financial Development in Sub-Saharan Africa'. *World Development* 37(1): 104–115.

Gurung, G. and K. Padma. 2013. *Nepali Women in the Middle East: A Situation Report*. UN Women Asia and Pacific. Available at http://asiapacific.unwomen.org/en/digital-library/publications/2013/10/nepali-women-in-the-middle-east. Accessed on 21 January 2018.

Hennebry, J. 2016. *Women Working Worldwide: A Situational Analysis of Women Migrant Workers*. New York: UN Women.

Hooks, Bell. 1990. *Yearning: Race, Gender, and Cultural Politics*. Boston, MA: South End Press.

Hosseini Hamed, S. A., Barry K. Gills, and James Goodman. 2016. 'Toward Transversal Cosmopolitanism: Understanding Alternative Praxes in the Global Field of Transformative Movements'. *Globalizations* 14(5): 667–684.

ILO. 2014. 'Labour Migration for Employment: A Status Report for Nepal: 2014/2015'. Available at https://www.ilo.org/wcmsp5/groups/public/---asia/---ro-bangkok/---ilo-kathmandu/documents/publication/wcms_500311.pdf. Accessed on 3 July 2019.

———. 2015a. 'No Easy Exit: Migration Bans Affecting Women from Nepal'. Available at http://www.ilo.org/global/topics/forced-labour/publications/WCMS_428686/lang-en/index.htm. Accessed on 11 December 2017.

———. 2015b. 'Realizing a Fair Migration Agenda: Labour flows between Asia and Arab States'. ILO Regional Office for Asia and the Pacific.

———. 2018. *Women and Men in the Informal Economy: A Statistical Picture*, 3rd edn. Available at https://www.ilo.org/wcmsp5/groups/public/---dgreports/---dcomm/documents/publication/wcms_626831.pdf. Accessed on May 14, 2018.

Johnson, Mark and Christoph Wilcke. 2015. 'Caged in and Breaking Loose: Intimate Labour, the State, and Migrant Domestic Workers in Saudi Arabia and Other Arab States'. *Migrant Encounters: Intimate Labor, the State, and Mobility across Asia*, edited by S. Friedman and P. Mahdavi. Philadelphia, PA: University of Pennsylvania Press.

Kharel, A. 2016. 'Female Labor Migration and the Restructuring of Migration Discourse: A Study of Female Workers from Chitwan, Nepal'. PhD dissertation. KS: Kansas State University.

Kilkey, M. 2013. *Gender, Migration and Domestic Work: Masculinities, Male Labour and Fathering in the UK and USA.*Migration, Diasporas and Citizenship. Basingstoke: Palgrave Macmillan.

Kofman, Eleonore and Parvati Raghuram. 2010. 'The Implications of Migration for Gender and Care Regimes in the South'. In *South-South Migration*, edited by Katja Hujo and Nicola Piper. London: Palgrave Macmillan.

Lan, P. 2008. 'Migrant Women's Bodies as Boundary Markers: Reproductive Crisis and Sexual Control in the Ethnic Frontiers of Taiwan'. *Signs* 33(4): 833–861.

Lohani-Chase, R., E. Grosz, L. Ahearn, B. Balliet, J. Diamond, and N. Fermon. 2008. *Women and Gender in the Maoist People's War in Nepal: Militarism and Dislocation*. Camden, NJ State University of New Jersey.

Lokshin, M. and E. Glinskaya. 2009. 'The Effect of Male Migration on Employment Pattern of Women in Nepal'. *The World Bank Economic Review* 23(3): 481–507.

Mahapatro, S. R. 2013. 'Changing Gender Relations and Its Influence on Female Migration Decision in India'. *Pakistan Development Review* 52(1): 69–88. Available at https://www.jstor.org/stable/24397874. Accessed on 7 July 2019.

Massey, Doreen. 2002. 'Globalisation: What Does It Mean for Geography?' *Geography* 87(4): 293–296.

Massey, D., J. Arango, G. Hugo, A. Kouaouci, A. Pellegrino, and J. E. Taylor. 1993. 'Theories of International Migration: A Review and Appraisal'. *Population and Development Review* 19(3): 432–466.

Massey, D., William G. Axinn, and Dirgha J. Ghimire. 2010. 'Environmental Change and out Migration: Evidence from Nepal'. *Population and Environment* 32(2): 109–136.

Ministry of Labour and Employment. 2018. *Labour Migration for Employment: A Status Report for Nepal: 2015/2016 – 2016/2017*. Kathmandu: Government of Nepal. Available at https:// asiafoundation.org/wp-content/uploads/2018/05/Nepal-Labor-Migration-status-report-2015-16-to-2016-17.pdf. Accessed on 10 July 2019.

Mohanty, C. 2003. *Feminism without Borders: Decolonizing Theory, Practicing Solidarity*. Durham and London: Duke University Press.

National Planning Commission. 2016. *Nepal and the Millennium Development Goals Final Status Report 2000–2015*. Kathmandu.

Nelson, Julie. 1995. 'Feminism and Economics'. *The Journal of Economic Perspectives* 9(2): 131–148. Available athttp://www.jstor.org.libproxy.wlu.ca/stable/2138170. Accessed on 8 January 2018.

Nonini, D. 2002. 'Transnational Migrants, Globalization Processes, and Regimes of Power and Knowledge'. *Critical Asian Studies* 34(1): 3–17.

Oksala, J. 2013. 'Feminism and Neoliberal Governmentality'. *Foucault Studies* 16: 32–53.

O'Neill, T. 2001. 'Selling Girls in Kuwait: Domestic Labour Migration and Trafficking Discourse in Nepal'. *Anthropologica* 43(2): 153–164.

———. 2007. 'Our Nepali Work Is Very Good: Nepali Domestic Workers as Transnational Subjects'. *Asian and Pacific Migration Journal* 16(3): 301–322.

Ong, A. 2006. *Neoliberalism as Exception Mutations in Citizenship and Sovereignty*. E-Duke Books Scholarly Collection. Durham, NC: Duke University Press.

Orrenius, P. and M. Zavodny. 2010. *How Immigration Works for America*. Annual report.Dallas: Federal Reserve Bank of Dallas.

Oso, L. and N. Ribas Mateos 2013. *The International Handbook on Gender, Migration and Transnationalism Global and Development Perspectives*. Northampton, MA: Edward Elgar Pub.

Panday, P. and R. Williams. 2011. 'Interplay between Conflict, Poverty and Remittance: The Case of Nepal'. *The International Business & Economics Research Journal* 10: 67–76.

Parreñas, Rhacel. 2001. *Servants of Globalization: Women, Migration and Domestic Work*. Stanford, CA: Stanford University Press.

Peterson, J. 2009. 'Life after Oil: Economic Alternatives for the Arab Gulf States'. *Mediterranean Quarterly* 20(3): 1–18.

Peterson, V. 2012. 'Rethinking Theory: Inequalities, Informalization and Feminist Quandaries'. *International Feminist Journal of Politics* 14(1): 5–35.

Poertner, E. M. Junginger and U. Müller-Böker. 2011. 'Migration in Far Western Nepal'. *Critical Asian Studies* 43(1): 23–47.

Prakash Nair, R. and Tobias Pfutze. 2009. 'The Impact of Gender and Remittances on Household Expenditure Patterns in Nepal'. Doctoral dissertation. Washington, DC: Georgetown University. Available at https://search-proquest-com.libproxy.wlu.ca. Accessed on 22 January 2018.

Rahman, Matiur, Andrew Foshee and Muhammad Mustafa. 2013. 'Remittances-Exchange Rate Nexus: The U.S.-Mexico Case'. *Journal of Developing Areas* 47(1): 63–74.

Rai, D. 2008. 'At What Cost the Remittance Economy? Female Migrant Workers are Especially Vulnerable to Exploitation and Abuse'. *Nepali Times*, 423, 31 October–6 November. Available at http://nepalitimes.com/news.php?id=15345#.VtHjeZwrLIU. Accessed on 10 January 2018.

Ratha, Dilip. 2003. 'Workers' Remittances: An Important and Stable Source of External Development Finance'. World Bank Global Development Finance. Available at https://ssrn.com/abstract=3201568. Accessed on 10 May 2019.

———. 2005. 'Workers' Remittances: An Important and Stable Source of External Development Finance'. *Economics Seminar Series*, Paper 9. St. Cloud, MN: St. Cloud State University. http://repository.stcloudstate.edu/econ_seminars/9. Accessed on 10 May 2019.

Sachs, W. 2013. 'Liberating the World from Development'. *New Internationalist* 460: 22–27.

Sapkota, C. 2013. 'Remittances in Nepal: Boon or Bane?' *Journal of Development Studies* 49(10): 1316–1331.

Sassen, S. 2002. 'Women's Burden: Counter-Geographies of Globalization and the Feminization of Survival'. *Nordic Journal of International Law* 71(2): 255–274.

———. 2007. *Sociology of Globalization*, 1st edn. Contemporary Societies. New York: W. W. Norton.

———. 2008. 'Two Stops in Today's New Global Geographies: Shaping Novel Labor Supplies and Employment Regimes'. *American Behavioral Scientist* 52(3): 457.

Scholz, S. 2010. *Feminism: A Beginner's Guide*. Oxford, NY: Oneworld.

Seddon, D., J. Adhikari, and G. Gurung. 2002. 'Foreign Labor Migration and the Remittance Economy of Nepal'. *Critical Asian Studies* 34(1): 19–40.

Shrestha, S. and S. Bhandari 2007. 'Environmental Security and Labor Migration in Nepal'. *Population and Environment* 29(1): 25–38.

Sijapati, B. and A. Limbu. 2012. *Governing Labour Migration in Nepal: An Analysis of Existing Policies and Institutional Mechanisms*. Kathmandu: Himal Books.

Simkhada, Padam, Edwin Van Teijlingen, Manju Gurung, and Sharada P. Wasti. 2018. 'A Survey of Health Problems of Nepalese Female Migrant Workers in the Middle-East and Malaysia'. *BMC International Health and Human Rights* 18(1): 1–7.

Sunam, R. 2014. 'Marginalised Dalits in International Labour Migration: Reconfiguring Economic and Social Relations in Nepal'. *Journal of Ethnic and Migration Studies* 40(12): 1–19.

Sunam, R. and J. McCarthy. 2015. 'Reconsidering the Links between Poverty, International Labour Migration, and Agrarian Change: Critical Insights from Nepal'. *The Journal of Peasant Studies* 43(1): 1–25.

Tiwari, P. C and J. Bhagwati. 2015. 'Climate Change and Rural Out-Migration in Himalaya'. *Change and Adaptation in Socio-Ecological Systems* 2(1): 8–25.

Wagle, U. R. 2012. 'Socioeconomic Implication of the Increasing Foreign Remittance to Nepal: Evidence from the Nepal Living Standard Survey'. *International Migration* 50: 186–207.

Weissbrodt, David and Justin Rhodes. 2013. 'Migrant Workers in the Middle East'. *Middle East Law and Governance* 5: 71–111.

Wichterich, C. 2000. *The Globalized Woman: Reports from a Future of Inequality*. North Melbourne, London and New York: Spinifex Press and Zed Books.

World Bank. 2013. 'Migration and Development Brief'. Available at https://siteresources.worldbank.org/INTPROSPECTS/Resources/334934-1110315015165/MigrationandDevelopmentBrief20.pdf. Accessed on 10 February 2018.

———. 2017. 'Migration and Development Brief 27, Migration and Remittances: Recent Developments and Outlook'. Available at http://pubdocs.worldbank.org/en/992371492706371662/MigrationandDevelopmentBrief27.pdf. Accessed on 10 February 2018.

———. 2019. 'Personal Remittances, Received (% of GDP)'. Available at https://data.worldbank.org/indicator/BX.TRF.PWKR.DT.GD.ZS?locations=NP. Accessed on 7 July 2019.

# 9

# Migration and Developmental Capital in a Punjab Village

ROSY HASTIR

## Introduction

India ranks among the top recipients of remittances from people settled in Western countries. The Punjabi community, scattered in different parts of the world, has been actively engaged in sending back remittances to family members in the homeland. The diaspora community has also contributed significantly to the development of their ancestral villages. When diaspora philanthropists sponsor projects in their ancestral homeland, they do not just make capital indiscriminately available for local use; rather, they fund particular kinds of activities that they consider necessary and valuable.

Scholars of migration have shown that historically and in the contemporary period, migration shapes the lives of people both in the places of origin and in places of destination. Migrant communities must, therefore, be studied as 'transnational' because they cross different kinds of boundaries, in terms of movements of goods, people, ideas, and cultures, creating and transforming spaces across the globe. It is this framework of the 'transnational' nature of migrants that I examine through my work on Punjabi migrants and the diverse links they maintain across national/ transnational boundaries. In Punjab, I selected Kharoudi village because of its transnational movements and the connections which migrants maintain with this village, especially the connections which are apparent in the form of capital flows that have driven development processes in the village.

## Remittances and Development

Diasporic communities are globally spread but at the same time linked back to their homelands. People from developing nations, such as Pakistan, Bangladesh, Sri

Lanka, Philippines, and India, move to various Western countries, such as the USA, the UK, Canada, and Europe. In the case of Pakistan, transnational migration of Mirpuri Muslims to Britain not only brings economic capital into the area through the flow of remittances, but also facilitates significant social development through the construction of schools, hospitals, and so on (Ballard, 2004).

Vertovec (2007) demonstrates that remittances are sent by all types of migrant workers—male and female, legal and illegal, permanent and temporary, low-skilled and highly skilled. They can be transferred through various modes such as banks, agencies, directly through the Internet, through professional couriers, or through the social networks of the migrants. Remittances influence the lives of local people who are left behind and transform the sociocultural settings of people in the homeland with respect to their status hierarchies, gender relations, patterns of marriages, and user habits.

Vertovec (2009) further discusses the role of remittances for development in migrants' hometowns. The frequent flow of remittances used for the development of infrastructure which includes roads, and other facilities such as sports complexes, schools, ambulances and hospitals, have changed the picture of the migrant's hometown. New forms of philanthropy and social investment in villages have been noted by Dusenbery and Tatla (2009) as well as by Thandi (2008). The rapid influx of social remittances is only possible through transnational practices. Efficient and rapid modes of travel and communication, especially mobile phones, facilitate the flows of ideas, values, and tastes which migrant bring or send back to their country of origin. Thus, migration is not a one-sided phenomenon but a continuous flow of ideas and practices between sending and receiving countries. It not only influences the life of the migrant but also influences the lives of the people in the homeland.

Ratha (2013), in his study of remittances, has shown their significant impact on economic growth and poverty reduction. According to him, remittances facilitate the growth of human sectors such as health, education, and gender equality. They have not only contributed to the earnings of many people and their families but have also acted like a life-support system for many poverty-stricken individuals. Ratha describes remittances as a form of insurance that has immensely improved the living standards of recipients and he also notes the impact of remittances in relation to education, as migrant households often provide private-school education for their children. Others, however, have been more sceptical and de Haas (2005), for example, has used the term 'remittances euphoria' in relation to the excessive enthusiasm for remittances among international policy-makers.

International migration across borders affects the lives of relatives left behind in ways that go beyond economic benefits. Frequent links with the migrants through various modes of communication and personal visits to homeland encourage their left-behind family members to experience life abroad. Thus, family and kin networks play a vital role in the process of chain migration from a particular place of origin. It is clear that the phenomenon of migration is not only a one-time movement but an intermittent and long-term flow. According to Chopra (2011), within the context of the village, migration is not considered to be just a single event but a process that is doubly experienced and that requires contextualizing before and after the event itself. In other words, it is a process of becoming a migrant and being a migrant, it 'begins' before any member of the family actually leaves the village.

The last half century has seen a huge movement of people across the globe. By the end of the twentieth century, the number of people residing outside their country of birth was estimated at 175 million, constituting 3 per cent of the world's population (United Nations, 2002: 20). Within a decade, from 1990 to 2000, the number of migrants in the world increased by 14 per cent, confirming the view that 'the closing years of the twentieth century and the beginning of the twenty-first will be the age of migration' (Castle and Miller, 1998: 3) with economic opportunity and family reunification as primary reasons for migration (United Nations, 2002, cited in Chopra, 2011: 87).

## Transnational Migration from Punjab

Punjab has had a long history of transnational migration. This history has been captured in numerous ways. The writer Prakash Tandon (1968) has written about it in his famous books, such as *Punjabi century (1857–1947)* and other subsequent volumes: *Beyond Punjab (1937–1960)* and *Return to Punjab (1961–1987)*. According to him, migration is captured in folk songs such as *vichorian* or the songs of separation (Tandon, 1968).

The Sikh community is scattered around the world while at the same time retaining strong ties with their homeland. 'Sikhs have become a paradigmatic transnational community charting what Arjun Appadurai has called "a new, post-national cartography"' (Dusenbery and Tatla, 2009: 3). The kind of vital links these diasporic Sikhs maintain with their homeland serve to channelize the resources, information, and values between the host and home countries (Barrier, 2007).

Dhesi (2008: 431) discusses the different waves of migration from Punjab to North America, Great Britain and the Middle East. On the one hand, amongst those who migrated to the USA, most were educated and professional migrants. On the other hand, migrants to the Middle East were mostly small-scale artisans from poor economic backgrounds. Therefore, as Dhesi shows, there are many reasons, phases, and periods of migration. Historically, labour migration was very important. The long history of Sikh communities abroad is illustrated, for example, by Rai (2014) in his study of Indians in Singapore.

Why does this particular community contribute so significantly to global migration? How actively do they maintain links to their homeland? What are the means through which they remain connected with their place of origin?

Tatla (1999: 6) argues that the diasporic Sikh community maintains strong links with its homeland through memories and religious connections. Initially, they were small in number in the Indian or Punjabi diaspora, but with the passage of time their numbers became significant. There were numerous features such as social values, religion, linguistic bonds, and ethnic identity that made them a distinct community within the Indian diaspora. Tatla further adds that a majority of Sikh migrants voluntarily migrated, while other communities were pushed to migrate due to political circumstances or to escape state violence. Broadly, there are three countries where the Sikh community has a significant population—Canada, Great Britain, and the USA. The period of decolonization also witnessed the remigration of Sikhs from East Africa and the Far East to various Western countries. Emigration of single male migrants largely occurred in the colonial period, while in the postcolonial period they started settling with their families.

According to Dusenbery and Tatla (2009: 3), the Sikh community from Punjab is a pioneering transnational community in sending back remittances to their families in the homeland. In a globalized world, India ranked as the top recipient of remittances sent by their people settled in Western countries and Punjab, in particular, has seen immense flows of capital which have contributed significantly to the development of migrants' ancestral villages.

Undoubtedly, philanthropic activities are primarily undertaken by non-resident Indians (NRIs) who are well-established and have accumulated wealth in their host country. The act of giving back to their ancestral villages provides them with a sense of gratification. Constructing a village gate with their names inscribed on it gives them popularity and status in the village. After landing in foreign countries, their prime purpose is to send remittances to family members in their village. Once settled in the host country, migrants start sponsoring their family members and fellow-kin members to migrate. When a migrant's family unites abroad in the country of immigration, their next target is to contribute their share of wealth for the development of the village community. They are usually aware of existing problems in their ancestral villages, whether it is drainage, sewerage, shortage of schools and hospitals or disorganized cultural activities, sports tournaments, and so on.

Dusenbery and Tatla (2009), in their discussion of diaspora philanthropy in Punjab, have described in detail the contribution of transnational migrants to the infrastructural transformations of Punjabi villages. The global dispersion of Sikhs, and the strong links which they maintained with their ancestral and spiritual homeland, encourages them to share some part of their income in different kinds of projects in Punjab, ranging from family consumption to political and religious agendas. Remittances for community development, social investment, and charitable or philanthropic work are also recognized. Dusenbery and Tatla describe this philanthropy as 'private giving for local good' in the ancestral homeland.

Dhesi (2008) has defined Punjabi people's outlook as broad, liberal, and cooperative, especially in some unexpected circumstances such as emergencies and external threats to collective security. NRI philanthropic contributions to their villages meet the social requirements of fellow villagers and overcome, at least partially, the inefficiency of the state, market, and formal and civic institutions. In attempting to provide goods and services not provided by others, they have earned a positive reputation as 'the good fellas' and 'the new VIPs' of Punjab (Dusenbery and Tatla, 2009).

Thandi (2008) notes the range of philanthropic activities by migrants in terms of charity, which includes gurdwara donations, clothes, and computers. As far as infrastructure is concerned, it includes hospitals, nursing colleges, parks, sports complexes, street paving and lighting, mortuaries, sewerage, and water supply. He also notes human development initiatives such as scholarships, libraries, computers, and health facilities as well as recreational facilities such as sports and sports tournaments. In the case of infrastructure investment, initiatives include various programmes for the improvement of village community life such as waste and water recycling.

Thandi (2008) also analyses how Punjabi diasporic communities benefit the homeland economy. Through their regular visits to Punjab, they have immensely benefitted the transportation sector. Besides this, they have also contributed to the market economy whether through marriage-related consumptions such as ethnic clothes and jewellery or the purchase of cultural goods such as foodstuffs, books, and VCDs and DVDs of films and musical instruments. However, the capital remitted by migrants to their family is the most popular and frequent contribution by diasporic communities. Another study by Walton-Roberts (2004: 85) on Palahi, situated in Hoshiarpur district of Punjab, observed that 'with the development of one communication resource that is a polytechnic internet connection, people of Palahi prided themselves. And in one local television story, Palahi was termed a Cyber village.'

## Developmental Capital in Kharoudi Village, Punjab

In the popular imagination, villages are thought of as places of sparse population, fresh environment, and natural beauty such as green fields and cultivated areas with pollution-free living spaces, far from the dense settlements of cities. M. K. Gandhi said, 'The soul of India lives in its villages.'[1] However, in contemporary India, wide-ranging social processes such as electoral politics, government policies, and internal and transnational migration amongst others, have transformed the stereotypical village. The village is no longer a homogenous place, where people are happy, living simple lives. Any village study in India in the twenty-first century shows that villages are transnational spaces, inhabited by people who think of the world as their homeland while retaining ties with their villages. This kind of dual, transnational identity is certainly characteristic of villages in late twentieth and early twenty-first century Punjab. To understand the changes that migration has produced within village society and culture as well as within the political economy of the village, I examined Kharoudi—a small village located in Hoshiarpur district—which is a part of the Doaba region of Punjab. This particular belt of the Doaba, that covers the areas of Jalandhar, Hoshiarpur, Kapurthala, and Phagwara, is considered most affluent, and represents the largest source of NRIs. Many people from this belt have migrated over a long period of time to different Western and Middle Eastern countries. This is quite obvious in the case of Kharoudi. Roughly 40 minutes by road from the urban centre of Jalandhar, Kharoudi lies off the main highway that connects the cities of Jalandhar and Chandigarh. However, the village settlement itself lies about 25 minutes away by road from the highway. The entrance to the village is marked by a large gateway, which was built in 1979 in memory of Swaran Kaur and Karam Singh Canadian and their daughter. The inclusion of foreign terms like Canadian within the name is marking the pride of achieving international identity. The inscriptions on the gateway are in Roman and Gurumukhi scripts which immediately signal the transnational nature and connections of those who live in Kharoudi.

My choice of village Kharoudi as a field site was inspired by a video on YouTube, called 'Modern Village Kharoudi' which features the prominent returnee migrant Baldev Singh, a retired engineer from Abu Dhabi.[2] In the YouTube video, Baldev Singh introduces the viewers to the conspicuous signs of transnational migration that are evident in the public spaces of the village as well as his own domestic space. For example, viewers are shown a water tank in the shape of an airplane, solar light panels, and paved roads. The viewer is also shown a hoarding (Figure 9.1) which reads, 'Village Kharoudi Lifestyle Improvement Project, a co-operative effort of Kharoudi NRIs and local villagers with the support of the government of Punjab.'

---

[1]  See 'The Soul of the Real India Lives in Its Villages', 1 October 2016, available at https://studymoose.com/the-soul-of-the-real-india-lives-in-its-villages-essay, accessed on 10 June 2012.

[2]  See http://wikimapia.org/.../Modern-Village-of-Distt-Hoshiarpur-Punjab-Kharoudi-Gill-House, accessed on 4 August 2012.

Figure 9.1 | A hoarding of Village Kharoudi Lifestyle Improvement Project

*Source*: Picture taken by the field investigator, October 2011.

*Note*: This hoarding is on the main street of village Kharoudi.

During the Gram Pushkar Awards ceremony in New Delhi held on 24 February 2005, the President of India, A. P. J. Abdul Kalam, referred to this village as 'The Model Village' in Hoshiarpur.

The pioneering NRIs who have contributed to the development of Kharoudi are Harman Singh from Canada, Raghubir Singh from the USA, and Baldev Singh from Abu Dhabi.[3] The inclusion of foreign terms like Canadian within the name is marking the pride of achieving international identity.

I interviewed Harman Singh and Baldev Singh during my fieldwork and in fact stayed with the family of Baldev Singh. My understanding of the transnational nature of the village is, therefore, based on 'public' information as well as my own fieldwork. Kharoudi is a well-known village across Punjab not only in terms of its long-established transnational connections, but also because of its infrastructural development such as a family theatre, primary schools with computer facilities, a sewerage system, two children's parks, solar heater systems, and solar street lighting.

According to the census records of 2011, there were 188 households in Kharoudi and the total inhabitants of the village numbered 806.[4] . However, during my period

---

[3] See wikimapia.org/7812733/Modern-Village-of-Distt-Hoshiarpur-Punjab-KHAROUDI-Gill-House, accessed on April 2012.

[4] See http://www.onefivenine.com/india/villages/Hoshiarpur/Mahilpur/Kharaudi, accessed on 27 June 2019.

of fieldwork from 2011 to 2012, five homes were locked during the entire period I spent in the village. These undoubtedly belonged to NRIs who had migrated abroad a long while ago. No one lived in these homes nor did anybody visit these homes during the period of fieldwork. Thus, when I did my fieldwork, there were 137 households and the total population then residing in the village was 644, excluding the 5 locked households. I interviewed 1 person from each household, which means the total number of interviewees was 137. Therefore, the person who answered my question was the household reference person who told me about all the other household members. Out of the total population of 644 of those who were resident of Kharoudi, 319 were men and 325 were women. Out of the total number of 137 people interviewed, 5 were caretakers in the homes of NRI people who have permanently migrated from the village but still retain their village homes. All of the caretakers were living in the employer's house; they are, therefore, treated as the household reference person for these 5 households. Out of the 137 households in the village, 93 households had one or more members who had emigrated overseas. Sometimes villagers refer to these migrant households as 'NRI de ghar' (NRI household). Migrant households include short-term NRI visitors, returned migrants, and migrants currently abroad. Respondents were from all castes, though the predominant two groups were Ad-Dharmi and Jat. Migration from the village was to diverse countries across the globe, including Canada, the USA, the UK, and other European countries and various Middle Eastern countries; the majority seemed to be going to Dubai. Men outnumbered women migrants and migration without family, rather than with family, was the predominant pattern. It is clear that migration was not homogeneous across castes or classes. The richer, higher castes and landholders had a different pattern of migration, connections, and linkages to Kharoudi in comparison to the poorer, lower castes and landless migrants. For example, landless lower castes migrated primarily to the Gulf countries. Most of them were employed as labourers in Dubai, Lebanon, Oman, and Abu Dhabi. A few people among the lower castes migrated to Italy and the UK.

Short-term NRI visitors had various reasons to visit Kharoudi. Some were there to look after an NRI project, others to meet family and friends or to look after their personal property. By and large, visits are a way of renewing ties with the village-based families and with the culture of the home village. Looking after personal property is another important reason for visiting. Many migrants still own or hold property in the village and this is a substantial and material link through which they maintain ties, and an important reason why they still speak of Kharoudi as 'home'. During my fieldwork, one of my respondents who was the founder of Village Kharoudi Lifestyle Improvement Project and on the Village Lifestyle Improvement Board (VLIB) said,

Twice in a year, I visit my village to look after the NRI project. I started this project for the welfare and development of my ancestral homeland.

Another respondent who is managing the Village Kharoudi Lifestyle Improvement Project is a retired engineer from Abu Dhabi, and he said,

After retirement, I have permanently decided to return to my village because I have a huge property in the village and I cannot rely on my relatives to look after it.

Kharoudi migrants have contributed immensely to the development of their village. The 'Pillar of Appreciation' in Figure 9.2 is the apparent picture of the sum of money they have donated to the village. As it is also mentioned in the picture, 'Pillar of Appreciation; Dedicated to those NRIs of this village who donated rupees lakh or more to make their ancestral village a shining example of the 21st century modern human habitat of India.' Although there have been wealthy individuals who undertook philanthropic work on their own and in their own way, most of the community remittances currently being mobilized are through the development of hometown or village-welfare associations. In the entire process of circular migration,

Figure 9.2 | Indicates the number of donations given by Kharoudi NRIs for the infrastructural development of the village

*Source*: Picture taken by the field investigator, October 2011.

remittances largely play a vital role in connecting the individuals back to their homeland. Social remittances are the other significant factors through which there is an exchange of ideas, values, and beliefs between the host and the home country. Figure 9.3 shows two different images of village Kharoudi, which was only possible with the tremendous contribution of NRIs. These are from open street to finished street, from polluted ponds to fish tanks, from the smelly marsh in the middle of the village to a square park with a pillar of appreciation in the middle, and a new main street with sidewalks and the computer room and library in the school. In the middle of this board, there is also the picture of Harman Singh and Raghubir Singh (main contributors to this project) monitoring the work. This picture was hung in the drawing room of Baldev Singh who is a returnee NRI from Abu Dhabi and also the caretaker of this project.

According to Rajwade (2005), with the development of a sanitation and water management system, the image of Kharoudi has changed entirely. This change was a result of the contribution of Kharoudi NRIs. The most significant part of this project was that it crossed the boundaries of caste and encouraged each and every villager to contribute their share of wealth for village development. Kharoudi was not only developed in infrastructural terms such as sewerage pipes, water pipes,

Figure 9.3 | A poster of Village Life Improvement Program. The poster is titled 'Village Kharoudi: Modernization in Progress (before) and (after)', November 2011

*Source*: Photograph by the author.

Figure 9.4 | Primary school with computer facilities, village Kharoudi, October 2011
*Source*: Photograph by the author.

solar-power lights, and panchayat community centre but also has advanced in the field of education. A primary school in the village is well equipped with five computers, and the presence of one computer teacher (Figure 9.4).

The fieldwork in Kharoudi has provided insights into the present scenario of migration and its future implications. In particular, this case study highlights the migration of two major caste-groups of villagers—the Jats (upper caste) and Ad-Dharmi (lower caste) migrants. An analysis of migration patterns reveals the complex picture that migration as a process presents in the life of the village itself and how the different categories of migrants affect the life of the village as a whole. I have categorized them as big fishes and small fishes. Big fishes are the main transformers of Kharoudi village. A majority of the migrants contributing to the gurdwara in the village were from upper/dominant caste households; however, the Scheduled Caste (SC) contributions to the gurdwara were also significant. Overall village development, which includes village infrastructure, the school, health club, and cremation centre, was an important focus of contribution for upper/dominant caste households; almost an equal number from among them donated for village improvement as well as towards the gurdwara. The SC contributions, on the other hand, seem to be towards religious institutions. During the interviews, I asked one of my migrant respondents, Harman Singh (the main contributor to the project in Kharoudi), what led him to begin the project and start giving back to his village. He told me that many years ago he brought his daughter to India to show her

Kharoudi. He proudly showed her the village where he spent his childhood. His daughter then said,

> If this is your village and you have your childhood memories here then you should improve the condition of the village. You should provide as many facilities as possible here to distinguish it from other villages.

This really struck him and he started thinking of about a project where all the NRIs of Kharoudi would contribute to their ancestral village. According to him, it was the joint efforts of the NRIs which brought better results for Kharoudi. When I asked him how much his contribution was, he told me that he does not even remember how many times he has contributed and he does not want to reveal it because as he said there is no use in contributing if one is counting one's money. During the interview, Harman Singh also expressed his views about his homeland. He told me that Gandhiji said, 'Villages are the soul of India', which according to Harman is absolutely true because in cities people live such congested lives that there is no space for roots. They do not have enough space for the family members. On the other hand, in the villages, you will find big open spaces. It is not congested like cities. He said,

> We are attached with our roots and want to see it developed over a period of time and want to avail all the modern amenities and facilities here but the only depressing thought is that the villagers do not maintain these later on. If NRIs in village contributed it is not their duty to maintain everything; in fact, it is the duty of the villagers who are living here. It can only be possible by sharing the same interests and collective efforts. It is not a responsibility of one person.

## Conclusion

In the present age of global movement, migrants no longer inhabit an enclosed space as their daily practices draw them between sending and receiving communities/countries. They can be conceived as 'transmigrants' which means those migrants whose everyday lives depend on multiple and constant interconnections across transnational borders and whose public identities are recognized by more than one nation-state. After migration, they have been called by different names in Punjab such as NRIs, the OPs (overseas Punjabis), *pravasi*s,[5] and new VIPs; the last term used by Tatla (2009) to characterize a new status of migrant in Punjab.

---

[5] *Pravasi* means emigrant in Hindi language, taken from https://www.collinsdictionary.com/dictionary/hindi-english.

The pattern of migration not only influenced the migrant but also influenced the families left behind.

The Jat caste is more prevalent in Kharoudi than the lower castes. Among the lower castes, the majority belonged to the Ad-Dharmi and Ravidasi groups. Caste plays a significant role in differentiating migration patterns from the village. Thus, for example, only upper-caste migrants managed to purchase agricultural land in the village after their migration. None of the SC migrants managed to purchase agricultural land; most SC migrants managed to build *pucca*[6] homes on the foundations of their old homes. Further, more upper-caste migrants managed to migrate with the help of relatives and friends by comparison to the SC migrants. Both the purchase of land and diaspora networks gives us a sense of how links with homelands are maintained and give us a sense of the differences between castes in creating 'transnational' people with 'transnational' links. Caste intervenes strongly in enabling or restricting the development of transnational links/networks and the very nature of transnationalism itself.

The people who migrated to the Middle East said that it was less expensive to migrate to any Gulf country. Most of them migrated on work permit visas, through agents. Caste enters the picture again; the SC migrants predominate among those who go to the Middle East with the help of agents. The financial sources for migration of upper-/dominant-caste migrants are mostly from family resources (either within the village or financed by relatives abroad) or sale of assets; the SC migrants largely borrowed money from relatives and friends. A small percentage of the SC migrants also took bank loans to finance their migration.

A majority of the migrants who visited their homeland for a short time did so mainly to visit their families and friends and to look after the NRI project discussed previously and take care of property matters. Those migrants who returned permanently did so mainly due to a lack of permanent jobs abroad.

The notion of transforming the village or giving back to the home depends on multiple factors such as ownership of land in the village, history of migration, country of immigration, and status of the migrant abroad—in other words on the nature of transnational links that migrants maintain and foster. The migration of upper-caste Jats is mostly to the USA, Canada, and European countries. On the other hand, Ad-Dharmi migrants mostly migrated on work permits or illegally with the help of agents to Europe or the USA. In the case of Jat migrants, they migrated with their families, whereas Ad-Dharmi migrants mostly migrated without families. The temporary migration to the Gulf countries is also because of citizenship/nationality/permit policies in this region. Irregular/illegal migration from Kharoudi was mostly to Western/European countries rather than to the Gulf countries. Migrants going to the Gulf countries were on work permit visas. The Gulf migration nevertheless

---

[6] *Pucca* home is made up of bricks and concrete.

is temporary migration, so it cannot be considered as a migrant's country of final destination.

Gidwani and Sivramakrishnan (2004) discussed circular migration as a facilitating factor of rural cosmopolitanism in India. According to them, a migrant's active involvement in both the places of origin and destination is not only limited to geographic space and ideas but also reaches the social space in different worlds. With the example of Manavalan village and a teenage girl, Gidwani and Sivramakrishnan (2004: 341) presented the picture of 'cosmopolitanism of circulating people, whose social space of reproduction encompasses—and disrupts—the space of the conventionally "urban and rural"'. The term cosmopolitanism which Gidwani and Sivramakrishnan (2004: 345) defined is that 'art of being which is able to straddle a political world of difference and deploy the technologies of one to some advantage in the other'. I find this to be true of Kharoudi. In the process of circular migration, culture is transformed. This is not a one-sided phenomenon but a dual-sided phenomenon. Transnational migration brings changes in the social world of the village and leaves a deep impact on cultural values, norms, ideas, and lifestyles. Setting themselves up as patrons of religious events, many Gulf-returned migrants are transforming wealth into status and power in culturally approved ways but with twists. On the other hand, Puri (2003: 212) analysed the different behaviour of migrants when they return to their motherland. They found themselves to be unique in term of attitude, behaviour, and beliefs. Their exposure to Western countries makes them distinct in their ideas and day-to-day behaviour relative to their village counterparts. Levitt (2001: 54–55) calls this 'social remittances in which the ideas, behaviours and social capital that flow from abroad'. According to her, these social remittances move globally with migrants to their country of destination. When migrants return to their homeland these same ideas and practices become problematic and challenging for those people who stay behind (Levitt, 2001). In the case of Kharoudi, these social and cultural changes are quite prominent. Those migrants who returned from abroad have brought along all the home appliances for their house such as microwave oven, air conditioner, computers, water purifier, sometimes induction oven, the trend of using tissue papers after eating food, using toilet paper in their bathrooms, or sometimes using foreign products for their skin and hair. Such material and ideological changes transform everyday life in the village. Another very crucial instance of their exposure to Western world was visible that quite a few NRIs visiting for short period preferred to give their interviews in English, like Harman Singh and Sohan Singh Deo. They prefer to promote their newly enhanced skill on language, demarcating sharp prejudice against the local natives.

The migration process was not homogeneous across castes and classes. For example, families of the Jat migrants have joined them later on, but the families of the Dalit migrants are left behind in the village. I have observed that there were mostly women who were alone with their children in the houses. Their husbands send back money which was used only for family consumption. There was only one lower-caste Ad-Dharmi from England who migrated quite a long time ago and has also contributed to the village like the Jat NRIs. It shows that there are some successful migration stories of the SC migrants in Kharoudi. Nonetheless, they are fewer in number than the upper or dominant caste.

Today, Kharoudi is known as modern or model village. The transnational villagers of Kharoudi keep on moving between their two homes, and sometimes more than two homes. One is the country of emigration, and the other is the country of immigration. The notion of 'home' and 'homeland' is more precise for the first-generation migrants who are born and brought up in the village because second-generation and third-generation migrants seem to consider only one home where they were born and brought up and usually get married there. However, even amidst their negative feelings towards village homes in Punjab, there is a relationship they acknowledge as their 'roots'. This acknowledgment translates through music, fashion, names, and often religious or ritual practices, to the formation of an idea of 'home'. It shows that attachment with the roots or with the ancestral village, though diminishing from generation to generation, is ultimately not totally absent. However, it does affect the contribution for village development and active involvement in philanthropic activities in the homeland. It would, therefore, be interesting to study the future prospect of many transnational villages like Kharoudi, after another two decades to see the effects of the subsequent generations and their links with village life in Kharoudi.

# References

Bailey, Ajay. 2011. 'In Search of Livelihoods: Migration and Mobility from Karnataka to Goa'. In *Migration, Identity and Conflict: India Migration Report 2011*, edited by S. Irudaya Rajan, 108–124. New Delhi: Routledge.

Ballard, Roger. 2004. 'A Case of Capital-Rich Under-Development: The Paradoxical Consequence of Successful Transnational Entrepreneurship from Mirpur'. In *Migration, Modernity and Social Transformation in South Asia*, edited by Filippo Osella and Katy Gardner, 25–57. New Delhi: Sage Publications.

Barrier, N. Gerald. 2007. 'Sikh Emigrants and Their Homelands: The Transmission of Information Resources and Values in the Early Twentieth Century'. *Sociology of Diaspora: A Reader*, vol. 2, edited by Ajaya K. Sahoo and Maharaj Brij, 663–689. New Delhi: Rawat Publications.

Castle, Stephen and Mark J. Miller. 1998. *The Age of Migration: International Population Movements in the Modern World*. New York: Palgrave Macmillan.

Chopra, Radhika. 2011. *Militant and Migrant: The Politics and Social History of Punjab*. New Delhi: Routledge.

Dhesi, Autar S. 2008. 'Overseas Punjabis and Rural Development'. In *Rural Development in Punjab: A Success Story Going Astray*, edited by Autar S. Dhesi and Gurmail Singh, 427–445. New Delhi: Routledge.

Dusenbery, Verne A. and Darshan S. Tatla, eds. 2009. 'Introduction: NRIs Are the New VIPs'. In *Sikh Diaspora Philanthropy in Punjab: Global Giving for Local Good*, 2–30. New Delhi: Oxford University Press.

Gidwani, Vinay and Sivaramakrishnan, K. 2004. 'Circular Migration and Rural Cosmopolitanism in India'. In *Modernity and Social Transformation in South Asia*, edited by Filippo Osella and Katy Gardner, 339–367. New Delhi: Sage Publications.

de Haas, Hein. 2005. 'International Migration, Remittances and Development: Myths and Facts'. *Third World Quarterly* 26(8): 1269–1284. Available at https://www.jstore.org/stable/4017714?seq=1#page_scan_tab_contents. Accessed on 21 August 2018.

Harriss, Kaveri and Filippo Osella, eds. 2010. '"Educational Transnationalism" and the Global Production of Educational Regimes'. In *Transnationalism and Institutional Transformations*, edited by T. Faist and P. Pitkanen, 140–163. Collected working papers from the TRANS-NET Project (Working Paper 87/2010). Center on Migration, Citizenship and Development, Faculty of Sociology, University of Bielefed.

Levitt, Peggy. 2001. *The Transnational Villagers*. London: University of California Press.

Puri, Harish K. 2003. 'Revolutionaries of Will: Pioneer Punjabi Migrants to North America'. In *Development, Gender and Diaspora: Context of Globalization*, edited by Paramjit S. Judge and S. L. Sharma, 207–227. New Delhi: Rawat Publications.

Rai, Rajesh. 2014. *Indians in Singapore, 1819–1945: Diaspora in the Colonial Port City*. New Delhi: Oxford University Press.

Rajwade, Gayatri. 2005. 'Village Shows Cleanliness Is Affordable'. *The Tribune Chandigarh*. 16 March.

Rajan, S. Irudaya and U. S. Mishra, eds. 2011. 'Facets of Indian Mobility: An Update'. In *Migration, Identity and Conflict: India Migration Report 2011*, edited by S. Irudaya Rajan, 1–8. New Delhi: Routledge.

Ratha, Dilip. 2013. 'The Impact of Remittances on Economic Growth and Poverty Reduction'. No. 8, September. Available at http://www.migrationpolicy.org/pubs/Remittances-PovertyReduction.pdf. Accessed on 21 August 2018.

StudyMoose. 2016. 'The Soul of the Real India Lives in Its Villages'. 1 October. Available at https://studymoose.com/the-soul-of-the-real-india-lives-in-its-villages-essay, accessed on 10 June 2012; http://www.onefivenine.com/india/villages/Hoshiarpur/Mahilpur/Kharaudi, accessed on 27 June 2019.

Tandon, Prakash. 1968. *Punjabi Century, 1857–1947*. Berkeley, CA: University of California Press.

Tatla, Darshan S. 1999. *The Sikh Diaspora: The Search for Statehood*. London: UCL Press.

———. 2009. 'Sikh Diaspora Philanthropy: Direction, Incentives and Impact on Punjab'. In *Sikh Diaspora Philanthropy in Punjab: Global Giving for Local Good*, edited by Verne A. Dusenbery and Darshan S. Tatla, 236–270. New Delhi: Oxford University Press.

Thandi, Shinder S. 2008. 'Evaluating the Potential Contribution of the Punjabi Diaspora to Rural Development'. In *Rural Development in Punjab: A Success Story Going Astray*, edited by Autar S. Dhesi and Gurmail Singh, 446–459. New Delhi: Routledge.

United Nations. 2002. *International Migration Report, 2002*. Department of Social and Economic Affairs, Population Division. Available at http://www.un.org/esa/population/publications/ ittmig2002/2002ITTMIGTEXT22-11.pdf. Accessed on 22 August 2012.

Vertovec, Steven. 2007. 'Migrant Transnationalism and Modes of Transformation'. In *Rethinking Migration: Theoretical and Empirical Perspective*, edited by Portes Alejandro and Josh de Wind, 149–180. New York: Berghahn.

———. 2009. *Transnationalism*. London: Routledge.

Walton-Roberts, Margaret. 2004. 'Returning, Remitting, Reshaping: Non-Resident Indians and the Transformation of Society and Space in Punjab, India'. In *Transnational Spaces*, edited by P. Crang, C. Dwyer, and P. Jackson, 78–103. London: Routledge.

Wikimapia. 'Modern Village of Distt: Hoshiarpur Punjab: Kharoudi, Gill. House. 24 Feburary 2005. Available at http://wikimapia.org/.../Modern-Village-of-Distt-Hoshiarpur-Punjab-Kharoudi-Gill-House. Accessed on 4 August 2012.

# 10

# The Production of Nurses for Global Markets
## *Tracing Capital and Labour Circulation In and Out of Asia*

MARGARET WALTON-ROBERTS

## Introduction

How do capital and labour mobilities interact in the context of Indian nurse training and migration, and what kind of institutional actors facilitate the multiscalar mobility of this labour? This chapter will address this question using the example of the global mobility of nurses. Nurses represent the largest, most internationalized and feminized section of the health profession, and developed regions of world have demanded well-trained nurses because of demographic and health care delivery changes. These changes are connecting regions of the world through increasingly globally oriented models of nursing training, skills development, and labour and related capital mobility. The nature of historic and new migration corridors marks the evolving spatiality of this labour mobility and associated capital flows. Novel state–market interactions structure these processes of labour mobility and mark new institutional forms of governance related to nurse training and deployment of migrant labour. Nursing is a specifically gendered occupation, and the cultural context allows us to understand the particular embodied nature of nursing—how this contributes to the disciplining and controlling of workers, and how their skills and capabilities are constructed and utilized. This chapter makes explicit connection between labour and capital mobility by drawing upon research conducted in India and Canada to highlight how labour and capital mobilities interact in global nursing labour circulation.

The health care services industry is one of the most significant and growing parts of the global economy. The United Nations' International Standard Industrial Classification (ISIC) categorizes the health care industry as hospital activities, medical and dental practice activities, and other human health activities that occur under the supervision of health professionals in various areas. In terms of value, a 2017 health care outlook report by Deloitte (2017) indicated that health care spending represents 10.4 per cent of global GDP in 2015 (US$7 trillion in 2015) and is expected to rise over the next 5 years, especially in low-income nations. Health care is witnessing neoliberal industrialization in terms of the division, standardization, deskilling of health care labour, and rise of managerial superstructures (Rastegar, 2004), including widespread but differentiated engagement with New Public Management approaches to increase efficiency and enhance innovation (Pollitt and Bouckaert, 2017).

The World Health Organization (WHO) estimates a global shortage of 4.3 million health care professionals, and the migration of these workers (mainly from low- to higher-income nations) represents a challenge, both in terms of losing workers and integrating internationally trained workers into national health systems (Clark, Stewart, and Clark, 2006). The international migration of health workers has long been an issue of state health policy concern, but as health services have become corporatized, privatized, and commoditized, health worker migration is increasingly orchestrated via global service mechanisms (Collyer and White, 2011), which can be seen as a commodity that is formed and exported by state and private capitalist interests. This is particularly relevant in Asia, seen as the primary driver of the globalization of health service delivery (Crone, 2008) and a key region for both internal and outward movements of health care workers, particularly nurses (Walton-Roberts, Bhutani, and Kaur, 2017; Castro-Palaganas et al., 2017).

Health care worker migration research has focused on the issues of brain drain, flight, and gain (Bourgeault et al., 2010; Khadria, 2009; Crush and Pendleton, 2011). This chapter follows earlier research (Walton-Roberts, 2015) and moves beyond a singular focus on the mobility of health workers; rather, the chapter contributes to theorizing transnational labour and capital mobility together in the case of the global mobility of India-trained nurses.

## Spatiality

The mobility of nurses into and out of India has a history woven together with colonial and global capitalism. India's engagement with British colonialism and American neocolonialism has shaped the very idea of nursing, its training structures, and its ongoing occupational evolution (Walton-Roberts, 2012; Healey, 2014). Colonial capital and labour mobility included forms of philanthropic and religious investment from institutes such as the Rockefeller Foundation and Christian missionary groups to support the development of the nursing profession in India, including the movement of Western-trained nurses and other health professionals into India (Healey, 2008; Reddy, 2015). In the 1950s, this directionality began to change as India-trained medical professionals, among others, were recruited into the service of the UK and other Western markets to staff the expansion of national health care systems (Raghuram, 2009). The reversals in the flow of health professionals are suggestive of a form of extraterritorial investment in labour training subsequently drawn upon by colonizing powers (Raghuram, 2009; see also Choy, 2003 in the case of the Philippines).

Since the 1970s, we have seen significant flows of health workers from relatively poor Asian, African, and Small Island States to the Global North, often leading to negative development consequences for sending nations (Mackintosh, Raghuram, and Leroy, 2006). Developed regions of the world demand well-trained nurses because of their ageing populations (England and Henry, 2013), the increased prevalence of chronic diseases, the shortage of primary care physicians, and the use of nursing in managing complex clinical cases (Gostin, 2008). Demographic and health care delivery changes are thus creating demand for nursing and other care workers in more developed states that cannot be satisfied through their domestic supply (Kingma, 2006; Connell and Walton-Roberts, 2016). Moreover, universal maldistribution of health workers means that rural and remote areas are often underserved, and Internationally Educated Health Professionals (IEHPs) have often been used to address these gaps (Mbemba et al., 2013). In response to these problems, in 2010 the WHO launched a voluntary code of practice to regulate and monitor health worker migration and international recruitment from regions of the world considered to be facing chronic health care shortages (Aluttis, Bishaw, and Frank, 2014). Despite these voluntary codes and efforts to curtail the negative development effects of health worker migration, the process continues. Census data from the early 2000s indicates that in Australia 48 per cent of doctors and 29 per cent of nurses were born overseas, the figures for Canada are 32 per cent and 17 per cent; the UK, 15 per cent and 33 per cent; and the USA, 19 per cent and 24 per cent respectively (WHO, 2014: 93). Recent high-level dialogues on health worker migration have confirmed, among other things, 'the accelerating and dynamic nature of international health worker movement', the blurring of distinctive source and destination countries, increasing interregional movements occurring alongside Global North to South movements, increasingly temporary migration, and increased source country production that is often disconnected from labour markets (WHO, 2017: 1).

These changing dynamics of international health worker migration are connecting regions of the world through increasingly globally orientated models of health training and professional mobility facilitation (Kingma, 2006). Linked to the increased scope and scale of IEHP global migration, professional standards and qualification assessments have become globalized and have significant implications for health worker regulation and the restructuring of occupational hierarchies (Baumann and Blythe, 2008; Segouin, Hodges, and Brechat, 2005). These international opportunities mean that spatial mobility is a core feature of health occupations, and candidates in lower- and middle-income nations increasingly select health careers because of the global migration prospects they offer (Connell, 2014; Walton-Roberts, Bhutani, and Kaur, 2017). Spatial mobility has thus become part and parcel of the very choice to enter the health occupations, and this spatial dimension informs the delivery, costs, and regulation of education and training in key supply markets in various ways, including reducing quality and increasing costs (Baumann and Blythe, 2008; Walton-Roberts, 2015). Internationalization also interacts with training in destination markets; for example, the Caribbean offshore medical training industry invests millions of dollars in order to access prized US-based residency spots, and this monetization is out-competing medical students from US schools (Halperin and Goldberg, 2016).

Within India, the geography of Indian nurse migration is diverse, including internal and international mobility. Across India, the capacity for training nurses varies, but a basic assessment of the number of recognized nursing programmes according to the Indian Nursing Council by state population numbers indicates that the largest training capacity exists in southern India, especially Karnataka, Andhra Pradesh, and Tamil Nadu (Walton-Roberts, 2015). This balance explains some of the internal migration of student nurses from Kerala to neighbouring Karnataka, since nursing is heavily oversubscribed in Kerala due to its historical role in nurse education (George, 2005). The popularity of nursing means that many students in Kerala are unable to get into the colleges of their choice and instead go to Bangalore in Karnataka to study, contributing to significant rates of internal migration for young people. Zachariah and Rajan (2007) found that after the unemployed, students constituted the second largest outmigration group from Kerala at 25.8 per cent, leading them to argue that Kerala's post-matric education capacity was underdeveloped. Relying on internal migration for the provision of nursing education is not without its risks, since the state of nursing education in Karnataka has been precarious; it expanded its capacity in the early 2000s (Walton-Roberts, 2015), but faced numerous charges of paper-only colleges and colleges with inadequate facilities (*Times of India*, 2008). In 2017, the Indian College of Nurses refused to license a number of Karnataka-based nursing colleges (*Times of India*, 2017).

In terms of international mobility, there are well-worn regional migration networks between southern India and the Gulf States and Organization for Economic Cooperation and Development (OECD) markets (Percot, 2016; George, 2005), together with international migration from northern India to North America, Europe, and Australia (Walton-Roberts, Bhutani, and Kaur, 2017). The UK has a long history of recruiting from India, and in the wake of the WHO voluntary code for ethical recruitment, India has remained a key source of recruitment because it 'has remained a disturbingly grey area so far, as a poor developing country with an apparently heaving mass of world-class employees' (Ahmed, 2001). Analysis of current global migration circuits from India suggests that colonial networks marked by the hegemony of the English language represent a preferential geographical circuit that includes the British Isles, Ireland, Singapore, and white-settler colonies of Australia, New Zealand, South Africa, and Canada. Indian nurses enter this network, but India itself does not often enjoy the same preferential entry into the network as nurses from other white-settler colonial states. This highlights one of the main policy concerns linked to IEHP migration, that of credential devaluation, and professional marginalization of immigrants.

This changing spatiality of migration flows into and out of India indicates the changes in how borders structure the value of labour. Transborder labour flows are subjected to variable training standards, credential and visa requirements, and health and other checks. These all represent forms of flexible control over the movement of workers but are also mechanisms of accumulation for the state and market actors involved. As Mezzadra and Neilson's (2013: 8) work on 'the border as method' suggests, 'the regulatory functions and symbolic power of the border test the barrier between sovereignty and more flexible forms of global governance in ways that provide a prism through which to track the transformations of capital and the struggles that mount within and against them'. Mezzadra and Neilson (2013) argue that borders are not only proliferating but also heterogenizing in their variable articulation with labour and other material transfers such as capital and goods. For instance, unlike earlier phases of colonial nurse deployment from the heart of the British Empire to the peripheries (Healey, 2008; Yeates, 2009), international mobility in the current period of health care workers is marked by regulatory barriers that exact immense costs, especially in terms of foreign credential devaluation (Bourgeault et al., 2010; Sweetman, McDonald, and Hawthorne, 2015). Scholars have begun to interpret this transfer as a new form of unequal exchange (Valiani, 2011; Wise and Covarrubias, 2012).

To understand further the spatial mobility of nurses from India and associated capital flows, we need to focus on the role of the state and market institutions as facilitators and regulators of both capital and labour mobility in nursing.

## Distinct Institutional Forms of State and Market Interaction

Nurses comprise two-thirds of India's health workforce, and the 2015 National Health Plan recognizes the need to enhance the specialist training of this group and expand employment opportunities (Ministry of Health and Family Welfare, 2014). The regulation of nursing education, however, has been dominated by attempts at deregulating the sector in the interest of private colleges, which in turn have marketed nursing as a conduit for international opportunity (Walton-Roberts, 2015). Recent growth in the nurse education sector is impressive, with a total of 300,000 training seats from auxiliary, to diploma, bachelors and MSc and PhD positions (FICCI, 2016). However, research-focused nursing programmes in India are extremely limited, only graduating 21 nursing PhDs in 2014–2015 (FICCI, 2016: 27), and continuous education for those in the profession is poorly organized. Those entering nursing desire highly targeted employment outcomes: 'Within India, nurses take up the profession with a clear goal: to use it as a bridge to get international placements, or, if they work in India, get placements in government hospitals as the compensation there is much better, and job security and working hours are much better managed' (FICCI, 2016: 29). Indeed, while over 60,000 nurses are graduated each year, it is estimated that over 20 per cent of them emigrate, and these are usually BSc and higher degree holders (*Times of India*, 2015).

Some are concerned about this exodus in terms of loss to the national health system, but national governments also gain a return from this exodus through migrant remittances (Walton-Roberts, 2004), diasporic investment (often in the health care sector itself), and the productive employment of their surplus working population abroad. State-led interest in health worker migration can be seen in terms of bilateral service trade agreements negotiated between India and other Global South partners (Crone, 2008; Walton-Roberts, 2015) as well as the multistage labour migration pathways that emerge as part of migration processes (Percot, 2016). The openness of key immigrant destination markets has been a matter of concern for the Indian government. For example, Donald Trump's efforts to tighten renewals of H1B and L1 visas for skilled workers in the USA (including health and IT professionals), resulted in the Indian government lobbying the US government regarding the economic and technical value of Indian workers to the US economy (*Economic Times*, 2017). The quality of the labour produced domestically can thus add value to a national workforce that is globally orientated; concomitantly poor quality can diminish the national reputation of this workforce.

International migration can spatially and socially distort the training and quality of domestic labour, and the degree to which this occurs is a highly contingent and complex phenomenon (Khadria, 2009). This form of export-led development represents the mobility of labour and related capital (both in terms of public and private investment in training, and returns in the form of international currency). Success, however, depends upon India positioning itself as a valuable source of well-trained English-speaking health professionals within relevant circuits or value chains constituted through a specific combination of state and market forces.

## State Regulation of Education and Skills Training

States play a role in helping suppliers to position themselves within value systems, 'state action and inaction creates the enabling conditions that shape whether and how firms, regions and nations are able to engage with global markets, and their capacities to upgrade these engagements' (Neilson, Pritchard, and Yeung, 2014: 8). Scholars have noted that although the complex international interactions occurring in global value chains have been explored, 'the national institutional contexts in which these new international strategies are played out, and their consequences for capability formation and skills development, are in the main absent' (Ramirez and Rainbird, 2010: 700). Skills upgrading is demanded as states and firms attempt to derive more from higher value processes and activities. A great deal of a firm's ability to achieve this value capture is based on national systems and institutional forms of skills development.

The Indian state's role in nurse training structures can be traced through to the Indian Nursing Act, which was framed in 1947 and is still currently the regulatory framework for the provision of nursing education. The Indian Nursing Council, the professional regulator for the profession, was formed in 1949, in part through the Trained Nurses Association of India (TNAI), which was instrumental in the overseas training of nurses under the colonial system. There have been a series of reports on nursing that have all attempted to modernize the profession. The Government of Indian formed the Sarojini Varadappan Committee in 1990 to report on nursing, finding numerous deficiencies including lack of nurses, a curative model of health, the practice of depending on student labour, shortage of nurses in hospitals, poorly resourced schools with a lack of necessary equipment and infrastructure, and poor pay and working conditions. The report also noted the severe lack of autonomy and respect for the nursing profession and commented that physicians usually made decisions and gave directions with regard to nurses and nursing care. The report offered numerous recommendations in both nursing education and nursing employment. Following this a working group on education and manpower was formed in 1991, which encouraged continuing higher-level nursing education, including the creation of a PhD programme, higher-level education for teachers, changes to the BSc programme, and the suggestion to phase out the three-year General Nursing and Midwifery (GNM) diploma by 2020.

In the recent past, the most active regulation of nursing education by the Indian state has come through phases of deregulation. In late 2008, the Indian Nursing Council announced a number of changes in the regulations guiding nursing programmes that would facilitate both an increase in student numbers and enhanced capacity. Admission eligibility criteria were reduced for all nursing programme categories. These changes aimed at increasing the pool of candidates, while other regulatory changes targeted increasing institutional capacity by reducing the standards demanded of educational facilities, one of the key means by which government and regulatory institutions determine the basis for providing licenses (Peters, Rao, and Fryatt, 2003: 254). Changes were also made to teaching standards, and super-specialty hospitals were allowed to start MSc programmes without having an undergraduate programme in place. At the time student groups expressed concern about these changes and how they might impact the quality and global reputation of Indian nurse training, but these changes were positively greeted by the private sector (*Times of India*, 2008).

Subsequent reports on nursing in India identify many of the same problems that have plagued the profession for some time in terms of training quality and regulation, the status of the occupation, and retention of trained nurses within the Indian health care sector (FICCI, 2016). Regulations of the many Indian health professional councils have been a challenge for the government, in part due to powerful vested interests connected to the financial returns made by colleges. Professional regulation of health workers is managed through four councils (medical, dental, nursing, and pharmacy), and despite charges of corruption, most acutely in the Medical Council of India (Berger, 2014), this system currently remains intact. The Indian central government's attempts to create a new National Council for Human Resources in Health have not succeeded.

> Reforms in each of these areas, but especially in professional councils ... is also facing resistance from certain stakeholders and will require considerable political leadership and public support to implement these reforms. There are also genuine concerns that it would bring back 'license raj' the unnecessary and inefficient Government interference in private sector growth. (Ministry of Health and Family Welfare, 2014: 11)

Nursing is intimately shaped by distinct Indian institutional formations, but national training systems reflect state–market interactions within a globally orientated and corporatized health sector.

## State and Non-state Interactions in Facilitating Nurse Migration

There is no formal Indian policy to promote the migration of health workers, rather there exists a range of contradictory views from employers, state and central governments, and nursing regulators that simultaneously support, suppress, and encourage international migration as a health workforce plan (Walton-Roberts et al., 2017). Private interests are keen to seize the opportunities linked to international migration, and their pressure on the state has eased some of the regulatory controls on training institutions. The role of the state governments, with support from the central government and national regulatory groups, indicates the active involvement of these actors in creating a training system that can satisfy international as well as domestic needs. The changing approach of the Indian central and state governments illustrates the internationalization and harmonization of nursing education that is evident in the sector (Baumann and Blythe, 2008). Transformations in nursing education are influenced by a multitude of factors that the state is often reacting to. Institutional groups such as recruiters, professional associations, state governments, private educational and medical interests, and internationalized health testing and education groups mediate this reaction. In India, as international demand for nurses has increased, national regulations of training institutions have eased, and private health groups have become more and more active in 'business process outsourcing' systems of training, recruitment, and placement of nurses overseas (Khadria, 2007). Currently, 90 per cent of nursing educational institutions in India are in the private sector (FICCI, 2016: 23).

Some states are active in promoting channels for international migration. The state of Kerala, for example, is actively involved in the overseas recruitment of labour, ostensibly to protect would-be migrants from unlawful recruitment agents. It does this through the Kerala-government-owned Overseas Development and Employment Promotion Consultants (ODEPC), a recruitment and travel consultant, 'soliciting only the best trained and high skilled Keralites for overseas deployment'.[1] The agency is active in health worker deployment, for example, a search on the ODEPC website in April 2018 using the keyword 'nurse' brought up seven advertisements for nursing positions in the UK, Ireland, Saudi Arabia, and the United Arab Emirates; these were mostly calls for interviews for ongoing recruitment drives.[2] States can also insert themselves into skilled migration circuits by attracting key testing centres into their jurisdictions. In 2003, the Kerala state government successfully lobbied the Philadelphia-based Commission of Graduates of Foreign Nursing Schools (CGFNS) to have Kochi become an exam centre in addition to Bangalore, Mumbai, and Delhi. The CGFNS identifies itself as the largest credentials evaluation organization in the world with testing centres in over 50 countries, and it administers the testing system required before nurses can take the NCLEX-RN® licensure exam required by the majority of US states (and most of Canada) prior to nurse registration. In 2015, CGFNS's revenue was US$10.8 million.[3]

---

[1] See http://odepc.kerala.gov.in/, accessed on 14 June 2019.
[2] See http://odepc.kerala.gov.in/search-job-results.html, accessed on 20 April 2018.
[3] See https://projects.propublica.org/nonprofits/organizations/232026352, accessed on 21 May 2019.

Once an office is located in the country, these organizations become important conduits for internationalization of education and training, for example, in 2008, the CGFNS rolled out two country-specific programmes which test nursing students in situ with the stated intention to improve the nursing education in those respective countries, not to act explicitly as a migration conduit. In India, a pilot programme, Assessment of General Nursing Knowledge (AGNK), was launched in combination with AHED Global Healthcare, an educational services company based in the USA with offices in Boston, New Delhi, and Seoul (Business Wire India, 2008). The AGNK is presented as an assessment tool valuable for local nursing needs but is also presented as valuable for international assessments. The implicit internationalization of this assessment offers a paradox that in seeking to advance the standards of nursing in India, the programme is, of course, another way to facilitate global mobility.

The central Government of India also supports forms of corporate investment in the health sector, including the health education field. The Ministry of Health and Family Welfare (2014: 9) plan includes these facilitative provisions in the areas of private health care investment:

> The Government has had an active policy in the last 25 years of building a positive economic climate for the health care industry. Amongst these measures are lower direct taxes; higher depreciation in medical equipment; Income Tax exemptions for 5 years for rural hospitals; custom duty exemptions for imported equipment that are lifesaving; Income Tax exemption for Health Insurance; and active engagement through publicly financed health insurance which now covers almost 27% of the population. Further forms of assistance are preferential and subsidized allocation of land that has been acquired under the public acquisitions Act, and the subsidized education for medical, nursing and other paramedical professional graduating from government institutions and who constitute a significant proportion of the human resources that work for the private sector; and the provision for 100% FDI. Indeed in one year alone 2012-13 … as per market sources the private health care industry attracted over 2 billion dollars of FDI much of it as venture capital. For International Finance Corporation, the section of the World Bank investing in private sector, the Indian private health care industry is the second highest destination for its global investments in health.

One example of the scale of private sector investment in health care and education can be seen in the example of Apollo Hospitals Enterprise Limited. Apollo is one of the leading private health sector actor in India which manages over 10,000 beds across 64 hospitals, more than 2,200 pharmacies, health insurance services, 15 academic institutions, and a research foundation, with revenues of

US$940 million in 2015.[4] Apollo has medical training programmes and in-house training facilities for nurses under the Apollo Hospitals Education and Research Foundation (AHERF). The Apollo College of Nursing was launched in 1997 and offers general diplomas in nursing and midwifery, bachelors of nursing, master's and BSc conversions across several of the Apollo sites, including Delhi and Hyderabad. The programme emphasizes the international dimensions of nursing.

> Our vision is to provide the best nursing education that combines continuous quality improvement, current technology and cost effectiveness within a mechanism to continually assess and improve student performance in learning and rendering compassionate patient care in the international environment.... Today our nurses are much sought after and find placements in India as well as the US, Europe, Singapore, Australia and other Asian countries.[5]

Recent growth in speciality and tertiary hospitals and related training capacity in India has been dominated by the private sector. In the Ministry of Health and Family Welfare (2014) plan, the need for the national government to invest in this health training is evident and includes the need to strengthen existing government medical district hospitals to become medical colleges and build more centres of excellence in medical and health education (Ministry of Health and Family Welfare, 2014: 35). The Ministry of Health and Family Welfare (2014) reveals deep awareness of the problems associated with the rapid increase in private medical and health professional training:

> The challenge with respect to expansion of medical colleges in the private sector is the high cost they charge for clinical care and professional education. The fees and the orientation make it less likely for graduates to take up public sector services or even serve in towns and cities outside the main metropolis.... The greater the gap between the need and the availability of specialists in a given domain, the greater the likelihood that many may just emigrate, given the need for specialists in developed nations as well.... Given that the private sector operates within the logic of the market and that they contribute to the economy through their contribution to the growth rate and by the national earnings from medical tourism, there need not be any major effort to persuade them to care for the poor, as long as their requirements and perceptions do not influence public policy towards universal health care. (Ministry of Health and Family Welfare, 2014: 36)

---

[4]  See https://www.apollohospitals.com/locations/india, accessed on 24 May 2019.
[5]  See https://www.apollohospitals.com/academics-research/courses/nursing, accessed on 14 June 2019.

The increased role of the private sector in health care training and the production of nurses for international circulation (export) are recursively related; one leads to an increase in tuition fees that must be repaid with higher earnings, often only available with overseas employment. This concentrates the cost of such training (often held as debt) in the household's finances and becomes a form of private investment to overcome the lack of economic options at home. Research in Kerala (Walton-Roberts and Rajan, 2013), found that the total cost of nursing education varied from as low as US$2,000 to as high as over US$10,000, and the majority of the respondents paid for their education using family savings (35 per cent) followed by a bank loan (30 per cent) and other methods (20 per cent) which are usually a combination of various sources. When asked about the repayment of debts, 56 of 125 people who reported on the nature of the loan they received had not been able to repay the debt at the time of the survey.

Understanding the distinct and diverse role of institutions in the case of nurse migration adds to the earlier focus on diverse spatialities. However, as with any occupational and nationally specific case, the issue of cultural context in terms of identity, the social construction of skills, and migration as a lived experience, are key dimensions to comprehending how labour and capital mobility are connected.

## Culture: Sex (Gender) and the Household

Every economic system reflects the gendered patriarchal norms of its society, institutions, and social geography (Dunaway, 2014). Gender hierarchies, divisions of labour, and existing patriarchal norms and systems of organization provide the opportunity structures by which women's labour is spliced into global productive systems. States, as well as market-based actors, can exploit these systems under conditions of socio-economic transformation (Silvey, 2004).

Nursing in India reflects the more widespread historical–cultural influence of patriarchy in nursing. Gamarinkow's (1978) incisive review of how the structural determinants of the sexual division of labour reflect the intersection of patriarchy with the occupational specificity of nursing is worth recalling. Gamarinkow notes how medicine relates to nursing through the patriarchal power structures of father–mother–child relationships, which maps onto the doctor–nurse–patient relationships. The nurse is under the control of the doctor and cares for the patient under the direction of the doctor. Tracing the historical evolution of nursing, Gamarinkow (1978) notes the mapping of occupational roles to those of family roles provides a naturalism that characterizes occupational divisions as merely extensions of biological functions (doctors cure, while nurses care). The focus on good hygiene that nursing developed under the guidance of Florence Nightingale also allowed for a transposition of the good nurse into the characteristics of the good woman in that her responsibilities on the ward become extensions of domestic labour. Nursing, with its origins in religious orders, was presented as a vocation of care, thereby limiting the possibility of militant action as part of the labour force. Women were historically inculcated into a role that was subservient to the state and to the (male) doctor. Transformations in the idea of nursing and its professionalism have significantly changed the nature of the profession globally over the last half century, but cultural patriarchy continues to frame the nature of nurse training, regulation, and status in India.

Under an increasingly transnational labour market, different types of gender hierarchies intersect to construct, materially and discursively, how workers are perceived. Sending states can exploit their patriarchal systems to create competitive conditions for the 'export' of labour or goods, for example, pretraining sessions for domestic workers that promote docility and femininity (Rodriguez, 2010), and the receiving states of such labour can likewise find opportunities in their own gendered and racialized hierarchies to facilitate cost savings (Pratt, 1997). More generally labour markets and migration policies undervalue women's skills:

> As immigration states become more competitive in the race for talent and as selecting nations place greater emphasis on human capital credentials, language abilities, vocational skills and work experience, the importance of gender is amplified. In short, the global race for talent is gendered, with significant implications for the skill accreditation, labour market outcomes, rights of stay, gendered family dynamics, including freedom from domestic violence and financial independence, of female immigrants. (Boucher, 2016: 3)

Gender considerations are centrally important in skills development (including decision-making at the household level) and the growing service sector (especially in health). Critical examination of these practices expands our understanding of contemporary global economic processes that incorporate more and more people and functions within the global market economy. The state and the household as well as non-state actors are intimately involved in the global deployment of nursing care labour. The gender implications of such migration are particularly significant, since women account for almost half of today's international migrants and are over-represented in health and personal care sectors of the global economy. These occupations are often undervalued in terms of income security and status (Valiani, 2011). While the specific policy context of IEHPs' integration into different national labour markets varies (Picot and Sweetman, 2011), there is a structural trajectory of convergence of IEHPs being incorporated into health systems facing restructured or diminished state spending (Williams, 2012; Yeates, 2009).

As previously discussed, the professional status of nursing in India is shaped by a history of colonial interest in the formalization of the occupation and in the more recent globalization period of its professionalization. Colonialism has played a role in the historical construction and reproduction of the nurse-training context within which the feminized caring profession has emerged. Healey (2008) provides a detailed historical assessment of impact of international nurse advisors sent to India post 1947 to introduce ambitious programmes aimed at remaking and professionalizing Indian nursing. The poor status of nursing in India during the colonial period resulted in the sector being mostly populated by the daughters of low-status families, orphans, or widows. In the postcolonial period, international nursing advisors worked hard to elevate the image of nursing through the introduction of formal degree-granting programmes offered by newly created colleges of nursing. The efforts of a cadre of highly trained Western nurses to create a formal degree-level nursing education in India was challenged by various groups (including doctors), and by social and cultural practices that stigmatized nursing in light of taboos, such as dealing with bodily fluids, and the need for women to interact with unrelated men, be they patients or doctors (Walton-Roberts, 2012).

Healey (2008) examines how the Indian state produces (trains) nurses, and she argues that rather than focusing resources on improvements in the training and education of nurses, more success might have come if those resources had been used to improve the working conditions within hospitals. This gets to the crux of the problem with regard to nurses' status in India; the reality of poor working conditions for nurses in many Indian hospitals contributes to the weak status of feminized nursing staff. Indeed, we can read in Healey's work how international advisors themselves, rather than introducing a generalized improvement in the sector, sought to radically remake nursing through its professionalization and formalization, part of which desired the replacement of poor-class women with higher-status ones. This focus on the social background of those attracted to nursing rather than a focus on improving the conditions in health care settings, more generally, can be seen as an important historically and culturally contingent process that has contributed to setting the course for the continued marginalization of nursing within India and thus sustaining interest in overseas opportunities. International nursing advisors also found that doctors were resistant to the professionalization of nursing, since they saw nurses as a form of hospital labour rather than medical professionals to be consulted. Despite the initial commitment of both the central and state governments to provide resources to create and support nursing, Healey found funding was often withdrawn or reduced throughout the immediate postcolonial period. International advisors sought to overcome the vestiges of a British system of nurse training that they felt had entrenched the idea of nurses and nursing students as merely 'a cheap source of labour rather than as students' (Healey, 2008: 66).

Under Prime Minister Nehru's bold postcolonial vision of a modernizing India, the elitism of higher education took hold in the vestiges of engineering and technology, but in nursing efforts towards educational elitism have produced contradictory outcomes for the health system itself. Healey (2008: 74) argues that the education system formed during this era elevated 'administration and teaching positions over bedside and practical nursing' to the point that 'what was constructed functioned more as a pathway out of clinical nursing, an outcome unlikely to address the serious and persistent problems of the majority of nurses'. The Indian educational system was thus imbued in its early years with a pervasively outward-looking focus, presenting the West as the site of better social relations as well as of better professional practice. As was characteristic of many programmes of development, the objects of international nursing projects were forced to remake their social relations 'in order to enter the promised new world' (Healey, 2008: 75). This has led to the current human resources situation in health where that state has acknowledged that

> the rules regarding setting up of medical colleges and the entire system of regulation of medical education would also be informed and guided by the needs of correcting the current distortions of medical educational policy that have led to this mismatch between needs and skills. (Ministry of Health and Family Welfare, 2014: 37)

Even in the current period in most Indian states, nursing is actually regulated through medical councils, formalizing the subservient positioning of the nursing profession to medicine and preventing regulatory autonomy (Sheikh, Raman, and Mayra, 2012). Workplace hierarchies exacerbate this relationship, since nurses are often seen as 'handmaidens to doctors', and in private hospitals doctors tend to be shareholders and executives, effectively making nurses their employees. The professional weakness of nursing devalues the status of the occupation in India but also has the potential to be transmitted outside of India to destination markets where non-hierarchical multidisciplinary collaborative teams are increasingly the practice model (Nancarrow et al., 2013). This was clear in research interviews conducted with hospital directors of nursing in Dubai, UAE; and Australia (2008–2009); and Canada (2010–2011), where Indian nurses were often seen as lacking autonomy and professional confidence and demonstrated less ability to advocate on behalf of patients.

All of these cultural factors translate into spatial differences that are generalized onto the profession. One of the most persistent reasons nurses and nursing students use to explain their interest in migration was the perception of the greater respect and professional opportunity nursing offers overseas; whether employed in private or public hospitals in India, nurses perceive their working conditions as poor (Simoens, Villeneuve, and Hurst, 2005; Walton-Roberts et al., 2017). As one of the major employers of nurses nationally, the Indian state has improved salaries in various pay commissions, and there are employment opportunities in private sector hospitals and rural community health centres, but these postings are less desirable, since the pay and conditions are unappealing. Recent cases have seen national commissions recommending revisions to the conditions of employment for nurses and increased salaries (even in the private sector), but such action has not, as of yet, been fully taken up by the central and state governments (Nair, Timmons, and Evans, 2016). The state has not used its potential to match overseas employment opportunities, and powerful cultural norms continue to frame the profession and its scope for educational and occupational improvement within a health system strongly orientated towards the dominance of medical doctors' power and authority.

To conceptualize nurse migration from India and associated capital mobilities, we need to consider the entire spatial spectrum, beginning with the household, including intervening sites of education, training and employment, and transit and eventual end destinations. At each stage of this system labour and capital mobility interact, but the directionality of movement and the main agents involved in shaping and benefiting from the process vary, and the cultural context always informs the process. Important factors in the process include educational and recruitment agents, and these can be public and/or private. The relative power of different nation-states is positioned as exerting meso-structural or macrostructural influences depending on their relative power to set or impose the recruitment terms for nurse migration. This relative power is informed by cultures of colonial history, as already discussed, which frame international relations as well as the terms of employment and occupational status of nursing within the Indian context. Women's international mobility is framed, constrained, and distorted by how the community perceives autonomous female mobility. In India, migrant nurses have been subjected to stigma and status devaluation when their work is associated with prostitution (Walton-Roberts, 2012; see also Silvey, 2010 on Indonesian domestic workers).

## Conclusion

The corporatization, commoditization, and privatization of health and personal care services mean they are an increasingly central feature of the global productive economy. In a 2016 report, McKinsey Global cites health care as one of the top areas for global growth, a sector where total spending is growing overall faster than GDP. Health care systems have long relied on internationally educated nurses (IENs) to meet structural shortages (WHO, 2010), and India has become one of the leading sources for health care worker migration. This chapter examined this reality in the case of nurse migration by examining transnational capital and labour mobility together using the categories of spatiality, institutional forms of governance, and cultural context.

In terms of spatialities, the circuits for nurse migration out of India can be seen as a legacy of colonial capitalism, where the bidirectional transfer of nursing labour has a long history. The UK and the USA both played a role in the development of nursing expertise over the last century in the form of labour and 'philanthropic' capital transfers from the 'core to the periphery'. The transformation of nursing in India occurred with an external orientation to developments elsewhere, and in the post-Second World War period the spatiality of nurse migration shifted to provide workers for the expanding social welfare systems of Europe and health demands in the USA. More recent petro-development in the Gulf region has seen new circuits of capital and labour transfer emerge as expanding health systems employ significant numbers of Indian health professionals, whose remittances and diasporic investments have become vital to the Indian state. The scale of health professional migration and its significance in terms of trade demands that we expand our conceptualization of internationalized labour markets, regulatory and credential systems, and the various transnational intermediaries that are active in these circulation processes.

In the Indian context, these institutional formations reveal a deep interaction between state and market actors, and the regulatory control of health worker training and credentials reveals itself as a complex struggle between these forces. The contemporary period reveals a landscape where training, education, employment, and the deployment of health workers overseas is organized through networks where markets often play the leading role (education), but the state also mediates the process (state control of overseas development offices that deploy labour). Significant capital transfers accompany overseas employment, both in terms of the fees paid to international training and credential agencies and migration and education agents, and after successful migration—the various capital transfers made between source and destination markets. A varied network of institutional actors facilitates this mobility: in Kerala, for example, ODEPC (the state recruitment agency) steps in to provide social protection for workers going overseas. However, deep cultural norms and patriarchal relations have preconditioned nurses within a system where their occupational standing is subservient to medicine in regulatory terms (nursing is regulated by medical education boards) and in terms of everyday workplace relations (nurses work under the direction of doctors for daily activities and also in terms of employee relations in private hospitals). These conditions of relative inequality create the preconditions for the stratification of Indian nurses into the global labour markets, where professional credentials have to fit into new organizational systems with different workplace expectations. The transnational mobility of labour and capital in the case of Indian nurses thus reflects historically variable spatialities, which are themselves reflective of particular institutional arrangements between states and markets and workplaces and lived experiences of mobility, marked by the intersection of states, markets, and community structures of cultural patriarchy.

# References

Ahmed, Rashmee Z. 2001. 'UK Looks Up to Indian Nurses'. *Times of India*. 18 July. Available at http://timesofindia.indiatimes.com/articleshow/msid-492441190,prtpage-1.cms. Accessed on 5 May 2009.

Aluttis, Cristoph, Tewabech Bishaw, and Martina W. Frank. 2014. 'The Workforce for Health in a Globalized Context: Global Shortages and International Migration'. *Global Health Action* 7: 23611. Available at http://dx.doi.org/10.3402/gha.v7.23611.

Baumann, Andrea and Jennifer Blythe. 2008. 'Globalization of Higher Education in Nursing'. *The Online Journal Issues Nursing* 13(2).

Berger, David. 2014. 'Corruption Ruins the Doctor-Patient Relationship in India'. *BMJ* 348: g3169. Available at https://doi.org/10.1136/bmj.g3169.

Boucher, Anna. 2016. *Gender, Migration and the Global Race for Talent*. Manchester: Manchester University Press.

Bourgeault, Ivy Lynn, Elena Neiterman, Jane LeBrun, Ken Viers, and Judi Winkup. 2010. 'Brain Gain, Drain and Waste: The Experiences of Internationally Educated Health Professionals in Canada.' University of Ottawa. Available at https://www.edmontonsocialplanning.ca/index.php/resources/digital-resources/f-social-issues/f13-immigration/768-2010-brain-drain/file. Accessed on 4 January 2019.

Business Wire India. 2008. 'CGFNS International Partners with AHEd Global Healthcare'. 2 September. Available at https://www.financialexpress.com/archive/cgfns-international-partners-with-ahed-global-healthcare/356389/. Accessed on 26 April 2018

Castro-Palaganas, Erlinda, Denise L. Spitzer, Maria Midea M. Kabamalan, Marian C. Sanchez, Ruel Caricativo, Vivien Runnels, Ronald Labonte, Gail Tomblin Murphy, and Ivy Lynn Bourgeault. 2017. 'An Examination of the Causes, Consequences, and Policy Responses to the Migration of Highly Trained Health Personnel from the Philippines: The High Cost of Living/Leaving, A Mixed Method Study'. *Human Resources for Health* 15: 1–14.

Choy, Catherine Ceniza. 2003. *Empire of Care: Nursing and Migration in Filipino American History*. Durham and London: Duke University Press.

Clark, Paul, James Stewart, and Darlene Clark. 2006. 'The Globalization of the Labour Market for Health-Care Professionals'. *International Labour Review* 145(1–2): 37–64.

Collyer, Fran and Kevin White. 2011. 'The Privatisation of Medicare and the National Health Service, and the Global Marketisation of Healthcare Systems'. *Health Sociology Review* 20(3): 238–244.

Connell, John. 2014. 'The Two Cultures of Health Worker Migration: A Pacific Perspective'. *Social Science & Medicine* 116: 73–81.

Connell, John and Margaret Walton-Roberts. 2016. 'What about the Workforce? The Missing Geographies of Health Care'. *Progress in Human Geography* 40(2): 158–176. Available at https://doi.org/10.1177/0309132515570513.

Crone, Robert K. 2008. 'Flat Medicine? Exploring Trends in the Globalization of Health Care'. *Academic Medicine* 83(2): 117–121.

Crush, Jonathan and Wade Pendleton. 2011. 'Brain Flight: The Exodus of Health Professionals from South Africa'. *International Journal of Migration, Health and Social Care* 6(3): 3–18.

Deloitte. 2017. 'Global Health Care Outlook: Making Progress Against Persistent Challenges'. Available at https://www2.deloitte.com/content/dam/Deloitte/global/Documents/Life-Sciences-Health-Care/gx-lshc-2017-health-care-outlook.pdf. Accessed on 23 April 2018.

Dunaway, Wilma (ed.). 2014. *Gendered Commodity Chains: Seeing Women's Work and Households in Global Production*. Stanford, CA: Stanford University Press.

*Economic Times*. 2017. 'India "Very Strongly" Raises H-1B Visa Issue with US'. 28 October. Available at https://economictimes.indiatimes.com/nri/visa-and-immigration/india-very-strongly-raises-h-1b-visa-issue-with-us-suresh-prabhu/articleshow/61287982.cms. Accessed on 4 January 2019.

England, Kim, and Caitlin Henry. 2013. 'Care Work, Migration and Citizenship: International Nurses in the UK'. *Social & Cultural Geography* 14(5): 558–574.

FICCI (Federation of Indian Chambers of Commerce and Industry). 2016. 'Nursing Reforms: Paradigm Shift for a Brighter Future'. Available at http://indiainbusiness.nic.in/newdesign/upload/nursing-reforms-paradigm-shift-for-a-bright-future.pdf. Accessed on 5 April 2016.

Gamarinkow, Eva. 1978. 'Sexual Division of Labor: The Case of Nursing'. In *Feminism and Materialism*, edited by Annette Kuhn and AnnMarie Wolpe, 96–123. Boston, MA: Routledge.

George, Sheba. 2005. *When Women Come First: Gender and Class in Transnational Migration*. Berkeley and Los Angeles, CA: University of California Press.

Gostin, Lawrence O. 2008. 'The International Migration and Recruitment of Nurses: Human Rights and Global Justice'. *JAMA* 299(15): 1827–1829.

Halperin, Edward C. and Robert B. Goldberg. 2016. 'Offshore Medical Schools Are Buying Clinical Clerkships in US Hospitals: The Problem and Potential Solutions'. *Academic Medicine* 91(5): 639–644.

Healey, Madelaine. 2008. '"Seeds That May Have Been Planted May Take Root": International Aid Nurses and Projects of Professionalism in Postindependence India, 1947–65'. *Nursing History Review* 16: 58–90.

———. 2014. *Indian Sisters: A History of Nursing and the State, 1907–2007*. New Delhi: Routledge.

Kingma, Mireille. 2006. *Nurses on the Move: Migration and the Global Health Care Economy*. Ithaca, NY, and London: Cornell University Press.

Khadria, Binod. 2007. 'International Nurse Recruitment in India'. *Health Services Research* 42(3p2): 1429–1436.

———. 2009. 'Adversary Analysis and the Quest for Global Development: Optimizing the Dynamic Conflict of Interest in Transnational Migration'. *Social Analysis* 5(3): 106–122.

Mackintosh, Maureen, Parvati Raghuram, and Henry Leroy. 2006. 'A Perverse Subsidy: African Trained Nurses and Doctors in the NHS'. *Soundings* 34(1): 103–113.

Mbemba, Gisèle, Marie-Pierre Gagnon, Guy Paré, and José Côté. 2013. 'Interventions for Supporting Nurse Retention in Rural and Remote Areas: An Umbrella Review'. *Human Resources for Health* 11(1): 44.

Mezzadra, Sandro and Brett Neilson. 2013. *Border as Method, or, the Multiplication of Labor*. Durham and London: Duke University Press.

Ministry of Health and Family Welfare. 2014. *National Health Policy 2015 Draft*. Available at https://www.nhp.gov.in/sites/default/files/pdf/draft_national_health_policy_2015.pdf. Accessed on 4 January 2019.

Nair, Sreelekha, Stephen Timmons, and Catrin Evans. 2016. 'Nurses in the Private Health Sector in Kerala: Any Lessons Learnt from Their Strikes in Recent Years?' *Indian Journal of Gender Studies* 23(1): 8–25.

Nancarrow, Susan A., Andrew Booth, Steven Ariss, Tony Smith, Pam Enderby, and Alison Roots. 2013. 'Ten Principles of Good Interdisciplinary Team Work'. *Human Resources for Health* 11(1): 19.

Neilson, Jeffrey, Bill Pritchard, and Henry Wai-chung Yeung. 2014. 'Global Value Chains and Global Production Networks in the Changing International Political Economy: An Introduction'. *Review of International Political Economy* 21(1): 1–8. Available at https://doi.org/10.1080/09692290.2013.873369.

Percot, Marie. 2016. 'Migration of Malayali Nurses to the Gulf Countries'. In *South Asian Migration to Gulf Countries: History, Policies, Development*, edited by Prakash Jain and Ginu Oommen, 247–263. New York: Routledge.

Peters, David H., K. Sujatha Rao, and Robert Fryatt. 2003. 'Lumping and Splitting: The Health Policy Agenda in India'. *Health Policy and Planning* 18(3): 249–260.

Picot, Garnett and Arthur Sweetman. 2011. 'Canadian Immigration Policy and Immigrant Economic Outcomes: Why the Differences in Outcomes between Sweden and Canada?' IZA policy aper, 25.

Pollitt, Cristopher and Geert Bouckaert. 2017. *Public Management Reform: A Comparative Analysis—New Public Management, Governance, and the Neo-Weberian State*, 4th edn. Oxford: Oxford University Press.

Pratt, Geraldine. 1997. 'Stereotypes and Ambivalence: The Construction of Domestic Workers in Vancouver, British Columbia'. *Gender, Place and Culture: A Journal of Feminist Geography* 4(2): 159–178.

Raghuram, Parvati. 2009. 'Caring About "Brain Drain" Migration in a Postcolonial World'. *Geoforum* 40(1): 25–33.

Ramirez, Paulina and Helen Rainbird. 2010. 'Making the Connections: Bringing Skill Formation into Global Value Chain Analysis'. *Work, Employment and Society* 24(4): 699–710.

Rastegar, Darius A. 2004. 'Health Care Becomes an Industry'. *The Annals of Family Medicine* 2(1): 79–83.

Reddy, Sujani K. 2015. *Nursing and Empire: Gendered Labor and Migration from India to the United States*. Chapel Hill, NC: UNC Press Books.

Rodriguez, Robyn Magalit. 2010. *Migrants for Export: How the Philippine State Brokers Labor to the World*. Minneapolis, MN: University of Minnesota Press.

Segouin, Cristophe, Brian Hodges, and Pierre-Henri Brechat. 2005. 'Globalization in Health Care: Is International Standardization of Quality a Step toward Outsourcing?' *IJQHC* 17(4): 277–279.

Sheikh, Kabir, V. R. Raman, and Kaveri Mayra. 2012. 'Nurturing Nursing in India: Need for Governance Reform'. *BMC Proceedings* suppl. 5: O32.

Silvey, Rachel M. 2004. 'Transnational Domestication: State Power and Indonesian Migrant Women in Saudi Arabia'. *Political Geography* 23(3): 245–264.

————. 2010. 'Stigmatized Spaces: Gender and Mobility under Crisis in South Sulawesi, Indonesia.' *Gender, Place and Culture: A journal of Feminist Geography* 7(2): 143–161.

Simoens, Steven, Mike Villeneuve, and Jeremy Hurst. 2005. 'Tackling Nurse Shortages in OECD Countries'. OECD Health working papers, no. 19. Paris, OECD Publishing (NJ1).

Sweetman, Arthur, James McDonald, and Lesleyanne Hawthorne. 2015. 'Occupational Regulation and Foreign Qualification Recognition: An Overview'. *Canadian Public Policy* 41(1): S1–S13.

*Times of India*. 2008. 'Nursing Institutes Have a Reason to Cheer'. 15 December. Available at http://timesofindia.indiatimes.com/articleshow/msid-3838449, prtpage-1.cms. Accessed on 5 May 2009.

————. 2015. 'Nursing Reality: Big Money Drives Many to Take up Jobs Abroad'. 27 November. Available at https://timesofindia.indiatimes.com/india/Nursing-reality-Big-money-drives-many-to-take-up-jobs-abroad/articleshow/49942668.cms. Accessed on 4 January 2019.

————. 2017. 'Nursing Council Warns Students Against Joining Karnataka Colleges'. 19 June. Available at https://timesofindia.indiatimes.com/city/thiruvananthapuram/nursing-council-warns-students-against-joining-ktaka-colleges/articleshow/59208833.cms. Accessed at 20 April 2018.

Valiani, Salimah. 2011. *Rethinking Unequal Exchange: The Global Integration of Nursing Labour Markets*. Toronto: University of Toronto Press.

Walton-Roberts, Margaret. 2004. 'Globalization, National Autonomy and Non-Resident Indians'. *Contemporary South Asia* 13(1): 53–69.

————. 2012. 'Contextualizing the Global Nursing Care Chain: International Migration and the Status of Nursing in Kerala, India'. *Global Networks* 12(2): 175–194.

————. 2015. 'International Migration of Health Professionals and the Marketization and Privatization of Health Education in India: From Push–Pull to Global Political Economy'. *Social Science & Medicine* 124: 374–382.

Walton-Roberts, Margaret and S. Irudaya Rajan. 2013. 'Nurse Emigration from Kerala: "Brain Circulation" or "trap"?' In *India Migration Report 2013*, edited by S. Irudaya Rajan, 206–223. New Delhi: Routledge.

Walton-Roberts, Margaret, Smita Bhutani, and Amandeep Kaur. 2017. 'Care and Global Migration in the Nursing Profession: A North Indian Perspective'. *Australian Geographer* 48(1): 59–77. Available at http://dx.doi.org/10.1080/00049182.2016.1266633.

Walton-Roberts, Margaret, Vivien Runnels, S. Irudaya Rajan, Atul Sood, Sreelekha Nair, Philomina Thomas, Corinne Packer, Adrian MacKenzie, Gail Tomblin Murphy, Ronald Labonté, and Ivy Lynn Bourgeault. 2017. 'Causes, Consequences and Policy Responses to the Migration of Health Workers: Key Findings from India'. *Human Resources for Health* 15(28). Available at https://doi.org/10.1186/s12960-017-0199-y.

Williams, Fiona. 2012. 'Converging Variations in Migrant Care Work in Europe'. *Journal of European Social Policy* 22(4): 363–376.

Wise, Raúl Delgado and Humberto Márquez Covarrubias. 2012. 'Strategic Dimensions of Neoliberal Globalization: The Exporting of Labor Force and Unequal Exchange'. *Advances in Applied Sociology* 127: 127–134.

WHO. 2010. 'International Migration of Health Workers'. Policy brief. Available at https://www.who.int/hrh/resources/oecd-who_policy_brief_en.pdf?ua=1. Accessed on 4 January 2019.

————. 2014. 'Migration of Health Workers: The WHO Code of Practice and the Global Economic Crisis'. Available at http://www.who.int/hrh/migration/14075_MigrationofHealth_Workers.pdf?ua=1. Accessed at 17 April 2018.

————. 2017. 'International Health Worker Migration: A High Level Dialogue'. Meeting summary. April. Available at https://www.who.int/hrh/news/2017/high_level-dialogue-int-health-worker-migration-meeting-summary.pdf. Accessed on 4 January 2019.

Yeates, Nicola. 2009. *Globalizing Care Economies and Migrant Workers: Explorations in Global Care Chains*. Basingstoke: Palgrave Macmillan.

Zachariah, Kunniparampil Curien and S. Irudaya Rajan. 2007. 'Economic and Social Dynamics of Migration in Kerala, 1999–2004'. Analysis of panel data. Thiruvananthapuram: Centre for Development Studies.

# 11

# The Mobility–Oligopoly Nexus in Philippine Property Development

KENNETH CARDENAS

## Introduction

What kinds of places do contemporary mobilities of capital and labour create, and what kinds of place-specific capitalism do they enable? This chapter addresses these questions through an examination of the restructuring and rise of the largest Philippine-nationality conglomerates (PNCs) from 2001 to 2015, a period which saw the emergence of property development businesses as a core interest among these companies. It situates this development within two place- and period-specific sets of labour and capital mobilities: the continued growth of the overseas Filipino workforce and their inbound remittances; and the emergence of a foreign direct investment (FDI)-driven, information technology-enabled business process offshoring industry in the country's major urban centres, and a concomitant strengthening of domestic rural–urban migration flows. While PNCs had played only minor and indirect roles in facilitating these two developments, they have been the primary beneficiaries of demand for residential, office, and retail property which these movements of labour and capital have created.

This chapter argues that meeting this demand was a matter of staying in place, in two senses of the term. First, the foremost advantage of PNCs over both foreign firms and smaller domestic firms was in the acquisition and development of newly privatized and brownfield tracts of urban land, which is restricted to juridical Philippine nationals—an advantage that also extends to the power, water, communications, and transportation infrastructure that undergird these developments. By diversifying into these sectors, PNCs thus became vertically integrated rentiers, able to capture substantial portions of capital flows through the built environment without any direct involvement in either the deployment of Filipino labour overseas or in the operation of business process outsourcing (BPO) firms. In its purest form, this is expressed as mixed-use development 'townships' that carry echoes of cash crop latifundism: the sources of demand are ultimately global, and the value is created through labour, but the basis of the key surpluses are rents on land and other inputs to production and reproduction.

Second, the place-based and place-specific opportunities presented by demand for urban property in the Philippines allowed PNCs to obviate the need to seek new markets for their former core interests elsewhere or to invest in new businesses that could plug into global production networks. With a few exceptions, the surpluses that were extracted from urban property have not been invested in value-adding, or job-generating, sectors. Instead, they had been reinvested in new land-like businesses, that is infrastructure, and to new sites of activity for the same rentier-type activities, both in second-tier and urbanizing areas of the Philippines and in other developing markets overseas.

Through the Philippine case, this chapter seeks to illustrate two crucial gaps in how labour and capital mobilities relate to each other and their implications for place as a dimension to political economy. First, the Philippines presents a clear case in which the mobilities of labour and capital cannot be considered in isolation from each other: wages remitted home by globally mobile Filipino labour, much of which is spent on real estate and consumption, have been a key driver for the investment patterns that Philippine capital have taken with respect to sectoral and geographical diversification. Second, the Philippine case shows how labour and capital mobility as transacted through inherently immobile land and land-like assets can reinforce the importance of place-based rentierism as an accumulation strategy. In contrast to the view of property development as a financialized, highly speculative, and placeless sector under 'advanced' capitalism, the advantages of Philippine capital in these sectors are inherently place-specific.

## Key Changes in the Philippine Economic Landscape

For much of the twentieth century, the capitalists that dominated the Philippine economy built their wealth and power on two sets of interests. One was landownership, upon which cash crops were raised for export to a quota-guaranteed US market, built allied industries such as food, milling, and liquor, and by way of tapping their workforce as vote banks, landowners accessed electoral office. The other was state patronage, either in the form of protectionist economic policies to corner and dominate domestic markets in light manufacturing or by extracting crony capitalist surpluses from state-owned enterprises and state-sanctioned monopolies (Yoshihara, 1988; Rivera, 1994; Bello et al., 2004).

Both these bases of wealth and power have gradually been eroded, to the point that neither can still be considered a viable basis for accumulation. Cash crop export began its gradual decline in 1974, when privileged access to the US market for sugar export ended with the expiry of the Laurel–Langley Act. Over the following decades, a combination of factors rendered the export of traditional cash crops, namely sugar, coconut, and tobacco, an unviable basis for accumulation. The most crucial of these were depressed world prices, the mismanagement of state-owned monopolies by Marcos cronies, as well as the partial successes and unintended consequences of agrarian reform from 1987 onward: the break-up of some large estates and the reclassification of many others into industrial and residential uses to forestall land redistribution (Borras, 2001; Kelly, 2003; Larkin, 1993) (see Figure 11.1).

Similarly, the protectionist policies that propped up domestic manufacturing have been dismantled by three decades' worth of structural adjustment programmes and trade liberalization agreements. In the 1970s, manufacturing accounted for over 25 per cent of the country's gross domestic product (GDP) and 11 per cent of its formal employment. The decades since have seen declines in both figures. The most important import-substitution industries, such as textiles and domestic appliances, have succumbed to foreign competition. Other major industries, such as cement and automotive assembly, presently survive only as local operations of multinational corporations. Finally, lucrative state-owned and debt-financed industries, such as oil refining, steel, and energy, have long been either privatized or dismantled (Cardenas, 2014; Ofreneo, 2006). And while the Philippines during this period did attract some foreign investment into export-oriented industrialization, these new enclaves of manufacturing did not offset the decline of domestic industry (Figure 11.2).

Yet despite losing their old sources of wealth, domestic political instability, and adverse global economic conditions, this century has so far been surprisingly good for Philippine capitalists. From 2000 to 2015, the Philippines' GDP grew, in real terms, by 112 per cent. The combined gross revenues of the 11 biggest Philippine-nationality conglomerates, meanwhile, grew by 545 per cent and now accounts for more than 15 per cent of the country's GDP, up from 5 per cent.[1]

Over the course of this boom, the largest and most successful Philippine conglomerates converged on remarkably similar blueprints for success. The businesses upon which they originally built their wealth have either been divested or now return very small shares of their incomes. In their stead, these conglomerates' portfolios are now built on urban property development, financial services, and liberalized infrastructure sectors, particularly energy generation and distribution, water utilities, transportation, and telecommunications; most recently, some conglomerates have started investing heavily in mining and casinos. Their businesses

---

[1] Figures computed from GDP data from Philippine Statistical Authority (various years) and World Bank (2018), and gross revenue data from annual reports of conglomerates from 2001 to 2015.

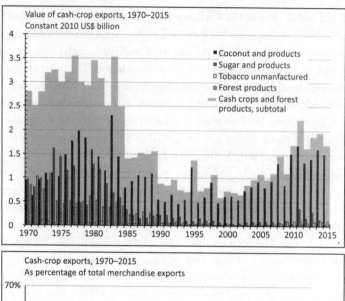

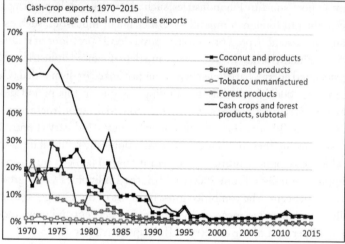

Figure 11.1 | The decline of cash-crop agriculture as a basis of accumulation, 1970–2015

*Source*: Data from *Foreign Trade Statistics of the Philippines*, Philippine Statistics Authority, various years; World Bank (2018).

*Note*: The top graph depicts the value of exports, in constant 2010 US dollars, for three key cash crops (coconut, sugar, and tobacco) and forest products, which played a similar role in the accumulation strategies of domestic Philippine capital; the bottom graph depicts the share of these four commodity groups in the country's total merchandise exports.

From a peak of 58 per cent of total merchandise exports, the share of these commodities dwindled to an average of 2.65 per cent from 2000 to 2015. The value of these exports has similarly shrunk: from a peak of US$3.5 billion in 1983, these four product groups generated an annual average of US$1.3 billion in exports from 2000 to 2015. The decline and stagnation of sugarcane and forest products have been particularly stark.

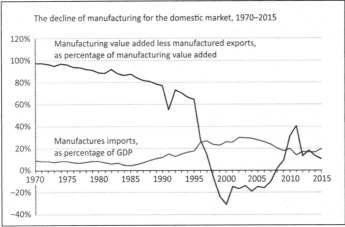

Figure 11.2 | The stagnation of domestic Philippine industry, 1970–2015

*Source*: Data from *Philippine Statistical Yearbook*, Philippine Foreign Trade Statistics, various years; World Bank (2018).

*Note*: The top graph depicts the share of manufacturing in GDP and total employment. The bottom graph depicts two indicators for the decline of manufacturing for the domestic market: manufacturing value added minus manufactures exports, expressed as a percentage of manufacturing value added, and manufactures imports, expressed as a percentage of GDP.

During the 1970s, manufacturing consistently accounted for more than 25 per cent of GDP and 11 per cent of employment. More than 90 per cent of manufacturing was oriented to the domestic market, and manufactures imports accounted for less than 10 per cent of GDP. In contrast, during the period 2000–2015, manufacturing had declined to an average of 22.57 per cent of GDP and 8.97 per cent of employment; manufacturing exports exceeded manufacturing value added for several years, and manufactures imports accounted for an average of 22.41 per cent of GDP.

in these sectors are relatively new operations, with most of the real property, energy, and infrastructure arms of the major conglomerates having been established from 2001 to 2015.

This retooling was not only quick, it was also thorough. Of the PHP1.14 trillion in profits that the 10 largest Philippine conglomerates made from 2000 to 2015, 25 per cent was from property development, 22 per cent from energy, and 16 per cent from financial services. They also appear to have discovered an edge in running these businesses in other markets: their overseas arms are now operating malls in southern China, power plants and water utilities in Vietnam and Indonesia, and electric grids in Nigeria; with the ongoing integration of the Association of Southeast Asian Nations (ASEAN) market, their banking, property development, toll road, and airline arms are prospecting for opportunities across South East Asia.

Why did the largest Philippine conglomerates, despite coming from widely divergent origins, converge on these businesses as their new core interests? What about these businesses explain their successes at home and their forays overseas? Conjecturally, sectors as diverse as property development, energy, and infrastructure demand very different forms of technical and managerial expertise; the countries to which these conglomerates have expanded also present very different regulatory and institutional environments. Yet by moving in a similar direction, these conglomerates appear to have discovered features common to these businesses and these markets, an affinity for making money off these features, and are exploiting these advantages in earnest. What might these common features be, and what might they reveal about the recent good fortunes of Philippine capital?

## Fictive Markets, Philippine-Nationality Firms, and the Mobilities of Labour and Capital

Situating these questions in terms of ongoing shifts in the movements of labour and capital, and the Philippines' changing position astride these flows, goes some way towards answering them.

The flow of labour overseas, the remittances they send back, and the inflow of investment into services offshoring are the most obvious examples, and indeed the Philippines in recent years has largely appeared in the literature as a metonym for these processes. But other aspects of Philippine political economy can also be productively interpreted through the vocabulary of flows. The privatization of state assets was motivated by the need to service decades-old debts incurred by the Marcos regime and to establish 'special-account' cash flows meant to address systemic fiscal weaknesses of the post-Marcos era. The investment of Philippine businesses in these land and infrastructure assets can be understood as capital seeking its own level, as returns in their former core interests diminished in the face of trade liberalization. But at the same time, their success was predicated on flows of FDI into the property and infrastructure sectors that were anticipated but did *not* materialize, as well as the withdrawal of state investment from these sectors. These factors allowed them to intensify their participation in the privatization process and to play familiar roles as oligopolists and oligopsonists, despite the decline of their former mainstay businesses. Meanwhile, flows of capital in the form of remittances and FDI into services offshoring and flows of labour, both overseas as well as to new urban centres within the Philippines, sustained demand for these businesses' new wares. From property development, whether in the form of starter apartments for the new, globalized middle classes, vacation homes for the Filipino diaspora, commercial space for the retail industry, or office space for the offshoring industry to the power, water, transport, and telecommunications infrastructures which undergird these developments, it has been Philippine-nationality conglomerates that had been in the best position to profit from the reconfiguration of these flows.

By taking a point of view which emphasizes flows and mobility, the success of Philippine big business and the way they have shaped the Philippines' recent development can then be studied in terms of their ability not only to tap but also to actively shape these flows. I argue that this ability can in turn be understood in terms of the 'fictitious' property of market exchange in these new core interests, in the sense invoked by Karl Polanyi (1944: 68–76). That is, they involve commodities which do not present themselves on the market ready for exchange. Rather, they become commodities only through sustained interventions from outside the internal logics of the self-regulating, institutionally separated market. The notions that these interests are commodities, that only some (but not all) actors can buy, own, or sell them, and that markets are the means through which they are best exchanged are fictions that must be created, continuously maintained, and optimized through human agency. Success in these businesses, then, is not necessarily a matter of developing some managerial, technological, or first-mover advantage; rather, it is a matter of developing the ability to write, rewrite, and persuasively interpret the fictions which sustain market exchange. In this chapter, I examine this ability through two entry points: the markets in these assets and the firms which participate in them.

I begin my analysis with a re-examination of market-oriented reforms that were inaugurated in the years immediately after the overthrow of Ferdinand Marcos in February 1986. This moment, popularly known as the 'EDSA Revolution' for the ring road on which the largest of the popular protests took place, created an opening for various interests to project their visions for Philippine society. These included not only its creditors and international financial institutions but also domestic technocrats, the gentry politicians that Marcos had usurped, as well as aspirations for a more democratic society from progressive circles. Many of the new core interests of big Philippine business trace to processes that were set in motion by these often-contradictory visions. Situated within this context, the Philippine privatization and public-private partnership (PPP) programmes, typically understood as triumphs of market-oriented reform, are instead better seen as products of historically contingent processes with uneven outcomes. They were shaped not only by structural adjustment programmes and financialized technocratic expertise but also by aspirations for a 'de-Marcosified', democratized economy. In practice, the interplay of these technologies and aspirations led to some unintended yet far-reaching consequences, and the Philippine state's forays into creating, maintaining, and finessing markets carry its imprints to this day.

For our purposes, the most important of these imprints is a shift in the role played by the Philippines' state-owned enterprises, known as government-owned and controlled corporations (GOCCs). GOCCs were transformed from instruments of direct, strategic intervention in the economy for achieving developmental ends to instruments of revenue generation for a periodically cash-strapped state. Two features of this shift are discussed in this chapter: the design and set-up of new GOCCs primarily as asset-disposition entities and the adoption and eventual proliferation of the practice of special accounts where privatizations are designed to generate funds for specific developmental or policy objectives. These features, in effect, dug new channels for investment to flow into, determined which kinds of flows could (and could not) enter these channels, and played a crucial role in reshaping the economic landscape.

I then turn my analysis to the firms that have taken part in these privatizations. Because of constitutional restrictions placed on foreign ownership of land and infrastructure, it was Philippine-nationality conglomerates, hereafter referred to as PNCs, that had the key to unlock the opportunities for accumulation presented by these privatizations. Whether these opportunities are supply-side, such as mustering the requisite capital to participate in big-ticket privatizations, or demand-side, such as meeting the demand for urban property development and infrastructure that the hollowed-out state was now unable to provide, it was PNCs that reaped the biggest gains from this system. In turn, the PNCs have been the vehicle for a wide array of interests: the families which incorporated and still maintain control and sizeable ownership over them; foreign capital, whether in the form of joint venture partners, investors, or lenders; smaller, illiquid, and/or peripherally located Philippine capitalists; and the Philippine state.

In addition to their legal status as Philippine-nationality persons, they also have at their disposal a range of other place-based abilities. Some of these emanate from their nationality and the protection it confers such as their ability to mobilize the largest volumes of cash within the country for big-ticket privatizations. Other advantages derive from PNCs' ability to write, rewrite, and selectively interpret other aspects of the fictiveness in their new core interests: their embeddedness within ethnic and/or kin networks, their deep familiarity with (and occasional influence over) the regulatory environment, and their ability to navigate the more inscrutable non-market aspects of market exchange. In turn, these abilities provide both the fuel for, and the underlying logic of, their geographic and sectoral expansions, while simultaneously providing an indirect reinforcement for the role played by the outbound orientation of the country's labour force.

Many of these abilities express themselves most vividly as advantages when they are applied to land. This period had seen billions of dollars ploughed into the land—but instead of sugarcane and coconuts for export, the new cash crops of the Philippine economy are condominiums, office towers, malls, and leisure developments, cultivated by PNCs to capture global flows of capital. And as in the past, the most successful enterprises diversified to both the inputs necessary for these crops' cultivation, as well as to allied products—in this case, the energy, communications, and transportation infrastructure that undergird these urban developments and enable the reproduction of the globally mobile labour force. Their fundamental advantages, again, are based on the restriction of the ownership of land to Philippine nationals, and their size as oligopolists and oligopsonists set them apart from other Philippine-nationality market actors.

## Market Creation and the Moral Origins of Cash Flow Privatizations

The overthrow of Ferdinand Marcos in 1986 inaugurated far-reaching changes to the Philippine economy. Various aspects of these changes have previously been scrutinized: in the literature, the perceived 'neoliberal' character of the reforms instituted by the first post-Marcos administration—which have also largely held as the policy consensus since—has been a crucial factor (Bello et al., 2004). At times, understanding the post-1986 economy as neoliberal deepened the analysis, and lent a welcome sensitivity to collusions between global financial institutions and the domestic political elite, the consistently thorny issue of servicing Marcos-era debt, and the role played by trade liberalization to the unravelling of domestic industries.

At other times, however, the neoliberal appellation overshoots developments as they 'actually exist', though not necessarily out of oversight: after all, the import of some features cannot be anticipated *a priori* by a framework and are only brought to light by retracing how features of the present landscape owe to path-dependent, institutionally fraught origins. In this section I locate the roots of the rise of PNCs in one of these aspects: the privatization programme, and the role assumed by the Aquino government (1986–1992) as a 'moral liquidator', designing and implementing it in a way that was strongly imbued with moral imperatives to democratize the country's economy and to purge it of the dictatorship's influence.

The origins of this moral imperative trace back to the practices of the Marcos dictatorship that was overthrown by this revolution. Typical of third-world dictatorships in the 1970s, a defining feature of the Marcos regime was debt-driven legitimacy: grand, countercyclical public investment, funded by cheap credit from Western banks awash with petrodollars. During this period, the creation of state-owned enterprises was the preferred vehicle for this investment. In 1970, there were 64 GOCCs, including 18 subsidiaries. But by the time that Marcos was removed from power, there were 296 GOCCs, with assets of PHP743 billion and about 156,000 people on their payrolls, by the World Bank's count. From 1975 to 1982, investments through the major GOCCs accounted for more than half of public investment, and about 5 per cent of gross national product. Many of these GOCCs could not sustain their operations through revenues: only 15 per cent of their capital expenditures were from internal cash generation, and thus depended on either direct foreign borrowing—which accounted for 60 per cent of their investment outlays—or fresh capital infusions from the Philippine government. The government itself had come to depend on short-term foreign commercial credit to finance its deficits, as well as to roll over its maturing obligations.

These practices became untenably expensive in 1980–1981, as a recession in developed countries triggered both a rise in interest rates and weakened demand for Philippines' exports. Businesses owned by Marcos's associates were particularly vulnerable to the crisis: they expanded rapidly on the back of so-called behest loans, granted by state-owned banks on the instruction of Marcos, and traded in sectors that saw very steep price declines. As these 'crony' businesses began to collapse, the 2 state-owned banks that had acted as the guarantors for their foreign credit took on 399 of these non-performing assets, with a total book value of PHP132 billion. The government corporate portfolio thus became an immense fiscal deadweight on the Philippine government, and the resulting period of fiscal tightening, capital flight, and structural adjustment directly led to the collapse of the Marcos regime.

After the ouster of Marcos in 1986, government corporate sector reform took on an emblematic significance. What was initially a reluctant effort on the part of the Marcos government was now taken up by the new government led by Corazon Cojuangco Aquino and imparted with revolutionary zeal. Beyond the immediate goal of relieving the state of an immense fiscal burden, the privatization of GOCCs and the sale of sequestered assets became an occasion to contemplate what the future of the Philippine economy ought to look like. It would be 'systematically de-Marcosified', with his cronies denied any lasting influence over the economy. The assets purchased with his behest loans were to be liquidated, and the proceeds used to address the inherited injustices of rural landlessness. It would also be democratic and 'people-powered', with the state using privatization to widen the benefits of capital ownership and wielding its responsibly streamlined portfolio of GOCCs to address developmental goals.

Among these objectives, only the broadening of capital ownership reflected the influence of the country's multilateral lenders, and they all owed to the influence of progressive voices within the Aquino cabinet, and more broadly to the democratic expectations pinned on the new republic. The causes and effects of these contradictions are better explored elsewhere; for our purposes the most relevant consequences involve the new roles played by GOCCs under the EDSA system.

The underlying logic for these new roles was in transforming GOCCs from instruments of direct state investment into instruments of cash flow generation. In reaction to the excessive formation and loose regulation of GOCCs during the Marcos era, very stringent criteria for creating new GOCCs were adopted and strict performance targets drawn up. These criteria reflected the backgrounds of the personnel tasked with the privatization effort in business and finance, with financial criteria often being better operationalized in performance targets than policy or developmental goals. It was also made a goal that GOCCs could no longer be a fiscal drain on the national government—they at least had to be revenue-neutral, operating independent of subsidies. Ideally, they should also serve as revenue sources. This has meant that new GOCCs are set up in a way that their ability to generate revenue is guaranteed, *despite* the narrowness of the market. The clearest examples are GOCCs set up for disposing of assets in two of the PNCs' most lucrative sectors: the Bases Conversion and Development Authority (BCDA), set up in 1995 to tap military lands and former US bases to finance the Philippine military's modernization, and the Power Sector Assets and Liabilities Management Corporation (PSALM), set up in 2001 to privatize the state energy generation monopoly's assets to service its debts. This locked them into relatively unsophisticated asset disposition forms that have a constant stream of saleable assets going up on the auction block, but with little latitude and incentive to pursue other strategies, which has persisted to this day. The most recent performance scorecards for BCDA and PSALM are illustrative in this regard: they are heavily weighted in favour of financial criteria, comprising 35 and 50 per cent of their respective scorecards. Meanwhile, other criteria that are not categorized as financial also reveal a financialized, revenue-oriented logic: an additional 25 per cent of BCDA's score are computed on the basis of 'actual investment in BCDA economic zones' (10 per cent), 'total remittance to the national government' (10 per cent), and 'adherence to the asset disposition schedule' (5 per cent). Curiously, the first two criteria are counted under the corporation's social impact score.

But to what ends were these cashflows to be used? Another practice that became entrenched during this period was the use of *special accounts*. This entailed locking the cash flows generated by specific privatizations to fund corresponding policy programmes. The roots of this practice appear to be in the design and set-up of Marcos-era GOCCs, when the cash crop-export monopolies (the Philippine Coconut Authority and the Philippine Sugar Commission, respectively) were funded by special levies on producers and exporters. But the practice was carried over into the EDSA system through Presidential Proclamations 50 and 82 of the Aquino government, which specified that the sales from the disposition of sequestered crony assets were to fund a new agrarian reform programme.

Special accounts have since proliferated across the Philippine state. A 2014 tally by the budget, audit, and finance departments identified 61 special accounts, spread out across no less than 31 state agencies. They are at the heart of the privatization of land and energy assets: BCDA, set up in 1993 to convert military bases, was designed to generate revenues for the Armed Forces of the Philippines' (AFP) modernization. PSALM, meanwhile, was set up in 2001 to service the debts incurred by the National Power Corporation (Napocor) by selling off its best assets. To date, these two GOCCs have generated PHP17.1 billion and 504.8 billion toward these ends, respectively. But one consequence of this practice is that it holds policy and developmental outcomes hostage to the ability of GOCCs to generate revenue, which in most instances translates into the speed and constancy at which they can liquidate their assets. Again, this served to reinforce the transformation of GOCCs: from instruments of direct, strategic intervention in the economy for achieving developmental ends to instruments of revenue generation for a periodically cash-strapped state.

Overall, the need to generate cashflows was in direct opposition to designing asset sales that would allow a wider base of asset ownership. As the overriding imperative was determined by the needs to service debt, as well as to fund specific policies, this meant bringing prime assets to sale in a way that would generate cash quickly and regularly. In practice, this meant designing their sales as winner-takes-all, highest-bidder auctions for large, consolidated assets. As conjectural alternatives, these privatizations could have been carried out as sales of smaller lots or as initial public offerings. This had two main effects: It effectively restricted participation in these markets to entities which could front the sums for these auctions. It also meant the prioritization of real estate assets. Often, lands were the only assets both ready for sale and attractive to potential investors as many of the GOCCs' capital assets had deteriorated from neglect. But as the ownership of land, as well as of utilities and infrastructure, is restricted to juridical Philippine nationals, this effectively meant that the market of privatized assets was restricted to Philippine nationals with the ability to mobilize the large amounts of capital to participate in these auctions. This artificial constraint on the pool of market participants laid the foundations for lucrative markets in consolidated urban land and energy-generation assets—to the almost exclusive benefit of PNCs.

The reform of GOCCs thus created new opportunities, but the ability of capital to flow into the new channels that have been dug up presents separate questions:

what kinds of capital could flow into, and profit from, these new markets? What were the vehicles for these flows?

The first-pass answer is that it was PNCs, neither the Philippine state nor its GOCCs, transnational corporations (TNCs), or smaller Philippine businesses, which benefitted the most from these opportunities. However, this answer presents two problems. First, the privatization of lucrative assets are supply-side opportunities; demand for land, energy, and infrastructure still had to be created for capital to see a return on investment in these opportunities. The PNCs, however, have played a rather slim role in generating demand. Their successes since 2001 have been accomplished with very little direct participation in the new export earners for the country: they do not facilitate the movement of Filipino workers overseas, though their recent forays into private education and healthcare provision in the Philippines might see them take on this role. With some exceptions, they do not participate in electronics manufacturing or IT-enabled services export, the country's two sunshine industries that involve actual value creation. Nevertheless, by building and operating special economic zones, PNCs have succeeded in capturing massive profits from demand generated by these sectors. Why was it that PNCs directed their investment into land and infrastructure, as opposed to either the new export-oriented sectors or to innovating in their old mainstays? Second, this answer specifies a kind of business organization, and not capital as a process. As corporations, PNCs can act as vehicles for varieties of capital that are as diverse as its stockholders. The question of the kinds of capital and capitalists that profit from these new opportunities, therefore, remains open. The next two sections attempt to answer these two questions by looking at the sectoral and geographical diversification of PNCs and the organization of their ownership and control.

## Privatized State Assets, Property Development, and New Flows of Capital and Labour

Along with the dismantling of the Marcos state, the Philippines' economic policy after 1986 also sought to replicate the FDI-fuelled, manufacturing-driven, and export-oriented economic miracles in the rest of East and South East Asia. To this end, all post-Marcos governments have committed to trade liberalization and investment promotion (Bello et al., 2004). But while it has been arguably quite successful in liquidating its prime assets, the Philippines' record in attracting this kind of investment has been spotty, and the hoped-for inflows of foreign capital were miniscule, especially in comparison to its South East Asian neighbours.

An immediate effect of the country's failure to attract foreign investment was that its export-oriented industrialization was at a much smaller scale than its neighbours and concentrated in just one region, south of Manila (Bello et al., 2004;

Kelly, 2000). This was further compounded by the decline of domestic industry, in large part due to their poor competitiveness against liberalized imported goods. As its impact on jobs remained modest, and with wages in other sectors and regions remaining stagnant, Filipino labour continued to seek greener pastures overseas, and migration for overseas labour contracts became a permanent fixture of its economy.

The privatization of Fort Bonifacio is illustrative of the way that flows of capital and labour, including flows that were hoped for but did not materialize, have implicated privatized state assets, transformed the interests of Philippine capitalists, and help account for their recent successes. It was one of the best assets in BCDA's portfolio, comprising 240 hectares of former military lands adjacent to Manila's premier business district. It was first acquired in 1995 by First Pacific with the intent of developing it as a magnet for the anticipated exodus of capital from Hong Kong after its 1997 handover from the British to Beijing. Practically none of this investment materialized, and by 2003 Fort Bonifacio was resold at a loss to a joint venture between Ayala Corporation and the Campos family's Evergreen Holdings, Inc.

The property fell into this joint venture at just the right time. The decade began with real estate development in crisis: the sector shrank from 2000 to 2002, hitting a 24.7 per cent year-on-year contraction in the first quarter of 2001. But beginning with 2003, real estate grew at a sustained double-digit pace, uninterrupted even by the global financial crisis of 2007–2008. The gross value added of the sector doubled in real terms between 2002 and 2010 (Cardenas, 2014). During this period, personal remittances grew from US$6.9 billion in 2000 to US$21.5 billion in 2010 and consistently accounted for more than 10 per cent of Philippine GDP. Much of these remittances, in turn, were spent on real estate (Cardenas, 2014; Faier, 2013; Ortega, 2016; Pido, 2017). Right around the same time, the Philippines' IT-BPO boom began to take off in earnest, fuelling demand for officespace leasing, to the tune of approximately an additional 300,000 square metres of demand per year (Cardenas, 2014; Kleibert, 2015).

Fort Bonifacio's new owners exploited this boom in earnest and set about to create a new business district attuned to these new sources of demand. Beyond real estate, however, the creation of an entirely new business district also presented other opportunities. The concentration of residential, commercial, and office use in these new business districts are treated by PNCs as demand aggregators for their other businesses, particularly telecommunications, transportation infrastructure, and most recently, retail energy. Malls are treated as trip generators for rapid transit infrastructure, and key elements of the design of Manila's new metro lines have been dictated by wrangling between PNCs over station placement. In the case of Ayala Corporation developments, tenants are made to connect exclusively to Ayala's telecommunications subsidiary. Finally, a recent development within the Philippines' liberalized energy sector created businesses that are called retail electricity suppliers

(RES). RES firms can buy electricity directly from power generators and sell it directly to consumers, provided they can aggregate a contiguous area exceeding a set amount of demand. Integrated developments such as Fort Bonifacio present a perfect captive market of aggregated demand: contiguous; bounded; and with commercial, residential, and office use generating a reliably large energy requirement. It is worth noting that of the 14 licenses for RES firms that were active as of 2015, 9 were subsidiaries of PNCs; all of these PNCs had interests both downstream, in real estate, as well as upstream, in energy generation.

By diversifying into real estate, PNCs thus became vertically-integrated rentiers; able to capture substantial portions of capital flows through the built environment without any direct involvement in either the deployment of Filipino labour overseas or in the operation of BPO firms. In its purest form, as seen in Fort Bonifacio, this is expressed as enclave 'townships' with an emphasis on mixed-use, self-contained 'live-work-play' development (Kleibert and Kippers, 2016). These townships carry echoes of cash-crop latifundism: the sources of demand are ultimately global, and the value is created through labour, but the basis of the key surpluses are rents on land and other inputs to production and reproduction.

The new interests of PNCs are important for understanding the patterns of their diversification and expansion and the role played by flows of capital and labour in structuring these patterns. The PNCs' new core interests are largely based in the Philippines—yet profiting from them would have been impossible if not for the peculiar form that globalization had taken hold in the country. The real estate boom, after all, is ultimately sustained by demand for and by Filipino labour, both deployed overseas and electronically mediated. And despite staying in the Philippines, PNCs have had to diversify away from their former core interests. Hence a distinction must be made between a company 'staying in place' on one hand, and the 'mobility' of capital on the other. This is underpinned by a conception of capital not as a thing (or an organization) but as a *process*—the firm itself might stay in place, but it might direct its capital into new locations and new activities. Capital mobility, in this sense, is about geographical and sectoral diversification within the same jurisdiction.

With a few exceptions, PNCs are not directly invested in the Philippines' sunshine industries, that is electronics assembly and export and IT-BPO services offshoring (see Table 11.1). Among PNCs, only Lopez Holdings and Ayala Corporation have investments in high-tech and/or export-oriented manufacturing. Only Ayala Corporation had an investment in IT-BPO, which it divested in 2016. All the other PNCs' manufacturing concerns are in mainstay food and beverage, refining, and automotive assembly sectors that are largely oriented towards the domestic market. Indeed, in expanding its food and beverage business internationally, JG Summit Holdings preferred to set up or acquire plants in their new markets, rather than export from their Philippine operations. Similarly, PNCs are not directly involved in labour export, though their recent investments in education and healthcare might present them with the opportunity for closing this loop.

Most, though not all PNCs with origins in manufacturing are divesting from it. It is worth noting, too, that most of the domestic-market manufacturers that characterized the Philippine economy in the mid- to late-twentieth century have not made a successful transition into PNC-hood: they have attained neither the size nor the diversification which sets this group apart. Among the largest PNCs, only San Miguel Corporation and JG Summit Holdings still derive a substantial portion of their incomes from manufacturing. This observation leads into a conception of land as playing a strategic role, similar to that played by banks in *keiretsu*: in transitioning into their new interests, PNCs without substantial real estate arms or assets have tended to rely on liquidating industrial assets, taking on new investors, and/or going into debt. Meanwhile, companies without banks but with property development arms get by just by having a property development arm. For instance, San Miguel Corporation appears to have been forced into a debt-driven strategy for its diversification precisely because it did not have a substantial real estate arm and was thus unable to tap into these flows of remittances and foreign investment.

Diversification into these new sectors also enabled a lower level of reliance on former core interests. However, it also reinforced the shift away from value-creation in the East Asian mould and towards rentier strategies for accumulation: Without much of an export-oriented industrial presence, Philippine capital had little incentive to transition into suppliers to multinational locators—which was the route taken by many firms in the second wave of industrialization across East and South East Asia. In this sense, the lucre of rentier sectors have indirectly abetted the overall pattern of lower-middle income industrialization, which in turn feeds into overseas orientation of the labour force and further entrenches these companies' dependence on their new interests.

Finally, while many of the PNCs' advantages are place-based, this does not necessarily mean that the abilities which underpin these advantages cannot be developed and applied in other jurisdictions. This period has also seen the international expansion of PNCs. But these are not, by far, the most noteworthy aspects of their recent successes. Their overseas operations return small shares of their revenues, and their management remains tethered to operations in Manila. Very few Philippine-based businesses, past or present, have managed to attain escape velocity; within the short- and medium-term, most PNCs will likely still rely on the markets created by the Philippine state, and by Filipino workers.[2]

---

[2] There are, however, some important exceptions. There are also Filipino-origin firms that have extensive overseas operations, and they tend to rely less on the flows of capital sent, or captured by, Filipino labour. Instead of diversifying into land, they instead expanded

One executive of a PNC-affiliated property firm described these movements as 'opportunistic' investments, whose tempo is dictated by the opportunities as they present themselves rather than by long-term strategic thinking.[3] There is some evidence for Philippine regulatory regimes being actively promoted, by the Philippine state and its development partners, to other lower-middle income, infrastructure-deficient, 'emerging' markets. The Philippine PPP programme is being showcased by the Philippine PPP Center as a template for the programmes being designed for Cambodia, Laos, Myanmar, and Vietnam. In this sense, their expansion is enabled (and constrained) more by market conditions than by borders. The offshoring of some ownership to corporations-in-boxes in known tax havens also presents a worrying possibility for a future where restrictions on foreign ownership are relaxed. Under such a situation, the owners of PNCs can offshore a larger share of their ownership—even while their other place-based advantages are maintained.

## Philippine-Nationality Conglomerates: Staying in Place, Directing Capital Flows

The key advantage of PNCs has been their legal status as Philippine-nationality juridical persons. The 1987 Constitution contained national patrimony provisions, which restricted levels of ownership by foreign nationals. Notably, foreign equity in the ownership of private land, condominium units, infrastructure franchises, and of public utilities are capped at 40 per cent. As previously noted, this effectively restricts the market for privatized state assets to Philippine-nationality firms that can mobilize large sums of capital.

But this advantage extends beyond these immediate sectors. Any form of economic activity which requires land will require the participation of a Philippine-nationality firm, whether this be a new suburban development, an export processing zone, an IT-enabled office tower, a new telecommunications operator, or even

---

their core businesses horizontally into other jurisdictions. The two most notable examples are International Container Terminal Services, Inc. (ICTSI), a port management firm with operations in 20 countries, and Universal Robina, a subsidiary of JG Summit engaged in food and beverage manufacturing across China and South East Asia. Finally, there is Jollibee, a fast-service restaurant chain, which on top of expanding the operations of its core Philippine brands to countries with large Filipino populations, has also acquired several brands in mainland China.

[3] It is worthy here to consider the positionality of my informants and the perspective it afforded them. They work for a company that takes a rather patient approach to cleaning up messy title structures, in one instance taking several decades to consolidate titles for a 2,290-hectare development in south of Manila.

a fast food restaurant. This is the primary modality through which PNCs have benefitted from the booms in remittances-fuelled homebuying, assembly and testing of electronics, services offshoring, and the new-found consumption power of the workers—often without directly participating in these activities.

But whose capital do PNCs mobilize? To whom do the flows of profit accrue? Historically, big business in the Philippines has been understood primarily through the lenses of family ownership and control, and of ethnicity (Yoshihara, 1988; Rivera, 2004). But an analysis of the corporate structure of PNCs—their ownership, the entities they own, and their management—reveals the need for an update of this characterization (Appendix 11.1). An analysis of SM Investments Corporation (SMIC), presently the biggest PNC by market capitalization, demonstrates this point. Founded in 1958 by Henry Sy, Sr as Shoe Mart, Mr Sy grew the business into the country's dominant department store, which for much of the succeeding decades was its core interest. Mr Sy, as well as members of the Sy family to the second generation, now have diverse interests in commercial, office, and residential developments; finance; casinos; construction; mining; and private education. Many of these new interests were inaugurated within the past 15 years: its real estate arm, SM Development Corporation, only sold its first condominiums in 2001, yet is now the largest residential developer in the country. The main vehicle for these new investments is SMIC, a holding company with 44.56 per cent of its stocks publicly listed on the Philippine Stock Exchange.

An analysis of SMIC's ownership and management shows how PNCs are a vehicle for a wide variety of interests: the families which incorporated and still maintain control and sizeable ownership over them; foreign capital, whether in the form of joint venture partners, investors, or lenders; smaller, illiquid, and/or peripherally-located Philippine capitalists; and the Philippine state.

Considering these interests in turn, 55 percent of SMIC proper and significant portions of its subsidiaries are owned by its progenitor family, the Sys. The Sys also maintain a tight managerial rein, and first- and second-generation members of the family sit on the boards of SMIC and its subsidiaries. Second-generation members of the Sy family have also ventured into businesses independently from SMIC, presumably by leveraging the wealth they have accumulated through it. This is most notable in the case of Hans Sy's joint venture with the State Grid Corporation of China for the National Grid Corporation of the Philippines, a privatized Napocor asset.

But PNCs can also be vehicles for foreign capital. In the case of SMIC, 33.45 per cent of its shares are owned by non-Filipinos. As with SMIC, foreign ownership in most of the other PNCs is similarly non-controlling and non-consolidated and primarily through publicly-traded shares. The only two exceptions are Ayala Corporation, in which the Japanese conglomerate Mitsubishi has had a stake since 1974 which stood at 10.15 percent of Ayala's shares in 2015; and Metro Pacific

Investments Corporation (MPIC). MPIC is exceptional as it is the only major PNC which is 55.8 percent owned by First Pacific Company Limited, a Hong Kong-registered holding firm for the international investments of Anthoni Salim of Indonesia. These shares are owned through a series of nine intermediate shell corporations, a structure which allows Salim to imbue his ownership of MPIC with juridical Filipino nationality while maintaining managerial control.

Foreign capital has a more substantial presence in the ownership and operation of PNCs' subsidiaries and joint ventures. This is particularly true for the local presence of prominent global brands: some smaller PNCs, such as the Rustans Group, specializes in brokering the local presence for brands such as Marks & Spencer, Muji, and Starbucks. In the case of SMIC, these include the Philippine operations of Sodexo (French, customer science), Forever 21 (American, fast fashion), and Uniqlo (Japanese, fast fashion). Other TNCs also maintain a presence in the country through the intercession of PNCs: for example, Honda through Ayala Corporation, Toyota through GT Capital, and McDonald's through Alliance Global. Typically, foreign involvement in these joint ventures involves both part-ownership of the joint venture, as well as a substantial presence in their top management.

A professional managerial cadre also features prominently on the boards of SMIC, its subsidiaries, and the family-affiliated holding companies which own stocks in it. It is unclear, however, if this is leading to the fusion of ownership and control in the managerial class, seen elsewhere in contemporary capitalism. These executives do not appear to be compensated in stock ownership and own negligible portions of these companies' stocks. There are, however, prominent examples of this trend in other PNCs, such as Ramon S. Ang for San Miguel Corporation and Manuel Pangilinan for MPIC.

In addition to their progenitor families, foreign capital, and the shareholding public, PNCs have also enabled other kinds of domestic capitalists to benefit from the transformation of the Philippine economy. Apart from Aboitiz Equity Ventures, which originated from Cebu in the central Philippines, most PNCs' operations in their new core interests began with Manila and its extended metropolitan region. Most PNCs, too, are headquartered in Manila. In expanding to other regions of the country, they have tapped smaller regionally based capitalists as joint venture partners. These companies play a role in mobilizing their own place-based assets, for example, clear and consolidated titles to parcels of land, centrally located properties, or connections with the local political elite. For instance, SMIC's own geographical expansion appears to have been facilitated largely, but not exclusively, by ethnic Chinese-Filipinos tapped as joint venture partners for their expansion to regional centres outside of Manila. Ethnicity, therefore, does matter within Philippine capitalism; however, its role needs to be restated in operationalizable, observable ways.

Another pattern of expansion of PNCs involves them supplying the necessary liquidity to dormant concerns. This has been especially evident in franchise rights-based sectors, such as mineral exploration, infrastructure projects, and casinos, where a smaller company may hold franchise rights but does not have the liquidity to exploit these rights, nor the asset base and track record to borrow the required sums. A high-profile example involved the bidding war between SMIC and Ayala Corporation for the assets of OCLP Holdings, which owns substantial tracts of land in Manila. OCLP, which was started by the Ortigas family, was once one of the country's largest real estate developers and had developed one of Manila's business districts in the 1960s and 1970s. However, it largely missed out on the ongoing property boom, and as such many of its assets remained idle.

Recently, inter-PNC cooperation has also emerged as an important feature. As the privatizations and PPPs grow in size, PNCs have sought partners. Joint infrastructure projects are perceived as demand drivers for their retail and development businesses. In describing a joint venture between SM Investments and Ayala Corporation for a planned rapid transit line, the president of Ayala Infrastructure Holdings noted, 'You might be wondering why two competing developers would go together and its very simple; your development is nothing without mobility. We do have people in Makati who want to go to Mall of Asia and vice-versa and this will help.'

The PHP122.8-billion Laguna Lakeshore Expressway Dike Project (LLEDP) has so far attracted the most ambitious attempts at joint ventures between PNCs. In February 2015, SM Investments, Ayala Corporation, Megaworld, and Aboitiz Equity Ventures put together a joint bid, under Trident Infrastructure and Development Corporation; the two other pre-qualified bids for the project came from Malaysia's Allyo-PAVI-Hanshin-LLEDP Consortium and the heavily leveraged San Miguel Corporation. However, by late 2015, interest within the Trident group had started to flag; its spokesperson had described the project as the 'most complex PPP to date' and one which 'exposes the concessionaire to extensive risks'. Ayala Corporation and SM Investments have also partnered up for an unsolicited proposal for a PHP25 billion elevated expressway in Manila which will form a new beltway. Meanwhile, Ayala Corporation also partnered with Metro Pacific for the operation and maintenance of one line in Manila's rapid transit system, through the joint venture Light Rail Manila Holdings, Inc.

## Conclusion: Accumulation, the Immobility of Land, and the Mobilities of Labour and Capital

A common perception is that market-oriented reform would undo the dependent, 'crony' or 'ersatz' forms that capitalism had taken in the Philippines and usher in a different form of capitalism after the EDSA Revolution of 1986. This was shared across political divides: on the part of its designers this was the intended effect. On the part of its critics, this represented a surrender of sovereignty to international financial institutions and thus to foreign capital (cf. Bello et al., 2004 and Robinson et al., 2000). But none of these outcomes really materialized. Understood within longer timescales, the relationship between Philippine capital and the state remained fundamentally the same, in that the former remained dependent on rentier-type opportunities created by the latter. What changed was the mechanism and the assets in question. In previous periods of Philippine capitalism, it was access to church lands being redistributed by the American colonial government; systematic plunder of the central bank; access to forex licenses, easy credit, and/or management of a state monopoly; or a state-backed hostile takeover of a lucrative business. For the post-1986 Philippines the mechanism became privatization, and eventually private–public partnerships; the opportunities again returned to land and land-like assets.

Considered in terms of capital mobility, the privatization programme was crucial in the Philippine state's continued participation in capital markets, as well in its ability to pursue a few costly flagship projects, despite having a weak revenue base. But in the process, it also created new opportunities for accumulation into which capital can now flow—opportunities that were restricted to a few participants, and opportunities in which returns precluded the possibility of Philippine big businesses being invested in the creation of jobs in the country. Similarly, other aspects of the country's market-oriented reform, particularly those meant to attract foreign investment, did not have the intended effect of spurring export-oriented industrialization and likely contributed to the stagnation of its domestic industry, and thus to the exodus of its labour force.

Furthermore, the direction of development taken by the Philippine economy from 2001 to 2015—with much of the growth being driven by rentier as opposed to value-added sectors, and with much of this growth, in turn, being captured by PNCs that have reinvested most of these returns into more rentier sectors—have arguably reinforced the position of labour export in Philippine society. An inability of the Philippine economy to create well-paying jobs at home has long been a crucial systemic factor behind its sizeable overseas workforce, and the same could be said of the present period of remittances- and offshoring-driven, real estate-based growth.

In contrast to how real estate has been understood in recent years, which emphasizes a placeless, frictionless quality to both its sources of demand as well as to the recirculation of the profits made from it, property development in early-twenty-first century Philippines shows how place, and thus fixity, remains an important dimension to economic life, even when considering the mobility of labour and capital. It also shows how accumulation strategies of capitalists from the Global South can remain dependent on rentierism, albeit a globalized, mobility-enabled, and urbanized form. This is again in contrast to how successful Southern capitalists tend to become visible in the literature with respect to their position along value chains and/or production networks, as the strategy of PNCs depends not on the creation of value, but rather on the extraction of rent. As the Philippines is not completely exceptional with respect to its position along global flows of labour and capital, the institutional configuration of its capitalism, nor in its characteristics as an urbanizing but largely non-industrial society, the possibility that PNC-like firms are important parts of contemporary capitalism elsewhere must be examined.

## Appendix 11.1: The Largest Philippine-Nationality Conglomerates as of 2015

| | Interests (**bold** indicates historical core interests) | Segment income as share of total net income | | |
|---|---|---|---|---|
| | | 2001–2005 | 2006–2010 | 2011–2015 |
| SAN MIGUEL CORPORATION<br>Financial position: PHP1.245 trillion in assets, of which 35% are land, power plants, and capital projects in progress. An additional 10% are in toll road concession, leasehold, mineral, airport concession, power concession and port concession rights PHP861 billion in total liabilities. PHP541 billion in noncurrent liabilities, of which 34% are floating rate foreign currency notes with maturities through to 2020, and 24% are PHP-denominated payable loans Ownership: 66% owned by Top Frontier Investment Holdings, Inc., out of which 59.6% is owned by Iñigo Zobel. 15.5% owned by Privado Holdings, Corp., which is wholly-owned by SMC President Ramon Ang. 10.09% of shares publicly traded of which 2.35% is foreign-owned Management: Eduardo Cojuangco, Jr sits as chairman and CEO. Ramon Ang is vice chairman, president, and COO. Iñigo Zobel is an independent director | **Beverage** | 115 | 55 | 61 |
| | **Food** | 19 | 30 | 18 |
| | **Packaging** | 26 | 6 | 6 |
| | Real estate | 0 | 0 | 0 |
| | Energy | — | 8 | 59 |
| | Infrastructure | — | 0 | 6 |
| | Telecommunications | — | 0 | -2 |
| | Mining | — | — | 0 |
| | Fuel and oil | — | 1 | 29 |

## AYALA CORPORATION

Financial position: PHP794 billion in assets, of which 38% are real estate (including overseas developments), 10% in water service concessions, 2% in investments in energy companies, and 0.7% in investments in overseas water and infrastructure PHP465 billion in liabilities, of which 35% are fixed-rate long-term debts and 11% are floating-rate foreign currency notes

Ownership: 49% owned by the Zobel de Ayala family through Mermac, Inc.; 10.2% owned by Mitsubishi Corporation; 37.1% is publicly traded, of which 11.1% is foreign-owned

Management: Brothers Jaime Augusto and Fernando Zobel de Ayala are chairman and CEO and president and COO, respectively. Yoshio Amano is an independent director and is also senior vice president of Mitsubishi Corporation

| Interests (**bold** indicates historical core interests) | Segment income as share of total net income | | |
|---|---|---|---|
| | 2001–2005 | 2006–2010 | 2011–2015 |
| **Real estate** | 43 | 38 | 53 |
| **Financial services** | 23 | 21 | 27 |
| Energy | — | — | 1 |
| Telecommunications | 33 | 26 | 12 |
| Water | 5 | 9 | 19 |
| Mass transit | — | — | 0 |
| Electronics | 10 | 2 | 2 |
| IT-BPO | — | -2 | 0 |
| Automotive | 2 | 1 | 2 |

## SM INVESTMENTS CORPORATION

Financial position: PHP771 billion in assets, of which 43% in investments in land, buildings, and improvements, construction in progress, and land held as investment (including investments in strategic landbank of Ortigas Holdings); 26% are in investments in associate banks; 13% in foreign currency-denominated financial assets, primarily time deposits; and 1.5% in investments in mining and casino companies

PHP389 billion in liabilities, of which 20% is foreign-denominated floating-rate notes with maturities through to 2019, and 15% is foreign-denominated fixed-rate long-term debt

Ownership: 55% owned by first- and second-generation members of the Sy family, both directly and through holding companies; 33.5% owned by foreign investors through publicly traded shares. A further 11.1% is publicly traded and owned by Filipino nationals

Management: Four members of the Sy family sit on the company's board of directors, including founder Mr. Henry Sy, Jr.

| Interests (**bold** indicates historical core interests) | Segment income as share of total net income | | |
|---|---|---|---|
| | 2001–2005 | 2006–2010 | 2011–2015 |
| **Retail** | 62 | 30 | 18 |
| **Commercial centres** | 85 | 37 | |
| Residential development | 8 | 16 | |
| Real estate | | | 61 |
| Financial services | 71 | 38 | 42 |
| Mining | | | 0 |

*Contd*

*Appendix 11.1 contd*

| Interests (**bold** indicates historical core interests) | Segment income as share of total net income | | |
|---|---|---|---|
| | 2001–2005 | 2006–2010 | 2011–2015 |

**LT Group, Inc.**
Financial position: PHP750 billion in assets, of which 50% are loans and receivables of its banking subsidiary. Of its nonfinancial, noncurrent assets, 27% is land and buildings and 11% is capital equipment for its manufacturing subsidiaries
PHP580 billion in liabilities, of which 75% are deposit liabilities of its banking subsidiary. Of its non-deposit, noncurrent liabilities, 13 % are fixed-rate peso-denominated long-term notes.
Ownership: 74% owned by the Tan family through Tangent Holdings Corp.; 29% publicly traded, of which 14% are held by foreign investors
Management: Three members of the Tan family sit on the company's board of directors, including founder Lucio Tan
*Data from 2012 onwards*

| Interests | 2001–2005 | 2006–2010 | 2011–2015 |
|---|---|---|---|
| **Distilled spirits** | | | 4 |
| **Beverage** | | | 7 |
| **Tobacco** | | | 35 |
| Real estate | | | 3 |
| Finance | | | 50 |

**JG Summit Holdings, Inc.**
Financial position: PHP596 billion in assets, of which 28% are in land, buildings, construction in progress, land use rights, and an investment in a real estate company with operations in Singapore; 19% are in capital equipment for its manufacturing and aviation arms; and 12% in an investment in Manila's electricity distribution utility
Ownership: At least 40% owned by members of the Gokongwei family, either directly, through shell corporations, or the Gokongwei Brothers Foundation, Inc. An additional 14.4% is owned through an account with the affiliated Robinson Savings Bank Trust and Investment Group. 47% public of shares publicly traded, of which 12.7% is foreign-owned
Management: Six members of the Gokongwei family sit on the company's board of directors, including founder John Gokongwei, Sr

| Interests | 2001–2005 | 2006–2010 | 2011–2015 |
|---|---|---|---|
| **Food and agro-industrial** | 40 | 33 | 33 |
| **Petrochemicals** | −18 | −12 | −1 |
| **Textiles** | 2 | −1 | — |
| Real estate | 21 | 46 | 29 |
| Finance | 60 | 25 | 1 |
| Energy | — | — | 11 |
| Airlines | 1 | 25 | 10 |
| Telecommunications | −12 | 2 | 15 |
| Olefins | — | — | 2 |

| | Interests (**bold** indicates historical core interests) | Segment income as share of total net income | | |
|---|---|---|---|---|
| | | 2001–2005 | 2006–2010 | 2011–2015 |
| ALLIANCE GLOBAL, INC. | **Brandy** | 22 | 18 | 24 |
| Financial position: PHP449 billion in assets, of which | Fast-food restaurants | 77 | 8 | 3 |
| 15% are land, buildings, condominium units, and | Real estate | 11 | 61 | 55 |
| construction in progress, and 13% are current real | Casinos | — | — | 18 |
| estate inventory | | | | |
| PHP218 billion in liabilities, of which 23% are | | | | |
| dollar-denominated bonds listed in Singapore, | | | | |
| 13% are peso-denominated long-term loans from | | | | |
| Philippine banks affiliated with other PNCs, and | | | | |
| 11% are foreign currency-denominated floating-rate | | | | |
| short-term loans | | | | |
| Ownership: 39% owned by the Tan family through | | | | |
| The Andresons Group, Inc. 42% publicly-traded, of | | | | |
| which 32% are held by foreign investors | | | | |
| Management: Three members of the Tan family | | | | |
| sit on the company's board of directors, including | | | | |
| founder Andrew Tan | | | | |
| | | | | |
| ABOITIZ EQUITY VENTURES | **Energy** | 69 | 73 | 73 |
| Financial position: PHP340 billion in assets, of | **Shipping** | 9 | 1 | — |
| which 40% are in energy generation and distribution | **Food manufacturing** | 8 | 9 | 7 |
| assets, including joint ventures, concession rights, and | Real estate | — | — | 1 |
| construction in progress; 7.5% is in an investment | Finance | 32 | 16 | 14 |
| in an associated bank; and 3% is in land, leasehold | Infrastructure | — | — | 0 |
| improvements, and buildings | | | | |
| PHP193 billion in liabilities, of which 49% are fixed- | | | | |
| rate peso-denominated long-term retail bonds, and | | | | |
| 26% is a finance lease obligation for an 'independent | | | | |
| power producer agreement' regarding a privatized | | | | |
| energy generation asset | | | | |
| Ownership: 49.25% owned by the Aboitiz family | | | | |
| through Aboitiz & Company, Inc. An additional 10% | | | | |
| is owned by holding firms associated with the family. | | | | |
| 21% publicly-traded, of which 10% is foreign-owned | | | | |
| Management: Four members of the Aboitiz family | | | | |
| sit on its board of directors | | | | |

*Contd*

*Appendix 11.1 contd*

| | Interests (**bold** indicates historical core interests) | Segment income as share of total net income | | |
|---|---|---|---|---|
| | | 2001– 2005 | 2006– 2010 | 2011– 2015 |
| LOPEZ HOLDINGS CORPORATION (formerly Benpres Holdings)<br>Financial position: PHP358 billion in assets, of which 28% are in energy assets, including plant and equipment, goodwill, concession rights, and geothermal exploration rights; and 10% are in land assets<br>PHP214 billion in liabilities, of which 25% are fixed-rate peso-denominated long-term loans and bonds and 24% are in floating-rate dollar-denominated long-term loans<br>Ownership: 52% owned by the Lopez family through Lopez, Inc.; 42% publicly traded, of which 13% are held by foreign investors<br>Management: Three members of the Lopez family sit on its board of directors | **Broadcasting and entertainment** | -20 | 13 | n.d. |
| | **Energy** | | | 77 |
| | Water | -2 | — | — |
| | Manufacturing | | | -10 |
| | Real estate | — | — | 13 |
| FIRST PHILIPPINE HOLDINGS (subsidiary of Lopez Holdings)<br>*Considered as a separate entity for 2001 to 2010. Data for 2011–2015 tabulated as part of Lopez Holdings.* | **Energy** | 87 | 36 | |
| | Real estate development | 2 | | |
| | Tollways | 7 | 5 | |
| | Manufacturing | 2 | 1 | |
| GT CAPITAL HOLDINGS, INC.<br>Financial position: PHP317 billion in assets, of which 26% are in real estate assets, including joint ventures and condominium inventory, and 7% in energy assets<br>PHP122 billion in liabilities, of which 67% are fixed-rate peso-denominated long-term loans<br>Ownership: 54% owned by the Ty family through Grand Titan Capital Holdings, Inc. 45% publicly traded, of which 36% are held by foreign investors.<br>Management: Three members of the Ty family sit on the board of directors, including founder George Ty<br>*Data from 2009 onwards.* | **Finance** | | 138 | 29 |
| | Real estate | | 27 | 14 |
| | Energy | | — | 24 |
| | Automotive | | 39 | 38 |

| | Interests (**bold** indicates historical core interests) | Segment income as share of total net income | | |
|---|---|---|---|---|
| | | 2001–2005 | 2006–2010 | 2011–2015 |
| METRO PACIFIC INVESTMENTS CORPORATION | Real estate | | 100 | — |
| Financial position: PHP302 billion in assets, of which 25% are water utility concessions, 23% are in energy generation and distribution, and 17% are toll road concessions. | Water | | 139 | 55 |
| | Toll roads | | 47 | 27 |
| | Mass transit | | — | 0 |
| PHP151 billion in liabilities, of which 45% are peso-denominated long-term loans, subject to repricing | Healthcare | | 15 | 6 |
| on the 5th year, with banks affiliated with other | Energy | | 14 | 37 |

PNCs, primarily Banco De Oro (SMIC), Chinabank (SMIC), BPI (Ayala), and PNB (LT Group); 16% are service concession fees for water, toll roads, and rail; and 6% are in fixed-rate long-term loans from Philippine state-owned banks and international financial institutions

Ownership: 55.8% of MPIC is owned, through a series of nine shell corporations, by First Pacific Company Ltd., a Hong Kong–registered holding firm for the international investments of Anthoni Salim in Indonesia. First Pacific also has large investments in telecommunications and mining in the Philippines

Management: MPIC and its subsidiaries are managed by a core group of executives, led by Manuel V. Pangilinan. None of the Salim family sit on its board

*Data from 2005 onwards.*

| | | 2001–2005 | 2006–2010 | 2011–2015 |
|---|---|---|---|---|
| DMCI HOLDINGS, INC. | **Mining** | 54 | 74 | 27 |
| Financial position: PHP148 billion in assets, of which 31% are energy generation assets, 18% are mining equipment and exploration rights, 8% are investments in water utilities, 6% are construction equipment, and 1.6% are land assets. | **Construction** | 2 | 11 | 6 |
| | Real estate | 4 | 16 | 17 |
| | Energy | — | 23 | 17 |
| | Water | — | 23 | 14 |

PHP74 billion in liabilities, of which 35% are fixed-rate peso-denominated long-term loans from Philippine banks affiliated with other PNCs

Ownership: 51.5% owned by Dacon Corporation, which through two layers of holding companies, are owned by members of the Consunji family; 18% owned by DFC Holdings, Inc., which is held by members of the Consunji family through a similar structure of intermediate holding companies; 37.3% publicly traded, of which 16.3% are held by foreign investors

Management: Six members of the Consunji family sit on the company's board of directors, including David M. Consunji, until his death in 2017

# References

Aboitiz Equity Ventures, Inc. 2001–2015. *Annual Report Pursuant to Section 17 of the Securities Regulation Code and Section 141 of the Corporation Code of the Philippines.*

Alliance Global, Inc. 2001–2015. *Annual Report Pursuant to Section 17 of the Securities Regulation Code and Section 141 of the Corporation Code of the Philippines.*

Ayala Corporation. 2001–2015. *Annual Report Pursuant to Section 17 of the Securities Regulation Code and Section 141 of the Corporation Code of the Philippines.*

Bello, Walden, Marissa de Guzman, Herbert Docena, and Mary Malig. 2004. *The Anti-Development State: The Political Economy of Permanent Crisis in the Philippines.* Quezon City: University of the Philippines Press.

Benpres Holdings Corporation. 2001–2015. *Annual Report Pursuant to Section 17 of the Securities Regulation Code and Section 141 of the Corporation Code of the Philippines.*

Borras, Saturnino. 2001. 'State-Society Relations in Land Reform Implementation in the Philippines'. *Development and Change* 32: 545–575.

Cardenas, Kenneth. 2014. 'Urban Property Development and the Creative Destruction of Filipino Capitalism'. In *State of Fragmentation: The Philippines in Transition,* edited by W. Bello, K. Cardenas, J. P. Cruz, A. Fabros, M. A. Manahan, C. Militante, J. Purugannan, and J. J. Chavez. Quezon City: Focus on the Global South and Friedrich-Ebert-Stiftung.

DMC Holdings, Inc. 2001–2015. *Annual Report Pursuant to Section 17 of the Securities Regulation Code and Section 141 of the Corporation Code of the Philippines.*

Faier, Lieba. 2013. 'Affective Investments in the Manila Region: Filipina Migrants in Rural Japan and Transnational Urban Development in the Philippines'. *Transactions of the Institute of British Geographers* 38(3): 376–390.

First Philippine Holdings, Inc. 2001–2015. *Annual Report Pursuant to Section 17 of the Securities Regulation Code and Section 141 of the Corporation Code of the Philippines.*

GT Capital Holdings, Inc. 2008–2015. *Annual Report Pursuant to Section 17 of the Securities Regulation Code and Section 141 of the Corporation Code of the Philippines.*

JG Summit Holdings, Inc. 2001–2015. *Annual Report Pursuant to Section 17 of the Securities Regulation Code and Section 141 of the Corporation Code of the Philippines.*

Kelly, Philip F. 2003. 'Urbanization and the Politics of Land in the Manila Region'. *The Annals of the American Academy of Political and Social Science* 590(1): 170–187.

————. 2000. *Landscapes of Globalization: Human Geographies of Economic Change in the Philippines.* New York: Routledge.

Kleibert Jana Maria. 2015. 'Islands of Globalisation: Offshore Services and the Changing Spatial Divisions of Labour'. *Environment and Planning A* 47(4): 884–902.

Kleibert, Jana Maria and Lisa Kippers. 2016. 'Living the Good Life? The Rise of Urban Mixed-Use Enclaves in Metro Manila'. *Urban Geography* 37(3): 1–23.

Larkin, John. A. 1993. *Sugar and the Origins of Modern Philippine Society.* Berkeley, CA: University of California Press.

LT Group, Inc. 2008–2015. *Annual Report Pursuant to Section 17 of the Securities Regulation Code and Section 141 of the Corporation Code of the Philippines.*

Metro Pacific Investments Corporation. 2007–2015. *Annual Report Pursuant to Section 17 of the Securities Regulation Code and Section 141 of the Corporation Code of the Philippines.*

Ofreneo, Rene. 2006. 'Development Choices for Philippine Textiles and Garments in the Post-MFA Era'. *Journal of Contemporary Asia* 39(4): 543–561.

National Economic and Development Authority. 1978–1990. *Philippine Statistical Yearbook.* Manila: National Economic and Development Authority.

Ortega, Arnisson Andre. 2016. *Neoliberalizing Spaces in the Philippines: Suburbanization, Transnational Migration, and Dispossession.* Lanham, MD: Lexington Books.

Philippine Statistics Authority (National Statistics Office). 1993–2015. *Philippine Statistical Yearbook.* Quezon City: Philippine Statistics Authority.

———. 1971–2015. *Foreign Trade Statistics of the Philippines.* Quezon City: Philippine Statistics Authority.

Pido, Eric J. 2017. *Migrant Returns: Manila, Development, and Transnational Connectivity.* Durham: Duke University Press.

Polanyi, Karl. 1944. *The Great Transformation: The Political and Economic Origins of our Time.* Boston: Beacon Press.

Robinson, R., M. Beeson, K. Jayasuriya, and H. Kim, eds. 2000. *Politics and Markets in the Wake of the Asian Crisis.* London: Routledge.

Rivera, Temario. 1994. *Landlords and Capitalists: Class, Family, and State in Philippine Manufacturing.* Quezon City: University of the Philippines Press.

San Miguel Corporation. 2001–2015. *Annual Report Pursuant to Section 17 of the Securities Regulation Code and Section 141 of the Corporation Code of the Philippines.*

SM Investments Corporation. 2001–2015. *Annual Report Pursuant to Section 17 of the Securities Regulation Code and Section 141 of the Corporation Code of the Philippines.*

World Bank. 2018. *World Development Indicators.* Washington, DC.

Yoshihara, Kunio. 1988. *The Rise of Ersatz Capitalism in South-East Asia.* Quezon City: Ateneo de Manila University Press.

# Notes on Contributors

**Preet S. Aulakh** is professor of strategy and the Pierre Lassonde Chair in International Business at the Schulich School of Business, York University. His recent research focuses on the internationalization of firms from developing economies. Within the geographical contexts of India, China, and Latin America, he explores how multilevel institutions influence the extent and diverse paths of organic and inorganic growth of organizations from these countries. His research has been published in leading management, marketing and international business journals and has co-edited two books and edited several journal special issues on institutions and organizations. He is currently undertaking a comparative historical project exploring how colonial regimes influenced the evolution of legal institutions related to land tenure.

**Alvin A. Camba** is a doctoral candidate in sociology at Johns Hopkins University (JHU). Prior to JHU, he acquired his degrees from University College London, Tartu University, and Binghamton University. His work aims to bring back the role of domestic politics, social protest, and place-based considerations in examining the determinants, impact, and modality of Chinese FDI in South East Asia. His work has received assistance from, and been funded by, the South East Asian Research Group (SEAREG), the Arrighi Center for Global Studies at JHU, the Asian Research Institute (ARI), and the Middle Eastern Institute (MEI).

**Kenneth Cardenas** is a doctoral candidate in human geography at York University and a graduate associate with the York Centre for Asian Research (YCAR), working on the new geographies of Philippine capitalism. He has previously worked on 'disasters' and the definition and control of urban populations and on corporate malfeasance. He maintains an interest in the overlaps between academic research, public due diligence, and investigative journalism. His work has been featured by the Philippine Center for Investigative Journalism, the *Philippine Daily Inquirer*'s 'Talk of the Town', and as a special report for ABS-CBN News.

**Mauricio Cervantes** is full professor of corporate finance and investment at Tecnologico de Monterrey, Mexico. His research interests are microfinance, base of the pyramid and cultural finance. He is executive director of the Asia Pacific Institute of Monterrey Tec.

He is a consultant in the areas of international finance, portfolio theory, risk coverage, and business in China. He has been a visiting professor at University of International Business and Economics in Beijing, China; Portland State University, USA; Universidad San Francisco de Quito, Ecuador; ESAN, Graduate School of Business, Peru. He holds a PhD in finance from the UT-Austin/Monterrey Tec.

**Xiangming Chen** served as the founding director of the Center for Urban and Global Studies at Trinity College from 2007 to 2019 and is currently Paul Raether Distinguished Professor of Global Urban Studies and Sociology at Trinity College in Hartford, Connecticut. He is also an adjunct professor in the School of Social Development and Public Policy at Fudan University in Shanghai and the Graduate School of the Shanghai Academy of Social Sciences, China. He has published extensively on globalization, cities, and economic development. His (co-)authored and co-edited books include: *As Borders Bend: Transnational Spaces on the Pacific Rim* (2005), *Shanghai Rising: State Power and Local Transformations in a Global Megacity* (2009; Chinese edition, 2009), and *Global Cities, Local Streets: Everyday Diversity from New York to Shanghai* (2015; Chinese edition 2016; Korean edition 2017). He has conducted policy research and constancy for the United Nations Conference on Trade and Development (UNCTAD), the World Bank, the Asian Development Bank, and the Organisation for Economic Co-operation and Development (OECD).

**Harald Conrad** is professor of modern Japanese studies at Heinrich-Heine-University Düsseldorf, Germany. Former posts include a senior lectureship at the University of Sheffield's School of East Asian Studies (2008-2019), a position as associate professor at Ritsumeikan Asia Pacific University (2007–2008) as well as a research fellowship and deputy directorship at the German Institute for Japanese Studies, Tokyo (2000–2007). Conrad holds a PhD in economics from Cologne University, Germany. His research focuses on Japanese human resource management, social policy, the organization of markets and intercultural business negotiations. He is a member of the editorial boards of *Contemporary Japan* and *Japan Forum*.

**Na Fu** is an ABD in the Politics Department, the New School for Social Research. After receiving a master's degree in community and regional planning from the University of Texas at Austin, she served as the head of the research department at the Shenzhen Center for Design in Shenzhen between 2014 and 2016. In Spring 2017, she was a Luce Foundation visiting scholar at the Center for Urban and Global Studies at Trinity College, Connecticut. She is currently conducting dissertation research on the politics of local economic development and restructuring across the urban-rural interface in southern China.

**Rosy Hastir** is an assistant professor of sociology in Lovely Professional University, Phagwara, Punjab. She was awarded her PhD in sociology in 2016 from the Department of Sociology, University of Delhi and her master's degree in sociology from the Department of Sociology, Guru Nanak Dev University, Amritsar. During her PhD research, her fieldwork in Italy was funded by the European Union Programme. The topic of her research was 'Transforming Homeland: Transnational Punjabi Migrants and Their Links with Home' in which she examined the transnational Punjabi community in their homeland in Punjab and their varied settlements in small villages in Italy.

**Hari KC** is a doctoral candidate in Global Governance at the Balsillie School of International Affairs, Wilfrid Laurier University. His dissertation examines the labour migration governance in Nepal with a focus on gender. Born and raised in the foothills of the Himalayas in Nepal, Hari's professional background comprises work in diverse areas, including academia, NGOs, diplomacy, and the media. From 2002 to 2010, Hari taught undergraduate English at the Tribhuvan University in Kathmandu. Hari has pursued his passion for volunteerism and community engagement through different organizations, such as the Mennonite Coalition for Refugee Support, Centre for Community Based Research, Ontario Council for International Cooperation, Rohingya School, Spiritual Heritage Education Network, St. Louis College, and Nepalese-Canadian Association of the Waterloo Region.

**Philip F. Kelly** is professor and chair in the Department of Geography at York University and a former director of the York Centre for Asian Research. His research examines the global dimensions of Philippine development, the employment experiences of Filipino-Canadian immigrants and their families, and transnational linkages between Canada and the Philippines. He has run several research projects, including the Filipino Youth Transitions in Canada, the Toronto Immigrant Employment Data Initiative, and currently, the Canada-Philippines Alternative Transnational Economies project. His publications include *Economic Geography: A Contemporary Introduction* (third edition 2020, with Neil Coe and Henry Yeung) and *Migration, Agrarian Transition and Rural Change in Southeast Asia* (editor, 2013).

**Jana M. Kleibert** is a junior research group leader at the Leibniz Institute for Research on Society and Space (Erkner) and the Department of Geography of the Humboldt University of Berlin. Previously, she was a visiting professor in economic geography at the Institute for Human Geography at the Goethe-University of Frankfurt am Main. She received a PhD in human geography from the Amsterdam Institute of Social Science Research, University of Amsterdam in 2015. Prior to this, she studied international relations and European studies in Maastricht, Stockholm and Amsterdam. Her research interests are economic geography, globalisation, global production networks, services, economic development and, more recently, global cities and urban transformations, in particular in the Philippines.

**Asha Kuzhiparambil** received her PhD from the National Institute of Advanced Studies (NIAS), India, under the Reserve Bank of India (RBI) Program on Interdisciplinary Approaches to Economic Issues. Her dissertation was entitled 'Dynamics of Labor Relations across Different Circuits of Globalization: Evidence from Garment Making and Cashew Nut Processing Circuits in Kerala'. Currently, her research focuses on the Government of India's skill development policies that aim to channelize the surplus labour resulting from the demographic dividend into the growing sectors of the economy.

**Hendrik Meyer-Ohle** is associate professor in the Department of Japanese Studies at the National University of Singapore (NUS). He studied business administration and Japanese studies at the Philipps University Marburg where he also obtained his PhD. Before joining NUS in 2000 he worked as a research fellow for the German Institute for Japanese Studies (DIJ) in Tokyo. He was a visiting scholar at Ritsumeikan University in 2008 and at Waseda University in 2016. His publications include *Japanese Workplaces in Transition: Employee Perceptions* (2009), *Innovation and Dynamics in Japanese Retailing: From Techniques to Formats to Systems* (2003), and *Corporate Strategies for Southeast Asia after the Crisis: A Comparison of Multinational Firms from Japan and Europe* (co-editor with Jochen Legewie, 2000).

**Miguel A. Montoya** is professor of international business and economics at Tecnologico de Monterrey, Mexico. He studies global Mexican companies and innovations at the 'base of the pyramid' in emerging markets. He received a PhD from the Autonomous University of Barcelona.

**Francisco J. Valderrey** is professor at Tecnologico de Monterrey, Mexico. His research focuses on international business strategy, as well as marketing in China, and negotiation in multicultural environments. He has published several articles on Asia Pacific topics and the China–Latin American relationship. He has co-authored two textbooks on the fundamentals of marketing. He earned a PhD in administration and marketing from the University of Valencia in Spain.

**Margaret Walton-Roberts** is professor in the Department of Geography and Environmental Studies at Wilfrid Laurier University and affiliated to the Balsillie School of International Affairs, Waterloo, Ontario. Her research interests are in gender and migration, transnational networks in the Indian diaspora, and immigrant settlement in Canada. Her current research project focuses on the international migration of health care professionals. From 2008 to 2012, she was the inaugural director of the International Migration Research Centre (IMRC), a research centre focused on international migration and mobility at the global, national, and regional scale.

**Gavin Xu** is a junior at Trinity College, Connecticut. He was born and raised in Beijing, China. Majoring in both urban studies and political science, he has interned for the Planning and Zoning Department of the town of Ridgefield, Connecticut, and conducted research on party politics in Taipei and Kaohsiung, Taiwan.

**Sam Zhou** graduated from Trinity College with a degree in mathematics in May 2019. He was born in Dongguan, China, and is currently enrolled in the Master's Program in Data Analytics of the Graduate School of Arts and Sciences, Fordham University, New York.

# Index

identity, 197
ethnograpy/ethnographic
 research on Chinese mining companies,
 73, 83
European integration project, 32, 33
Evergreen Holdings, Inc., 246
expatriate(s)
 community, 98
 managers, 52, 65
 mobility, 56, 57
export-led growth, 77
export-processing zones (EPZs), 36, 7

family ownership, 250
feminization of migration, 188
 in garment factories, 165
 of mountain agriculture, 183
 of work, 175, 176
fictitious commodities, 33
Filipino labour, 233, 234, 246, 247, 248n2
foreign direct investment (FDI), 1–4, 23, 86,
 111, 114, 115, 138, 220, 233, 239, 245
 controlling expatriates, 51, 52
 investment by China in Philippines, 72,
 73, 77–81
 inward, 5
 outward, 5–7, 23, 77, 95
foreign employees, 50, 53, 55–61, 64–68
foreign investment, 3, 48, 76, 78, 138, 145,
 235, 245, 248, 253
Fort Bonifacio, 246, 247

garment industry in India, 18, 21, 33, 38, 137,
 138, 142. 160, 161
 cluster, 155–159
 requirement of skilled labour for, 162–168
gender/gendered, 8, 17, 42, 68, 166, 184, 188
 -based discriminations, 172
 class-based forms of exploitation, 21
 -differentiated vulnerabilities, 179
 division of reproductive labour, 176
 equality, 195
 hierarchies, 222, 223
 occupation, 211
 policy, 222–226

relations, 195
 transnational labour market, 38
 violence, 179
geopolitics, 78
global, 98, 185
 capital, 2, 173
 capitalism, 35, 43, 174, 175, 212
 capitalist economy, 36
 circuits, 153
 cities, 39, 40, 139, 153, 174, 226
 city formation, 2
 city networks, 153
 city zones, 39
 commodity
 chains, 1
 gut in mining sector, 74, 75
 deployment, 10
 dispersion of Sikhs, 197
 economy, 32, 34
 financial crisis of 2008, 137
 flows, 34
 inequality, 83
 investors, 4
 labour markets, 33
 -local dichotomy, 174
 middle class, 175
 migration, 9, 197, 213–215
 migrants, 9
 production networks, 1, 37, 168
 remuneration, 56
 scale, 11
 space, 16
 territories, 36
 value chains, 33
globalization, 31, 32, 34, 36, 39, 52, 103, 169,
 172, 173, 185, 188, 224, 247
 capital accumulation under contemporary,
 43
 of Chinese capital, 3
 counter geographies of, 173, 186
 economic, 173, 187
 fragmented, 44
 of health service delivery, 212
 myths and realities of, 174–180

inbound, 233
migrants, 16, 40, 216
  inflow and outflow, 4, 7
  from overseas, 19
monetary, 173
and Nepal economy, 180–184
social, 19, 189, 203, 207
rentier(s), 248
  integrated, 233
  -type activities, 234
  -type opportunities, 253
  vertically-integrated, 247
rentierism, 254
  place-based, 234
rent-seeking, 92, 94
resistance, 16, 20, 21, 23, 79, 173, 174, 185–
    188, 218
resource(s), 73, 184n3, 196, 198, 206, 220,
    224, 225
  access, 22
  economic, 139
  economies, 6
  financial, 183

San Miguel Corporation, 248, 251, 252, 254
Singapore, 3, 10, 39, 40, 48, 50, 52, 60n2, 77,
    90, 100, 122, 123, 124, 131, 196, 215,
    221, 256, 257
Skill Development Initiative Scheme (SDIS),
    India, 154, 159, 168, 169
Skills for Employment in Apparel
    Manufacturing (SEAM) by IL&FS,
    161–169
Skills for Manufacturing of Apparel through
    Research and Training (SMART),
    161
skill training, 159–61, 163, 166, 169
smart power, 100, 116
SM Investments Corporation (SMIC),
    250–252, 255
social capital, 11, 184, 184n3, 207
soft power, concept of, 63, 113, 114, 116
  definition of, 99
  in Mexico and Peru, 105–108
  origin of, 100
  use of, 100

South East Asia, 3, 4, 9, 15, 21, 24, 32, 34, 36,
    43, 48, 61, 64, 72, 73, 78, 87, 89, 90,
    95, 135, 245, 248, 249n2
  China trade and commerce relationship
      with, 121–127, 139, 142, 146,
      147
  gated communities as porous enclaves in,
      35n4
  network utilization by Chinese investors,
      86
  and overseas Chinese, 99, 103
South–South FDI, 6
special accounts, 238, 240, 243, 244
special economic zones (SEZs), 23, 31, 32,
    34, 35, 43, 130, 135, 245
  border, 38
  Chinese, 37
  extraterritorial, 38
  rise in, 37
  in urban India and Philippines, 40
state capitalism, 12–14
state owned enterprises (SOEs), 4, 99, 126,
    234, 240
  controlled by state, 14
  funded by government, 12
  role of, 13
student migration, 11, 22, 58, 214
systems approach
  definition of, 49
  proponents to migration, 64, 66

Taiwan, 3, 8, 61, 90, 101, 102, 108, 123, 135,
    136, 140, 144, 145
tax havens, 31, 249
territory(ies)/territorial, 39, 42, 73, 101, 102
  disputes, 122
  enclosed, 31
  global, 36
  moment, 43
  national legislative, 35
Tiruppur, 156–159, 162, 165, 167
trade, 115n5, 124, 227, 235, 241
  barriers, 13
  bilateral, 110